Many years ago William Gross was intrigued by the development of the character of Herod from the brief mention of him in the Gospel narrative to the crude but vigorous caricature of him in the medieval miracle plays. The players, who every year would try to "out-Herod Herod," must have had some historical basis, the author felt. Thus began a lengthy investigation which led, finally, to this reconstruction of another man nobody really knows. Using the *Antiquities* and the *Wars of the Jews* by Josephus as his base, William Gross has ranged widely through the centuries, gleaning where he could. He has searched both the *Talmud* and the *Apocrypha* (such as the Arabic "Gospel of the Infancy" and the "Protoevangel of St. James"). He has used the writers of antiquity as much as possible—Suetonius, Plutarch, Cicero, Strabo, and even Virgil have offered their grains of fact and insight. With these and modern historical researchers from Mommsen to Minkin and Perowne, William Gross has achieved his penetrating and sometimes surprising interpretation.

HEROD THE GREAT

HEROD THE GREAT

By William J. Gross

HELICON PRESS Baltimore—Dublin

Helicon Press, Inc.
1120 N. Calvert St., Baltimore 2, Maryland

Helicon, Ltd.
Dublin

Library of Congress Catalog Card Number 62-18775

Printed in the United States of America
by Garamond Press, Baltimore, Maryland

To Louise

Contents

I Prelude in Various Keys (536–167 B.C.) 1

II The Hammer of God 11

III Enter the Idumean 19

IV Rise and Ebb 29

V And Now the Parthian 40

VI Flight to Glory 56

VII Of False Allies and Battles 70

VIII A Marriage and a Siege 91

IX King of the Jews 107

X Death of a Boy Priest 125

XI War of Women 152

XII An Empire Lost 170

XIII A Kingdom Won—A Queen Lost 187

XIV Bread and Circuses 206

XV "Herod's Temple" 228

XVI Mariamne's Sons 248

XVII Return of the First Born 268

XVIII Plots and Confessions 286

XIX Two Trials 309

XX Penumbra 322

XXI We Have Seen His Star 340

XXII Night Falls 351

  List of Characters 368

  Genealogical Charts 371

Contents

I   Prelude in Various Keys (256–107 BC) 1
II   The Hammer of God 11
III Enter the Inhuman 19
IV Rise and Ebb 30
V   And Now the Puritan 40
VI Flight to Crécy . . . .
VII Of False Allies and Battles . . . .
VIII A Marriage and a Siege . . . .
IX Star of the Tea 107
X   Death of a Boy Born . . . .
XI War of Women 127
XII An Empire Lost 150
XIII A Kingdom Won, a Queen Lost . . . .
XIV Bread and Circuses 200
XV Herod's Temple . . . .
XVI Mohammed's Sons 244
XVII Return of the Free Born . . . .
XVIII Heirs and Conquests 280
XIX Two Trials 300
XX Penumbra . . . .
XXI We Have Seen His Star 340
XXII Night Falls 357
List of Characters . . . .
Chronological Charts 381

HEROD THE GREAT

CHAPTER I

PRELUDE IN VARIOUS KEYS (536–167 B.C.)

THAT THE NAME OF KING HEROD THE GREAT has not been long since lost in the mists of antiquity is due in large measure to a single chapter near the beginning of the Gospel according to Saint Matthew. Magi out of the East follow a strange star that portends the birth of a king. Near Jericho their guide disappears. Undaunted, they go up to Jerusalem and beard the tyrant Herod in his palace demanding, "Where is the newly born king of the Jews? For we have seen his star in the East and have come to worship him." Thereupon Herod calls together the priests and scribes, who indicate that according to the prophecy Bethlehem should be the birthplace of the Messiah. With soft words, though the very suggestion of a rival fills him with rage, he requests the magi to come back to tell him of their experiences. On their way to the hill town they again find their star—a lovely tradition says in the reflection at the bottom of a well—and then the Child whom they adore, and to whom they give their treasures of gold, frankincense and myrrh. Warned in a dream not to return to Herod they go back to their own lands by another route. Herod, "exceedingly angry" at their deception, orders the massacre of all male children in Bethlehem under the age of two. In his sleep Joseph is commanded by an angel to take the Child and his mother and flee to Egypt. Later, again through a dream, he learns that Herod is dead. So Mary, Joseph, and the Child return and live at Nazareth in Galilee.

Magi, whose very names are tradition, trailing an errant star through the sky's vastnesses across desert and mountain waste; a score of baby boys savagely killed; and a royal carpenter's family that follows a dream to safety. Only so much Scripture tells us about Herod. And so little keeps his name accursed as long as man shall endure.

The real Herod is all that Scripture intimates. Still, there is more which has no place in the sacred annals. Rarely has history recorded the story of an abler, more gifted, more ruthless, more misunderstood ruler. A zealous builder, a consummate diplomat, an eloquent orator, a brilliant general, a violent, unbridled despot—this man, a non-Jew, sat on the throne of David. He ruled a land far more extensive than that of Solomon and a people who attained under him their peak of material prosperity. His tortuous course crossed the thundering careers of Julius Caesar, Cassius, Marc Antony, Cleopatra, and Caesar Augustus; and from every precarious contact he emerged safely and with increased power and fame. He married ten times; divorced, dismissed, or simply ignored the wives he grew tired of, and never ceased loving the wife he murdered. He killed his uncle, his brother, his son-in-law, his mother-in-law, and the three sons he loved best; he slaughtered infants and graybeards, and died an old man, of natural causes—miserably.

The power of Herod was rooted in the evolution of Jewish life and ideals dating from the Second Captivity (586 B.C.). The attempts of Ezra (458 B.C.) and Nehemiah (445 B.C.) to re-establish a spiritual state by closest adherence to rule and ritual withered in the mass emigrations of the Diaspora, and the abominable excesses of the mingling. The glorious Indian summer of the Maccabees was blighted by the weakness of their successors and the polluting touch of the Herodian clan. Finally the regal, neo-Jewish pomp of six generations of Herods was engulfed in the holocaust at the destruction of Jerusalem (70 A.D.). After six hundred uncertain years, political Jewry was dispersed and left as its sole tangible monument a line of matched stone from Herod's Temple, the Wailing Wall.

We are told that when Cyrus captured Babylon in 538 B.C., God "stirred up" his spirit to return the Jews to their fatherland.

Perhaps Cyrus was motivated by practical considerations as well. In Palestine the "fertile crescent" of the Near East narrows to a land bridge joining the fertile lowlands and red brick metropoles of the Mesopotamian plain with the granary of Egypt. It was imperative that only a friendly people inhabit this narrow strip of sea plain and forested upland, for it afforded the only practicable passage for commerce or military operations.

If Cyrus had expected a mass exodus of Jews to their reestablished homeland, he was disappointed. In their own country the Jews had been an agricultural race. Canaan was cherished as "a land of wheat and barley—and vines and fig trees and pomegranates, a land of olive trees and honey"; wealth was counted in flocks and barns; sacrifice was evaluated by first fruits, and the pick of the flock. Denied the right to farm, the exiles had turned of necessity to commerce and developed a latent bargaining and acquisitive talent. In Assyria, which Ezekiel called "a land of traffic and a city of merchants, a fruitful land," many Jews became wealthy. It is not surprising then, that while a quarter of a million people had been driven into exile some fifty years earlier, only about fifty thousand of the more patriotic and pious—callously referred to as "foundlings, proselytes, and bastards" by those who refused to return—made the difficult trek to their homeland. Cyrus generously granted them a subsidy for the rebuilding of the Temple, gave them the sacred vessels seized by Nebuchadnezzar, and appointed Zerubbabel, grandson of King Joachim of the House of David as governor, while Joshua, grandson of the High Priest Jozadak was named high priest.

A dreary existence faced the returned exiles. Cushites, Moabites, Edomites, and Amonites had flocked into the fields of the dispossessed Jews. Jerusalem was a desolate ruin.

Zerubbabel was no administrator. Consequently, after a token sacrifice on a hastily erected altar, "each man went into his own country," a few remaining in Jerusalem, but most of them passing on to the towns and country to the south. Frequent clashes with other races resulted, which were settled by Persian intervention in favor of the Jews. After three years the cornerstone of the Temple was laid. Then, when it was suspected that cedar, a rare commodity in Judea, went into the construction of private homes instead of the Temple for which it had been purchased, Zerubbabel returned to Babylon in disgust.

Zerubbabel's departure definitely dimmed the glory of the House of David. For some five hundred years it would flicker ever more feebly, finally to expire with the death of the carpenter Joseph in the windowless cubicle at Nazareth.

For fifteen years rebuilding of the Temple was abandoned, until goaded by the reproaches of the prophets Haggai and Zechariah, the Jews resumed work and in four years finished the edifice. The young rejoiced; their elders, recalling the glories of Solomon's temple, wept, "so that one could not distinguish the voice of the shout of joy, from the noise of the weeping of the people."

During the next half century Jewish culture and faith languished. Alien races married with Jews, and pagan rites mingled with the sacrifice to Yahweh. In Babylon, however, when the scribe Ezra of the line of Zadoc heard of the defection of the Palestinian Jews, "he sat down and wept for days, fasting and praying before the God of Heaven." Appealing to the emperor, he was granted the authority and financial aid he requested. "And thou Ezra, appoint judges and magistrates that thou may judge all the people that is beyond the river." In 458 B.C. he led into Jerusalem some fifteen hundred Babylonian Jews, including a great-grandson of Zerubbabel.

With the ire of a zealot he went into action. Gold and silver were carried into the Temple; altar fires glowed anew; courts re-echoed to the sonority of priestly chants. But all this was meaningless unless he could reach the core of the problem—the defilement of Jewish blood and faith by intermarriage. Calling together the heads of families, he exhorted them to put away their foreign wives and children. After three bitterly indecisive months the Jews finally heeded his plea and returned home to eject their wives and children.

Ezra, while a dedicated enthusiast, was also an opportunist. He could not let his people brood in empty houses. In their sad hour, he felt he could substitute love of God, and the Law, for the lost creature comforts. From dawn to mid-day he read and expounded the Law they had transgressed. The next day he resumed reading and gave instructions for celebrating the Feast of the Tabernacles. For seven days he continued reading and teaching. Following two more days of strict fast the Jews stood and confessed their sins, and "the iniquities of their fathers." The covenant with God was renewed; marriage with gentiles, forbidden; regulations for keeping the Sabbath and Temple worship established; synagogues, organized; and books that were canonical defined.

Ezra, no doubt, felt that he had conditioned the Jews for acceptance of pure faith and unflinching adherence to dogma and ritual, however harsh. Yet even among the most sincere there was some subconscious revolt against an ordinance that shattered their domestic bliss, some doubt of the reasonableness of laws that seemed so exclusive. This wavering faith found expression in the "Book of Ruth," the romance of the beautiful Moabitess, who by intermarriage became the ancestress of David; and in the story of Jonah, who in his arrogance thought that God cared only for Jewish souls.

Ezra saw his people slipping back into the old forbidden practices. For fourteen years he watched his beloved Law crumble. Saddened, he could only pray.

Yet, though Ezra never sensed it, his reformation was more extensive than he could have foreseen. The Pentateuch, the basis of his insistence on rigorous ritualism, became the cornerstone of subsequent religious practices. Even more important, through his teaching ancient Israel perished, and Judea was born.

At this point (445 B.C.) a new figure enters the Judean scene. In Susa, the wealthy Jew Nehemiah, cupbearer to Artaxerxes I, hearing of the state of affairs in the land of his origin, obtained authority to attempt to remedy conditions. Unlike Ezra, Nehemiah was interested in the prosperity and safety of his people. He began by erecting the walls of Jerusalem, an operation enlivened with derisive remarks from an interesting old sinner, the Samaritan, Sanballat, whose crowning ambition was to have his own temple at Gerizim recognized as the hub of Jewish life. Sarcasm ineffective, Sanballat had dead bodies thrown into the project to make it ceremonially impure; cut off small bands of workers, and sniped at masons. Nehemiah's patrols thereupon circled the city, discouraging interference, while the building proceeded almost incredibly fast. After two years and four months, according to Josephus—fifty-two days by another account—walls that had been in ruins for one hundred and fifty years were rebuilt, and the fortress of Baris (or Akra) erected.

Secure from attacks from without, Nehemiah turned his attention to internal reform. He curtailed the privileges of the Levites, long suspected of laxity, if not downright dishonesty, in handling the tithes; he re-emphasized the observance of the Sabbath. Above all, he curbed the power of the wealthy moneylenders by prohibiting usury and the enslavement of a debtor and his family. Then, satisfied with the success of his mission, Nehemiah returned to Susa.

His social reforms proved no more lasting than the religious regeneration of Ezra. More and more power passed to the priests, who in turn were guided by the interpretations of the scribes and lawyers. As a result formalism and elaborate ritualism supplanted the simplicity of the Mosaic code. Moreover, the system of democratic priesthood ended. Only the tribe of Levi could minister in the Temple; only those of the family of Aaron of the tribe of Levi could offer sacrifice; only a direct descendant of Solomon's high priest Zadok was eligible for the office of high priest.

Effectively these restrictions resulted in a diminution of sanctity in the priesthood. Scandal and intrigue hung about the office of the high priest, culminating in the murder in the Temple of a grandson of the High Priest Johanan by his older brother on suspicion that the victim was plotting with the Persian overlord to supplant him.

In 323 B.C. the visit of Alexander the Great to Jerusalem marked the end of an era in Jewish history. During the two centuries since the return from the Second Captivity tremendous changes had taken place. There is, to be sure, no continuous history available. Gaps occur for which the reader of Old Testament history must substitute surmise or conjecture, or resort to legend and tradition. Yet, through this historical patchquilt, it is possible to discern a regular evolutionary pattern.

The Jews who returned at Cyrus' invitation were few and poor, and in many cases practiced trade and barter instead of restricting themselves to the old callings of herdsmen and tillers of the soil. Also, even before Ezra and Nehemiah, the failure of Zerubbabel to hold the loyalty of the people eclipsed the influence of the House of David, and foreshadowed an eventual Herod.

With the religious reforms of Ezra, and the social projects of Nehemiah, four additional essential changes took place. First, the ancestral Hebrew tongue became a dead language, to be replaced by Aramaic, spoken locally. Second, since the Jews were really free only in religion, they quite naturally looked upon their priests as champions of their liberties. Thus, through priestly influence, the Temple became the living symbol of Jewish individualism and the exclusive center of his creed. Third, in the practice of faith, emphasis was fixed upon ritualistic exactness, to the exclusion of simple devotion and piety. Consequently, the prophetic movement, which depended on inspired spontaneity and fervor, disappeared. And lastly, as the strictest observance of the minutiae of the Law was considered essential to salvation, the need arose for precise interpretation of this Law, resulting in the ascendancy of the Scribes, the predecessors of the Rabbis and Pharisees.

In brief, sectarian jurisprudence had displaced the love and fear of God. The Law served as a hedge to shelter and separate the Jew from the gentile, a ritualistic hedge so impenetrable that even acts of charity, such as the succor by the Samaritan of the man who fell among robbers, would have rendered the priest and the Levite unclean. Later, it will be seen that Herod, too, spent more than fifty vexatious years in trying to break through this hedge.

Under the beneficent despotism of the Persian and the brief, efficient domination of Alexander the Great, the Jew was at least immune from religious persecution. During the century and a half from the partition of Alexander's empire to the Maccabean revolt, however, life among the Jews became increasingly precarious. While Judea in time of peace prospered as the land bridge between Asia Minor and Egypt, in war it became a bridgehead held in turn by Alexander's Syrian and Egyptian successors, and a battlefield whose encompassed position denied the Jew even the safety of flight.

Still, the constant retrogression in racial and moral virtues during this period in Judea was not solely the result of war. One most important factor was the Diaspora or dispersal of individuals and masses, under compulsion or for reason of profit, into every part of the Alexandrine world. Multitudes flocked into newly-founded cities like Alexandria and Antioch. Other thousands, who picked a loser during the perennial Syro-Egyptian campaigns, were exiled to Cyrenaica and Phrygia and Lydia. Cosmopolitan life appealed to still others, so that Greek cities, especially Corinth, had large Jewish colonies. Eventually Rome, too, was to have its quota, as Cicero discovered to his annoyance when a Jewish mob noisily broke in upon one of his perfectly turned periods. Strabo perhaps best describes the omnipresence of the Jew in his petulant comment that it is not easy to find any place on earth free of them.

Living abroad usually made the Jew the more devoted to his race and creed. To keep his faith pure, he chose for his neighbors other Jews and thus established his own ghettos. Only in this regard did he differ outwardly from the gentile. He paid his taxes as cheerfully as he donated his tithe to the Temple; he was respected for his integrity and his patriotism. Essentially a lover of peace, he dutifully fought in one of the numerous Jewish brigades renowned for their valor, when his adopted country needed his help.

In Judea, the Jew was too often a less creditable character. Jews who left in the mass migrations were replaced first by Greek colonists, later also by Egyptians and Syrians, rarely of the best type. Associating with these, the Jew at home gradually succumbed to Hellenistic influences although his brother abroad remained almost invariably a devout Jew.

As warfare between Egypt and Syria grew more intense, the lot of the Jew became increasingly unhappy, particularly during the years between the conquest of Palestine by Antiochus the Great (219 B.C.) and the Maccabees. History presents no complete picture of these perilous years. It leaves the reader, rather, with unfinished tales of gore and glory; with alluring vistas terminating in blank walls; with sagas of courage and stories of treachery confounded into a phantasmagoria too confusing to comprehend and too horrible to contemplate. There is the story of the saintly high priest Simon the Just (about 302–283 B.C.) who built great reservoirs under the Temple, and repaired the walls of Jerusalem, rounding out a holy life by dying placidly after being greeted by a figure in brooding black as he entered the Holy of Holies. In a lighter vein we read of the nephew of the grasping high priest Onias, the Hellenist Joseph, who saved his country from the wrath of Egypt by persuading a Samaritan moneylender to entrust him with the tribute money required to placate Egypt. Later, on a visit to Egypt, Joseph fell violently in love with a native dancer of easy virtue and was determined to marry her. To prevent this his brother, a strict Jew, at the proper stage of the lover's befuddlement substituted his own daughter for the bored Egyptian. When dawn came, we are told, the demure little Jewess slipped from her uncle's arms and eventually married him—happily.

There are shameful tales, tales of intrigue and violence: of the traitorous Simon, Priest-Captain of the Temple, informing the Syrians of the Temple treasury, and of the horrible vision seen by the Syrian intruder before he fled empty-handed back to his master; of Jason, who unsuccessfully tried to buy the high-priestly office, and eventually died wretchedly at Sparta, where his dismal epitaph reads he was "buried among strangers"; of the high priest Menelaus, who outbid Jason, and was detected trying to steal the golden vessels of the Temple to sell at Tyre; of naked priests, the marks of circumcision artificially concealed, rushing from the Temple to the gymnasium adjoining the sacred structure.

Persecution of decent Jews reached its peak during the reign of the Emperor Antiochus Epiphanes (170 B.C.). Tired of the bickering among the Jews themselves, and irked by Rome's increasing interference in Syrian affairs, he stormed Jerusalem, killed 80,000 and enslaved 40,000 more. Guided by the high priest he strode into the Temple and helped himself to one thousand talents of gold, whereupon he ordered pigs sacrificed on the altar, had their meat boiled, and the unclean broth sprinkled in every part of the Temple.

Eradication of everything Jewish ensued. Circumcision of children and possession of copies of the Law were treasonable; refusal to eat pork was rebellion.

To the eternal glory of the Chosen People, unnumbered gallant souls suffered martyrdom. To the inspiring heroism of the venerable Eleazar, who died rather than pretend to eat pork; to the unparalleled courage of the nameless mother who saw her seven sons, one by one, tortured to death rather than break the Law, must be added countless other mothers whose circumcised children were hanged from their own beams, and numberless other families butchered because they cherished copies of the Torah.

But still greater numbers bowed the knee to the despot. The Temple was rededicated to Zeus Olympias, whose features were unmistakably those of a bearded Antiochus, while Jewish priests crowned with ivy reeled in Bacchic processions.

On December 25, 167 B.C., on the pagan Feast of Lights that celebrated the rebirth of the sun, daily sacrifice and oblation in the Temple stopped. The "abomination of desolation" foretold by Daniel had come.

CHAPTER II

THE HAMMER
OF GOD

A TIRESOME DAY'S JOURNEY WEST OF JERUSA-
lem, the hamlet of Modin, drowsing amid its vineyards and
barley fields, had seemed a sure refuge to the priest Mathathias
and his five sturdy sons fleeing the persecution at Jerusalem.
But early one morning in 164 B.C. the flinty pavement rang with
the tread of the king's troops. The people were rounded up; an
altar made ready; and Mathathias commanded to apostatize.
Normally the troops would have quickly cut down the reluctant
priest and moved on to find other victims. But a sycophantic
Jew, eager to demonstrate his loyalty to the crown by being the
first to commit the act of renunciation, unknowingly changed the
course of history by provoking the Maccabean revolt and thereby
making possible the reign of Herod. Hardly had the impious
hand of the renegade scattered the incense on the altar when
Mathathias' dagger pierced his heart. The startled shouts of the
soldiers were drowned in the explosive yells of the crowd. Overwhelmed in the surge of their enemies, the king's commissioner
and his men gasped out their lives in the dusty road.

The revolt of the Hasmoneans—later to be known as the
Maccabeans, after their great leader, Judas Maccabeus, the Hammer of God—marks the beginning of the most successful revolt
and the bravest period in Jewish history.

At first the rebels hid in the hills. Soon others joined them,
mostly recruits drawn from the Chasidim or Assideans, a secret
society founded to counteract Hellenism by the most scrupulous

11

observance of the Law. Minor revolts broke out everywhere, abetted by propaganda as the Book of Daniel (written almost four hundred years earlier) began quietly to circulate.

A serious setback occurred when about a thousand rebels barricaded in a cave near Jerusalem calmly submitted to butchery rather than defend themselves against an attack by the governor because it was the Sabbath, when any kind of work (including fighting) was forbidden. Mathathias, who by this time had effected some kind of an organization, decided with a majority of his followers, against the bitter opposition of the minority, that the law of the Sabbath did not deny the Jew the right to defend himself against attack. Thus at the very outset of their battle to free Judea, the Maccabeans were split into irreconcilable factions that would eventually help to deliver their descendants into the power of Herod.

The Syrian ruler, busy fighting the Persians, promised the rebels amnesty on condition of surrender. Scornfully rejecting anything less than complete freedom, they continued to wage guerilla warfare, burning and killing at widely scattered places, casting down pagan altars, circumcising children, and punishing apostate Jews—in their success constantly attracting recruits.

Within a year Mathathias died, after appointing Judas, his third son, as commander-in-chief. The deeds of this doughty "Hammer of God" are recounted in the two books of the Maccabees, supplemented by the works of Josephus. Acting on the principle that "in the sight of God there is no difference between saving the many and the few," he never avoided pitched battles, whatever the odds against him. Like Cromwell, he combined a fanatical faith in God with an unwavering belief in himself. With three thousand men, he routed an enemy army of fifty-seven thousand; with forces increased to ten thousand he had little difficulty in scattering sixty-five thousand foes.

On December 25, 164 B.C., three years to the day after the Temple had been befouled, Judas entered Jerusalem and purified and rededicated the holy place by instituting Chanuka, the Feast of Lights.

The following year, Antiochus having died, the Syrians made two more attempts to crush the Jews. The first failed, whereupon the Syrian commander killed the apostate Menelaus who had instigated the attack. In the final battle elephants, a mode of attack new to the Jews, threw the Maccabeans into disorder. In an effort to avert utter panic, Judas' brother Eleazar proved the vulnerability of the monsters by diving under an elephant and ripping open his belly. But it was at the cost of his own life, as the dying beast toppled upon him. The battle, nevertheless, was lost. Tired of constant bloodshed, the Jews agreed to submit to Syrian rule, in exchange for religious freedom.

The new king, Demetrius, shrewdly gave his approval of Alcinius, "a priest of the seed of Aaron," as high priest.

Alcinius had really nothing but the legitimacy of his spiritual ancestry to commend him. Nevertheless the Assideans, in no wise interested in national independence or the possible dynastic aspirations of the Maccabeans, almost at once withdrew their support of Judas. Onias, son of the high priest Onias III, supported by Judas and most of the Jews, in chagrin left for Egypt where he founded the heretical Temple of Yahweh at Leontopolis. His departure left the Maccabeans a merely nationalistic element, seemingly, in a land that (in the words of Mommsen) "was a church without a state; it retained a national character in religious forms, while ignoring the existence of a national state." No devout Jew, understandably, would transfer his allegiance from a validly functioning high priest to a purely military commander.

Judas, in an effort to show the weakness of the incumbent as well as to draw strength from the partisans of rival priestly candidates, chased Alcinius out of Jerusalem. To restore him came the army of Nicanor, a mean character, who daily raised his right arm in the direction of the capital with the ejaculation, "Oh when shall I be able to lay thee waste!" In the ensuing battle Nicanor was killed and his head and blasphemous right arm hung over the Temple Gate.

Wearied by victories that never seriously weakened his enemy, Judas turned to Rome, a gesture that would further facilitate the rule of Herod. The Senate listened to the Maccabean delegation and promised help. But before it could arrive, Judas, with eight hundred men, fought his last fight against the host of General

Bacchides. The epic numbers of I Maccabees tell the story, ending:

And Judas was slain and the rest fled away.

And Jonathan and Simon took their brother and buried him in the sepulcher of his fathers in the city of Modin.

And the people of Israel bewailed him with great lamentations and mourned for him many days,

And said, "How is the mighty man fallen that saved the people of Israel."

History records no more amazing miracle than the feat of Judas. He had literally the dregs of a Jewish nation to work with, a tiny minority among a host of enemies, a minority in which both the worldly Jews lured by Greek culture, and the pious seeking only to perpetuate a ritualistic demagogy, wrought and plotted against him. He strove at a period which was nearing the zenith of Jewish culture and was killed, deserted by all but a handful of those he died for. Overcoming almost hopeless odds, he established a Jewish state after four centuries of serfdom; he confirmed Jerusalem as the capital of international Jewry; he rolled down pagan gods from the slopes of Moriah.

Forlorn remnants of the Maccabeans hid in the trans-Jordanian wilderness, where they maintained a semblance of warfare by occasional raids and forays, during the course of which John, brother of Judas, was killed by Arabs. Alcinius strutted into Jerusalem where to demonstrate his authority he ordered that part of the Temple wall be torn down. Immediately he was stricken by a mysterious malady and died in horrible agony.

His death sobered the Jews. In increasing numbers they joined the rebels. Failing to subdue them, the Syrian commander solved the problem by killing the leaders of the Hellenizing Jews and making peace with the Maccabeans.

Jonathan, one of the two surviving brothers of Judas, had a flair for diplomacy. He renewed the alliance with Rome and, it is thought, made a compact with Sparta. When Demetrius I and Alexander Balas fought for the Syrian crown, he accepted favors from both before he openly espoused the cause of Alexander, the eventual winner. In gratitude, the conqueror appointed him high priest with the rank of prince, and three years later assigned him sole religious and civil authority throughout Judea.

Yet, like all the sons of Mathathias, Jonathan together with his sons was destined to die violently—in this instance at the hands of a certain Tryphon, a Syrian general with imperialistic designs.

When Simon, the last of the five brothers, finally did rule (from 143–135 B.C.), he consolidated Jewish power and prestige to a degree hitherto unrealized. In return, a grateful people ordained that supreme civil authority as well as the priesthood should be hereditary in the Asmonean family, an action that in a sense served notice that the newer Judaism would identify religion with nationalism, rather than subordinate national progress to traditional hierarchy.

The Syrians granted him exemption from taxation; the Roman Senate, graciously accepting his gift of a shield of gold, recognized him as an independent prince and ally of Rome. All omens seemed to portend a long, prosperous reign for this last of the Maccabean brothers.

Simon, however, established no family precedent by dying peacefully. Invited with his wife and sons to a feast at his son-in-law Ptolemy's palace, he became "heavy with wine" and was slain, while the other guests, excepting one son, John Hyrcanus, who escaped to Jerusalem, were imprisoned.

Vengefully raising an army and beseiging Ptolemy, John Hyrcanus was shocked by the sight of his mother and brothers undergoing torture on the city walls, the mother meanwhile imploring her son to disregard her suffering and to redouble his assaults on the city, until with the besiegers looking on helplessly, she and her captive sons were cut to pieces. With the advent of the sabbatical year 135 B.C., the seige was raised, and Ptolemy, despairing of success, fled beyond the Jordan.

Somewhat later, when Antiochus the Pious was killed fighting the Parthians, John Hyrcanus threw the Syrian garrisons out of Judea—the last Syrians ever to be seen in Judea as conquerors. In 129 B.C. he subdued the Idumeans, many of whom during the Captivity had settled in southern Judea with Hebron as their capital. Unaware that he was thereby hastening the doom of

his own family, he offered the defeated the choice between exile
and accepting Judaism. They accepted the Law, and gradually
were absorbed by the Jews. Until his death in 106 B.C. John
Hyrcanus consolidated his kingdom by new treaties with Rome
and further enhanced the dignity, wealth, and power of his
country.

But he was the last good Jewish king. In the remaining three
generations of his line, mediocrity and vice would becloud the
glory of Judea's brightest days, with only a dying flicker cast by
the hapless form of Herod's beloved Mariamne.

John Hyrcanus left his power to his queen, but his oldest son
Aristobulus I (105–104 B.C.) threw his mother into prison and
left her there to starve to death. Of his four brothers Aristobulus
imprisoned three, but through some twist in his ruthless mind,
he liked and trusted his second brother Antigonus. When the
king fell ill ("his entrails were corrupted"), Antigonus, honestly
concerned, arranged to visit the Temple to pray for his recovery.
Told by the queen and other envious persons that Aristobulus
would like to see him in his new armor, Antigonus, happy to
please the sick man, agreed to visit him on his way to the Temple.
Meanwhile, as the king had been convinced by the plotters that
his brother was on the way to murder him, he ordered him killed
in a dark corridor in the palace. As soon as Aristobulus I heard
of his brother's murder, he was shaken with grief and remorse,
and vomited blood into a basin. A servant carrying it through
the corridor where Antigonus had been killed slipped and spilled
the king's brackish blood on the very stones still encrimsoned by
his brother's gashed arteries. Within a year the king died, half-
mad with remorse.

His brother Alexander succeeded him after killing another
brother who seemed inclined to dispute his right. Although a
great warrior—he conquered Moab, Ammon, Gilead, part of
Petra and the lands of the Philistines—Alexander was also a
morose savage, whose reign was one unending wrangle with the
Pharisees.

This party, the Pharisees, began as a sect in the days of the
high priest Jonathan (161–143 B.C.). Traditionally priests had
been interpreters of the Law. But after Nehemiah, when the

Pentateuch circulated among the people, others, too, felt they could interpret the Word. Along with the Law, there began to grow an increasing mass of tradition that perplexed the simplicity of the Pentateuch. In the second century B.C., a class of legal experts arose—scribes in the synagogues; priests in the Temple— who constituted most of the Pharisaical sect. Almost from the beginning many Pharisees were proud, turbulent, and uncompromising. They began carping at royal authority during the reign of John Hyrcanus, but were thwarted by the king's humility. Alexander, lacking that humility, threw his support to the Sadducees, the liberals, who rejected tradition and cut down religious observances to a minimum.

The Pharisees decided to fight. At the most sacred moment of the service for the Feast of the Tabernacles, Alexander as high priest, instead of pouring the lustral water on the altar simulated sprinkling it upon the ground (a quite legitimate choice between two rituals). Crowded about him were the Pharisees, palms in one hand, citrons in the other. As one man they hurled their citrons at Alexander. The infuriated monarch called upon his Pisidian and Cicilian guards to bar the gates and slaughter all within. Six thousand Pharisees died.

Still, the king made one more effort to conciliate his enemies, but he was informed that peace would result only on condition that he kill himself. After nine years of fighting and fifty thousand casualties, the civil war ended with the seizure of eight hundred prominent rebels. Alexander's revenge was characteristic. Eight hundred crosses were erected in terraces above the palace. Carousing with abandoned women, he and his harlots jeered at the crucified captives whose agonies had been intensified by cutting the throats of their wives and children beneath their crosses. Six years of vice, drunkenness, and sloth followed before Alexander died, a diseased hulk, at the age of forty-nine.

Nevertheless, he retained his cunning to the end. He realized that his wife, Alexandra Salome (she had also been his brother's wife), could not continue the quarrel with the Pharisees. He therefore advised that news of his death be withheld until after she had offered them a share in the government. What would happen to his remains was to him a matter of complete indifference. Immediately after his death, she made her peace with her late enemies, who voted their late persecutor a splendid funeral as a "glorious king."

Months of terror followed as Pharisees purged Sadducees and other enemies. Thousands were hunted down, other thousands fled to remote villages. Of the murder of her former adherents, the queen seemed quite oblivious. Formally pious, and superstitious, she was the willing tool of her new masters. In fact she suited them so well that the Talmud reports that in her reign "grains of wheat were as large as kidneys, the grains of barley like olive kernels, and beans like golden denarii." And rain fell only at night and in just the right quantity!

But neither the gloating Pharisees nor their terrorized victims noted that a new force was almost imperceptibly expanding that would stifle what miserable residue of Maccabean glory still persisted and supplant it with vigorous alien stock. For during Alexandra's reign we become increasingly aware of the Idumean, Antipater, father of King Herod the Great.

CHAPTER III

ENTER THE
IDUMEAN

ANTIPATER HAD BEEN PROMINENT IN IDUMEA.
Ostensibly like all his countrymen a Jew in faith, he was at heart
a pagan who nurtured deep within him a gnawing urge to rule
as an Idumean, and a rankling hatred of the Jewish god who
thundered his anathema against the unfortunate children of
Esau. He was rich and had improved his social status by marrying Cyprus, daughter of an Arabian chief. His children—four
sons, Pharsael, Herod, Joseph, and Pheroras, and a daughter,
Salome—sharpened his determination to assure them a life of
freedom and opportunity not to be thought of so long as Judea
looked upon Idumea merely as a half-alien state of subjugated
men.

To free Corsica, Napoleon first had to win France. More than
eighteen centuries earlier Antipater formulated a similar security for his little country, through making himself master of a
vastly more powerful neighbor.

Combining the urbanity of the courtier with the candor of
the provincial, he easily won the confidence of Queen Alexandra.
His seeming simplicity, frankness, and lack of self-seeking were a
solace to the miserable woman, harassed by bickering Pharisees,
anguished by the growing friction between her sons, haunted by
the ghosts of her husband's fierce reign. Soon he was her agent,
her counselor, and, as she believed, her friend.

Still Antipater, despite his success, must have foreseen a
troubled future. Alexandra was an ailing, neurotic woman, old

19

before her time. Her death would leave the country in a sadly muddled state, with the Pharisees supporting the older son and logical heir, Hyrcanus, while the liberal elements and much of the army would wish to see the younger son, Aristobulus, king. Alexandra actually did name Hyrcanus as her successor and thereby pleased only the Pharisees. Hyrcanus himself would have been most happy to be high priest; the attendant office of king implied action and decision which his unambitious nature abhorred. Aristobulus, on the other hand, had all the fire and recklessness of his father. He had already incurred the hatred of the priestly clan by persuading his mother (in one of her rare reasonable moments) to put a stop to the hounding of his father's followers and to permit them to inhabit all but three of the frontier posts, including gloomy Macherus, where most of her treasure was stored.

After her appointment of Hyrcanus, the queen became seriously ill. This was obviously no time for Antipater to identify himself with either faction. The violence of Aristobulus and the fanaticism of the Pharisees could prove equally dangerous. He accordingly acted purely as a faithful minister of the queen, seemingly quite disinterested in who her successor might be.

When Alexandra was obviously near death Aristobulus made his move. In the dead of the breathless Judean night, with barely a glance at the single lighted chamber where women were ministering to his pain-tossed mother, he stole away from Jerusalem. Slipping like a wraith in the silver stillness, he passed from town to town, everywhere encouraged by pledges of loyalty. Within fifteen days, twenty-two communities had proclaimed their allegiances. The dying queen was bestirred from her torpor, and had his wife and children imprisoned. In retaliation, Aristobulus snatched the royal treasuries in a number of towns, therewith purchasing the support of foreign mercenaries. Unquestionably, he was the most powerful figure in the country.

The ensuing clashes between the brothers resembled on a small scale the former wars between Egypt and Syria, which had drained the manhood and wealth of Judea.

At first, King Hyrcanus saw his troops, tired of Pharisee arrogance and contemptuous of the king's lack of decision, going over to the enemy, as Aristobulus, swaggering up the country, seized one stronghold after another. Placing himself in the midst of his brother's hostage family, King Hyrcanus tremblingly awaited the almost unopposed approach of his brother. Aristobulus was unexpectedly conciliatory. He recognized Hyrcanus as king and requested an audience.

The upshot of their meeting was mutually satisfactory. Hyrcanus resigned the crown he had never coveted, embraced his brother before the eyes of a jubilant throng, and paced contentedly to his new home, while the new king strode proudly to the palace.

Had matters remained so, Aristobulus II might have enjoyed a successful reign. While the Pharisees hated him, the mass of the population wanted only peace.

A lasting peace, however, could readily mean the end of Antipater. Shorn of influence and power through Alexandra's death, he retained only a questionable prestige as counsellor of a Pharisee-dominated woman whose rejection of Aristobulus would probably cost Antipater his life. It was essential that he act quickly to terminate such a peace; not by instigating some sporadic outbursts which could be quickly suppressed, but by nothing less than a general uprising.

For this three elements would be required: the Pharisees to spearhead the rebellion; Hyrcanus to lend it dignity; and outside help to counter Aristobulus II's mercenaries.

The support of the Pharisees came almost unsolicited. They hated and feared Aristobulus II; he hated them. Hyrcanus was more difficult to win over. He liked his easy life and only the argument that his existence presented a potential danger to the king which Aristobulus II would sooner or later remove persuaded the high priest to strike for the crown. Since the royal troops were unquestionably loyal to Aristobulus II, Antipater prevailed upon the Arabian king Aretas, a visionary with delusions of conquest, to align himself with Hyrcanus.

Although the plot was Antipater's, he had been so circumspect in his operations that to the country in general he remained merely the discredited counsellor of a defunct regime. In fact, through most of the ensuing conflict he kept himself sedulously in the background. The time was not yet when he might declare himself irrevocably.

In the opening battle the Judean king's troops, confused by traitors and agents of Antipater within their ranks, were routed and Aristobulus II barely escaped to Jerusalem. During the siege of the capital occurred an incident not of vital importance, but characteristic of popular reaction to the war. Relentless heat and lack of water exhausted besieger and besieged alike. Someone in the shadeless inferno about the city remembered that a certain holy man, Onias, had once during a drought, called down by prayer rain from a blazing sky. Hyrcanus ferreted him from his cave and ordered him to curse Aristobulus II. Instead Onias prayed, "O God, the King of the whole world, since these that now stand with me are Thy people and those that are besieged are also Thy priests, I beseech Thee that Thou wilt neither hearken to the prayers of those against these; nor bring to effect that these pray against those." Following this prayer, Onias was quite consistently stoned to death.

Came the time of Passover, which even the Syrian Antonius the Pious had respected by offering sacrificial beasts to the Jews. Hyrcanus scorned such generosity. The exorbitant price of two thousand drachmae for each head of cattle was lowered from the walls in baskets. The besiegers thereupon gleefully kept both money and cattle. There is an additional account in the Talmud that someone (one tradition names Antipater) put a pig in one of the baskets but that the beast, conscious of its uncleanness, squealed all the way up as it tried to cling to the wall. As a result, states the tradition, an earthquake shook the land, destroying crops, so that starvation stalked through both camps.

In desperation, Aristobulus II appealed to Pompey, then waging war against Mithradates in Armenia. An agent of Pompey's, Scaurus, after accepting bribes from both sides, concluded that the king would be harder to conquer. He therefore ordered Hyrcanus to raise the siege. Hyrcanus at first demurred, but as Aretas, tired of fighting, willingly complied, the war came to an end at least temporarily.

For a year Pompey deferred final judgment, hoping the matter would amicably adjust itself. Instead a year of anarchy ensued.

Then once again the claimants appeared before the Roman. The proponents of Hyrcanus were described as more than a thousand Jews "of the best esteem"; the followers of Aristobulus II were "both young and insolent, whose purple garments, fine heads of hair, and other ornaments were detested by the court." A third faction, rabid theocrats, rejected both brothers since the Law ordained that a high priest, not a king, should rule. Pompey, essentially a just man, agreed to consider the dispute, and come to Jerusalem with his decision.

Aristobulus II could read between the lines. He was convinced that Pompey, unlike Scaurus, would prefer docility to strength in a subject ruler, and raised the standard of rebellion in Jerusalem. At the advice of Antipater, who decided this was the proper time to assert his adherence to the party of the high priest, Hyrcanus opened the city gates to the Romans, and Aristobulus II fled to the Temple. For three months hostilities raged. On every Sabbath, however, when the Jews were restricted to defending themselves against actual attack, the Romans made ready their machines, erected towers, and built mounds.

The final charge swept the Romans into the sacred precincts. Priests, departing not one jot from traditional procedure, were cut down at their altars. Others jumped off the walls or incinerated themselves in their houses. Altogether some twelve thousand died, while Aristobulus II and his sons were sent captive to Rome.

Pompey, disregarding Hyrcanus' plea, entered the Holy of Holies. Curiously he looked about him. He saw the golden table, the precious candlesticks, the censers, heaps of rare spices, and two thousand talents of the Sacred Treasury. But he could discover none of the reputed appurtenances of demon worship, of child sacrifice, no asses' heads or idols. Slowly the scented twilight settled upon him. With a half-fearsome glance over his shoulder, he stole out of the sanctuary, touching nothing that was within.

Hyrcanus had won a hollow victory. Confirmed as high priest and appointed ethnarch of Judea, he held only a barren scepter. The defenses of Jerusalem were demolished, tribute to Rome was exacted, Jewish soil was joined to Syria. Hyrcanus himself might not wear the crown, nor add territory to his country.

Antipater was really the only winner. Instigating the shabby bickering that disgusted Pompey, he had kept in the background, ingratiating himself with the Romans by practical suggestions and unostentatious display of his understanding the country and people, thereby convincing Pompey that he was the only man capable of conducting Jewish affairs to Rome's advantage.

This opinion was officially enacted in 57 B.C. when Alexander, son of Aristobulus II, escaped from Rome and stirred up a brief rebellion. The Romans, their cavalry led by Marc Antony, scattered the rebels after which Gabinius, the Roman commander, "settled the affairs of the Jews according to the wishes of Antipater."

These "wishes," apparently only a system of more democratic organization, were actually a subtle assault on the power of the Pharisees. In place of the previously existing twenty-three lesser sanhedrins functioning throughout the country with quite limited authority and subordinate to the great sanhedrin of seventy-two members in Jerusalem, he located five sanhedrins with equal power in Jerusalem and four other cities. This pleased the ordinary citizen who had up to this looked upon Antipater as a partisan of the Pharisees, because it greatly weakened the priestly clique at the capital.

The subsequent replacement of Gabinius the moderate by the detestable Crassus tried to the utmost all the patience and diplomacy of Antipater. Crassus had been a usurer, a purchaser of estates at times of conscription, a gang leader, head of an arson ring, and all-round grafter. By making promising young men like Julius Caesar his financial dependents, he had gone far socially and politically. Antipater tried, to the limits of his own safety, to stem the greed of Crassus. In vain. All the treasures (to the value of ten million dollars) that Pompey had spared, disappeared in his insatiable maw.

History has recorded his punishment. One short year and he blundered into a Parthian ambush, his packed legions wilting in their armor under a rain of arrows that blackened the sky, his matlocked foes led by an effeminate giant with painted face and long curls, thumping leather drums and banging gongs with maddening insistency as they rode round and round his stunned troops. His son, all besides gold that Crassus ever cherished, led a desperate charge. It failed and the youth's head was fixed on a stake in sight of the agonized father. When night fell, officers fled with their mumbling commander, in a last attempt at escape. Treacherous guides bogged them in a quagmire; Crassus was killed; his head and hands cut off and exhibited in triumph.

But meanwhile Antipater had to bear patiently the depredations of Crassus. His mind was fixed on a new, turbulent star that was mounting the imperial sky. He was determined to follow in the wake of Julius Caesar's meteoric sweep. For the first time, Antipater thought he recognized a patron who could assure stability to himself and provide for the future of his children, now approaching maturity in the clean air of the desert.

That Judea must be ruled by Rome to him was dogmatic. Keen student of men and affairs, he knew that Rome had long outgrown the sturdy period when it was truly *res publica*. He believed that the end of a transitional period between democracy and absolutism was near, during which strong but not quite strong enough leaders would destroy each other. He reasoned (and history has shown how short was his margin of error) that the time was ripe for one-man supremacy. The Romans he had hitherto known failed to qualify for sole rule. Pompey was too impractical; Crassus, too mean; Cassius, too impetuous. But Julius Caesar, he was certain, had the wisdom and strength and ambition required to dominate the Roman world.

Antipater was aware of how little he could offer that Caesar might want. Caesar was essentially a military genius while Antipater's achievements were in the field of statecraft. Nowhere in his record was there evidence of loyalty, bravery, and strategic skill. If the Roman had heard of him at all it was as a clever politician able to get along with characters as diverse as Pompey and Crassus, who could administer profitably and reasonably peacefully one of the more intractable Roman possessions. This for Antipater was not enough. Caesar must be made to admire his loyalty, and bravery, and military acumen.

His chances looked bleak. When Pompey fled Rome, Caesar immediately freed Aristobulus II, putting him in command of two legions to stamp out a rebellion in Syria. Here, however, he was poisoned by Pompey's agents, and his body, long un-

buried, preserved in honey, until Marc Antony sent it to Judea
where the restless spirit might sleep with his ancestors. Pompey's
waning strength was still potent enough also to bring about the
execution of Aristobulus II's son, the daring Alexander.

So the Idumean's luck still held. Only Hyrcanus the vacillating, and his nephew Antigonus II, only surviving son of
Aristobulus II, constituted the sorry survivors of the Hasmonean
line that reared a crumbling barrier between Antipater and
undivided rule.

Antipater's decision to support Caesar demonstrated vision
(and perhaps good fortune) of no mean order. Julius Caesar was
not destined to spring to power overnight. Before him stretched
five uncertain years of civil war with enemies in Spain, Africa,
Greece, and Egypt that must be crushed. A less far-sighted
statesman would have waited before committing himself irrevocably to a cause. But Antipater knew that a supreme ruler would
have thousands of camp followers, that to be in the favored inner
circle, he must have risked career and life while the conqueror's
present was still uncertain and his future dark.

His opportunity came when Mithradates, willing though un-
gifted ally of Julius Caesar, was stalled at Ascalon on the Palestinian coast. The troops were tired, their supplies exhausted, the
way to Egypt blocked by the fortress Pelusium. Antipater rushed
to their aid with three thousand seasoned Jewish troops, re-
enforced by a host of Arabs, born fighters, who knew every foot
of the desert wastes ahead. He also persuaded wealthy Syrian
leaders, as yet uncommitted, to solve the supply problem by
declaring for Caesar.

The heartened troops resumed the offensive. By an impetuous
charge which he personally led, Antipater cut through the enemy
lines and was the first to burst into the doomed fortress. The road
to Egypt was now open.

But Egypt was a hostile camp. Everywhere were garrisons of
Jewish mercenaries, warriors somewhat of a cross between Ireton's
fanatical Ironsides and the rollicking medieval men-at-arms. At
Onion Antipater conferred with their commanders. Ties of race
and religion, he argued, should preclude bloodshed between
them. To support this contention he produced letters from

Hyrcanus appealing to all Jews to support Julius Caesar, the enemy of Pompey who had violated the Holy of Holies. The Jews of Onion welcomed Antipater, as did those at Memphis and almost everywhere else. Only the Delta still held out.

At a place called the Jew's Camp their armies met. As usual, Mithradates miscalculated and was in danger of annihilation. Antipater, however, scattering the troops opposing him, wheeled and attacked the assailants of Mithradates on rear and flank, routing them completely at a loss of only eighty men.

Mithradates, though commander-in-chief, in his report to Caesar insisted that all the credit for victory should go to Antipater, the savior of his life. Caesar was impressed, and entrusted Antipater with a number of dangerous missions, all of which he accomplished, fortunately—as it turned out—getting himself wounded in the process.

After Egypt had been pacified, Caesar returned to Syria. Here he bestowed on Antipater the privileges of Roman citizenship and exempted his estates from taxation. Publicly, he proclaimed him as friend; almost as an afterthought, he confirmed Hyrcanus as high priest.

It was Antigonus II who unwittingly fixed Antipater still more firmly in Caesar's favor. After the deaths of his father and brother, this Hasmonean prince and his sisters were taken from their mother by Philipsio, son of Ptolemy of Chalcis. Philipsio promptly fell in love with Alexandra, the younger sister, and married her. Fascinated by his new daughter-in-law, Ptolemy quite as promptly murdered his son and married her himself. Antigonus II fled this alarming household and went to Caesar. Foolishly, instead of reminding the Roman of his former generosity to his family, and of Pompey's vindictive treatment of them, he indulged in a vicious tirade against Antipater, accusing him of fostering civil war for his own advantage, and charging that the Idumean's support of Caesar was purely selfish.

Antipater listened unmoved. He threw off his clothes, and pointed to his battle scars, for "there were many wounds almost all over his body."

Caesar brusquely dismissed Antigonus II. To prove his complete faith, he asked Antipater to designate whatever authority he wished for himself. Modestly—because he understood Caesar—Antipater asked for nothing.

Caesar's response was truly generous. He appointed Antipater Procurator of Judea, with these rights: 1) absolute control of all local civil and religious authority; 2) nomination and deposition of high priests; 3) charge of all priestly equipment, to be let out for use at his discretion. In addition, the country was declared free from tribute and levy; the Judean government was entrusted with the defense of frontier towns and forts, and (probably at Antipater's suggestion) the walls of Jerusalem might be rebuilt.

Antipater hurried back to Jerusalem, and refortified the capital. Hyrcanus was, of course, cosily ensconced in the high priesthood.

The procurator, though not an old man, was tired. Perhaps he had the child of the desert's premonition of death, and wanted to see his estate settled on his sons in his own day. Calling them together he appointed his oldest son Phasael, governor of Jerusalem and its environments; the rule of unquiet Galilee he entrusted to his second son, Herod.

CHAPTER **IV**

RISE AND EBB

IN THE CAREER OF HEROD THE GREAT, THERE is lacking the usual array of significant childhood incidents and omens that make the lives of most great men such object lessons for unaspiring youth. He breaks into the Judean scene full-blown at the age of twenty-five, a husband and a father, abundantly gifted with the talents for rule. As we see him first, he is brave, handsome, able, and ruthless—an organizer and a reformer—one obviously quite competent to play his role. So much is evident from the moment he stepped into his office, despite our almost utter ignorance of his antecedent life.

Undulating dunes dozing by a sapphire sea; sand-blasted ruins that now and again push a shattered spine through the shroud of burning desert; silences, interrupted only by the guttural calls of passing Arabs, or the incongruous wail of a locomotive coasting along the inland flats are all that mark the birthplace of Herod.

Called Ashkelon by the Philistines, it had gloried in the noise and color and smell of the Phoenecian mart; Semitic lads had thrilled to the tales of gypsy-like seamen, of the towering Pillars of Hercules, of tin mined by squat, dark barbarians in distant foggy Cornwall; of the lush shores of golden Ophir. Under Roman occupation it lost much of its charm and became work-aday Ascalon, a busy naval port and embarking place, whence, with a short, pleasant sail, the heat and dust of the land bridge between Egypt and Syria could be bypassed. Crumbling blocks of black stone mark the fortress erected by Richard the Lion-hearted, recalling the fervent movement that, defeated in its objective of ransoming the Sepulcher of the Lord, brought back, as a solace, the wisdom of the East.

Though Herod named and beautified this city as his birthplace, it is probable that little of his childhood was spent here. His mother Cyprus—although she may have had a remote Jewish ancestor—had the desert denizen's dislike of crowded alleys, preferring the windy horizons, the tortured hills, and the drowsy oases of the wilderness. His father, sane and sensible in raising a family as he was cautious and crafty in ruling the state, knew the inevitable danger of subjecting his children to the vehemence and meanness of Jewish political life. It is almost certain that Herod, with his brothers and sister, was carefully brought up with his mother's people, in the wild gravelly stretches of the Arabian desert, where the luxury and treachery of Jerusalem was but another mirage.

Yet their knowledge of statecraft, their ability to set a value on the words and deeds of men, were never acquired in the uncomplicated society of the desert. In that acquisition, we see the hand of Antipater. His children might be brought up as nomads in their black tents, but they must never be allowed to forget that over the horizon were council chambers, and ravaging armies, and golden thrones.

Very little is told of Herod's childhood, and what little there is might be considered prophetic. When he was twelve, his teacher Manahem, an Essene, predicted that the boy would one day be king. When Herod laughed at the prediction, Manahem slapped him, bidding him "remember my prophetic words by this blow." That an Essene, a follower of the extreme right wing of Judaism, one whose religion was so utterly unworldly as to be almost mystical, was his teacher is a commentary on the type of moral and spiritual guidance which Antipater provided for his children.

Meager though enthusiastic accounts of Herod's physical prowess particularly stress his accomplishments as a rider. "His lance was quick," we are also told, "and his arrow seldom missed its mark." Like young David, he fought off wild beasts that raided his flock; along with other adventurous Arabs he loved clan fights and marauding expeditions.

When his older sons had attained maturity, Antipater, as we have seen, appointed Phasael, loyal, cheerful, and rather stupid, to rule Judea. Phasael's task was for the time being not very trying. Antipater himself was at hand; priestly authority was vested in Hyrcanus, who could be counted on to exercise his sacerdotal functions adequately and with popular approval; the country was well policed; in fact no situation was likely to arise which Phasael, with perhaps some help from his father, could not cope with.

Galilee, Herod's proving ground, was quite another problem. Unlike barren, "gloomy" Judea, it was a pleasant land. Rainfall was ample, thanks to the rain clouds caught by the heights of the Lebanon. The soil was fertile. Figs, walnuts, vines, palms, in fact all Mediterranean fruits and grain, grew profusely. The Sea of Galilee, in Herod's day ringed about by a diadem of gleaming villages, teemed with fish. A sixth-century writer described it as "a paradisal country, rivaling Egypt with its grains and cereals, and, although so small, surpassing her in wine, oil and fruit." Nor was it all farms and vineyards and fisheries. Dotted on its verdant surface were some two hundred and forty towns and villages. Manufacturing flourished chiefly along the coast, where potteries and dyestuffs, known throughout the East, were made.

While the Galilean was racially akin to the Judean, there were, nevertheless, differences which the Judean delighted to emphasize. Historically, Galilee was not altogether Jewish. King Solomon had given over ten of its cities for colonization to King Hiram of Tyre, in part payment for his help in building the Temple. Because of his somewhat mixed blood, the Galilean was despised in Judea. He was made the butt of jokes, cruel and humorless, as were all the pleasantries of the Judeans. His accent and his countrified appearance were scoffed at and his breathless piety in the Temple derided by the sanctimonious sophisticates at the capital. "Can anything good come out of Galilee?" they asked of Christ. "Thy speech doth betray thee," the serving maid told Peter. "Search and look, for out of Galilee there arises no prophet," was the verdict of Jerusalem.

The Galilean himself was never conscious of any inferiority.

He was good-natured, brave, tenacious in his opinions and fanatically devoted to his faith. He made an ideal soldier and a perfect missionary. (It will be recalled that it was an apostolate of Galileans, if we except the cosmopolite Saint Paul, who carried the creed of the Master to the earth's far corners.)

Had Galilee been even moderately at peace, Herod's task as governor would have been relatively simple, testing only his powers of organization and development. But Galilee was at this time overrun by bands of robbers, highly organized, working in collusion with many of the nationalistic elements in the country, and abetted by the people as a whole. Many writers have described these gangs as patriots waging incessant war against Rome, to keep the flame of insurrection aglow in the glens and caves of Galilee after it had been crushed under the iron heel of the legionary in Judea.

In part only is this accurate. They did cut off small Roman detachments; they did attack Roman transport trains and isolated army posts. But they went beyond such military activities. They terrorized neighboring villages across the border in Syria, took toll of caravans passing through Galilee, and robbed and killed foreign travelers. Only remotely might they be called successors to the Maccabees. Rather they resembled the hijackers of the Prohibition Era.

Immediately Herod took office, he was besought by many of the peace-loving Galileans, as well as by the Romans, to destroy what Josephus describes as a "nest of robbers." The term specifically refers to a powerful and vicious band, led by Hezekiah and his son Judah.

Herod had one great advantage over the Romans, who had been unable to exterminate the robbers. He knew how to deal with ambushes and raids and forays. Calling on his desert experiences, he checkmated surprise with surprise, snare with snare; and, having as much of bravery as his enemies and greater skill and means, he soon destroyed them, accepting the submission of the less contentious, relentlessly killing those who persisted in their resistance. He was particularly severe with Hezekiah and Judah; he had these self-appointed Maccabeans tortured to death.

In Syria, Herod became overnight a popular idol. Lebanon

villages vied with each other in composing ballads in his honor. Even the Roman commander in Syria, the hard-bitten Sextus Caesar, was so affected by the personable young warrior that "he loved Herod."

In Jerusalem, Herod's exploits excited a quite different response. Pharisees looked sourly on the administrative successes of Antipater and his sons. So long as the people in general were satisfied, they could do nothing. Here was their opportunity. Herod had overstepped himself. Instead of a Jewish ruler, he could be depicted merely as a minion of Rome. By executing robbers who had not been condemned by the Grand Sanhedrin at Jerusalem, he had done what even the Roman rarely dared to do to Jewish citizens. For according to Jewish law, the Grand Sanhedrin was the only agency that might condemn a Jew to death.

This sanhedrin held a place of peculiar importance in the history of Jewish jurisprudence. According to tradition, it grew out of a council of seventy elders of Israel whom God commanded Moses to assemble in the "tent of meeting." It is more likely that it originated in the time of Antiochus the Great (223–187 B.C.). In form, it was a combination of a high court of justice and an administrative council. Its membership numbering seventy-two included probably the priestly nobility of the Sadducees and the doctors of the Pharisees. During the earlier reform of Antipater, its power had been limited to its own district of Jerusalem. When the government was centralized in Jerusalem after the rebuilding of its walls, its former state as a sort of Jewish supreme court was restored.

The authority of the court was unquestionably flouted when Herod ordered the killing of the robbers. It could, and would, therefore, call Herod himself to account, and so it informed Hyrcanus.

The high priest was not anxious to stir up trouble. As always he wanted to be left at peace. Only when that peace was threatened could he be prodded into action.

This the Pharisees proceeded to see done. They harped on the usurpation of his authority and of his priestly office by Herod. Eventually, by nagging repetition over this disturbing theme, they convinced him that his security, even his life, depended on the removal of so ambitious and arrogant an adversary.

Even more disturbing to the sensitive high priest was the continuous heckling by the mothers and other female relatives of the dead robbers. The Pharisees had brought them to Jerusalem with generous maintenance and very specific instructions as to conduct. Wherever he went, they dogged the footsteps of Hyrcanus, weeping and wailing. On the way to the Temple his path was blocked by throngs of disheveled women, decrying with oriental abandon and vividness his failure to avenge their men by calling their murderer to account. Even his nights were made sleepless by relays of mourners, tirelessly shrieking maledictions at the spurner of the Jewish law. And always on the outskirts of the bereaved stood the Pharisees, sniffing their distress at the timidity of the representative of Aaron.

As a matter of fact, the Jews of Jerusalem had absolutely no interest in the fate of the Galilean robbers. Most of them must have felt that their extermination was a good thing for the country. Nevertheless, the Pharisees made skilful use of the Galilean women. Eventually, to obtain respite from the insistence of the Pharisees and the complaints and abuse of the women, Hyrcanus summoned Herod to appear before the sanhedrin to answer for his actions.

It is not likely that, left to himself, he would have obeyed the summons. He was, in truth, not a little upset by the procedure. He felt that to keep order in his province was a duty assigned him by his father and by Rome and that it was his task to ensure safety to the neighboring towns of Syria, as well as to foreign travelers and merchants passing through Galilee. To do this he had had to break up the robber bands that infested the land. Where possible he had acted moderately; when the robbers were stubborn, he had them killed.

Perhaps, he granted, he had been unduly severe with Hezekiah and Judah. But these were notorious malefactors, rebels as well as robbers, and their fate would serve as a warning to others. It was, of course, true that the law required that the death sentence be passed only by the Grand Sanhedrin at Jerusalem. Still, this was war of a kind, where martial law supplanted the civil courts.

Galilee was essentially a Roman province, and Herod's conduct had greatly pleased his Roman overlords as well as the great mass of peaceful provincials. It would be beneath his dignity to stand before a court of pietistic fuss-budgets to submit his well-intentioned actions to the myopic judgment of formalists.

The mediation of Antipater and Phasael was all that prevented Herod's defiance of the sanhedrin. Flouting the law would only outrage the people as a whole, they persuaded him. It would cool the enthusiasm of the Galileans and intensify the hatred of the Pharisees. His great deeds in Palestine would be forgotten; all classes would unite behind Hyrcanus as the champion of the law. To a people whose concept of patriotism was largely the inviolability of their law, disregard of this law, however silly or unjust it might appear, could prove fatal. Let him, therefore, attend the trial, but not as a criminal. Rather let him go confidently, proudly. Let him be accompanied by a guard, not so many as would seem to defy the court, but strong enough to assure his safety.

Herod acquiesced. He saw that the plan had possibilities never visualized by its proponents.

In Jerusalem, Hyrcanus was fidgety, clearly anxious to have the hateful ordeal over with. His apprehension grew as a messenger brought him a letter from Sextus Caesar, demanding that he free Herod under fear of his displeasure. That displeasure could have but one meaning. If the Jews executed a Roman citizen (Herod's father had been granted citizenship), Rome would certainly be revenged on Jerusalem from Hyrcanus down.

The day of the trial dawned in a ferment of excitement. No other trial till that later infamous trial of Christ ever caused so much tumult. Long before the sun's first beams ignited the burnished dome of the Temple, crowds began to converge on the "Hall of Hewn Stones." By noon the courtyard was jammed. A twisting, squirming mass of humanity filled every converging lane. No one wanted to miss being in at the kill. For it was common knowledge that, hours before the time of trial, the jury huddled in the chill shadows of the hall of judgment had agreed on its verdict. Hyrcanus eventually made his appearance. The mob, with mocking obsequiousness, had not failed to cheer his passage. So dejected he seemed, however, that the sanhedrin, while formally respectful, could hardly conceal their contempt at his timorousness.

The hall in which the sanhedrin met was not calculated to raise the spirits of the defendant or to move his judges to mercy. Its architecture has been called daring and austere. Stone walls of relatively great height closed in upon a semicircular room, lighted only by latticed windows near the roof. At the center of the long, straight wall, opposite the squat, angular entrance was a table upon a stone dais, where sat the "high rabbi" (Hyrcanus in this instance), with "the father of the house of judgment" (the authority on law) at his right.

Down three short flights of steps on the floor of the hall were semicircular tiers of seats where sat the members of the sanhedrin. Between the judge and the sanhedrin was space for the defendant. Behind him were three benches for the Law, with small tables at each end for the secretaries, one of whom took down the testimony of the defendant, the other, that of the prosecutor and the judgment of the court. Designedly, the defendant and the jurors were placed in the lower gloom. High up, benefiting by the half-light that sifted through the narrow windows, sat the judge, symbolizing the lofty, and sometimes unscalable heights of justice.

The hour of trial came and passed. Still no Herod! Would he dare come? Suppressed elation at his seeming defiance swept through the council. He was playing into their hands. Dire threats were muttered and transmitted to the sweating throngs in the steaming alleys beyond.

Then, of a sudden, sounds swelled never before heard in that dismal hall. Clang of arms, crisp words of command, and a group of stony-faced Romans and keen-eyed Arabs bored through the spectators and halted before the sanhedrin. From their ranks, bold and debonair, his garments purple, hair and beard curled and perfumed, voice resonant and unafraid, stepped the culprit Herod.

The assembly was dumbfounded. Always in trials by the sanhedrin the accused presented himself humbly and meekly, with disheveled clothing and woebegone appearance, almost literally with his throat in a halter, in order to stimulate a sense of pity in his judges. Here was so violent a departure from custom that it left the judges stunned. His death was already decided. They loathed him.

Yet they feared him even more. Sidewise glances at gleaming spears and business-like swords made life seem too dear to be squandered on reckless threats and accusations. For a time no one dared raise his voice. It seemed likely that the charges would go by default.

At length the most venerable person in the hall, the sage Sameas, "a righteous man and for that reason above all fear," arose. Looking quite through the handsome, sneering figure that fronted his cowering judges, he spoke in tones low but unafraid which carried beyond the dim judgment hall to the hushed courtyard beyond:

"O ye that are assessors with me, and O thou that art our king (Hyrcanus), I neither have ever myself known such a case, nor do I suppose that any one of you can name its parallel—that one who is called to take his trial by us ever stood in such a manner before us. But everyone, whosoever he be, that comes to be tried by this sanhedrin, presents himself in a submissive manner, and like one that is in fear of himself and endeavors to move us to compassion, with his hair dishevelled, and in a black and mourning garment. But this admirable man, Herod, who is accused of murder, and called to answer so heavy an accusation, stands here clothed in purple, and with the hair of his head finely trimmed, and with his armed men about him, so that if we shall condemn him by our law, he may slay us, and by overbearing justice may himself escape death. Yet do not I make this complaint against Herod himself. He is, to be sure, more concerned for himself than for the laws. But my complaint is against yourselves, and your king, who give him a license so to do. However, take notice, that God is great; and this very man, whom you are going to absolve and dismiss for the sake of Hyrcanus, will one day punish both you and your king also."

As he finished, the suspicion of a flush crept over the hard features of the Romans; the beady eyes of the Arabs darkened to animated jet; the tanned face of Herod burned with vexation. The hall was a turmoil of yelling and cursing, of hoarse cries and threatening fists. The judges to a man shrieked their condemnation; the multitude without echoed their malediction—a generation later their sons would clamor, "Crucify him—his blood be upon us and on our children," when a gentle, innocent victim faced his judge.

Through all the uproar, three figures stood out: the wise Sameas, foreseeing perhaps the day when Herod would ironically give the letter of his prediction the lie by sparing him while slaughtering the rest of the sanhedrin; Herod, hand on sword, upset, but not unnerved by this revulsion; and Hyrcanus, against his will, the one person with power to still the storm.

For perhaps the only time in his life, Hyrcanus acted with force and decision. In a strangely ringing voice that carried through the bedlam he declared the session ended for that day, to be resumed on the morrow.

Like a storm passing into the distance the shouts and cries died away to a sullen muttering. The high priest had spoken. However hateful his words, they must be heeded. Herod, ringed about by the spears of his guard, turned his back to his judges, and the troops pressed through the jeering, spitting mob, down from the Temple to the castle of Antigonus.

Later that day Herod received a message from Hyrcanus imploring him to quit Jerusalem that very night.

Although Hyrcanus has been accused of self-interest and cowardice in suspending the session just when the conviction of Herod seemed certain, it is probable that he acted in accordance with the rules of the sanhedrin. Exactly what the proper procedure was then, we do not know. Certainly a few years later the death sentence might be passed only after a night had elapsed since the trial.

Herod went to Damascus to lick his wounds.

The fury of the mob, the deep-rooted hatred of the judges did not make him afraid. Instead it aroused a corresponding fury and hatred in his heart. He felt deeply injured. His destruction of the robbers was an act that benefited the Jews. Instead of gratitude he found opposition and enmity because he had ventured to snap a thread of the formalism twisted about the core of Jewish life. From that shameful day in the Hall of Hewn Stones he hated the religious and judicial leaders of the Jews with a cold, purposeful malignity that he bore with him to the grave.

To console him, his friend Sextus Caesar appointed him governor of Coele-Syria and Samaria. (It is unlikely, in view of the relationship between the two, that, as Josephus says, Herod bought the office.)

With power and prestige re-established, Herod raised an army and started for Jerusalem. Furious plans raced through his mind. He would unseat the poltroon Hyrcanus; he would let his troops loot and rape the scurrilous Judeans; he would batter down the walls of the detestable city, and raze the Temple where they chanted their hypocritical hymns.

Antipater and Phasael once again curbed his precipitancy. Patiently, as with a sullen, hurt child, they argued, not excusing the sanhedrin—they were too discreet for that—but Hyrcanus. The high priest was naturally a timid man, they told him, who could be easily convinced that Herod with an army and most of Galilee to support him threatened his security. Even so, Hyrcanus did not act with malice. Under duress, he was compelled to summon Herod. Yet he suspended the session of the sanhedrin and thus saved the prisoner from the death sentence. That night he advised him to escape when a sojourn in that inflamed city might have cost Herod his life. Impress Hyrcanus, frighten him, by all means, but go no farther. Above all, do not by violent action give the mass of Jews cause to believe that there is truth in the accusation of the sanhedrin.

Grudgingly, Herod postponed his plan for vengeance. As an outlet for his energies he accompanied Sextus Caesar in a campaign in Syria.

The rebuff by the sanhedrin was a minor setback to the progress of Herod. On the horizon lowered clouds portending stress and storm, in the wake of which would be strewn the broken bodies of the wise Antipater and the loyal Phasael and a Herod, shaken and beaten, plotting suicide because he was as yet blind to the miracle of the Roman rainbow beyond.

CHAPTER V

AND NOW
THE PARTHIAN

SUETONIUS NEED NOT HAVE EXPRESSED SUR-
prise that the Jews in Rome should pass night after night in
bitter wailing after the murder of Caesar. Their grief was a
grateful response to the passing of a benefactor. Unwittingly
these exiles were bewailing as well the impending dissolution
of their country, and a second, more permanent diaspora. The
three-and-thirty daggers that "hacked each other in the sides of
Caesar" as surely struck at the heart of Jewish hopes. It is but
one stumbling step from dead Caesar to triumphant Herod; with
Herod happily gone, to the shameful admission, "Away with
him, we have no king but Caesar"; less than four decades more,
to the last awful cataclysm when the lanes of the sweet towns
that ringed Lake Galilee ran red, and the tawny heights of
Jerusalem were seared with blasting destruction.

Caesar was a leader whom his men followed implicitly, an
incomparable military analyst, and a supremely great general.
When Antipater, however, accounted him another Alexander the
Great, he—from a deceptive distance—missed one great fault.
Caesar consistently misjudged the quality and ability of all men
except soldiers. With money and amusements, he planned to
win the support of the citizens of Rome; his soldiers, he knew,
were faithful. Therein he miscalculated tragically.

This attitude was not the result of the soldier's disdain of the
civilian, nurtured in the rarer atmosphere of the military camp.
It was an integral part of Caesar's makeup. Even before he held
any public office he had already spent thirteen hundred talents

to cultivate popular acclaim. As surveyor of the Appian Way he poured borrowed money into his work to get himself talked about. As aedile he provided the people with as many as three hundred and twenty gladiatorial contests a day, at enormous personal expense. While he was contesting for the office of pontifex maximus, one of his opponents offered him money sufficient to clear all his debts to withdraw. Caesar answered that he was prepared to borrow even a greater amount to win.

When his big opportunity came to rehabilitate his fortunes as governor of Spain, his creditors so hounded him that only the willingness of the vulpine Crassus to take over a debt of eight hundred and thirty talents left him free. That there were men with neither the dog-like devotion of the soldier, nor the purchasable friendship of the commoner, Caesar never learnt until too late.

This weakness Antipater was naturally not in position to discover in time. So, when he and his sons were identified with the fortunes of Julius Caesar, they took over all the enmities and hatreds of the very considerable following of Pompey which was still strong in almost every part of the Roman empire.

The first threat came from Syria. There, Cecilius Bassus, protégé of Pompey, assassinated Herod's patron, Sextus Caesar. The army of Sextus, with the easy assimilation of most mercenary soldiers, transferred their allegiance to Bassus. Other Roman troops, natives of Syria, and auxiliaries sent by Antipater besieged Bassus in Apamia.

The war dragged on long enough to irritate Caesar at Rome, who sent Marcus to restore order. Before this could be accomplished, the assassins let open the flood gates of chaos to inundate the whole Roman world.

Peace of a sort came when Cassius, the practical, effected a reconciliation between Bassus and Marcus, before turning to the serious business of proving true the contention that he had "an itching palm."

With the Jews, whom he justifiably considered friendly to Caesar, he was particularly severe, imposing on them the gigantic fine of seven hundred talents, roughly half the annual income of the entire country. Antipater, of necessity, set about raising the money, dividing its collection among Phasael, Herod, and Malichus, an intimate of Hyrcanus. Phasael, with difficulty, accomplished his quota, while Herod showed such avidity in raising his share (a hundred talents) in Galilee that he won the applause of Cassius. Malichus, because of a spirit of rebellion or through mere ineptitude, was so remiss in collecting his part that only a last-minute contribution of a hundred talents of Hyrcanus' own money saved him from being killed by Cassius. As it was, four cities in his district, including Emmaus, were reduced to slavery and their inhabitants sold to raise the money.

All the sullenness, the bitterness that simmered in the pharisaical soul of Malichus seethed into every fiber of his fanatical being. He blamed Antipater for his own predicament, for the weakness of Hyrcanus, and for the lack of spirit among the Maccabees generally. And so Malichus plotted, with a deplorable lack of discretion, to kill Antipater.

Antipater knew what was going on. He might have forcibly disposed of his enemy. To do this, however, at a time when the people were desperate because of the crushing taxes, would almost certainly invite rebellion, give Cassius an excuse to take over the country, and depose him and his sons. He gathered together a loyal bodyguard of Idumeans and Arabs and sped across the Jordan to the desert.

Malichus boldly made his way to the camp in the wilds. Under the cold desert starlight, surrounded by faces savage in the writhing flames of thorn bush, he convinced Antipater that he erred. How could anyone dare plot his death, so long as Phasael commanded the garrison of Jerusalem and Herod numbered the military might of Galilee and Syria among his following?

Perhaps the persuasive mouthings of the Pharisee prevailed, with the winy desert air, in confounding the senses of the Idumean. Intrigue and plots seemed very remote there around the fitful fire, under the velvet heavens hobnailed with stars, with the fierce loyalty of the sons of the desert between him and danger.

They reached Jerusalem just in time to encounter Marcus. So transparent were the designs of Malichus that the Roman had rushed down from Syria to kill the plotter and nip a Jewish uprising. Antipater quieted Marcus' uneasiness and half convinced him that Malichus was harmless.

It was a fatal error. Jealousy and hatred had blinded Malichus to every consideration of gratitude. At a banquet in the palace of Hyrcanus, meant to seal their reconciliation, the cup of friendship—in this instance a goblet of poisoned wine—was passed to Antipater by a butler, a creature of Malichus. Antipater, the instant his lips touched the cup, knew himself doomed. Groping for the table edge that suddenly became elusive, he half pulled himself to his feet, then crumpled on his couch. Darkness, that swooped in foglike banks, bit by bit blotted out the glitter, and scent, and turmoil of the chamber. His glazing eyes tried ineffectually to stab the dark to see, beyond this perjured land, the flinty sands and ruddy cliffs of his home. Instead they closed on the horrified bewilderment of the high priest and the triumphant sneer of the Pharisee.

For terseness and dignity, no epithet can excel that of Josephus. To him Antipater was "a man that had distinguished himself for piety, and justice, and love of his country."

The death of Antipater (43 B.C.) left Herod without any real restraining influence, except a canny understanding of his own position and interests. Phasael—even had he lived—would have had the calmness to curb Herod but not his father's acumen to guide him. Herod, hurt by the attitude of the sanhedrin, sickened by the treachery that destroyed his father, was hurled, not entirely of his own volition, into a maelstrom of passions and plots that excited his genius, and unfortunately his intemperance. While Antipater lived, he was an impetuous, ingenuous child of the desert, bred to organize, and control not only his subordinates but also his own faculties. Thereafter he became by degrees, and slowly at first, an oriental despot, abler, crueler than most, but essentially a descendant of Sennacherib and Darius.

His conduct toward Malichus was the surest evidence that his impetuosity was tempered by his unhappy experiences before the sanhedrin and with this by an appreciation of the vicissitudes of subject princes under inconstant Rome. Two years before, regardless of consequences, he would have killed Malichus with as little compunction as he had slain the Galilean robbers.

Now, even though Cassius had shown his favor by making him general of an army in Coele-Syria and commander of a fleet as well, he made little objection to his brother's plea to postpone their revenge until such time that civil war might not result. The desert law of the clan was annulled, giving place to the slow guile of diplomacy. Seemingly he accepted Malichus' protestations of innocence in good faith and contented himself with erecting a noble monument to his father's memory.

Chaotic conditions in Samaria, always a plague spot to Jews and Romans alike, gave him an outlet for his pent emotions. He threw himself into the thankless task of establishing order amid anarchy, in a district not worth considering from either a political or a military viewpoint. He settled reasonably the differences among factions, relieved the distress of a starving people, and set up a workable government.

This accomplished, he started for Jerusalem with a considerable army. Malichus, fearing the worst, prevailed upon Hyrcanus as high priest to send messengers to Herod, forbidding him to enter the city during the period of Purification. Herod ignored the messengers and marched into Jerusalem, taking pains, however, to give the impression that his was merely a routine visit.

Malichus, in friendliest manner, was the first to welcome him. He recalled the sterling qualities of Antipater, and, working himself into a frenzy of grief, threw himself on Herod's shoulder in a tempest of tears. Herod matched tear with tear and the two parted with protestations of everlasting friendship.

Neither could have believed he was deluding the other. Malichus' entire career was ingrained with fanaticism and hypocrisy. As for Herod, never in his life could anything deviate him from his purpose, whether it were the death of a foe or the rebuilding of the Temple. All that was uppermost in the minds of both was to kill the other. But each was as firmly determined to kill him safely.

Herod's procedure was legitimate and shrewd. He sent a complete, impersonal record of all that happened to Cassius, who saw in Malichus a malcontent whose continued existence was a challenge to himself. Cassius ordered Herod to have him killed. To expedite his death, he instructed his officers in Tyre to place themselves under Herod's orders.

The capture of Laodicea after a protracted siege provided the occasion. Nobility, including Herod and Malichus, from all the nearby states met at the stricken city to present its captor with garlands and gifts—a practice made politely compulsory by Cassius.

Malichus so far had shown himself bold and hypocritical, but transparent. Now he conceived a plan so logical and daring that it translates his customary folly into the field of grand strategem. His son was held hostage in Tyre. Under cover of the excitement of the celebration, he arranged to spirit him away. Then knowing that Cassius was feverishly anxious to leave for the campaign against Antony, he felt the occasion opportune to rebel against Rome and kill Herod.

Unfortunately for Malichus, Herod foresaw the same possibility; the invective "that fox," applied to Herod's son, describes Herod as well. After telling Cassius' officers his suspicions, he invited Malichus to supper.

It was an invitation that he could not readily refuse without disclosing his hand. After all, it need not disrupt his plans. When the guests were tipsy with the sweet eastern wines and absorbed in the undulations of the Syrian dancing girls, he could slip away and free his son.

He never reached the supper. On the baked sands outside the city Roman bravos buried their daggers in his false heart.

For a while the still form lay solitary on the blinding beach. A regal figure strode from behind the shelter of a dune, threw one divining glance at the crimson blood welling now more slowly, matting the victim's perfumed beard, and turned away with firm step. Herod had accounted for another enemy.

When Hyrcanus heard of Malichus' death, he was for the moment speechless with fright. But shortly he issued a statement in which he "commended the action; for that Malichus was a very wicked man, and one that conspired against his country." Malichus, too, had committed the unpardonable sin of threatening Hyrcanus' security.

Safe for the moment, Herod began to build for the future. It was galling for him to think that as a result of a juvenile infatuation he had married Doris, a Jewess of no great family connection, but wise and virtuous enough to insist on a legal union.

His mortification was not lessened because he had, for a time at
least, genuinely loved her and was proud of Antipater, the robust
son born to them. Doris, despite her commonplace origin, was
attractive and apparently, save for a headstrong strain that resulted in violent if transitory disputes, a fit mate for her husband.

Yet Herod knew he could never completely command the
support of the Jews—he was not interested in winning their
affections—unless he had some sort of hereditary claim on them.
Like Napoleon, eighteen centuries later, he was willing to put
away the wife he loved and supplant her with one who could
bring him prestige.

Still quivering over the Malichus affair, Hyrcanus received
from Herod a plea for the hand of his granddaughter.

Mariamne was most completely a Maccabean princess. Hyrcanus, in an attempt to cement peace in his family, had arranged
the marriage of his daughter Alexandra with his nephew Alexander, the son of Hyrcanus' brother, Aristobulus II. The child
of first cousins, both of them lineal descendants of the Maccabees
—no purer Hasmonean blood could flow! To marry her, to found
an unassailable throne for himself and their children, Herod
would willingly dismiss Doris.

To Doris, Herod's action could not have been unexpected. She
had been permitted to share her husband's love; never his position. Aware of Herod's ambition, she knew she must eventually
be thrust aside. The realization was a gnawing fury, which she
transmitted to her unfortunate child, doomed to be Herod's
final victim at the very time when his father was squirming and
blaspheming in the throes of his death agony.

Hyrcanus gave a qualified consent to the marriage, which
seemed, after all, a pledge to his safety. But his very timidity
made him firm in one respect. The wedding must not take place
until Herod himself was assured of the throne.

Alexandra, Mariamne's detestable mother, furthered the match
with all the insistence of her vile nature.

As for Mariamne herself, a sweet, gay, loyal, pretty young
lady—in many respects she is the prototype of the unhappy
Desdemona—there is little question that the glamor of her masterful lover put to rout any stray qualms that might have crept
into her romantic mind.

So were espoused the dreamy, sensitive Jewish princess and the cynical, relentless Idumean. Four years were destined to drag by before they were married in the calm quiet of Samaria, where the din of Jerusalem's tumbling walls seemed only the distant echo of the bridal song of this fairest and most pitiful of the Maccabean line.

It is almost a truism that the moment a conqueror turns his back on his victims, the dogs of revolt begin to worry his heels. No sooner had Cassius left Asia to join Brutus than rebellion broke out at Jerusalem and at Tyre.

In the former city, the Roman commander Felix, a conceited, foppish weakling, seized the strong points in the city and as far afield as Masada in the south. Felix's outburst was actually a grudge fight, the combined results of jealousy of Herod's success and chagrin at being buried in the cold, hostile tomb of Jerusalem while more able and favored officers had an opportunity for glory and plunder elsewhere. While Herod was away, Felix planned to kill Phasael and then dispose of his greater enemy later.

When news of the outbreak reached Herod, he was with Fabius, Roman governor of Damascus, who was by heavy bribes secretly aligned with the cause of Antigonus II. He had planned immediately to march to his brother's aid. But before he was able to do so, he was stricken with a mysterious malady that laid him helpless. Josephus calls the affliction a "distemper," a comprehensive term for whatever illness could not be readily diagnosed. It is conceivable, however, that excitement, worry, and disappointment brought on a temporary fit of madness, the precursor of many violent mental attacks that grew more and more virulent as his declining years were harried by unhappiness and mistrust.

Phasael did not need his brother's help to subdue the Roman incompetent. In a short time, Felix was glad to sue for terms and to be allowed, after his claws were drawn, to keep his former office. With Hyrcanus, Phasael took a harsher tone. He berated him for being at the bottom of the trouble, both by his former aid to Malichus and by his taking no steps to prevent Malichus' brother from seizing the fortress at Jerusalem.

Meanwhile Herod recovered in time to round up the rebels

that were waging guerrilla war about the countryside and to receive the surrender of the remoter forts and posts.

The Tyrean sedition threatened to become a more serious affair because of its Galilean repercussions. Marion, local tyrant, one of a type that throughout the East obtained power by purchase from Cassius, thought his dominion too inconsiderable for his spacious ambition. He burst into Galilee, seized three forts, and by a combination of generosity and shrewdness won many of the people to his side.

This was a threat to the very core of Herod's power, the loyalty of his Galileans. Once and for all to grapple the provincials to his cause he scraped together every soldier and engine, and with unnecessarily overwhelming power took fort after fort with laughable ease. After every conquest he called together his shamefaced, cringing captives. Like a father smiling patiently at the silly mistakes of his children, he spoke to them, and not only left them the lives they forfeited by rebellion, but loaded them with presents as well.

It is easy to understand the rebirth of loyalty and affection such a course engendered. Yet it is characteristic of Herod that always he played the childlike, thick-headed Galilean and the inhibited Samaritan, hungry for friendship, against the inflexible Judean. In the course of the war it developed that the force behind vain, incapable Marion was Ptolemy, first father-in-law, later, after he murdered his son, husband of Antigonus II's sister, so that, in smashing the Galilean revolt, Herod also crushed a conceivable attempt at restoring the Maccabean line.

For all too brief a time the future seemed serene. Rebellion was overcome (in most instances with kindness); Antigonus II stood repudiated; Samaria and Galilee were definitely loyal; and even in Judea, Hyrcanus, as grandfather and guardian of Herod's espoused wife, was at least for a time converting to his side all but the most bitter of the priestly clan. As for the ordinary Judean, he was ready to accept any ruler whose reign would guarantee peace.

No action more cataclysmic than the Battle of Philippi had ever recast the complexion of Rome. Actually, amid most violent birth throes, it marked the natal day of a new, strangely different

Roman world. Brutus and Cassius, key figures in post-Caesarian Rome, killed themselves; and their adherents in every part of the empire could entertain little hope of escaping their fate.

Spurts of violence flickered up wherever rulers with the threat of Brutus or Cassius to bolster their arm had flailed the spirits of their subjects. Jerusalem seethed with schemes to overthrow Herod. Men hitherto docile or disinterested became ranting rebels. Was not the tetrarch the favorite of Cassius? Did he not drain his country's wealth to a degree to please even the bottomless greed of the Roman? In return, had he not been honored and trusted by his overlord? All the world recognized him as a creature of the discredited tyrant's. Would not the mortal enemies of Cassius eject this Idumean upstart from their land and permit them to select a ruler of their own blood and creed? Jostling porters and fishmongers shrilled rebellious yells down the reeking alleys of the city; in council chambers gloating Sadducees and Pharisees, for once on common ground, plotted the course of overthrow.

After Philippi, Octavius returned to Italy; Antony to the East —and Cleopatra.

At Bithynia Antony was awaited by a delegation of Jews. Hyrcanus, they were prepared to charge, their rightful king, was so in name only. Herod and Phasael, through bribes to Cassius, had been permitted to seize control and to rule the country in a manner detrimental to the interests of its people, and of Rome.

Herod was on hand to defend himself. Since, however, he had had the foresight to send Antony a large gift of money and since Antony was impatient of bickering that postponed his return to Cleopatra's embraces, the charges were not even listened to.

Hyrcanus, demonstrating one of his few glimpses of practicality, put the lesson of the failure to use. At Ephesus, Antony's next stopping place, he was met by an embassy bearing the gift of a heavy crown of gold from Hyrcanus, and a petition that the Jews whom Cassius sold into slavery for non-payment of tribute be released. The crown was a weighty argument. Antony graciously acquiesced and the slaves were ordered freed.

With traditional Hebraic persistence, the anti-Herodean delegation would not let initial failure discourage their efforts. At

Antioch, by a combination of bribery and downright refusal to be put off, they managed an audience with Antony. The Roman's slow progress through Asia Minor increased his ardor for Cleopatra; he begrudged every moment that kept them apart. Listening to the graybeard prolixity of strange priests on a matter of rule in a remote, unimportant cranny of the Roman domain was what he wanted least to do.

Still, the dignity and sincerity of the Jews, in spite of their guttural, uncertain Greek, could not but impress him. Their charges seemed well founded and logical. On the other hand, his comrade-in-arms Messala heatedly defended Herod. If only there were a way to render judgment hastily and yet properly. On the outskirts of the crowding throng his eye spied Hyrcanus, whose generosity was a pleasant memory. He beckoned the diffident Jew to him, asking whom he considered best qualified to rule. To the confusion of his party, Hyrcanus, probably from honest conviction, possibly prodded also by the recollection that his ward's espoused was on trial, replied that Herod was most eminently fitted to govern Judea.

Antony rose from his judgment seat, relieved. What had seemed so disquieting a matter was after all not so hard to settle. During the stunned moment, before the shouts of imprecation had time to form, he gave his decision. Under the new regime Herod and Phasael were to be recognized as tetrarchs and their power in their country was confirmed by the might of Rome.

The chamber was the scene of wild uproar when the import of the crushing verdict broke on the minds of the delegates. Wailing and shrieking, they shook their fists at Hyrcanus; only the thought of his sacred office kept them from spitting at the cowering figure of the high priest. From Hyrcanus they turned on Antony, grasping his robes and blocking his egress. Guards seized fifteen of the noisiest demonstrators and ungently plowed a way through the rest.

Once again Herod by his understanding of the kind of person he had to deal with achieved a triumph. His adversaries had seemingly everything, possibly even justice, on their side; he only an unsavory (to his present judge) past. He countered with the base move of a judiciously expended bribe the aroused dignity and patriotism of the champions of a nation, and over the most

exalted and perhaps weakest of his opponents he exerted a calculated influence that would cause a disastrous breach in their
solidarity at a critical moment. The Jews knew and loved their
cause, and lost; Herod knew the weaknesses of Antony and
Hyrcanus, and won.

Even now the delegates refused to admit defeat. They stormed
back to Jerusalem. The city flamed with hatred and mortification. A delegation augmented to a thousand hastened to Tyre,
where Antony would next rest on the road to Egypt. Herod and
Hyrcanus, knowing the temper of Antony and his increasing
anxiety to see Cleopatra, begged the Jews not to attempt to see
the Roman.

Their pleading was in vain. An angry, noisy mob, they pushed
their way into Antony's presence and demanded that he rescind
his judgment. The Roman was fed up with these Jewish squabbles. He had heard their case and had made a final decision.
Now he would resort to other methods. A word to the governor
of Tyre, and troops with thrusting spears and hacking swords
poured into the defenseless throng. Almost every demonstrator
was killed or hurt. Hyrcanus tenderly cared for such as were not
beyond cure, having them conveyed to Jerusalem in his own
litters. No sooner were they well, however, than their outcries
against Herod and Antony became so boisterous and abusive that
Antony, on being informed of their actions, ordered that the
hostages be executed.

The family of the Hasmoneans had by this pretty well run its
course. Still surviving were Antigonus II, son of Aristobulus II
(executed at Pompey's command); his uncle, the high priest
Hyrcanus; his cousin and sister-in-law, the malicious Alexandra
(Hyrcanus' daughter), and the latter's children, Mariamne and
Aristobulus III.

Antigonus II, the last of the family to clutch at the crown, was
in many respects the most despicable of the lot. During the two
years following his defeat in the Tyrean revolt he worked under-
ground, never endeavoring to ingratiate himself with the Jews
to be regarded as their champion, but rather plotting with gentiles and strangers.

In the successful revolt of the Parthians and their subsequent
overrunning of Syria he saw his main chance. With a son of his

precious father-in-law Ptolemy as go-between he made a bargain
with the Parthians. The terms picture clearly the revolting nature
of this decadent scion of a noble family. The Parthians agreed
to depose Hyrcanus from the high priesthood and to kill the
tetrarch Herod. This accomplished, Antigonus II promised to
give them a thousand talents and five hundred Jewish women.

At the outset of the invasion, an advance unit of Parthians and
their Jewish allies cracked Herod's advance lines and chased the
tetrarch's troops all the way into Jerusalem. Jewish rebels momentarily swelled the ranks of the invader. In the market place a
pitched battle was fought. Herod's men, seemingly unable to
check the overwhelming mass of attackers, gave ground slowly.
Every street became the site of a new battle; every alley clanked
with clashing arms. From roof tops frenzied men and women
heaved stones that shattered indiscriminately on the skulls of
invader and defender. It seemed a chaotic hurly-burly in which
planless, formless fights to the death occurred in a hundred
places and fifty directions at once.

As the fighting progressed, however, it became apparent that
the master hand of Herod was at the controls. Bit by bit the
invaders were lured or driven into the Temple, the trap was
sprung, and the Parthians, deserted by their fainter-hearted
allies, were walled in, with Herod's troops blocking every avenue
of escape.

Herod, believing the day's carnage would have a sobering
effect on the Jews, withdrew his troops, except for a guard about
the Temple. In so doing he failed to take into consideration the
raving hatred of the people of Jerusalem. With clubs, stakes, and
stones they rushed the guards from every side. The front ranks
crumpled under the thrusts of well-armed troops. Eager thousands took the place of the fallen. The never-ending masses of
attackers wore down the tiring guards. One by one they fell, to
be pounded or yanked into oblivion. When the last soldier had
been beaten to the ground, the quick and the dead were thrown
on one churning heap; wood was piled on the mass, and a torch
applied. Outside the Temple the smudge of smoldering humanity
spiraled to the heavens, where it mingled with the fainter haze,
drifting from the sacrificial altars within, and hovered foreboo-
ingly over the city.

Although Herod paled with fury when a trembling messenger brought the news of the massacre, complete revenge was temporarily not to be thought of. It was the season of Pentecost. The city, even normally packed within its constricting walls, was now glutted with thousands of pilgrims from every part of the Roman and barbarian world.

The presence of the Parthian invader, far from curbing the religious emotionalism of the visitors, actually augmented it. About 70 B.C. a legend sprung up that the Parthians would make straight the way for the Messiah. Now the Parthian had come, seemingly an impossibility when the legend originated. Should an alien invader alone shed his blood for the coming Messiah?

Natives and visitors alike caught the anti-Herodian fever. The fetid air was surcharged with fanaticism. Compact units of regular troops dashed from their fortified camps, killed until they tired, and cut their way through living barricades back to safety. Other units less fortunate were borne down and literally torn to pieces by mobs whom losses but infuriated the more. The city became an inferno of raids and counterattacks, of sudden death and lingering torture. And above all rang the shrieking, cursing leitmotif of hatred of Herod.

Naturally no effective preparations could be made to meet the main army of Parthians sweeping down the country in two columns. One under the governor Barzapharnes marched inland along the sloping valleys of Galilee and Samaria; the other, commanded by Pacorus, the king's son, traversed the level coastal plain.

As the armies converged on Jerusalem, they halted instead of proceeding immediately to the attack. That a victorious army, overwhelming in size, should hesitate to assault an overcrowded, seditious city, the majority of whose inhabitants would welcome the invader, is not as puzzling as it might appear. The Parthian army consisted in greater part of slaves whose military ardor in the face of determined resistance was questionable. Such free men as there were fought remarkably well on horseback but were totally unaccustomed to any other kind of fighting. In the maze of alleys in the city and against the frowning castle and towers of the tetrarchs their strategy would be almost futile.

The slippery mind of Antigonus II suggested the solution of

the Parthian difficulty. Accompanied by the king's cupbearer
(also named Pacorus), he sought audience with Phasael. He loved
the city; he assured the guileless Idumean he would rather sacrifice his own prospects than to see the capital his family had
restored, and the Temple of his God which his great ancestor
had rededicated, looted and desecrated by pagan barbarians. The
Parthians had no quarrel with the rulers or the people. Their
one object was plunder. If some satisfactory tribute were paid—
to save face, it might even be termed a loan—the Parthians would
withdraw and leave Phasael and Herod to re-establish order.
The tense atmosphere of Jerusalem was, however, not conducive
to orderly deliberation. If Phasael and the high priest under
solemn assurances of safe conduct would meet the Parthian commanders in the quiet seclusion of Galilee, he was sure that
Jerusalem could be spared the horrors of a siege.

Phasael and Hyrcanus, too guileless to fathom the consummate
treachery of Antigonus II, agreed, permitting, moreover, five
hundred picked Parthian horsemen to enter the city to help
restore order.

Herod vainly pleaded with his brother and the high priest to
discredit the sincerity of the enemy. With the stubbornness of
simple, single-minded men they rejected every objection and
accompanied Antigonus and Pacorus to the Galilean headquarters of Barzapharnes to arrange, as they fondly imagined, a peace.

In Galilee, Phasael learned the shocking truth about the thousand talents and five hundred Jewish women, listed among whom
were many of his relatives and acquaintances. He discovered also
that, after he was disposed of, Herod was to be lured outside the
walls to be murdered.

Though Phasael was deplorably stupid, he was a very brave
man. He was offered a chance to escape. Saramalla, wealthiest
of Syrians and admirer of Herod for wiping out the Galilean
robbers that waylaid his Syrian caravans, had a galley at the dock
with oars fixed and sails set. The guards were bribed. Phasael
had only to step aboard to be whisked to freedom. Since that
would involve abandoning Hyrcanus, who was detained apart,
he refused to flee.

Instead he demanded that he be taken before Barzapharnes.

Boldly he disclosed his knowledge of the plot and offered the Parthian a more generous monetary bribe than Antigonus'. Playing for time, Barzapharnes denied the accusation, and then hastily sent word to Jerusalem, quickly to deal with Herod, since Phasael knew of the plot and might attempt to warn him.

Thereupon Hyrcanus and Phasael were thrown into a dungeon.

In Jerusalem, Herod was uneasily pacing his chamber. Intermittent yells of mockery from the crowds that passed before his castle in never ending streams reached his subconscious ear but failed to touch off any flash of resentment. His mind was in Palestine with that lovable, simple-hearted brother of his and that nincompoop of a high priest. It was not bad news, but rather no news that worried him. As a concession to his misgivings Phasael had grudgingly consented to despatch a confidential messenger to Jerusalem in the event that any of Herod's suspicions might seem well-founded. This messenger had not arrived, not in itself an alarming symptom were it not for the fact that no communication of any kind had been received either from his brother or from Hyrcanus.

Phasael had in fact sent the messenger the instant he was aware of Antigonus' duplicity. The Parthians, however, captured the messenger. It was imperative now to get rid of Herod before he might learn the truth from another source. A Parthian captain entered the castle. Courteously he told Herod that a messenger from his brother was outside the gates of the city but was apprehensive of passing through the streets of the turbulent city with an important personal message. With a Parthian guard, Herod was assured, he could move through the city with impunity and personally receive the message.

Herod suspected a trap. Otherwise, could not the guard escort the messenger in safety to his castle? He dismissed the Parthian with a noncommittal answer and hastened to tell his suspicions to Hyrcanus' daughter Alexandra, as wily and calculating a woman as ever disgraced the Hasmonean name. Her answer was direct and immediate. He must seek safety in flight. Herod himself could see no other way to save himself against the day of revenge. For the only time in his life he was faced with a problem that he could solve only by running away.

CHAPTER VI

FLIGHT TO GLORY

IN THE DEEP OF NIGHT HEROD, WITH HIS FAMily and body guard, stole from the fortress of Baris on the north of the Temple. At the same, still hour, trembling men and women, almost indistinguishable from the enveloping shadows, slithered through little doors that opened upon lifeless streets. Slipping around every random pool of moonshine that lost itself among the sullen walls, they made their fearful way to the south gate. They were the friends and followers of Herod accompanied by those whom the arrogant hand of Antigonus II would strike first and the women who were listed for parceling among the Phasael.

It had never occurred to Herod that he could escape more speedily and safely alone. Throughout the day until the hour of the sunset sacrifice trusted Idumean guards passing in the Pentecostal crowds for pilgrims went from house to house wherever there was a Herodian sympathizer, urging him if he valued his life or cherished his women to flee that very night.

Except for an occasional roaring Parthian, too drunk to be dangerous, the fugitives met no one. Fortunately for them the Jews were not a nocturnal people. After dark, decent citizens stayed within houses that turned windowless backs or high garden walls on unlit streets, deaf to commotion that would be only drunken troops or lawbreakers. A wagon, its wheels muffled with damask ripped from the palace walls, bore Herod's immediate family: his mother, his sister Salome (not the one of the Gospel but a far more vicious specimen), Mariamne, her mother Alexandra, his youngest brother Pheroras, and the young son of Phasael.

Amid hushed sobbing and muttered objurgations, the fugitives left the brooding walls of Jerusalem behind them. Southward, their way wound over the shallow brook Kedron, by the Mount of Olives, past the cave dwellings of hilly Bethlehem; still south across bleak slopes, where, as a generation later, there were shepherds, "watching their flocks by night."

From the shepherds, simplest and kindest of Judah's children, there was nothing to fear. But some of the Parthians had sobered sufficiently to appreciate what the forms that had passed by them like wraiths in the night were. It was, after all, impossible entirely to conceal the escape of several thousand persons, each stumbling through the dark, burdened with what he most wished to save. Fast-driving horsemen began to harass the rear of the long, slow train of fugitives. There was no time to organize an effective defense; the terrain was too steep and rugged to permit deploying about the country side; the straggling, lumbering line appeared singularly vulnerable. But luckily the moon was down, and the assailants unfamiliar with the land.

All night long, Herod was with the rear guard, fighting incessantly—almost hopelessly, it seemed at times. At daybreak they were in the Idumean wilds, still twenty dreary miles from their haven, the Dead Sea fortress of Masada.

Exhausted with worry and lack of sleep, Herod had never been so near the cracking point. The road, littered with discarded valuables and jammed with querulous refugees snatched at an instant's warning from lives of wealth and ease, labored endlessly over the hills already white-hot and choked with dust.

Reinforced and emboldened, the enemy hovered by, darting in to transfix a straggler and scampering off on wiry little horses that seemed as wily and vicious as their riders.

An arrow swished by Herod's head and buried itself quivering in the back of one of his guardsmen. Sudden squeals of terror, and enraged curses, were almost lost in swelling whoops of triumph. A wagon, bearing his mother, had overturned. Seeing the mishap, a band of Parthians, brothers to the vultures that hung high in the clouded dust, swooped upon the disorganized rear guard frantically trying to right the wagon. Cyprus in an instant realized her son's danger. She implored him to abandon her and flee, before he would be quite cut off. Instead he put his shoulder to the wagon and lifted with the rest. All efforts seemed unavailing. The little band had delayed long enough to be cut off from the rest of the fugitives.

For one brief moment he was completely unnerved. He braced the hilt of his sword against a rock, and steadied the cruel blade, preparatory to hurling himself upon its lethal point to put an end to a career of frustration. A sudden elated yell, almost in his ear, distracted him. With a desperate heave the wagon had been righted.

The fit of despair passed as quickly as it came. With newborn courage he charged the engulfing mass of Parthians and slashed a way back to the relative safety of the main body.

At length, with alarm and excursion, and loss and repulse, the fugitives moved into the Satanic landscape of the hills of Edom, and their assailants drew off, fearsome of this weird land. Then the unsmiling glint of the Dead Sea, the black basalt walls of gloomy Masada, and safety.

Herod saw that the fugitives were comfortably established in this impregnable pile manned by eight hundred troops under his brother Joseph. He then paid off his own men with money he had had the foresight to transport from Jerusalem, and ordered them to scatter into the Moabite hills, to reassemble at his command. With all arranged he toppled into a sleep of complete exhaustion.

Twenty-four hours later, in the company only of Phasael's son, he turned away from the perils of the north, away from the safe haven of Masada, south to the domain of the Nabatean Arabs. Long did Mariamne and his mother watch the waning figures—the strong man on his mount, so bent and tired, the child so keen and avid—until their brown figures merged into the dun of the sandy wastes.

In Jerusalem the escape of Herod and his party filled the Parthians with chagrin. Carelessness had filched from them the noble Jewish girls they had been offered as prizes. Even the loot fell far below their anticipation. Bulky furniture and costly fabrics were there in abundance. But the little precious things, the gold and jewels, that a man might carry off on horseback and count himself wealthy, were taken away by the fugitives themselves.

Herod himself left little of value to the enemy. Practiced in the hard school of the desert, and profiting from the wisdom of Antipater, he had provided for just such an exigency. His wealth, instead of being concentrated in Jerusalem, was distributed in many places in Palestine, so as to be immediately available under any condition.

The Parthians and Antigonus II drew cold comfort from seizing what little was left and butchering several thousand Jews whose remoter connection with the Herodians falsely assured them immunity.

Furious at his discomfiture, Antigonus II dashed to Galilee. At any rate he would not be deprived of his revenge on the high priest and Phasael. First he must make certain that Hyrcanus would never again reprove him from the unscalable heights of the high priesthood. The even more delectable experience of torturing Phasael could wait.

A diabolical thought began to possess his cruel mind. He recalled the edict: "Whoever of the seed of Aaron, the priest, hath blemish, he shall not approach to offer sacrifice to the Lord." There was no sport in killing a senile carper. He could better satisfy his revenge by disfiguring him, at once hurting him and forever disbarring him from the office that carried with it the esteem of all Jewry. He strode into the dungeon of Hyrcanus, hurled himself on the trembling old man and yanked him by the hair toward himself. His teeth closed on the shrieking priest's ear. One brutal wrench, and he flung the mutilated figure fainting on the stone floor.

Eventually the blubbering priest was released from prison and after a short captivity in Parthia was taken to Babylon. Here he lived, and, had he been wiser, would have insisted on dying, loved and venerated by the kind, scholarly Jews of that city.

Phasael in his dungeon calmly deliberated on his prospects. A jailer told him of Hyrcanus' fate; he could surmise his own doom and the savage delight Antigonus would derive from carrying it out. With inexorable pagan logic—for unlike Herod, who

was a circumcised Jew, Phasael was always essentially heathen—
he concluded that only by his death, escape being impossible,
could he atone for the inexcusable credulity that had involved in
misfortune those he loved. Death imposed by Antigonus II would
hardly suffice, since that would further gratify the author of his
calamity. It must then be by suicide.

To prevent such eventuality jailers had bound his hands behind his back and removed every semblance of weapon or utensil
with which he could do himself harm.

All their precautions were vain. Propelled with all the force
of his cramped limbs, he projected his body through the air,
crashed his skull against the stone wall, and lurched over senseless and mortally wounded. (There is also a less likely account
which has him recovering from his hurt, whereupon a doctor in
the pay of Antigonus II pours poison into his wounds.)

Whatever the immediate cause, his death was not unhappy.
A woman dressing the stricken man's wounds told him of Herod's
escape. The dying figure smiled, "I now die with comfort, since
I leave behind me one alive that will avenge me of mine enemies."

It is a provoking picture—first sapient, judicious Antipater;
now loyal, sturdy Phasael, treacherously slain, mainly because of
Herod's activities, yet dying willingly because they were certain
that the record of Herod's coming glory would justify their
sacrifice.

Following hard on the death of Antipater, Phasael's suicide was
more unfortunate for Herod than he knew. There now remained
no check on his unbridled will except perhaps the soft curb of
Mariamne's love. At a period when sudden misfortune, or equally
sudden good fortune to come, would intoxicate him to the ex-
tremes of depression or elation, there was lacking an evening,
modifying leaven—an unselfish, reasonably unprejudiced influence that would still excessive passion and temper extravagant
hope. How greatly Herod would miss his father and his brother
would become apparent only later, when the impetuous king
would tear vainly at the meshes of intrigue and jealousy that
tangled his unhappy court.

For the moment, though, Herod was far from impetuous. Resting during the burning heat of day in the warped shade of tor-

tured rocks, forcing their jaded horses through the chilling night across merciless flats of flinty gravel, pausing again to rest when day flushed the frigid sands with stifling heat, the wondering lad and the proud, sad-faced ruler neared the miraculous city of Petra.

Even today Petra is one of the wonders of the past. Once magnificent cities, now mounds of mud and prone, broken pillars abound in Eastern wastes that were flourishing gardens. But Petra was always a flawless architectural gem set in a wasteland of blasted rock and arid flats. Through some quirk of pride, the Arabs poured their hard-won wealth into its maintenance to make it a matchless capital of a desert land.

Its only entrance, a long, narrow gorge, wound serpent-like between unscalable cliffs, to disclose around an unimposing bend the exquisite buildings and tombs—pink, cream, coral, and gold in the white sunlight that blinked away the first rapturous glimpses of the city. Herod could reasonably expect a kind welcome and practical support from the Petrans. Malchus, their king, still owed a great sum of money that had been lent him by Antipater. Kindred of the desert, the Idumean understood the chronic impoverishment that the maintaining of Petra imposed upon the Arabs. He appreciated their pride in their extravagant irridescent towers and never pressed for repayment. Herod, himself, came with no intention of demanding the money owed him. He hoped that by leaving his nephew as hostage he might obtain the loan of three hundred talents, an amount ordinarily ample— he as yet knew nothing of his brother's suicide—to redeem Phasael from the Parthians.

At the hidden entrance of the city his path was blocked by an Arab, courtly, sympathetic, but inflexible. The Arab conveyed his royal master's best wishes, in the ornate, oriental idiom proper to the occasion, but he regretted that Herod must not be permitted to enter. To give him sanctuary would incite the anger and greed of the Parthians. Not once did he even hint at the real reason behind Malchus' inhospitality: the fear that Herod might want money rightly his.

Herod made no effort to dam the Arab's flowery drone. When the litany of excuses was ended, his burning eyes shot a single

shaft of indignation at the uneasy ambassador; his parched lips
went through the motion of spitting disgustedly at his feet. Without a word, he roughly grasped the arm of the puzzled boy and
turned his back on the ungrateful city. Throughout the endless
day, his sun-glazed eyes stared at the boundless horizon; heedless
of the lengthening shadows, he pushed ever on. The child beside
him whimpered; he but increased his pace. He was bound for the
sea. He was determined, by whatever means, to reach Rome. His
father had been right. Why waste time cultivating petty princes
and royal underlings, who would smile, and double deal, and
cheat? Rome was a stern mistress, but generous. Henceforth he
was resolved always to act in collusion with her; to make his
interests synchronize with Roman policy; and thus rule safely
and securely.

This newborn determination, as he contemplated the boundless horizons it unfolded, eased the harsh journey. That night
he slept at a temple where some of his men were quartered. From
them he learned of his brother's fate. Another reason why he
need not hasten back to his ungrateful country—until he had
perfected plans for its subjugation at Rome!

Haggard, penniless, and in rags, he reached Pelusium, near the
present Port Said. Stopping only to put his nephew in the care
of one of the omnipresent Idumean clansmen, he turned to the
quays. No ships were sailing for Rome, but a naval vessel was
about to embark for Alexandria. It was, of course, not a passenger ship and ordinarily would certainly not be available as
transport for an impoverished foreigner. Yet there was that
nobility of bearing and impressiveness about Herod that induced
the captain on his own responsibility to take him as passenger.

The ship was already tacking in the hot desert wind, when a
fleet messenger from Malchus dashed into the city. Too late, the
king realized how terribly he had sinned against hospitality and
gratitude, and he wanted to recall Herod. . . .

At Alexandria, the marks of travel and hardship removed, and
once again a handsome, regal figure, he immediately caught the
attention of Cleopatra, who made it her concern to be informed
of whoever or whatever might be of interest or importance. The
sturdy bearing, the melancholy, noble demeanor, the virile

bearded face, above all something of the desert mystery and charm that was his birthright intrigued the queen.

To depict Cleopatra as a sensual Circe spending her charms promiscuously upon glistening Nubian giants and clumsy blond barbarians from the northern wastes, is traditional but hardly factual. Writers have called her "The Serpent of the Nile" and have pictured her as a heavy-lidded, negroid Aphrodite. Yet the real Cleopatra was pure Greek; at most Alexandrine, never a true Egyptian. For less than three centuries her family, founded by Ptolemy Lagos, one of Alexander the Great's generals, ruled in the land of the ancient Pharaohs. Constant inbreeding to prevent the contamination of their pure Greek blood by any foreign infusion had not wrought for family loyalty, or affection.

Murder was a family tradition; and its women were more ruthless than the men. Cleopatra's childhood and youth were violent and unhappy. At fourteen she was a guerrilla fighting the Romans. At eighteen, when her father died, she married—a merely formal union—her ten-year-old brother. Family quarrels broke out anew. Her loutish brother-husband was shanghaied and never more heard from. Her sister Arsinoë, after being declared queen, was murdered—it is thought at Cleopatra's direction.

As queen, Cleopatra was popular with the masses of Egypt, excepting partisans of Arsinoë and some Alexandrine Jews. The Egyptians were not especially affected by the crimes or the erotic escapades imputed to her. In their queen they saw no cold, disdainful Greek whose very excesses lacked passion, but rather one of themselves, with a nature abundant as the Nile valley and hot as the desert. Still they regretted that she had no masterful mate by her side, one who was a ruler by nature, not merely by imperial edict. Cleopatra, almost psychic in appraising the popular pulse, sensed this feeling, which so perfectly synchronized with her own.

But, until she met Herod, this mate had existed only in the realm of the unattainable. A familiar emotion, yet charged with a fiery, volatile difference, surged through her turbulent being as she tried to sound the glowing, black depths of Herod's eyes. Other men she had entrapped, solely for the good she might do, by bartering her beauty for her country's welfare. Her Caesarion was Julius Caesar's; Antony had sired her recent twins, Alexander and Cleopatra, called the Sun God and Goddess of the Moon by their infatuated father.

But Caesar was dead, and Antony had been whisked away to marry Octavia.

And now Herod!

Here was no aging, fidgety, bald-pated Caesar to ensnare by the humiliating expedient of being unrolled from a carpet, disheveled and half-naked at his feet; no debauched, exacting Antony, coarse in his pleasantries, and vile in his passion.

This was a soul akin to her own, impassioned and intense, with discretion, ability and ambition. Together they might vitalize her lifelong dream of a regenerate Egypt. Joined with a free Palestine, coast and hinterland, it could challenge and over-bear the might of Rome itself.

But she caught Herod in no mood for dalliance. She saw in her infatuation the fulfilment of her hope for a greater Egypt; he could see only a delay in his absorbing need, the aid of all-powerful Rome. When she offered to make him general, he curtly refused. Only the animal sensuality of Cleopatra occurred to him. He had no wish to amuse her for a time and then be cast aside.

Had he known the consequences, he might have handled the situation more delicately. This slur Cleopatra never forgave. Henceforth the shadow of the Alexandrian harpy brooded over him. She became his relentless enemy, slandered him, harried him, spied upon him, and at length brought upon him lasting domestic misery.

His rejection of Cleopatra's offer threw the Jews of Alexandria into a ferment. This city, next to Jerusalem, had the largest Jewish population, its proportion of Jew and gentile being simi-lar to that of New York City today. If anything, the factional squabbles of the mother city were here intensified by distance. Those favorable to Herod were stunned by his action; the parti-sans of Antigonus II, savagely elated. By his attitude Herod had alienated his supporters and strengthened his enemies.

His situation was far from happy. Considered by his own race as a scoundrel or a fool, pursued by the hatred of a slighted queen, he found it imperative to embark for Rome at once.

New difficulties arose. Political and meteorological storms were sweeping the horizon. At Rome the issue between Antony and Octavius was so confused and so portentous that no sane Egyptian would risk his ship's being sucked into the vortex. Besides, a terrific storm had spattered the eastern Mediterranean coasts with wreckage. Reports of almost unbelievable havoc were brought in hourly by dazed survivors. What ships were in the harbor pulled and groaned at their hawsers, uneasy at the tempest beyond.

Selecting the fastest ship, Herod prevailed upon the captain to steer for the open sea. He had little money, no power or authority. But such was the dominating presence of the man that the unwilling captain and his cowering crew pointed their vessel into a storm, the worst in the memory of man.

Wind and wave, nevertheless, were not so readily impressed. The storm raged more and more furiously. Off the coast of Rhodes the ship foundered. Yet once again the Herodian luck held. While the ship was sinking, a vagrant gale reversed itself and spewed it, almost miraculously, into a quiet cove where it settled calmly on the sandy bottom while the crew safely walked ashore.

Sea-stained and spent, Herod stumbled up the steep streets of the city of Rhodes. All about him were ruin and desolation, battered walls, and heaps of stone. Nor could most of the damage be attributed to the recent storm, for the city had suffered singularly in a devastating battle during the war with Cassius. The citizens, living timidly in the hills, seemed too helpless and dispirited to set about rebuilding, particularly since their sorry attempts had been flattened by the same gale that cast Herod among them.

To resume his journey immediately was unthinkable. No ships were available, and even if there had been it would have required more than a fixed purpose and a dominant will to galvanize these timorous Rhodesians into action. The plight of the

city awoke in Herod that nascent genius for building that later
marked him as one of the world's master builders. He drew plans,
prepared specifications and offered them to the citizens.

At first it was hard to poke them out of their lethargy. But
his energy and enthusiasm was contagious. The wealthier citizens supplied him with means; the poorer were conscripted to
clear away rubbish, tear down shaking walls, and lay the founda-
tions of the new city. The work progressed unbelievably fast.
From the rubble of a slipshod mercantile and trading settlement
sprung the first shoots of a charming modern town that tier by
tier would mount from practical docks on the shore through
substantial artistic public buildings and dwellings to wood-
ensconsed temples and flower-enveloped villas on the hillside.

While Herod threw himself unsparingly into the work of construction to keep dormant the gnawing realization that for a
long time to come no ship headed for Rome would be likely to
put in at the stricken heap of ruins that the world took Rhodes
to be, grateful citizens were secretly constructing a trireme that
would take him to his destination in becoming fashion.

The building of the ship was a labor of love, and soon completed. A delighted Herod, with full purse and finest apparel,
strode aboard and watched the green hillsides of the friendly
island merge into the purple of the eastern night. Favoring
breezes, as if atoning for past harshness, caressed the ship across
the middle sea. With decks gleaming, colors streaming, oars
dipping in rhythmic silver, she slid into the harbor of Brundisium, where at that moment the grim warships of Antony
jostled each other at anchorage.

Because of his delay at Rhodes he arrived at a most fortunate
crisis in the quarrel between Antony and Octavius. To keep
within bounds the errant affections of his partner, Octavius had
married him to his sister, pretty, complaisant Octavia. With every
symptom of reformation, Antony suffered the boring experience
of a wedding journey with his adoring wife; then impulsively
shot off to Cleopatra. Octavius, perceiving the inevitable rupture
of their interests, set about drawing up forces for the fight to
come. Poor, unhappy Octavia saw only disaster ahead in the
clash of the two she loved most in the world. Tearfully, she

appealed to her brother to attempt to win Antony back to both of them, especially since she was soon to give birth to Antony's child. She, who should be the most fortunate woman on earth with the foremost men of the world as husband and as brother, was in danger of becoming the most unhappy, she moaned. "I shall be miserable without redress; for on what side soever victory falls, I shall be sure to be the loser." Touched by his sister's tears as well as by the desire of saving Rome, if possible, from another debilitating civil war, Octavius agreed to make another effort at reconciliation. Antony, with all his faults not ungenerous nor heartless, cast off, momentarily, Cleopatra's silken shackles and penitentially returned to his Octavia.

This reconciliation of old comrades in arms was a second honeymoon, less intense, but more sentimental and thoughtful than the first flush of conquest at Philippi, where they had quenched the smouldering hopes of Caesar's assassins.

Octavius gave Antony two of his legions to help him in the war against the Parthians, which was going rather badly. Not to be outdone in generosity, Antony presented Octavius with one hundred armed galleys, a gift he would bitterly regret when his ships were scudding before Octavius' stabbing triremes at Actium.

Amid the pomp and blare of this love feast, Herod approached Antony, not obsequiously, but with halting dignity. This modesty, ordinarily so foreign to his imperious nature, was not assumed. His spirits had been badly buffeted by the upheaval at Jerusalem, the ingratitude of the Arabs, and the self-seeking designs of the Egyptian queen. Dejection had set in after the buoyant excursion from Rhodes. Tired in mind, and heartsick, he knew that more than his own future condition and his happiness with Mariamne depended on the outcome of this interview. He visualized also the fugitives at Masada, perhaps even then beset by yelping Parthian savages, while in Jerusalem Antigonus II was smacking his sensual lips in anticipation of their destruction— through the failure of him whose star they followed.

His fears were baseless. Antony greeted him warmly as an old friend who recalled the kindness and cooperation of Herod's father, and Herod's own gifts. From a purely practical viewpoint it was, incidentally, the policy of both Octavius and Antony—

though at present, no doubt, pushed into the depths of their subconscious minds under the surface emotion of their new-forged brotherhood—to supplement their own strength with every strong individual they came upon. Antony was moved to tears by the account of Herod's peregrinations; he foamed with fury at the picture of Antigonus II consorting with the Parthians—the people who had disgraced his army—and sporting the crown that Rome had given to his friend, Herod.

Octavius took a less emotional, but a quite as friendly view. he, too, saw that the alliance of Antigonus II with the Parthians foresight of the Idumean seer will redound to his son's credit— he, too, saw that the alliance of Antigonus II with the Parthians menaced Rome.

They took Herod to the capitol. To stamp their actions with a semblance of legality, they convoked the senate. Messala, pro-tagonist of Herod on a previous occasion, presented the triumphant refugee to the senators, dilated on the contribution of Antipater to Rome, enlarged on Herod's record of good will to the Imperial City, and drew a harrowing picture of the deviltry of Antigonus II and his Parthian allies.

The senate awaited only Antony's signal as to how they should decide. Unanimously in 40 B.C., they voted that Herod should be king of Judea, whereupon Antony declared Antigonus II deposed and a rebel against Rome. Arm in arm, between Antony and Octavius, crowned with the royal diadem, Herod paced from the senate in solemn procession with the chief officials of the city to sprinkle incense at the temple to the Roman gods; thereafter to file the decree of royalty at the capitol.

Antony, to whom a day without debauchery was a day lost, topped the formal festivities with a banquet. Amid the luxury, and gaiety, and swilling, the gyrating dancers and the exotic foods, the dripping perfumes and saturnalian revelry, the new king seemed strangely bemused. Not even to himself did he care to admit that he was really overwhelmed at the extent of his good fortune. It had been his intention to plead only that his young brother-in-law to be, Aristobulus, be appointed tetrarch with himself as his minister. He sat, bedazzled, still trying to digest a fact he would never again overlook. This Rome, this resplendent mistress, must be wooed and importuned regally, as befits a queen. To beg a gift unworthy of her bestowal was to slight the dignity of the donor, and to cheapen the cause of the pleader.

Shivering almost perceptibly when he recalled that only the impetuousness of Antony had precluded his asking the greater honor for someone else, he drained goblet upon goblet. The white bodies of the fluent dancers left him cold; the dainties of distant tropics and fog-banked Britain evoked no responsive taste. Only in the heady Falerian wine, gay with a score of Italian summers, and the heavy bouquets that imprisoned the fruity souls of Iberian vineyards, could he find warmth to check the chill thought of hardly missed disaster.

Slaves carried him to his couch, drunk, King of Judea.

CHAPTER VII

OF FALSE ALLIES
AND BATTLES

ON THE THIRD MORNING AFTER THE ORGY
following his investiture Herod boarded a warship put at his
disposal by Antony. Accompanying him was Dellius, Antony's
purveyor and go-between in half the shady deals of the East.
Dawn broke dull and heavy like Herod's own mood. The head-
ache that followed his unaccustomed debauch was gone. But a
remorseful aftertaste lingered, compounded of doubts of the
significance of his commission and fears for the safety of his
family, and especially Mariamne.

His concern was not unreasonable. The Romans had been
sincere enough in offering him the crown. Unfortunately there
was not now, and possibly never would be, any way in which
he could impose his sovereignty upon the Jews. Antony, within
whose realm Judea lay, was a poor administrator. Too prodigal,
too impetuous, too impatient with the details of government, and
above all too enamored of Cleopatra, he was constitutionally dis-
inclined to spend his talents on administrative affairs. Local
Roman government in Judea, instead of being an asset, was
actually an additional problem. Ventidius, Antony's representative, was concerned primarily with driving out the Parthians, a
prerequisite to a more complete elimination of all rebellious
elements.

Herod suspected with reason, being acquainted with the administrative and ethical standards of Roman commanders, that
Ventidius was probably not disposed to proceed too far beyond

70

his immediate objective, in which he had at least the tacit good
will of most Jews, who were growing increasingly alarmed at the
savagery of their allies. But to help put another foreigner in
power, above all one qualified to bring about order and put a
stop to the Roman's policy of enrichment by bribery and blackmail, would certainly not be a likely proceeding on Ventidius'
part. Even though ordered to assist Herod, he would more likely
regard him as a deterrent to legitimate profit, a needless burden
fixed upon him by impractical brass hats in Rome.

A consideration of the viewpoint of the Jew, whose king he
hoped to be, did nothing to lessen Herod's apprehensiveness. He
could not ignore the fact that Antigonus II belonged to the rightful royal family. However much decent Jews might abominate
their present ruler's excesses, he felt certain they would not be
willing to deny his right, as a Hasmonean prince, to rule their
land. Herod knew also that what Jewish governing body there
was detested him, Sadducees and Pharisees alike, or perhaps even
more bitterly the former. The Parthian remnants naturally
hated him as the cause of their loss of promised spoils. Antigonus
II most of all would feel the presence of Herod as an affront to
his country and a deadly peril to himself. More completely than
any of his predecessors, this last Maccabean ruler identified himself with the kingship. He had coins struck commemorating his
reign—something no other Jewish king except Alexander Jan-
neaus, to a very limited extent some forty years before, had dared
to do; every official act, every order and proclamation, however
insignificant, exuded an aura of hereditary royalty.

From Roman commanders in other provinces, Herod could
expect but little help. In Syria, Judea's nearest neighbor, Sosius
was a potential enemy. Herod had seen his coins, stamped with
the boastful legend, "C. Sosius, Imperator," with the figure of a
trophy flanked by a male and a female Jewish captive. As for
Silo, Ventidius' second in command, Herod knew him to be
utterly venal, a soldier of fortune of the basest type.

So Herod sat at the prow, shielding his eyes from the flying
scud, trying to solve the puzzle of his kingdom. When the flat top
of Carmel, floating on massive cloud banks, drifted into view,
he tried vainly to stir up the feeling of elation and enthusiasm

he felt was appropriate. He realized that he was not a prince to be welcomed by his yearning people as their leader and redeemer. Rather, as his eyes vainly searched the forbidding coast for some token of welcome or support, he must have felt as did a later Macbeth,

> *Upon my head they placed a fruitless crown,*
> *And put a barren scepter in my gripe.*

At a lonely spot near Ptolemy, under the somber shadow of Mount Carmel, they stepped ashore. Dellius with a guide immediately started inland. Herod, ringed about by a tough Roman guard, made camp on the dreary sands.

In spite of attempts at secrecy, the report of Herod's landing speedily reached Antigonus II. Characteristically, as whenever swift and decisive action was imperative, Antigonus II fell into a fit of hurt, panic-stricken rage.

It is hard to understand the utter incompetence of this man. Rome, in particular that part of the empire assigned to Antony, was badly organized. What Roman commanders were on the scene would selfishly prefer the continuance in rule of a weak king, and given the slightest excuse would color their reports to Rome in his favor.

Regarding his own people he surely need not have been concerned. With even a modicum of prompt action Antigonus II could have pinned his rival to an untenable beachhead. The rugged mountaineers of Galilee to a man were loyal to the ideal of Hasmonean authority. The caves of Arbela were packed with recalcitrant fanatics who hated the Idumean upstart. The arsenal of Sepphoris in Galilee could arm a willing countryside against the invader.

Had Antigonus II demonstrated even a semblance of resolution, it is likely that Antony and Octavius would have been compelled to abandon Herod to his fate. After all, the interests of Rome and their personal ambitions took precedence over the designs of an oriental kinglet, however much they might like him personally. Yet during the ensuing three years' conflict Antigonus II would commit one military and political blunder after another, with the result that he would not only alienate the loyalty of the Pharisees, the priestly clan, and the sanhedrin but also lose the esteem and support of the people.

For several weeks Herod remained undisturbed but fretful in his camp. Through the grapevine of the East, news of his arrival spread rapidly. Gradually small bands of his former troops joined him. Jew-hating Syrians crossed the border by night, singly and in groups. The poor, despised Samaritans flocked to his encampment in almost embarrassing numbers; there were hardly enough arms for all.

A swift messenger arrived with the information that Dellius and Ventidius would arrive the next day.

It would be a night of decision for Herod. Should he, on the morrow, begin the long march that would lead to the throne or to the scaffold? The swift shadows of the southern night swooped sullenly on the camp. Mournful wisps of hot wind mingled with the sad cadence of the ebbing tide. He tossed fitfully on his camp bed, vainly trying to stifle his uneasiness in sleep. After a time he rose, muttered a word to the sentry, and walked to the shore.

Throughout the sultry night he paced, conjuring grim visions, jumbled phantasmata: his father poisoned; his brother's treacherous capture and suicide; his wife's hatred; his betrothed's peril; the malice of the Jews; and the Romans' infidelity. The rasping screech of a gull, flying with the turning tide, broke in upon his gloom. In silly exasperation, he felt for a stone. All was thick, smooth sand underfoot. His prosaic occupation snapped the dismal chain of thought. The gull still scolded, provokingly near. For an instant it recalled his childhood days on the docks of Ascalon. Half-smiling, he searched in his purse for a copper coin to throw at the raucous fowl. His fingers clasped a coin—strange, greasy to the touch—not the sharp, hard mintage of Imperial Rome. He remembered how Antony laughingly had given it to him as a good-luck token on his departure. He needed no light to read the inscription. Every minute detail was branded in the tablets of his mind—the Hebrew motto "Mathathias (Antigonus) the High Priest, the Commonwealth of the Jews," and on the reverse, in Greek, "Of King Antigonus" with the representation of a cornucopia, and mathematical symbols, which would not violate the injunction against graven images.

It was growing perceptibly lighter—the smaller stars had already withdrawn. The sky was an inverted pewter bowl smudged with pearl and purple. With an almost boyish grin Herod scaled the coin toward the gull across the serried wavelets. Skimming from crest to crest, its sinking surface caught the first glint of a glorious sun breaking over Mount Carmel, and disappeared.

When Ventidius arrived, he was amazed not more at the numbers that had assembled apparently out of nowhere than at the enthusiasm of their leader. The mercenary Roman weighed the prospects of continuing to accept the bribes of Antigonus II or of marching openly under the standards of the invader. He gambled on Herod, at the same time covering possible losses by favorable, if meaningless, gestures in the direction of the Jewish king.

With the spirited rabble that passed for his army Herod began a foot-by-foot invasion of Galilee. Finally conquered, that province flared into rebellion almost at once. By a combination of cruelty and cunning he quelled the uprising. Those leaders likely to prove loyal, as well as the simple, sturdy common folk, he won over by gifts, generous promises, and, no doubt, more by the contrast his appearance made with that of ranting, sniveling Antigonus II. Those whom he could not hope to win over he killed.

Galilee and Samaria now secure, he marched on Masada, which Antigonus II was besieging.

The position of the defenders was precarious in that mountain stronghold. Too strong to be overborne by assault, too well provided with food to be starved into submission, they were nevertheless on the point of succumbing through lack of water. So extreme was the plight of the besieged that Joseph, addleheaded in an emergency rather than downright cowardly, had concocted the scheme of trying to escape with some two hundred of his friends and associates to the court of Malchus, of whose penitence for Herod's harsh treatment he had been informed. But, as Josephus piously remarks, God by sending rain during the night prevented their flight and filled the cisterns and reservoirs to overflowing.

As Herod drew near, Antigonus II raised the siege and returned to Jerusalem to test the efficacy of further bribery on Ventidius and Silo, as an alternative to battle with the invader.

Herod did not immediately enter Masada. The strong fortress at Joffa was a threat to his rear, and, unsubdued, might imperil the prospective campaign against Jerusalem.

In the capital, Silo had bled Antigonus II to the limit of his expectations. He used the proximity of Herod as an excuse to withdraw his troops and aid the invading army as he had been commanded to do by Rome. Enraged at such duplicity, Antigonus II pursued the Romans with overwhelming numbers and would have annihilated them had not Herod rushed to their aid. A sizable skirmish developed, but neither commander was willing to risk his army in a general engagement. Thereupon Antigonus II returned to sulk behind the bastions of Jerusalem, while Herod went to work on the walls and towers of Joppa.

The quick reduction of this fortress, more than anything else, fixed Herod as a great leader in the popular mind. On his swift march to Masada, his numbers were swelled very considerably, "some induced by their friendship to his father; some by the reputation he had already gained himself; and some to repay the benefits they had received from them both. But still what engaged the greatest number on his side was the hopes from him when he should be established in his kingdom."

By this it can be ascertained that Herod's army both in number and in achievement was formidable. There were good men who joined out of gratitude; self-seeking men, out of hope for gain; types that will fight furiously and unquestioningly for a commander in whom they have full faith. Such Herod had proved himself to be. As he reviewed his army, whatever echoes remained of the doubts that had racked him on the beach in Galilee were drowned out in the thunder of his faithful thousands.

To dispose of his family safely in the friendly shelter of Samaria was a simple, rapid operation, in spite of futile ambuscades and attacks by Antigonus II. This done, he made ready for the assault on Jerusalem, the last real stronghold of the enemy, the reduction of which would mark finis to an unbelievably brief and brilliant campaign.

That Herod showed consummate tactical skill cannot be dis-
puted. The difficult terrain of Galilee he conquered completely,
painstakingly; the more open country of the south he swept
through in blitz fashion, isolating or bypassing fortified positions
and then overrunning them with irresistible numbers.

The attack on Jerusalem, he knew, must be a reduction of a
walled city along more or less traditional lines. The defending
force would be cut off from fresh supplies of food and water and
harassed day and night by attacks at scattered points to conceal,
if possible, the spot where a breach in the walls would initiate
the grand assault. Once his troops were within the city, the
enemy might still resist with bitter and costly house-to-house fighting. Nevertheless, in his own mind at least, the doom of the
capital was certain.

Herod went into camp below the western wall of Jerusalem.
In the act of deploying his troops to stop every avenue of escape
from the city he was joined by Silo, haughtily demanding his
right to partake in the assault. Even had Herod needed more
men, this would have been a reinforcement of dubious value.
Only in the taking of bribes did the Romans demonstrate any
aptitude. As fighting men they showed little prowess against
either the Parthians or Antigonus. As it was, Herod's forces were
large enough to dispense entirely with Silo's aid. Besides his old
troops—mostly Idumeans—with many Samaritans, some Galileans,
and Judeans who joined him after Joffa, his numbers were augmented by a great many deserters from Jerusalem, who fled the
city either out of hatred of Antigonus II or out of fear of the
vengeance of Herod.

Still, because of policy, he felt forced to accept Roman help.
It would never do, thus early, to give Rome cause to believe that
he considered himself an independent monarch, rather than an
imperial agent. Grudgingly, he assigned Silo to a post of honor,
near the south wall.

He placed his troops skilfully, blocking off every avenue of
escape from the city. In regal garb, in plain view of the defenders,
he drew up near the wall barely beyond arrow range. A shower
of missiles fell harmlessly before him. Restraining the nervous
fingers of his bowmen, to whom the packed walls and the dumpy

figure of Antigonus II quite dancing with rage offered an almost irresistible target, Herod summoned his heralds. The shrilling trumpets sounded, and a hush fell upon both armies.

With a display of his strength Herod hoped to intimidate his enemies; with the eloquence of his speech he was confident he could win them over. His words were warm and resonant.

"Citizens of Jerusalem, subjects of Rome and Herod, hearken to the words of your true king, who is come not like the vile Parthians to seize your wealth and to dishonor your daughters, nor yet like the base son of the noble Maccabees, disgracing his blood and his religion by his wicked life and savage misdeeds. Herod is coming as your true king, to receive what is his by right and by the will of all-powerful Rome. Not as a conqueror laying waste your fields, slaughtering your manhood, and enslaving your wives and children would he appear before you, but as a kind, loving father, forgetting the transgressions of his children, anxious to fold them, even the greatest sinner among them, to his forgiving heart. Open the gates of the city and taste his kindness, for you cannot hope to withstand the might of his army, nor may he be able to protect you from the rage of his troops or from the vengeance of the Romans once they have become aroused by your vain resistance."

The speech might have been effective had it been heard in its entirety. But Antigonus II, sensing the danger, ordered his followers to shout down the speaker. He knew how wavering were many of his supporters—those who disliked him personally and were joined to him only by ties of temporary interest.

The proclamation of Antigonus II soon followed Herod's attempt to avert a siege. Ranting and abusive, it had nevertheless a substratum of low cunning that served to unite various factions against the usurper of the Judean throne.

"Who is this Herod," it began, "that would seat himself on the throne of David and Solomon? You men of Jerusalem know him; an Idumean, a slavish upstart; a half-Jew, who though circumcised burnt incense before the false gods of Rome. Behold his army. Gentiles: Romans, Syrians, Idumeans; and renegade Jews, accursed Samaritans, traitor Galileans, even natives of your own city, who so hate you, that they are fighting on the villain's

side. What if Antigonus may have forgotten always to keep
every commandment of God? Did not David and Solomon also
sin! Did not even our great father Moses incur the frown of
Yahweh! Antigonus has flowing in his veins the true Hasmonean
blood, as have others, Hyrcanus and young Aristobulus. Among
these must you elect your king, and not meekly, like driven,
stolid cattle, bend the neck to a barbarian selected by the lustful
rulers of Rome."

Herod might have continued the war by proclamations were
it not for an innate sense of dignity that shunned whatever was
ridiculous or degrading.

He had honestly hoped to take Jerusalem without fighting,
and, if possible, at least so long as he thought he could safely
do so, live at peace with his former enemies. But bits of the
diatribe from the walls, accusations utterly hateful and vile, reopened old sores, reanimated forgotten hatreds, and locked his
heart against mercy. By fire and the sword he must conquer
these stubborn subjects of his.

His troops were ready; of the outcome there could be no
doubt. Jerusalem, though strong, could hardly be intelligently
or long defended against the onslaught of his fiery warriors and
their Roman allies. It was the Romans that made Herod hesitate
before giving the final word for battle. They would fight only
for plunder and they hated all Jews without distinction of faction
or party. He was about to attack a city that must serve as his
capital, fortifications that he would wish to keep as nearly intact
as possible and people whom he wanted to keep alive, happy,
and prosperous.

The order to attack never came; a commotion in the Roman
ranks froze the words on Herod's lips. Silo, intelligent enough in
military lore to anticipate the almost sure success of the assault,
wanted no easy victory for Herod. As long as there were two
factions operating, he could make both pay. Should Herod win
quickly and easily, he would have no source of blackmail left.
Some of his blackguards, well rehearsed for the occasion, began
clamoring for back pay so they might buy food and supplies—to
provide which, incidentally, came within the province of Silo,
himself. Throwing down their arms, they called on other Romans

and Asiatics alike to follow their lead. Why, they screamed, should they, for the sake of an ambitious barbarian, spend their strength and waste their lives on a waterless slope, breathless with heat by day, icy cold by night, at all times without enough food or fuel, and without receiving the pay due them?

In a cold rage Herod saw his great opportunity slipping through his closing fingers. Concealing his anger and disappointment behind a mask of conciliatory words, he appealed to the Romans, officers and men alike, not to abandon him now. Though Silo might see fit to forget his duty, they like himself had been given this assignment by Antony, the commander-in-chief of them all. He appealed to their sportsmanship, their heroism, their love of him. That very day he would provide supplies; in the near distance there was the promise of unlimited loot—a prospect he disliked intensely to hold before their greedy vision.

True to his promise, within twenty-four hours, his scouts and raiders having collected food, fuel, and other supplies, he stilled the immediate complaints of the malcontents.

Within these same twenty-four hours he thought out his problem. Dissatisfaction within his ranks—however instigated—made impossible a quick conquest. The presence of the Romans, as well as that of other less dependable allies, constituted a threat since a repulse by the defenders or a long, costly siege might encourage their turning openly against him and place him between two enemies.

Bitterly dejected, he kept contact with Jerusalem only through the medium of a skeleton force. With his main body he set about preparing a gigantic commissary with headquarters at Jericho. Samaria agreed to furnish corn, oil, cattle, and wine, which would be shipped to the valley of the Jordan and thence distributed to the army. Gradually, as the commissary began to function more efficiently, Herod planned to increase the small force before Jerusalem, until the full army, amply supplied and conditioned, would resume the siege.

At this time there appeared one Phocus, a general of Antigonus II, who for over a year was to demonstrate a talent most disruptive of Herod's plans. Passing through the thin line en-

veloping Jerusalem, by stealth or by force, he organized and
directed guerrilla bands in a manner that indicated sheer genius.
With sudden swoops he destroyed lightly guarded supply trains
or trapped sizable fighting units in the recesses of the hills. Food
and supplies for the growing army before Jerusalem dwindled to
the point where grumbling at the shortage—naturally instigated
by the Romans—threatened a second revolt.

Herod, like any skilful commander, was never irrevocably
committed to a single plan of campaign. As soon as the ravages
of the enemy lowered the flow of supplies below the danger line,
he at once ordered all of the Romans and a considerable part of
his own army to the danger zone.

Phocus and his guerrillas could not make an effective resistance
against the disciplined, angry troops. Such bands as fought were
wiped out; others slunk to the hillside caves of Galilee or the arid
wastes beyond the Jordan.

Before proceeding with the siege of the capital—a logical final
step in his campaign—Herod took stock of the situation. His
Roman allies were once again a problem aggravated by the late
shortage before Jerusalem and by the lean opportunities for
plunder during the recent fighting. He loosed the Romans upon
Jericho, which he wished to teach a salutary lesson for its failure
willingly to co-operate with him. The rapacious hordes descended upon the city like a plague of locusts, looting and revel-
ing in the tropical paradise about the Jordan.

His brother Joseph with twenty-five hundred men—the size of
the force shows the task was not formidable—he commissioned to
eradicate what little resistance there was in Idumea. Then, leaving enough men to harass Antigonus II in Judea, he took the bulk
of his army to Galilee, where fighting had flared up anew, once
and for all to pacify that rebellious province.

Galilee was a hard nut to crack even with the might of the
Herodian pincers. Rebels had strongly garrisoned the towns,
while roving bands of robbers, hiding, when pursued, in caves in
all but inaccessible hills, made his task tremendously difficult.

A stroke of good fortune, growing out of a daringly conceived
surprise assault, resulted in the easy capture of the great Galilean
arsenal of Sepphoris. During a raging snowstorm Herod attacked

the weakly guarded outposts. Dismayed at the fury of the assailants that burst out of the whirling blizzard, the guards ran away, helter-skelter, neither making any kind of stand nor spreading the alarm. As a consequence Herod won, at the cost of hardship only, the chief arsenal in all Palestine as well as a headquarters from which he might operate to exterminate the robbers.

He let his troops regale themselves a while among the bountiful luxuries of the captured city and then proceeded to pacify the rest of the province. His immediate objective was Arbela, focal point of Galilean fanaticism. Here the robbers, abandoning their usual hit and run tactics, decided to make a stand. The armies closed in furious battle; it required all Herod's tactical skill and personal inspiration to save the day. His left wing reeled under the impact of a thunderous charge.

In a flash Herod saw the danger. Wheeling suddenly with his right, which had beaten off its adversaries, he attacked the exultant robbers in the flank and at the same time prevailed upon his defeated wing to re-form for an attack. He was successful; the casualties of the foe were tremendous; when the sun sank on a field red with slaughter, there no longer was a Galilean army. Small groups escaped across the Jordan; other units hid in the caves among the hills.

Herod, a great leader of men, knew when to drive, and when to rest and reward his army. Desperate bands were still at large in the wilderness, but his men were weary, many of them sick or wounded. Ignoring what rebels still were at large, he sent his troops into comfortable winter quarters at Alexandrium. To remove any temptation to desert or loot, he presented each soldier with a bonus of one hundred fifty silver drachmae, in addition to his share of the spoils. That there might be adequate means of spending this money, he ordered his youngest brother Pheroras to establish a market with provisions and luxuries, and to build a wall about their quarters to insure safety against the remote possibility of a surprise attack.

To Alexandrium came also Silo with the crestfallen remnants of his cohorts. After draining to the dregs the fertility of even Jericho, they had vainly appealed to Antigonus II for help. The Jewish king, instead, ordered the natives, wherever Romans were stationed, to flee to the hills so as to hasten the starvation of the arrogant pagans. After great difficulty and many losses Silo appeared before Herod and pleaded for relief. As though disdaining, himself, to deal with such bungling confederates, Herod committed them to his brother's care.

While the bulk of his army was still basking in the pleasant warmth of the winter at Alexandrium, Herod, as well as Silo, was called upon by Ventidius for help against their old foes, the Parthians. Glad of an opportunity to get rid of his unwelcome guests, Herod immediately despatched Silo to the front. Before he himself would leave the province, he wanted first to eliminate the robbers, who, reorganizing after their escape at Arbela, were again jabbing at his lines of communication and cutting down stragglers and outposts.

Herod hoped to achieve a quick victory and then overtake Silo, who was never overhasty in joining battle. The task he set for himself, however, took longer than he expected. To get at the enemy seemed almost impossible. Precipitous cliffs in the rugged Galilean highlands, known even in early Old Testament days as the "Hill of Robbers," are honeycombed with natural caves which the occupants had extended and fortified until they were apparently unassailable. Narrow, winding paths—where a single misstep meant certain death in the jagged depths below— offered the only direct approach to the caves. With every foot of the precarious way open to showers of stones from the caves above, Herod realized that an assault from below would be suicidal.

Out of range, though not out of earshot of the decisive, howling robbers, he halted his troops. His military genius had conceived a plan for victory at a minimum of risk. He took picked men, chiefly tough Idumean mountaineers and Syrian daredevils, to the plateau topping the cliffs. At his direction heavy wooden chests reinforced with iron chains were constructed, each capable of holding a score of heavily armed men. By means of an ingenious mechanism the chests, laden with their fighting freight, were let down the face of the cliff. When opposite the caves, the soldiers shot their bolts at the group huddling within the dim interiors or transfixed the cursing robbers as they flung out blinking into the sunlight. Those who escaped the arrows were yanked out, squirming and cursing, on long, barbed hooks, and dropped over the cliffs.

Where the caves were too deep or too irregular in contour to make effective such direct assaults, Herod ordered combustibles to be piled just within the entrance and ignited. The resultant indraft bore the choking fumes upon the defenders and drove them blinded and gasping upon the waiting spears of their assailants.

From a vantage point above, Herod watched the carnage. Magnanimous in battle, he deplored the wastage of brave men and the slaughter of their innocent families, who had fled with their men folk into the treacherous security of the caves.

The brassy echoes of a trumpet shrilled through the baneful gullies, calling a momentary halt to the butchery. Heralds shouted into every cave where symptoms of life still existed that all rebels submitting would be pardoned.

Herod's generous gesture was cast into his teeth. Doomed eyes still glared venomously through the billowing smoke; drooping arms continued feebly to hurl rocks and cast darts at the implacable aggressors. To a man they chose extinction rather than surrender. Josephus cites a typical example:

"And here a certain old man, the father of seven children, whose children, together with their mother, prayed him to give them leave to go out, upon the assurance and right hand that was offered them, slew them after the following manner. He ordered every one of them to go out, while he stood himself at the cave's mouth, and slew every son of his successively that went out. Herod was near enough to see this sight, and his compassion being moved at it he stretched out his right hand to the old man and besought him to spare his children. Yet did the old man not relent at all upon what he said, but reproached Herod on the lowness of his descent and forthwith slew his wife as well as his children. And, when he had thrown their dead bodies down the precipice, he at last threw himself down after them."

After the conquest of the cave dwellers Herod supposed—little realizing how intense and unrelenting was the Galilean spirit— that all rebellion was finally crushed. Leaving token garrisons under command of his friend Ptolemy in the principal towns, he determined to make a sudden attack on Antigonus II before going to the aid of Ventidius. No sooner was his back turned on Galilee than rioting provincials surprised and killed Ptolemy and besieged his little garrisons.

Herod hurriedly turned back from Judea. Systematically his enraged soldiers swept across hills and bogs, wiping out all resistance. This time Herod was not lenient. All prisoners were killed; a tribute of one hundred talents was imposed on Galilee.

The delay in Galilee cost Herod a chance to distinguish himself in the sight of Antony. Ventidius had proved strong enough to disperse the Parthians and kill his old enemy Pacorus, without Herod's help. Not that Antony considered Herod at fault for delaying. He appreciated the gravity of Herod's position and his successful beginnings in the pacification of a rebellious kingdom. Under orders from Antony a thousand cavalry and two legions were detached from the Syrian army to help Herod against Antigonus II.

Macheras, the commander of the Roman troops, was a peculiar personality, typical of the wide range of queer characters who rose to limited prominence in the Roman provinces. Knowing him to be absolutely vain and corruptible, both Herod and Antigonus II offered inducements to win him to their respective causes.

Antigonus II mistakingly made glowing promises, coupled with a diffuse account of Herod's injustice to his own people and his duplicity toward his benefactress, Rome. Herod, on the other hand, in lieu of promises, bought the Roman's good will with hard silver and gold, and Macheras was his man.

Assailable though he was, Macheras had a quixotic streak that would not let him be satisfied merely with taking money from the highest bidder in exchange for his good will, as did Ventidius and Silo. He approached Herod with a crackbrained scheme of seeming to acquiesce to Antigonus' pleas, then taking his money and escaping with a knowledge of his plans.

Against the repeated objections of Herod, Macheras stubbornly insisted on carrying out his project. Not for long was the wily Antigonus II, with his omnipresent spies, ignorant of the silly plot. Macheras was permitted to enter Jerusalem and then thrown out amid the laughter and derision of the people.

Here again, Antigonus II in his desire for revenge, his wish to humiliate an adversary who had flouted him, overreached his better judgment. Far wiser had he been to hold the noble Roman as hostage.

Hurt in his touchiest part, his vanity, Macheras spewed his revenge on every Jew he came across, killing indiscriminately the adherents of Antigonus and of Herod. Always loyal to his men, Herod in his first fury made ready to fight Macheras; on sober second thought he decided instead to protest to Antony. Macheras, too, by this time feeling both foolish and scared, hurried after Herod and implored him with every sign of contrition not to report to Antony what he had done.

A reconciliation followed. Herod henceforth had an ally whom, unlike Ventidius and Silo, he could blackmail.

Meanwhile, Antony was having his troubles at the siege of Samosata on the Euphrates. The legions supported him half-heartedly. They felt that Ventidius' killing of Pacorus had been poorly rewarded by Antony's dismissal of their commander. This time Herod was determined to let nothing stand in the way of aiding the Romans. He hurried to Antioch with an army of picked troops. From there on he convoyed a large number of Romans who had been afraid to proceed to Antony's aid because the roads were controlled by the enemy. Herod's reinforcements plus his personal valor and brilliant strategy infused vitality into lethargic siege operations. In a short time the city was subdued.

Antony renewed his protestations of friendship, publicly repeated to Herod the appellation "Rex Socius and Friend of Rome," and made profuse promises of help in the coming campaign against Antigonus II.

If Herod knew how badly affairs were going in Judea, his elation at Antony's professions of regard would have abated. On his departure he had left his brother Joseph, the weakest and dullest of the family, with full powers to represent him. He had, however, given Joseph strict injunctions not to move actively against Antigonus II, especially since he had grave doubts about the constancy and ability of his Roman ally, Macheras.

No sooner was Herod's back turned than ambition, long thwarted by his brother's ascendancy, began to buzz in Joseph's empty head. An armed truce prevailed which he decided to break by driving off Antigonus II's reapers in the fertile Jordan valley and seizing the grain himself, thereby reducing the enemy to near starvation.

With the help of Macheras' five Roman cohorts he easily scattered the reapers and harvested their grain. Laden with plunder, and carelessly singing their way through the mountains, they were set upon by Antigonus II's angry troops. The Romans, green troops, unbraced by any admixture of veterans, were cut down to a man as they fled in panic. The troops immediately under Joseph fought bravely, but were also annihilated, their commander among them.

Antigonus II, striding across the scene of battle, in a paroxysm of rage buffeted and kicked Joseph's bleeding body, and then cut off his head. On being informed that Pheroras was willing to pay fifty talents in exchange for a proper burial for his brother, Antigonus II scornfully laughed away the offer and left the carcass to the dogs.

Mass massacres followed. Groups of Herod's partisans, garnered from all over the province, were put on barges, which were sunk in the Lake of Tiberias to provide entertainment for gloating Jewish mobs.

When Herod, near Antioch, received news of these disasters, he was grief-stricken rather than shocked. Like many Orientals, he was obsessed by a belief in dreams and divinations. On this night a sense of foreboding made sleep difficult. When rest at length came, it was broken by repeated dreams, in which he saw his brother killed. A final vision was so real that he leaped from his couch with a cry of horror. Outside his chamber he could hear the somber voice of the messenger from Judea.

Against the pleas of his friends, he would tarry neither to mourn the dead nor to collect an adequate army. Unreasoning anger and a blind will to revenge goaded him on. Something seemed to snap in his brain; his appalled associates observed for the first time that insane rage that would recur more and more frequently with the passing of the years. Near Mount

Lebanon he collected eight hundred of the hardy Syrian high-
landers, always loyal to him, and a Roman legion. Before daybreak he struck devastatingly at the borders of Galilee, picking
up everywhere his scattered units, who caught from their leader
a spark of his ungovernable, irresistible fury.

In his stronghold, Antigonus II girded himself for battle. A
wave of depression had extinguished the blast of fury by whose
grim flare he had dishonored the body of Joseph. A foreboding
pulse insistently throbbed in his ears: this would be his final
fight, his doom.

Still, the elements granted him a respite. A storm too savage
for even the embittered troops of Herod to withstand drove them
back to Syria. There a second legion, the gift of Antony, joined
Herod. Resistance on the frontier collapsed. He was again on
the march.

The invasion followed the jungle road, along the humid valley
of the Jordan, to Jericho. That city, destined to be the occasion
of his quarrel with Cleopatra, and finally the scene of his pitiful
death, always held a peculiar place in Herod's affections. In its
moist warmth and balmy fragrance a sensual oriental strain,
buried shallowly under his desert breeding, and incompatible
with the austerity of Jerusalem, was given full play. Under a
happier star, he might have spun out contented years in its soft
palaces and gardens. As it was, he would try, always and vainly,
there and only there to find surcease from depression and despair.

But on this occasion it was no emotional impulse that prompted
him to march on the city. Jericho was anti-Jewish; the country
about, "the divine region," was the most fertile in the land; the
climate and defensive possibilities offered an ideal year-round
headquarters.

Soon after he arrived in his temporary capital, a fortuitous
incident convinced him that he was destined to escape all dangers and to accomplish great deeds. A grand dinner, tendered
him by the prominent men of Jericho, had come to a close—
early, for Herod, abstemious since that unforgettable banquet at
Rome, would let nothing infringe on the rigorous life of a
soldier on campaign. Hardly had the guests left the hall when
by accident or more probably as the result of a plot—since

patriotic Jews may have recalled the feat of lusty, heroic Samson—the walls caved in. As a result of his narrow escape, his followers concluded that Herod must be "very dear to God." Whatever Herod thought, he must have regarded his escape as a favorable omen, for the very next morning he pushed toward the western hills and Jerusalem.

About six thousand of the Jewish defenders attacked the Roman van—carefully avoiding actual contact with the terrible short spears and double-edged swords of the legionaries, but harrying them from a distance with stones and arrows. In the encounter Herod himself was wounded, though not seriously, by a dart in the side.

Antigonus II trembled at the potentialities of an immediate attack on his city. While he held Jerusalem, he could either bargain or fight; with its loss, all was lost. His best chance to temporize was by creating a diversion that would force Herod to turn aside. His really gifted general Phocus had disappeared somewhere in the Galilean debacle; his present commander Pappus was somewhat less able.

His strategy, nevertheless, was sound. He led a foray into Samaria, where Mariamne and Herod's family were sheltered under the sulking wing of Macheras. Herod, divining his strategy, deflected his army north of Jerusalem, taking ports along the Samarian border and cutting off reinforcements from Pappus.

With the Antigonians stalled in the hills, Herod withdrew to field headquarters at Cana, to watch the next step. Pappus had a choice of fighting his way back to Jerusalem or strengthening his army with sympathetic elements, risking once more the fortunes of the field. He chose the latter course. Galileans, various anti-Herodian factions throughout the country, even hot-bloods from Jerusalem made their way to his camp.

Herod, for his part, made very little effort to keep down the growing strength of Pappus' army. He had reached the conclusion that the greater the number he could eliminate on the battle ground, the fewer would be available for the defense of Jerusalem.

Herod first maneuvered Pappus into a position that was militarily hopeless, and then attacked. The battle was a one-sided slaughter; the battlefield a shambles, with the victors hardly more imperiled than if engaged in a gigantic bout of pig-sticking. No quarter was given, and, for that matter, rarely sought. Herod was determined to kill and kill; in one battle, to wipe out those irreclaimable enemies who, alive, might in the future endanger his reign. The fanatics in Jerusalem, behind their stone barricades, he would later dispose of. Their extinction, possibly long drawn out and spectacular, would be, nevertheless, only an anticlimax.

Heaps of casualties, the dead stiff and still in agonized poses, the feebly twitching wounded, hurried out of their suffering by merciful spear thrusts, choked every road and pass. Survivors, all order and discipline gone, flocked into a large village and hid in the dim interiors of the houses. Systematically, house by house, Herod's troops clambered up the ladders or outside staircases prevalent in Jewish houses, to the roof, and hurled and shot their missiles into the cowering refugees below. If any managed to escape the deadly hail, walls were pulled down and every last fugitive massacred.

Disaster to Antigonus II's cause was complete and overwhelming. His downfall was delayed for a season but at the cost of the cream of his army.

On the evening of his greatest triumph another incident occurred which convinced Herod that by some special dispensation of fate he was destined to escape extraordinary dangers that would be fatal to other men.

Three enemy soldiers, miraculously escaping the general slaughter, hid in Herod's quarters, grimly resolved to rid their country of this killer of thousands of their comrades. Stained with blood and grime, exhausted with the fatigue and the excitement of victory, Herod dismissed his attendants, stepped out of his soiled garments, and flung himself into a bath. The first of the assassins rushed upon the helpless king, raised his arm to strike, then recoiled before the glaring eyes of the naked figure and slunk into the street. The second and third fared no better; the kingly presence, alone and undefended, seemed proof against the aggression of lesser men.

Herod later gave the three their lives; possibly they were the only hostile survivors of that awful day.

Well might he be generous. Their failure created in Herod a disposition of utter fearlessness in personal peril, and complete contempt for the machinations of his enemies. He finished his bath and before sinking onto his couch sent the severed head of Pappus to his brother Pheroras. The headless shade of Joseph, avenged, could now rest.

As the blasts of winter shrilled along the Judean uplands, Antigonus II despairingly strengthened the defenses of Jerusalem for a final tussle. Herod, with thoughts of battle seemingly remote from his mind, sent his troops to recuperate in the languid warmth of Jericho.

When the early green of the hills quickened into fire and gold during the short, sweet Judean spring, Herod moved his army before the west wall of Jerusalem near the temple. Pompey, a generation earlier, had forced this passage, and the damage incurred then had never been fully repaired. First Herod ordered all buildings near this wall razed and all trees about the city, excepting a little olive grove on the Mount of Olives, cut down. Then he had skilled engineers build up three great mounds, surmounted by armored towers, whence projectiles might be hurled at the walls and into the city.

All preliminaries attended to, he left for Samaria and Mariamne.

CHAPTER VIII

A MARRIAGE
AND A SIEGE

NEARLY FOUR YEARS HAD DRAGGED BY SINCE
Herod and Mariamne had proclaimed their betrothal, and almost
three since his landing in the shadow of Lebanon. With the fall
of Jerusalem assured, there was no longer any necessity for putting off the solemn nuptial feast ending the long period of
betrothal. His position as king of the Jews would be weakened
ineffably were there no queen to share his throne. Conversely
no queen could be a more valuable helpmeet than the fairest of
the Hasmoneans, the royal race of postcaptivity Judea.

When Herod told her to prepare for the wedding, Mariamne
was rapturously happy. The duration of her betrothal had been
a disquieting time, not only because of uneasiness over the safety
of her husband-to-be, but also because of the insecurity of her
own position. In the eyes of her people she was neither maid nor
wife. From the day Herod paid the "mohar"—the groom's dowry—
to her family, her fate was fixed. With the Jews the betrothal
was the essential marriage ceremony; the nuptials were only its
culmination. All this time she was definitely Herod's. Even if
he canceled the betrothal, she could not marry without first procuring a divorce.

So she lingered and languished in bucolic Samaria, in alternate
fits of depression or elation, as the news that belatedly reached
her was bad or good.

Her associates were as checkered as her moods. Her guardian,
the dour, headstrong Macherus, bound to Herod in everything
but friendship or gratitude, invariably showed his disapproval at

91

her venture. On the other hand, the generous, unaffected Samaritans took the capricious little Jewish princess to their hearts, and made her worries and joys theirs as well. Of her family there were only her young brother and mother to turn to. Her cousins—Antigonus II and his family—were raucously resentful of what they called her treason to her faith and race, while her grandfather, Hyrcanus, was happy in far-off Parthia, soaking up the adulation of the gentle Eastern Jews. Aristobulus, her brother, was a gay, charming lad in his early teens, too young and unsettled to share her problems. Nor could she confide in her mother, Alexandra, an unprincipled Jezebel, who looked on her child merely as an attractive asset by whose investment she hoped to fulfil her own ambition.

The months passed tediously for her, listening to constant strictures by her mother on how to get the most out of her position as wife to the king, or discussing with her brother the unromantic trivialities that interest boys, or, worst of all, endlessly awaiting news that she felt, in her frequent moods of depression, must be bad. Then when her worries or her mother's scolding became unendurable, she would steal to her room, to reread with tearful smiles the most recent homily from her grandfather, or fleeing the constricting atmosphere of the palace, hurry to the fields and meadows to sport and gossip with her Samaritan hosts.

Her attitude toward Herod had changed since her betrothal at the age of sixteen. At first she saw in him a man far older than one she might have chosen, were the selection of a husband left (as it rarely was) to the girl. Still, with his knowledge of the world, his reputation for bravery and integrity, and his attractive appearance, he was a man in whom, in her romantic fancy, she gradually began to see the ideal husband. For beneath her gentleness there was an almost immoderate pride in family and race. As she read his letters with their glowing accounts of his hopes and triumphs, or on his infrequent visits listened in mute ecstasy to the story of his ambitions from his purposeful lips, there was fostered in her inmost heart the conviction that this man, provided she were by his side, would bring back the ancient glories of Judah.

Rumors of the scathing censure of the Jews, and the brutal insinuations of Antigonus II might momentarily have dimmed her spirit. There was, besides, the inescapable fact that to marry Herod would place her in a sense outside the pale of Orthodox Jewry, since marrying outside her tribe was equivalent to putting herself beyond its protection. But such dim shadows were quickly brushed aside by the strength of her own ardor or disappeared in the cold light of Alexandra's reasoning.

Now, a mature twenty, she was prepared to live with Herod, not alone from a sense of obligation, but because she loved him devotedly for what he was to her, and could be to her race and faith.

That the match had been engineered by Alexandra for the sole purpose of getting her hands on the royal power through the charm of her daughter's beauty the bride could not or perhaps preferred not to realize.

To Herod the match was in every way appealing. Through it his position would be in the highest degree respectable and, he hoped, acceptable. Stiff-necked Jews might still mutter "Idumean upstart" into their beards, yet Mariamne's children would have Hasmonean blood running in their veins. Even the Pharisees could not too easily disregard a king who professed himself a Jew and was married into the first Jewish family. With her, entering a Jerusalem spared by his liberality (such was his intention), he might soften the hatred of the conquered and transform it into homage and even affection.

Besides, he really loved the tender little Jewess. At thirty-seven, he combined in his manner toward her something of the devotion of a father with the rapture of a youthful lover. He would protect, cherish, and above all love his royal princess.

There was, of course, the matter of Doris and their son—an unlovable brat, even the father had to acknowledge. He had put her aside without divorcing her—a mistake, since if once divorced, and she chose to remarry, she could never make a claim on him.

Expediency aside, the truth was that they ceased to love each other. Doris had most of Herod's impetuosity with none of his generous qualities to offset it. She demanded, as her right, luxury, constant attention, and complete subservience to her whims. Hard, impatient with mistakes of judgment, unwilling to risk any suspension of her soft, easy life, she broke with Herod when he insisted on undertaking what she considered his foolhardy course in the pacification of Galilee and the defiance of the sanhedrin. As the pampered, willful darling of a Darius or a Croesus she might have had a contented existence. As the wife of an ambitious, impetuous, audacious man she was impossible.

Legally there was no impediment to the marriage with Mariamne. According to the Talmud, an ordinary Jew might have four wives; a king was entitled to eighteen.

Shortly before the wedding day the sleepy landscape of Samaria was unusually animated. Guests were streaming into the capital from all directions, singly and in jovial groups: the poor, on foot; those sliding up the social scale, in appropriate vehicles, on braying donkeys, spirited Arab steeds, or evil-tempered camels. Herod wisely decided on a typically Jewish wedding, since he was marrying a Jewish bride, whom he would place on the Jewish throne of her ancestors. Accordingly everyone was invited, for he knew that the omission of a person expecting an invitation to a wedding was a serious offense. "He who does not invite me to his wedding will not have me at his funeral," say the Jews. (As a commentary, it might be recalled that over sixty years later Herod's hospitality on this occasion was still sufficiently remembered to make effective the parable of the "Wedding Feast.")

Came the long awaited day.

In the apartment of Alexandra, the bride was decked, primped, and painted. She looked rather tired. The ordeal of dressing had been a long one; the demands of her attendants, exacting. In fact, all were a bit weary and passed the interval before the coming of the groom in the traditional manner—in praising to the point of tedium the beauty, the goodness, and the other estimable qualities of the bride.

To the sympathetic eyes of her attendants and even in the hypercritical scrutiny of her mother, Mariamne made a delectable bride. The immediate effect was that of dark—overwhelming, but dark—beauty. Braids of blue-black hair framed effectively the sweet heart-shaped face, the limpid brown eyes, fringed with eyelids made ebon with kohl, the faint olive skin suffused with a light rosy flush. A single pear-shaped pearl hung over her fore-head; a wire-thin nose ring and earrings studded with rarest gems sparkled with every slight movement. Her bridal robe was of finest flax dyed a Phoenician purple, surmounted with a white linen veil. About her waist was fastened an unfolded kerchief of amber silk, striped with cornflower blue. The nails of her hands and feet were stained with henna. Sandals of softest crimson leather, strings of matched pearls, bracelets and anklets of thin-beaten gold completed the enchanting picture.

Little embarrassed yawns were suppressed, as still the intermin-able round of praise droned on. Out of sheer nervousness, attend-ants left their places to administer perfecting dabs to the bridal array that was already perfect.

As darkness seeped into the apartment, ears grew keener, and a spirit of restless expectancy displaced the boredom. A little gasp compounded of alarm and relief swept through the room as a far-off amazingly shrill cry rang out. It was the strange, wavering wail, carrying almost unbelievable distances, that heralds the approach of the groom. A female watcher, stationed near Herod's apartment, had given the first warning. The cry was repeated by other watchers placed at regular intervals along the groom's route, and carried to the bride, long before his actual advent, news that the groom was on his way.

Along the winding road, its dust laved with scented water, and lined with palm branches and blossoms, swept the happy groom and his noisy attendants. Flaring, crackling torches rent the blanket of darkness; clanging cymbals and booming drums shat-tered the nocturnal stillness. Those with neither torches nor instruments danced giddily, or sang or shouted a chaotic paean in praise of the groom.

With all the turmoil and excitement dear to the Jew in joy or in sorrow, the party approached the bride's home, then by degrees quieted as Herod drew near.

Quickly the attendants anointed Mariamne's hair and the exposed parts of her body with violet, and made certain that the "maiden's cincture," which only her husband might untie, was securely fastened.

His demeanor combined humility and pride as Herod stepped

from among his friends, "the sons of the groom," to face his bride. A single, enraptured glance Mariamne permitted her husband, then modestly dropped her bridal veil.

Herod bore the crown and habiliments of a king. Prudently, he wore also the "tallith" or prayer cloak of a priest, often worn at weddings by pious Jews. The cloak, however, was folded so as to expose rather than cover the broad arm bands of graven gold, borne on the upper arm as a sign of royalty. Herod was come as a Jew, as a lover, but, above all, as a king to fetch his queen.

Back streamed the procession, its confusion and noise intensified with the shrill cries and high-pitched laughter of the bride's party. It thrashed a serpentine path between lanes of beaming Samaritans, with here and there a furtive-eyed Judean or a sardonic Roman, back to Herod's apartments.

The royal pair entered first and seated themselves on thrones erected under a canopy of palm branches and figured Babylonian embroideries. Then entered the guests in order of rank, each handed a lighted taper as he came to make his obeisance before the thrones. Again, according to rank, he took his place about the bridal pair or was herded into one of the other chambers or even into the gardens or adjacent streets—so extensive had been Herod's hospitality.

After the preliminary ceremonies, singers and dancers regaled the guests with artistic or sophisticated performances in the throne-room and more boisterous and vulgar entertainment for the rabble beyond. Then came the jesters with time-honored witticisms, and, just before dinner, the riddlers to awaken the mind and quiet the body, to appreciate the feast to come.

The common herd was fed bountifully wherever they sat or stood. The immediate guests of the bride and groom were conducted into a gorgeously decorated banquet hall. Bronze candelabra, burning perfumed oil, diffused a soft fragrant light. Festoons of fruit and flowers—symbols of fertility—hung from pillar to pillar. The walls were hidden behind gay rugs and matchless needlework.

The ordinary procedure of men and women dining separately was not observed. Instead they remained together. The men,

half reclining on cushions, rested on their left elbow, while the
women as a gesture to decorum sat upright.

Then began the traditional marriage ceremony. A priestly
associate of Hyrcanus, acting in place of the bride's father, took
the hands of the nuptial pair between his own and called upon
the Almighty to grant them all the blessings necessary to their
state of life. Then, taking the ring from Herod, he imposed his
hands upon it in a gesture of benediction, and returned it to
the groom, who slipped it on Mariamne's finger. The bridal
couple thereupon seated themselves while the priest raised a
goblet of wine toward heaven imploring further blessings. The
cup was then handed to Herod, who drank first and then lifted
Mariamne's veil while she drank. Having finished what remained, he smashed the cup on the floor to signify that there
could be no complete happiness until Jerusalem was freed from
pagan domination.

Then came the simple ceremony, the reading of the marriage
record and the injunction, "Take her according to the law of
Moses and Israel." Garlands were then placed upon the heads
of the celebrants as the groom signed the "kethubah," the contract in which he agreed to support, honor, keep, and love her
"as is the manner of the men of Israel." The ceremony essentially completed, bride and groom were showered with wheat
as a symbol of fertility, and little packages of corn were distributed to the guests as assurance that the bride was a virgin.

A group of singers accompanied by zithers, flutes, and harps
intoned the nuptial hymn from the Canticle of Canticles, the
floor was strewn with fresh flowers and leaves, and the guests
started upon the serious business of eating.

The dinner was oriental in profusion and quality, modified by
what Herod had observed at that memorable banquet in Rome.
Rare meats and fish from the Persian highlands and Caspian
coasts, honeyed sweets and cooling sherbets of the East, spicier
viands that awakened the appetites of jaded Rome, heavy wines,
the "strong drink" of the Bible, passed in endless variety, in
golden dishes and crystal goblets.

Between courses entered other singers, voicing the traditional
lays in praise of wine and laughter. Lesbian dancing girls fol-

lowed, placing fresh garlands on the heads of the diners before performing their dances, their ordinary obscenity refined in accordance with the solemnity of the occasion. As time passed, the wine bowls were refilled with increasing frequency; almost constantly fresh garlands replaced wilted ones on heated brows. A spirit of pagan abandonment crept into the hall. The more godly began to exchange uneasy glances.

But at the table where Herod and his most intimate guests dined, there was little hilarity. Each was, in his way, too full of his own thoughts to be distracted by the general gaiety. Mariamne, in her quiet pride, discerned beyond the befuddled guests a royal throne in the ancient castle at Jerusalem, a loving, noble husband and fine sons, new Maccabees, the homage of a happy people, and quiet years declining to a calm end, when her name would be lovingly chronicled with that of Ruth, and Judith, and Esther. Herod, with an air of ill-concealed triumph, felt that this, with only the final formality of seizing Jerusalem still pending, was infallibly the end of struggle, and hatred, and plot. Once crowned in Jerusalem, with the gracious queen by his side, he could surely heal the scars of over three decades of bloodshed, and bring prosperity, and glory, and contentment to his adopted people.

Even young Aristobulus was affected by the happy turmoil. The union of his beloved big sister and the idol of his boyish adoration filled his being with solemn, silent bliss. Old Saramalla, shrewd, honest, the prototype of all Syrian peddlers, beamed with good humor. Macheras, usually cackling over his unsolicited responsibilities, sank into a moody quiet. Costobarus, the Idumean sheik, Herod's latest protégé, was casting his hawk eyes covetously at Salome, who returned unashamed the inflamed glances of her latest lover, heedless of her doltish husband Joseph, lolled into drunken stupor by the wine which, this night, he was permitted to drink. And gloating with greedy, hungry speculation at the bridal party, sat the queen-mother Alexandra, already ominously spinning the web from whose meshes—except for that other spider, Salome—would escape only Macheras destined soon to the limbo that awaits fourth-rate Roman officials once their task is completed and their fortune made, and Saramalla, who would timely flee the septic atmosphere of Jerusalem and lose himself in his Syrian village. That she herself would be crushed in the convulsive fury of her ensnared son-in-law, and that countless other innocent victims would be lured to her noxious den, she could not as yet anticipate.

At the insistence of Saramalla the wedding lasted the full fourteen days, the period of rejoicing prescribed for those of the highest rank and state. Herod and Mariamne were ecstatically happy. Yet there were moments when his ear, lulled by the dulcet tones of his soft-spoken wife, heard as from a great distance the clang of armor and the rasping call to battle; nights, when the leering face of Antigonus II banished further sleep. Before the end of the fortnight, he was as if straining at the silken leash of Mariamne's love. When the guests, crammed and glutted with thitherto unimaginable hospitality, betook themselves to their various ways, to preserve for their children and their children's children the account of this incredible feast, Herod informed Mariamne that his place was before the walls of Jerusalem. Sensibly, she did not object. She was no Doris; she realized that a king has other obligations that take precedence even over his deference to his queen.

From a purely military viewpoint, there was really no need for his presence at the siege. Under the experienced eye of Sosius the besiegers were systematically reducing the outer defences. About sixty thousand troops, forty-five thousand of them battle-hardened veterans, were encamped before the walls, in greatest strength along the northern section. In spite of showers of missiles from the defenders, trenches were dug and embankments put up almost to the very foot of the walls. Thereupon heavy battering rams were erected, ponderous oaken beams ending in a brass ram's-head, suspended from massive framework. In never ceasing cadence these beams, propelled by the eager strength of the besiegers, battered at the walls, crunching bit by bit from the huge stone blocks. The Jews shot stones and darts, then flaming arrows and projectiles steeped in bitumen; but beneath the iron-sheathed roofs of their hurdles the operators continued, with maddening regularity, to crash at the walls.

Behind the battering rams were the catapults, hurling heavy

rocks in deadly parabolas over the walls into the cowering city, or, when defenders ventured into view, projecting huge arrows, against which the heaviest armor was useless, from a sort of crossbow arrangement. Ever alert among the machines were keen-eyed archers, with fingers wedded to bowstring. Behind them crouched the heavy armed troops, ready at a word to repel a sortie or charge the crumbling walls.

Within the city, horror stalked, beyond the ordinary terror of a siege. It was the sabbatical year, when no soil might be culti-vated, a year of scarcity even during normal times. Civil war, the wastage of man power in Galilee, pillage and counterpillage, the loss of crops in the granary about Jericho, and the general incompetence of Antigonus II had prevented normal provision against the lean year.

To make the situation more terrible, faction raised its dis-cordant voice above the cry of starving children. Religious fanatics needlessly courted death, on the premise that "it was the happiest and most devout man that would lay down his life in a sacred cause." At the other extreme, the most lawless ele-ments formed gangs that indiscriminately stole out of the city to stab a Roman sentry, or cut a Jewish throat within the walls for food or revenge.

Party strife fanned the flames of dissension. The Sadducees, to a man, supported Antigonus II and urged a vigorous, to-the-death defence of the city. Among the Pharisees, however, there was difference of opinion. Some, especially the famous Pollio and Sameas (who had advised the death of Herod as a menace to the party and state, before the sanhedrin some years before) now pleaded with the Jews to open the gates to Herod. In the over-throw of the Hasmoneans this group—a minority, but a very influential one—saw the judgment of God. "They have profaned the sanctuary. Their luxury and sins are worse than the heathen. The ordinance of God in favor of David these usurpers have set aside. Therefore God has overthrown them and sent their seed out of the land."

The more intelligent and moderate Pharisees in general saw in Herod the enemy of unorthodox Sadduceeism, and the displacer of Antigonus II, who in his festering violence might serve his

Pharisaical critics, as his ancestor Alexander had done, with mass crucifixions, and slaughter of their families. Herod, on the other hand, though only part Jew by birth, and more than part gentile by choice, might be tractable.

All the while that faction and party disputes tore asunder the morale of the defenders, the never-ending thud of the battering-ram and the vicious boom of the catapult bore to the ears of the doomed citizens a burden of havoc and despair.

Sorties and attacks on the deadly machines having invariably ended with a bloody repulse, the Jews, as a desperate expedient, planned a tunnel. They dug with painful care under the middle of one of the thirty-foot stones on which the wall was anchored and inched ahead in the sticky, black heat, muffling each sound so as not to alarm the Romans, meanwhile propping the narrow passage with crossbeams lest it collapse and entomb them. With incredible effort, but exasperatingly slowly, they pushed the tunnel under the most formidable of the rams. Willing hands passed along wood smeared with pitch and bitumen.

The miners drew back some yards except a besmudged giant, assigned to the perilous duty of flinging a burning torch into the inflammable mass.

He knew, as they all knew, the inevitable effect. Only one fact was questionable. If he rushed back quickly enough, he might escape the darting flames. In any case the earth would sear and blister; flames would shoot through the cracked earth and lick up the oaken ribs of the ram. With good fortune the fire might spread among the other machines. A well executed sortie at this point might discourage the enemy to the point of raising the siege.

His brave vision could not make the sputtering torch burn faster. Impatiently, he returned to his mates for a better one.

The momentary delay was fatal. A horrified shout from the mouth of the tunnel pulled every eye in that direction. The next instant, choking dust and flinty stone engulfed them. The Romans, suspecting the ruse and laying a countermine, had trapped them. Only with difficulty was the entrance into the city sealed off. It was the Jews' last offensive gesture.

As the fall of the city drew inexorably closer, Herod became more and more restless. He wanted a peaceful surrender, followed by his entrance with Mariamne, not as a triumphant conqueror, but rather as a forgiving monarch returning to his erring subjects. Every conciliatory offer, whether made formally, or deviously through his agents within the city, was insultingly rejected. Reluctantly, he consented to Sosius' demands to make the final assault.

Under the stimulus of a speedy victory, the besiegers redoubled their efforts. Like some prehistoric monster, the ram's horrid brazen jaws champed off great stone chunks and spit them on the pile of shattered rock that sloped up the tottering wall. A final mad thrust of the relentless ram and the massive wall, like a live thing, reeled and collapsed. A thunder of crumbling rock was scarcely heard above the tumultuous cheer of the besiegers and the hacking curses of the defenders. A cloud of dust, ghastly white, shot smoke-like to the coppery sky. Twenty picked men— Herod was with difficulty dissuaded from heading them—piled up the still churning rocks, close behind them a group of dashing young centurions, eager for promotion under their commander's eye. Then the close ranks of Roman cohorts, and the auxiliaries in impetuous disarray.

The triumph of the attackers was short lived. A second wall, seemingly as strong, had been constructed a short distance behind the first. The Romans were dispirited at this unexpected obstacle. Instead of a quick end to the fatigue and tedium of siege, they would have to begin all over. Piles of debris, sections of walls and buildings still standing, made it difficult to set up the battering rams within range. "What if there is a third wall beyond the second, and a fourth beyond that?" they asked querulously. "Don't these Jews know when they're beaten? The plunder will hardly be worth the risk and the time spent in taking this accursed city."

Their grumbling was premature. Whereas it had required forty days to break through the outer wall, within fifteen days Roman shock troops streamed like an army of ants up the heavy scaling ladders, and down into the teeming lower city.

Madding mobs pressed about the snarled lanes, obsessed with the sole idea of escaping the inferno of flaming steel. Above the wailing and cursing rang the horrified cry, "The Temple is afire! The Idumean has touched the torch to the sacred precincts of the Lord!"

Actually there was a fire in the cloisters of the Temple—set probably at the instigation of Antigonus II in order to allay the panic and substitute a determination to resist to the end.

Such, as a matter of fact, was its effect. Men hitherto indifferent in factional fights and anxious only to be let live, even men favorable to Herod, with women and children fought as one, to repel those who would defame the Temple. After appalling slaughter, which included hundreds of Romans engulfed in the sudden resurgence of fighting spirit in the fleeing population, the lower city and the outer courts of the Temple fell.

Now Herod made a final attempt to spare what was left of the city and its people. Prisoners brazenly demanding to be released that they might perform their duties in the Temple actually were freed. When the priests, unable to obtain sacrificial beasts in the hungry upper city, appealed to Herod for help, he sent them what they required, with a dutiful message. Instead of being propitiated by this conciliatory gesture, they offered their sacrifices for the destruction of the upstart, praying for the extinction of the pagan oppressor.

Against his wishes, Herod gave the word for the onslaught against the upper city and the Temple. With a sinister *"Vae victis"* on their lips the Roman regulars and their allies pressed home the charge.

The battle was a satanic nightmare. Romans died with a look of incredulous horror, stabbed by those they thought already dead. Stones propelled from roof tops by the jeweled hands of women crushed the skulls of legionaries who had survived the perils of Gaul and Parthia. Children snarled and clawed at the invader in the very instant that they were split by his sword. Old men, too weak to fight, poured pitch or oil over their clothes, and, igniting themselves, lunged upon an enemy to incinerate him also on their patriotic pyre.

The Romans for their part fought with a cold, unthinking fury, killing every Jew they came upon regardless of his party affiliations. Unfortunate partisans of Herod, who had joined

his forces to exact revenge upon their countrymen, found themselves unwillingly fighting shoulder to shoulder with their late
enemies, in a despairing effort to stem this avalanche of steel.
Even the unimpressionable Dio Cassius is moved to comment on
the bloodthirstiness of the Romans, explaining it thus: "The
Jews had committed many outrages upon the Romans, for the
race is very bitter when aroused to anger." Rarely had Romans
been so engrossed in the business of killing as to overlook the
main chance to loot. But here their single idea was to burn, to
destroy, to uproot every trace of the hated Jewish race.

Valor and desperation can at best but delay the bite of steel
and the unyielding fighting organism of an army like that of the
Romans. The upper city was cleared of opposition by the decisive expedient of killing all who could be found. Thereafter the
floodgates of fury were vented against the tight-packed mobs in
the Temple. Arms almost too tired to lift swords slew and slew
with a facility that had become second nature.

Vainly, Herod's officers tried to stem the slaughter. If fortunate, they were merely scoffed at; otherwise their lives paid for
their interference. Herod, deeply disturbed at his failure to stem
the massacre, appealed in person to Sosius to call off his men.
"Would you leave me king of the desert?"

The Roman shrugged his shoulders. "You can see my men
are out of hand. The treachery of the Jews has lost them all
claim to pity. Besides, where is the rich booty we promised them
for their long, perilous struggle? Buried, destroyed, burned by
your fanatical countrymen."

In agonized desperation Herod made his last appeal. "I will
give your men, from my private means, more than they could
expect from plundering the city. You, and your officers, too, will
be recompensed beyond your expectations."

The Roman appraised the offer shrewdly. This Idumean
evidently meant what he said. "I can restrain my men for
twenty-four hours. If payment is on hand at this hour tomorrow,
what remains of the city and its people will be spared. Otherwise—." He turned sharply on his heel.

A trusted party under Costobar sped through a ruined gate.
The glitter of steel flashed only spasmodically through the cloud
of blinding dust that rolled speedily along the gravelly highway.

The principal reservoir of what still remained of Herod's wealth lay concealed in a gully south of Jerusalem. His prudence spoke out against such enormous expenditure, but the occasion warranted the sacrifice. He must lose most of his wealth to save the remnants of the city and some thousands of the people over whom he had been appointed king.

Hardly had the cavalcade dashed out of the city when a second crisis threatened an abrupt termination of the truce. Impelled by curiosity to see the fabulous holy objects and ornaments their enemies held in such reverence, the Romans, in fact all the non-Jews, moved on the Inner Temple. When the news of this action reached Herod, he acted with incisive decision. If the Holy of Holies were profaned, he could never hope for any response from the Jews except undying hatred. Instantly, he sped with his Idumean guards to block the entry to the sacred precincts. The armed mob, its appetite whetted by hard fighting and little booty, thronged up to the gateway, bantering and cursing, boisterous and ugly at once. The better-disposed he dispersed by his pleading and promises. A little bloodletting cooled the zeal of the others. Herod had saved the Holy of Holies; perhaps, he ventured, the Jews would remember that gratefully, once he was really their king.

Exhausted, he flung himself down where he stood. Through the chill highland night he slept, on the hallowed tiles, the leaden sleep of the unendurably tired. An Idumean covered him with his own cloak, and stood shivering in the shadowy court until the sun emerged blazing behind the pink hills of Moab.

Costobar did not fail in his mission. (Loyalty to Herod aside— he must not appear incompetent to Salome.) Panting under sacks of gold, his men proceeded to Sosius' quarters. As Herod entered the gloomy chamber, he stared at a sight that numbed what Jewish blood ran in his proud veins. Antigonus II was groveling at the feet of the irate Roman, who spurned him aside with the sneer "Antigona." Nothing thus far had troubled Herod quite so much as the sight of this abject figure. Half-fainting, he grasped the arm of Costobar. "The coward, the bestial coward!" he muttered, as though to himself. "Could he not at least die as a Jewish king!"

The heavy clink of the gold restored the commander's good

humor. Hand outstretched he greeted Herod. "Antigona"—he repeated the slur—would no longer annoy Rome and Rome's good friend, Herod. He would be taken in chains to Antioch, later to Rome, to grace the triumphant procession of Antony.

The gold, though it all but scoured the bottom of Herod's treasure throne, sufficed to satisfy Roman demands. "All went away, laden with spoil," and there was "a most royal present for Sosius as well," in return for which, with the tolerant catholicity that marked the attitude of impious Romans toward the faiths of conquered peoples, he "dedicated a crown of gold to God."

After this edifying act, Sosius left with Antigonus II, the most royal of Jews and the only Jew to demonstrate fear and cowardice, in a capital that fearlessly died for him. On a Sabbath of 37 B.C., exactly twenty-seven years after the previous entry of the city by Pompey, and one hundred thirty years after the first Hasmonean proudly raised the crown to his head, the last king of that unfortunate race began his journey to a disgraceful end.

CHAPTER IX

KING OF THE JEWS

WITH THE FALL OF JERUSALEM, THE DEPAR-
ture of the Romans, and the reunion with his bride in the palace
vacated by his craven predecessor, it would be pleasant to be
able to summarize the story of the reign of the royal pair with
the traditional ending "and they lived happily ever after." Almost
inevitably, this would seem the appropriate comment on the rest
of their lives.

Of Mariamne, it might be said that she would have graced
any throne in the world. Birth, intelligence, beauty, courage,
and devotion fitted her pre-eminently as queen of this little Jewish throne, which to her and her husband marked the summit of
every conceivable human ambition. When we consider Herod
on the day when he ascended the throne of David, we perceive
him endowed with gifts and talents for a prosperous reign, and
a character and disposition for a happy one. There is, in fact,
an almost unbelievable difference between the Herod of his
coronation day and the morose monster that ordered the slaughter of the Innocents at Bethlehem in seeking the life of the
Christ Child.

Morally, he was actually better in some ways than his con-
temporaries. Though he might have thought himself one, he
was not really a Jew in faith. His experiences with skeptical Sadducees and hypocritical Pharisees had stifled what urge there
might have been to submit himself wholly to the dictates of the
Torah. But decidedly he was no pagan, bowing his will and
stultifying his intelligence in the worship of the sensual demi-

gods of Rome or the debased version of sun worship practiced by the Parthians.

Perhaps he might most correctly be listed as a deist. Even allowing for the empurpling touch of Nicolaus of Damascus (Herod's personal biographer, whose work has been lost) in his speeches as Josephus quotes them, they are, nevertheless, stripped of the rhetoric, the words of a man convinced of the existence and might of a God. That this God is no Old Testament Yahweh, speaking directly to his chosen children, is equally evident from the note of remoteness with which Herod speaks of him. There is a God, Herod knew, but a dim, perhaps unknowable God, approachable and sympathetic at times, especially if properly besought, but not too constantly concerned with the affairs of men.

To this belief in God Herod added a faith in his destiny, not the blind fate of the Greeks and Orientals, but a benign destiny demonstrating an intelligence by a God, and expressed in his own case by a special preternatural manifestation in the form of preservation from the physical dangers that beset ordinary men.

In discussing Herod's morals, it is well to consider the times he lived in. Though there were, of course, isolated instances of individual sanctity and wholesome family life, world decency had sunk to its nadir. Violence, rapine, corruption, adultery, and the absence of international morality and personal probity were the accepted standards of conduct. Nowhere was this festering rottenness more prevalent than in the courts of rulers and palaces of the wealthy. Even the common people, too weak or poor to transgress on the stupendous scale of their masters, found a thrill in sinning vicariously, by enjoying and spreading the tales of the colossal deviltry of their betters.

Yet in days when men commonly thought, acted, and talked obscenely, they agreed that Herod's emotional life bordered relatively on asceticism. He had loved Doris and cast her off. He loved Mariamne with all the love and devotion that charged his volcanic soul. Besides these, no woman seems seriously to have aroused his desire. Had he been a truly Jewish king, his sex life would unquestionably have been held a model and an inspiration for his people. Where David sinned and repented, and

Solomon sinned, and succeeding Jewish rulers became slaves of their passions, Herod lived an unimpeachable sexual life.

As he controlled his passions, he was equally abstemious in food and drink. Except for his single fling in Rome—it is possible that his new honor might have excited him quite as much as wine—there is no suspicion of his having drunk to excess. Gluttony, hypersensitivity in food, which signalized the voluptuaries of the day, were non-existent in Herod. He dined grandly with the Roman lords and the chieftains of his own people; he was quite as content with the rations of coarse barley bread and the brackish water he and his army consumed in the field. Effeminacy and the grosser forms of lust, rarely divorced from wealth elsewhere, as yet at least were not sanctioned in Herod's presence.

One fault he had not overcome, an impetuousness which when checked turned into wild rage, unreasoning anger that approached, if it did not actually identify itself with, madness.

Apart from this irascibility, his moral and mental traits were apparently of a superior type. To his family he had shown (and they in part at least had shown to him as well) an almost clannish loyalty, engendered, in part, of his patriarchal forbears. His older brother had died gladly on hearing of his escape; Herod would have given his own life as willingly for those of his family.

This loyalty extended also to his troops and subordinates. Unquestioningly they obeyed his orders, knowing he would, whenever possible, be in the front rank incurring their risks and sharing their hazards. Since loyalty begets loyalty, no other commander, until Napoleon, enjoyed quite the same confidence and homage.

Still on the topic of loyalty, it might be recalled that Herod had the happy faculty of attaching to his person and his cause the weak and misunderstood—the Syrians, and Idumeans, and Samaritans, who perceived in him a source to assuage their griefs and lift up their spirits, in a word to re-establish belief in themselves and their destiny.

Needless to say, he was a courageous warrior. Better than that, he was an inspired tactician. In every form of battle he showed supreme skill: in the open-field fighting against Pacorus, in swift or protracted siege operations at Jaffa and Jerusalem, in guerrilla warfare and ambuscade in Galilee and about Jericho, and in the terrible onslaught in the caves in the Hill of the Robbers. Master of the supply problem and keen appraiser of the limitations of human endurance, he managed always to feed and pay his troops regularly, and periodically and generously provided them with rest and relaxation.

Too often we think of Herod as a raging tyrant, turbulent, boisterous, and crude. Sixteen centuries after his death the charge would still be brought against a tiresome ranter, "He out-herods Herod." But his actions and speeches, until physical agony and madness had taken their toll, belie that charge. He was a dignified man. even a proud man, where dignity and pride were appropriate. Before Cleopatra, and Octavius, and Antony, he kept his head high, his pride and dignity undimmed. But with his Idumeans and Syrians, with his friend Saramalla, and his intimate Nicolaus, he was a hale, bluff man, somewhat burdened by responsibilities, saddened occasionally by worries and trials, but essentially a man like themselves.

Of his generosity, there is little need to speak, whether it be his material generosity in providing with open hand for the comforts of his troops or that finer generosity which would have spared his bitterest enemies at Arbela.

Prodigality with state funds was the fashion among potentates. Yet Herod was discreet and saving. His wisdom in distributing public money, as well as his private fortune, in various easily accessible places saved him an army-in-being during his flight to Rome; it made possible gifts to Antony when they would do the most good; it preserved him in the supreme hour at the fall of Jerusalem, when failure to procure great amounts quickly would have meant the utter destruction of the city and the annihilation of its inhabitants.

In the arts of peace, particularly architecture, he showed the greatest promise. Except for the tiers of attractive villas climbing up from the harbor of Rhodes, he had, as yet, had little opportunity to prove his outstanding talent as city planner and architect. Later, after the New Temple, and Sebaste, and Caesarea Philippi, he became recognized as a master builder, and men could say of him, as of the other great architects of the ages, "They did their days in stone."

Physically, he is said to have been a handsome, virile figure, generally inured to hardship and nervous strain. There is, to be sure, the disquieting record of a three months' "mysterious" malady that laid him low while he was hurrying home from Syria. Josephus seems intentionally obscure about that weakness. A similar vagueness makes it difficult to understand Herod's spasm of despair that prompted him to attempt self-destruction because of his mother's danger, when all about him men were taking practical measures to alleviate that danger.

Whether a secret physical taint—if it was physical—preyed upon his mind until the bounds of reason snapped; whether his suicidal impulse (certainly not understandable from any other logical premise) was a symptom of a gathering madness, is difficult to ascertain and impossible to prove. Such theory does, however, provide a reasonable and charitable explanation for the crazy excesses this brave, manly monarch would commit with increasing frequency and violence.

At the present, at any rate, Herod was a most promising king and a reasonably good man. What lives he had taken were in defense of his own or in furthering a cause, legally just, against opposition that knew only violence as a weapon. The putting away of Doris, at least its manner, was a blunder, but according to Jewish law strictly legal. In regard to his defiance of the sanhedrin let it be recalled that that legalistic assembly was angered not so much that he killed the robbers, but because he was too impetuous to wait for them to order the killing.

In brief, King Herod, in ascending the throne of Judea, was a better man than most men of his time, and certainly an able man—possibly, if given proper scope for his talents, the ablest man in the Roman Empire.

To the credit side of the ledger, as Herod opened the annals of his long reign, might be added the favor of Rome (an unstable asset at best), the devoted love of his queen, the attachment of a rather small group of Jews drawn to him by friendship or self-interest, the loyalty of a larger number of non-Jews who had fought under his banner, and the tentative support of the bulk of the inhabitants, sick of uncertainty and violence, and ready to subscribe to the leadership of anyone who could offer them peace and reasonable prosperity.

Yet despite his strength and ability, despite the superficially favorable auspices under which he began his reign, the situation that faced Herod was fraught with almost insurmountable difficulties. In dealing with Rome he must maintain a balance between Octavius, who would peremptorily remove a creature ruler for any lapse of perfection, and Antony, whose insatiable financial demands, on top of Cleopatra's subtle persecution, would make such perfection almost impossible. The political situation in his own domain was chaotic, party banded against party, except in common hostility against a king who was not wholly of their blood nor of their faith.

Even these obstacles, distressing and complex as they were, Herod, with consummate courage and ingenuity, would be able to master. The most pernicious problem, for which even the destiny in which he placed such unquestioning faith offered no solution, was disunion, intrigue, and hate in his own family. A Salome or an Alexandra singly could corrode the happiness of the most devoted family. Herod was unlucky to be cursed by both.

In the country generally, and more especially within the capital, political anarchy prevailed. As one critic states, "Judea was not a nation, but rather an agglomeration of sects, united in blood but separated by distrust and hatred." In these sects or parties was vested practically all local authority, judicial and religious. Yet, in the aggregate, the political parties comprised a surprisingly small part of the entire population. The largest of them, the Pharisees, consisted according to Josephus of no more than six thousand. Certainly unlike the American or British party systems which include practically all citizens, and different also from the one-party system that prevails in Fascist and Communistic nations, the Jewish political situation embodied all the faults of both systems with the advantages of neither.

The Jewish partisan (excepting the gentle, harmless Essene) had all the arrogance of the Nazi, and the guile of the Communist, without a redeeming semblance of devotion to his country; he habitually practiced the graft and intolerance of the seamier side of the multiparty system, without the participation of the general public in this system.

In a word, the Jewish party system, so involved in its ramifications, so vague in its delineation, enmeshed with theological and dynastic complications, placed before Herod an almost insoluble difficulty, which he must solve, and soon, or forfeit the confidence of the people and the approval of Rome.

Strangely enough, the parties varying so essentially in principle grew from a common root. It will be recalled that the Chasidim, or Pietists, came into being in the time of Judas Maccabeus. At the outset the Chasidim were little concerned with political government and devoted their lives to a rigorous adherence to the outward forms of religious worship and to the fostering of an inner piety, their prime purpose being, by strictest conformity to the letter of the Law, to inspire love for its inner meaning and to arouse disgust with the Hellenism that infected even the ancient priesthood of the land.

As time passed, the Chasidim split into three factions. One, by the exercise of the most extreme self-abnegation, developed a spirit of mystical asceticism. This group—naturally the smallest— became known as the Essenes. A second faction, later called the Sadducees, through an exaggerated nationalism gradually discarded their pietistic beginnings and grew to be utterly materialistic—intensely Jewish in national aspiration, but indifferent, if not antagonistic, in spiritual matters. With the third, and largest, party, the Pharisees, implicit compliance with the minutiae of the Law degenerated into a stilted formalism that they no longer considered merely the expression of piety, but identified with piety itself.

To Herod the Essenes presented no problem at all. They were simple, devout recluses, their habitat in the green oases or little remote villages, never in the swarming markets or political centers of the cities. Unconcerned with politics, they lived an orderly, almost monastic existence, with definite periods for prayer, work, ablutions, food, and rest. Their tastes were abstemious; they refrained from eating meat and the more delicate foods.

In personal habits they were scrupulously clean. The sight of an Essene, wearing at his side the little shovel he used to bury evidences of human necessity, afforded the uninhibited Orientals no little merriment. If the Essene left his peaceful community, it was on an errand of mercy: to teach the young, to cure the sick, to impart peace to those at war with themselves. Possibly, since it was his own tutor, an Essene, who first predicted Herod's greatness, the king took this unworldly, gentle sect into his favor and would have welcomed their presence in Jerusalem had they seen fit to emerge from their happy retreats.

It was almost impossible, however, for Herod to regard the other Jewish sects with anything like tolerance. Of the two, the Sadducees were the more irreconcilable. Frankly worldly, they rejected the doctrines of Divine Providence, the immortality of the soul, and the resurrection of the body. If a Messiah were to come—and they even more eagerly than other Jews were ready to throw their strength into any movement for independence headed by a strong Jew—he would be no God, but an ordinary mortal like themselves. His advent and success would be purely natural operations, disassociated completely from prophecy or divinity.

Most Jews disliked them intensely. They bore the reputation of being self-seeking, vengeful, avaricious, and cruel. Behind their backs, people referred to them as "hot-hands." Since they believed only in worldly success and temporal happiness, they naturally fell away from the observance of the Law of Moses, and embraced the laxity and worldliness of Hellenism without, however, being affected by its appreciation of aesthetic beauty.

Nevertheless it must not be supposed that they lived solely for sensual gratification. At the final fall of Jerusalem, for example, an impassioned patriotism and a fanatical hatred of the forces and individuals that obstructed Jewish freedom made them, on different principles, every bit as reckless and tempestuous as the Zealots. Obviously, Herod could come to no accord with a sect whose policy was an adamantine "rule or ruin."

There were too many shades of Pharisaism for Herod to adopt a uniform policy toward all. Still, he was safe in assuming the premise that his relations with them would be conducted, at best, in a spirit of alert suspicion. He knew that from their incipience in the days of the high priest Jonathan (161–143 B.C.) they had opposed every regimen they were unable to dominate, reaching a climax of violence in their struggle with John Hyrcanus (135–104 B.C.). He realized their tremendous influence on the unlettered mind. The priests might offer their sacrifices, and make an impression, particularly on the pilgrim from afar, with their processions, and shrilling trumpets and choric odes in the Temple. But the Pharisees worked more subtly. Daily they taught in the synagogues not only the Law itself, but unauthorized additions and commentaries. Since the listeners were usually ignorant of Hebrew and had to accept on faith the translation into the vernacular Aramaic, it was a quite simple matter for the Pharisees to submit their observations and interpolations as part of the actual Law.

That all Pharisees so took advantage of popular credulity is quite untrue. We have become habituated to thinking of all Pharisees in terms of the "whitened sepulchers" and "brood of vipers" that commonly represented this party some seventy years later. In Herod's day, there were among them many learned scholars, combing the Scriptures for clues and hints by which they might recognize the coming Messiah, whose time, they were sure, was close at hand, and many simple saints, yearning to worship and die for this Messiah.

Yet, granted the Talmud's distinction between "true" and "painted" Pharisees, there is little doubt that when Herod conquered Jerusalem most of the sect were of the less worthy type. Whereas the Sadducees abandoned the written Law completely, the Pharisees saddled on traditions and oral law, for which, with no authority or proof, they claimed equal antiquity and force. Thrusting aside the insistence of faith and charity as basic principles of human conduct, they regarded as their chief function the establishment of a "hedge around the Law," a protection for those within and a barrier against those without.

They attached an extraordinary importance to the externals of worship, to the distinction between clean and unclean, to the threads on tassels and the boxes on doorposts, to the observance of the Sabbath, and to ablutions. Often the quibbles that evoked stormy discussions in Pharisaic circles seem even more absurd than some of the reputed discussions in the decadence of Scholasticism among the schoolmen of the medieval universities: whether or not it was lawful to eat an egg laid on the Sabbath; whether water poured from a clean into an unclean vessel also contaminated the source.

Involvement in the minutiae of discussion made many of

them arrogant. They considered ordinary people "unlearned and ignorant men, whose talk is of oxen."

Consequently, the less gullible element disliked them almost as heartily as they did the Sadducees. But, peculiarly, women flocked to them in droves, seemingly welcoming the "abdication of reason" that the Pharisees called for from the female sex.

Herod's attitude toward the sects might be summarized as follows: not to molest the Essenes; to destroy the Sadducees; to deal with the Pharisees individually according to their dispositions and deserts.

Many of the Sadducees had already perished violently in the savage battles for the city. Those still alive whom he could reach, Herod had summarily executed; and he had seized their wealth as a most welcome legacy for his sadly depleted treasury.

It is significant that the slaying of these partisans and the confiscation of their property was the first time that Herod had men put to death because their continued existence constituted a potential threat to his safety. It was also the first time that he profited financially by a death that he ordered. In a sense, the execution of the Sadducees, understandable as it was, marked the turning point in a career hitherto honorable and humane. His chagrin at the failure of Jerusalem to accept its defeat as final, his annoyance at the stubbornness of partisans who would not admit the inevitability of his reign, and more than all his disappointment that he could not present a cheering, loving capital to his beloved consort—these brought on sanguinary reprisals.

But behind the resentment and the anger lurked the growing conviction that murder can be a profitable panacea for the ills and worries that beset a monarch. Vistas, terrible in their allure, began to unfold which would never completely fade out of his imagination. Eventually they would seem to engulf reason itself.

The Sadducees whom Herod disposed of were rich men; their wealth made a sizable contribution to the yawning Herodian coffers. Herod recalled that there were other sources of wealth also. Many of the Pharisees were affluent men; mostly they were his enemies. They controlled the sanhedrin; and in Herod's memory still rankled the shameful recollection of his trial before that body twelve years previously. Of the seventy-one members of the sanhedrin forty-five who had served during that trial were executed and their property was seized.

A wave of terror spread among the upper classes of Jerusalem, nonpartisans as well as Pharisees. A general exodus began. Men carried what gold and jewels they could hastily assemble and fled out of the city. Attempts to escape were generally futile. Anticipating such action, Herod had placed Costobar in charge of guarding all gates and patrolling the country about the capital. Those caught were returned and immediately put on trial. To the credit of the king it must be admitted that such as ran away out of pure panic and were not actively associated with the opposition were freed. Unlike what marked the tribunals during the French Revolution, there was no official policy of satisfying the popular blood lust, nor were spectators at the trial permitted to influence the decision of the judges. If, however, evidence demonstrating their enmity was offered, they were forthwith executed, and their property, of course, was absorbed by Herod.

While a semblance of legal justice characterized the formal trials, a new terror against which there was no safeguard gripped the harried upper classes. A spy in the household of an opulent Jew discovered that his master swallowed his most valuable jewels before attempting flight. It became known that others as well, before undergoing a trial whose issue they had reason to fear, gulped down their finest gems to insure their families at least against penury in the event that their estates were confiscated. This disclosure resulted in the practice of cutting open the dead to recover what jewels were secreted. The story spread. Riff-raff attached to Costobar's guards and thugs and assassins pouring out of the city's stinking alleys, waylaid men they suspected of so hiding jewels and ripped them open on the spot.

For a while, Herod turned a deaf ear to the agonized pleas for protection of what still remained of the upper classes of Jerusalem. By devious routes, most of the wealth seized by his creatures eventually made its way into his own treasury. But when the killings increased to the point where the proceeds were entirely disproportionate to the number of lives lost and to the unrest and confusion caused, he ordered a halt, and granted amnesty to all still under suspicion.

The most gruesome phases of these trials and murders are attributable to Costobar and his rowdies rather than to Herod. Yet Herod condoned the atrocities, profited tremendously by them, and stopped them only when they ceased really to pay. More and more it becomes evident that the fine edge of his warrior's sense of honor was being dulled by the determination to assure his safety and to satisfy his need for money.

It must not be thought, however, that the executions constituted a general reign of terror. Save for some indiscriminate butchery by Costobar's ruffians, only those who had reason to fear the heavy retributory hand of Herod were molested. To try to impress the populace that he really wanted to rule justly and leniently, he even forgave some of the less violent of the Pharisees.

Prominent beneficiaries of his clemency were the famous Sameas and Pollio, the foremost Pharisee scholars and members of the sanhedrin, who twelve years earlier were foremost in advocating his death. It was Sameas, in fact, who predicted that once Herod became powerful enough he would cause their death and who ironically escaped execution himself, to give a partial lie to his own forecast.

It is possible that Herod extended these judges his leniency and his friendship out of respect for their scholarly attainments. More probably, however, he took into consideration their attitude during the siege. The Pharisees already killed had on that occasion urged the people to resist to the uttermost, with the promise that supernatural aid would turn the scales in their favor at the hour of direst need. Sameas and Pollio, on the other hand, had advised surrender, since the will of Heaven pointed to Herod as the preordained ruler. Unquestionably this fact, more than any consideration for erudition, prompted Herod to spare their lives, the brief remainder of which, incidentally, they devoted to the elaboration of the Halakoth—the technical religious rules derived from the Law of Moses.

Gradually, as order was restored, the city quieted; men began to move about without fear; and the natural flow of commerce and industry ran its unimpeded course. The mind of Herod, alone, was unable to attune itself to the common tranquillity. Ever present in his waking hours, impinging on his fitful slumbers, was the haunting thought that his archrival, the pretender Antigonus II, was still alive and therefore a constant threat to his peace and safety.

When Sosius despatched Antigonus II as a cringing captive to Antioch, destined eventually to accompany Antony to Rome, to take part in his triumphant procession, Herod had to pretend to be pleased. Yet if the last of the Maccabean kings had died fittingly in battle, or, failing that, were he securely planted in some stone dungeon, within Jerusalem, awaiting a quiet strangulation after the departure of the Romans, Herod's mind would have been more at ease.

He knew, naturally, that it was fixed Roman policy to choose a new client king from the old line. In naming him king, Octavius and Antony had broken with precedent. Acting on a generous impulse, at a time when both were emotionally elated, they committed themselves to an irregular course that either or both might readily regret, as long as a scion of the old reigning house were alive. Herod feared, not without reason, that Antigonus II if permitted to reach Rome might eventually prevail on Octavius to rescind Herod's authority to rule. True, Antigonus II was a convicted rebel, unlikely to worm himself into the favor of the unimpressionable Roman. Still, it would be quite within the nature of the cowardly, waspish Jew to renounce his own claim to the throne and urge the substitution of his son, Alexander. So long as Antony had control of the prisoner, Herod felt he need not worry. But if Antigonus II were confined at Rome, under the eye of Octavius, Herod would have good reason to be troubled about his own status.

Of his two masters, it was only Octavius whom he really feared; he felt he could handle Antony. The latter was venal, but generous, and to a degree loyal. Herod could pander to his weakness and move his better nature with an appeal to friendship. But Octavius, while almost equally unprincipled, was cold, canny, and selfish. It was quite conceivable that he might prefer an enemy of Antony's on the throne of one of the puppet kingdoms assigned to Antony to a skilful, energetic ally like Herod.

Unluckily for Antigonus II, Antony was once again inundated by unpaid bills and creditors' claims. Spies of Herod having

informed him of the precise time when that spendthrift would
be crying most urgently for money, the king by drastic scraping
together of funds managed to present him with a truly princely
donation just when Antony's plight seemed most hopeless.

Accompanying the gift was the respectful suggestion that, while
Antigonus II remained alive, Herod's ability to continue to send
such evidences of esteem and friendship to his respected patron
was contingent, in part, on the continued good will of Octavius
and on the disposition of his own subjects. If the Jewish rebel
could be put to death, not as befits a hero, but rather as a common murderer, his Jewish partisans could neither call on their
leader to head a rebellion, nor invoke his memory to inspire a
revolt. And, of course, Octavius could not possibly entertain any
qualms concerning the somewhat irregular selection of Herod as
king. The message closed with a subtle reminder that Pompey
had made the mistake of being generous with the sons of King
Aristobulus II, as a result of which ill-timed benevolence one of
those sons, the present captive, had cost the Roman Empire
money and lives. A second instance of Roman forbearance might
be regarded as weakness and might encourage outbreaks elsewhere.

Antony was overwhelmed at the stupendous windfall. On
second thought he also recognized the wisdom of Herod's suggestions. Lictors were called on. They tied Antigonus II to a stake,
beat him, and then cut his throat. No other king in the history
of the Empire had been so ignominiously treated. Dio Cassius
reports (probably wrongly) that Antigonus II was crucified—an
indication, at any rate, that Romans were impressed with the
unusual indignity of his death.

When the news reached Jerusalem, a pall seemed to drop over
the spirits of every Jew. Even the most avid partisan of Herod
shared in the common gloom. There was little sorrow for the
scoundrel who died; it was the disgraceful manner in which
Jewish royalty was put to death that hung heavy over the hearts
of his compatriots.

But in the chamber of Herod there was an almost unholy joy:
he was breaking the pride of this stubborn race. Could he completely effect that, his most tantalizing problem would be solved.

Herod had still another reason to feel elated. He had necessarily given much thought to the methods by which he might remain in the favor of men so diverse in everything except sensitiveness and mutual distrust as Octavius and Antony. Were he stronger, or they really dependent on his aid, he might, by playing one against the other, constitute himself a sort of balance of power that both would find it expedient to cultivate. As it was, however, he was relatively too weak: either one could with an angry word shake him from his throne and shatter the work of a lifetime.

With Antony, in any case, his method had proved workable. The coarse, direct method he had decided on brought results. By properly spaced gifts of money, coming opportunely, at Antony's moments of greatest need, and in amounts greater than his patron could expect, he anticipated keeping him on friendly terms.

To keep Octavius favorable, if not actually cordial, he had projected a quite different procedure. If the Roman could be brought to realize that Herod was ruling effectively in Jerusalem, that the Jewish state paid relatively better than other client states, and that the king was loyal and reliable in his relations with him, he would have no occasion to want a change in rulers. Briefly then this was his scheme: to be efficient in the sight of Octavius; to be prodigal in dealing with Antony.

By filling the places of the executed members of the sanhedrin with his own followers, Herod held control of that august body. In the internal affairs of Judea he had never for one instant thought of his kingdom as any other than an absolute monarchy. He was nevertheless sensible of the limitations of one person's strength. There were duties and rights he was quite willing to assign to friends of proven loyalty to his cause and carefully selected for proficiency in particular departments of statecraft. The result was a cabinet responsible to him only, a cabinet that was not representative and certainly not Jewish, yet on the whole better than he could have picked in Judea.

Joseph, his brother-in-law, alert enough in manipulating money, however blind to the frailty of his wife, and a certain hard-headed Dositheus, were treasurers. Costobar, secretly proud of the scandal his behavior with Salome occasioned, the Iturean Sohemus, and Herod's cousin Achiab were appointed commanders in chief of the army and guardians of the caravan routes. Saramalla was named secretary of foreign affairs, an ideal post for a merchant prince, familiar with all parts of the world, though really content only in his drowsy Syrian birthplace. Herod had called on his old tutor Manahem to serve as a kind of house minister and royal guide. The Essene turned aside the offer, softening his refusal with the prophecy that the king would reign for over thirty years.

Two Damascenes were assigned to important posts. Ptolemy, astute financier, with a fabulous income, originally derived from hijacking on the caravan trails, became chief banker. Nicolaus, a Hellenist with all Aristotle at his finger tips, authority on rare plants, a dramatist whose *The Chaste Susanna* would be acted in the court, a historian with one hundred forty-four books including the biography of his patron, was named Herod's secretary.

In addition to the official family of the new king, a horde of hangers-on and opportunists flocked to the court: distant relations heretofore unheard of, native parasites, and especially foreign adventurers like the bombastic rhetorician Ireneus and the Spartan blackguard Eurycles, whose manifold villainies were in part redeemed by an exquisite gift in painting miniatures.

When it became evident that Herod was trying to conduct the business of government on a peaceful, orderly basis, elements still antagonistic but quiescent of late through terror began to agitate, somewhat tepidly, to be sure, but openly enough for reports of their action to reach the king. There was no sharp reaction on his part; in fact, he seemed anxious to avoid any excuse for further violence.

When his first coinage was about to appear, wild rumors flared through the city that he had his head engraved thereon and that Jews would have to use and even cherish these images. The rumors were foundless; the designs on the coins were chastely innocuous engravings of grain and fruit.

Emboldened by his apparent timidity, acts of nonconformity and petty rebellion became more numerous, and still the king took no action. But the refusal of some six thousand Jews to take the oath of allegiance to him and to Rome was an act of defiance he could not ignore. Legally, he might have ordered their deaths. Instead, in lieu of their pledging loyalty, he meekly accepted a fine, which was paid for them by the wife of his brother Pheroras, with money supposedly provided by the king himself. He was clearly making every effort to efface the reputation for brutality he had acquired during the cruel days following the fall of Jerusalem.

A congenital spirit of non-cooperation with civil authority was undoubtedly the cause of much of the opposition to Herod. There was, however, also a more immediate reason for the present unrest. For some years the coming of the Messiah was being eagerly awaited. So certain were men of his imminent advent that it would have caused tumultuous joy, but little surprise, had he suddenly appeared, to lead his people to victory and freedom. Prophecies began to circulate, symbolic utterances, prayers, and poems, all centering on the theme of veiled or open hostility to the usurper and longing for the rightful King.

The following extract from the then popular "Psalm of Solomon" is characteristic of the trend of thought among believing Jews of the period:

See, O Lord, and raise up for them a king,
The Son of David, at the time thou hast appointed:
That he may rule over Israel, thy servant.
Gird him with strength to crush unjust rulers,
Purge Jerusalem from Gentiles who tread it down to ruin.
In wisdom and righteousness let him drive out sinners from our
    heritage,
Breaking in pieces the pride of the sinner like a potter's vessel;
With a rod of iron breaking all their strength.

That Herod took no resolute steps to curb this incipient rebellion was due in part to a new perspective, rather more to the softening influence of Mariamne.

From a purely common-sense view, he could afford to be magnanimous. His crown was safe, his wealth more than restored, his government functioning smoothly. To fan the barely glowing embers of rebellion into flame by a persecution of the malcontents (most of whom were blessed with more piety than property) would be folly.

Yet his forbearance was due in largest measure to Mariamne. Having joined her husband just as he was recovering from a spree of bloodletting that in his quieter moments he must have regretted, she found him more than ordinarily susceptible to her suggestions and pleas. "Be patient and forgiving. Rule wisely and justly and make your subjects, in spite of themselves, love you." These mottoes she reiterated with gentle insistence, until the king half-believed in them himself.

Mariamne's ideal was the sweet, courageous Esther, captivating the will of her royal husband, to the preservation of her people. Left to herself, there is no reason to believe that Mariamne might not have succeeded almost as well as her prototype.

But her mother Alexandra seemed almost a reincarnation of the dreadful Athalia, insanely determined to dominate even if attainment of her ambition involved the sacrifice of her family and her happiness.

It was she who first suggested to Mariamne that Herod in his present mood might agree to the re-establishment of the high priesthood. What dark plans fomented in the recesses of her mother's mind she had no way of suspecting. The suggestion seemed eminently reasonable. A temple without a high priest was an anomaly; the Jewish people without a descendant, spiritual if no longer actual, of Aaron to offer their sacrifice were spiritually barren.

Mariamne broached the subject to Herod. After surprisingly brief consideration he agreed. It would be formally proclaimed by his own heralds that through the intercession of their queen the ancient sacred institution of the high priesthood, vacant since the death of its latest unworthy incumbent, the priest-king Antigonus II, would be re-established.

CHAPTER X

DEATH OF A
BOY PRIEST

CONCEIVED IN DIVINE GRANDEUR, THE HIGH priesthood had fallen upon evil days centuries before its prostitution in the reigns of Herod and his successors. When its first incumbent, Aaron, was anointed with the holy ointment of myrrh, cinnamon, cassia, calamint, and olive oil, so that it ran "down his beard to the skirt of his garment," he was truly a "priest according to the order of Melchisedech."

As long as he lived he was privileged annually to enter the hallowed penumbra that ringed the Ark of the Covenant, there to sprinkle the blood of the offering for sin, to efface the sacrificial odor with smouldering incense, and by direct or indirect communication with the Deity to make manifest to his chosen people the will of their God. The death of the high priest—not that of the king, be it noted—marked the closing of an epoch; leases, business agreements might be amended; bargains, reconsidered; criminals who had cheated the law by flight could freely return home from their places of refuge. From the very beginning the office was hereditary, descending directly from father to eldest son.

Though the high priest was sacrosanct, he was an institution rather than a person. As priest, the utmost reverence was due him; as man, the utmost contempt might be his portion.

Such was repeatedly the case. As early as the struggle between Samuel and Saul, he was at odds with civil authority. Often he abused his powers; occasionally he engaged in timeserving, or simony; but rarely did he completely subordinate his office to the interests of royalty.

After the return from the Second Captivity, the attempt was made to restore to the high priesthood, in the incumbency of Zerubbabel and his immediate successors, the sublimity and sanctity that marked it in its earliest days. It failed. A majestic pontificate requires revenue, culture, wealth and power. All these attributes were singularly lacking in the tattered remnant of Jewry that drifted back to the homeland.

When Nehemiah died, almost the last semblance of ancient priestly dignity passed. Anointing with oil, all the impressive solemnity characteristic of the inaugural of the high priests of the past, gave way to a simple ceremony of investiture. What was worse, the high priest ceased being a purely spiritual functionary. Gradually the Jews came to recognize him as head of the Jewish nation, a spiritual head of a religious and racial, rather than of a geographical entity to be sure, but nevertheless as the leader of whatever Jewish state might be considered to exist. This viewpoint received official sanction of a kind when the Jews exchanged their Alexandrian for Seleucid masters. Syrian satraps found it expedient and profitable to administer the country through the spineless agency of the high priests.

Increased temporal power resulted in disgraceful family brawls, scandals and plots, and greed for profit that further sapped the sanctity of the office. With few exceptions, unworthy priests manipulated their holy office for personal gain. Irregularities in descent began to appear, conspicuously, when Antiochus Epiphanes removed the high priest Jesus and conferred the office on the priest's younger brother Onias.

During the reign of the Maccabee Jonathan the office of high priest lost its distinctive nature by being united with that of king. (The Hasmoneans were descendants of the oldest branch of the family of Aaron.)

A final irregularity, preceding Herod's cavalier treatment of the office, occurred when the last Maccabean king, Antigonus II, mutilated his brother Hyrcanus and seized the priesthood for himself under the title of the high priest Mathathias.

Significant of the deterioration of the high priesthood thereafter is the fact that during the first fourteen hundred years of its existence, that is, up to the time of Herod, fifty-five men had held the office, serving an average of about a quarter of a century, while in the hundred years between the coronation of Herod and the destruction of Jerusalem by Titus there were no fewer than twenty-eight high priests, for an average tenure of less than four years.

No well-disposed Jew could have entertained any feeling but shame at the picture of Antigonus II in the sacerdotal robes of Aaron, and Samuel, and the good Onias. But, relieved as the pious believer was at the removal of the rapacious priest-king, the thought of the unfilled office, and the empty priestly chamber, left him restless and disconcerted. Though the synagogue had supplanted the Temple as the core of religious thought, the performance of the age-old ceremonies and rituals, which somewhat paradoxically the Pharisaical schools emphasized, required a priesthood under a high priest. Even before Mariamne pleaded with her husband for the restoration of the traditional dignity, Herod was convinced of the desirability of such a procedure. A high priest, pliant to the royal will, could take from Herod's hands all the unpleasant details of jurisdiction in religious matters, the inflammatory nature of which he was quick to recognize.

Consideration of the activities of the sanhedrin and its influence on the synagogues did much to prevail upon him to take rapid steps for the re-establishment of a high priest. The sanhedrin, stripped of real authority, had degenerated into a school of discussion characterized ordinarily by verbosity and bombast, but impinging occasionally on dangerous doctrine. Such an incident arose—according to a well-established legend—when the text, "One from among thy brethren shalt thou set king over thee; thou mayest not set a stranger over thee, who is not thy brother," was proposed for exhaustive examination and debate. When discussions on the same text were undertaken in the synagogues, Herod in a paroxysm of fury (according to the same legend) had the chief debaters put to death, excepting one of the Baba ben Buta, whom he spared after putting his eyes out "because he valued his counsel."

True or not, the legend is illustrative of a growing uneasiness, which Herod could appease only by restoring the high priest-hood. The deaths of Sameas and Pollio and the filling of their places by Babylonian priests increased the popular discontent and made imperative the need of a tractable high priest to assume responsibility for Herod's interference in matters pertaining to the spiritual government of the Jews.

In pondering the appointment of a new high priest, the name of Hyrcanus recurred to Herod with relentless insistence—not as actual nominee for the post, since his disfigurement prevented his eligibility, but more as a sort of high priest emeritus in whose venerable shadow a lesser figure might perform the priestly func-tions, his shortcomings and weaknesses hidden in the memory of the elder's virtues.

One only principle directed the king in the matter of giving the Jews a high priest. Since he could not himself serve in that capacity, the high priest must be completely and entirely his creature. Moreover, the king would have in his power the only living ex-high priest.

Since his cruel abuse by his brother, Hyrcanus had led a not unhappy life. It will be remembered that after Phasael's suicide Antigonus sent him to Seleucia in Babylon, a prisoner of the Parthians. Contrary to the king's hopes, the Parthians treated the timid priest with unwonted mildness, according him every consideration and honor on the journey, and placing him in charge of the Babylonian Jews after his arrival. Here he lived in exile, not in the steaming purlieus of Babylon itself but on the cool banks of the great irrigation canals—the rivers of Babylon, where Jeremiah had hung his harp.

To these Jews, the care of Hyrcanus was a labor of love. Descendants of the richer, more cultured elements of the race, who had declined Cyrus' permission to return to their homeland some five centuries before, these Eastern Jews retained all the essential fervor of their faith, while departing gradually from the complexities of its practices. The disfigurement of Hyrcanus was an irremovable bar to his service at Jerusalem. In Babylon it was merely evidence of a shameful atrocity that endeared its victim the more to his hosts, without affecting in the slightest the influence or the dignity of his position.

For some five years Hyrcanus actually basked in the deference and kindnesses of his compatriots. He was free to study, to expound to appreciative listeners abstruse aspects of dogma that the hot-blooded scoffers of Jerusalem found so boring, to celebrate with enraptured piety, unbroken by the fanatical undertones of Judea, the ceremonies his poor mutilated face made impossible at home; in brief, to live the prayerful, studious life for which his nature had fitted him.

Yet when news of Herod's victory reached him, uneasy stirrings began to agitate his serenity of mind. The placid Babylonian plain, the unexciting orderliness of the life he was living (and had always wanted to live) began to weigh upon him like a physical burden; his spirit fluttered uncertainly toward the heady Judean heights. In conversation with his erudite friends he shamefacedly hinted, then hysterically blurted out, his determination to return to Jerusalem. Their shocked remonstrances he stubbornly repelled. Herod would welcome him, he assured his friends; the king could not forget that it was he who had saved the heedless young Idumean at the trial before the sanhedrin; his place, especially now that his beloved granddaughter was married to Herod, was at the new king's side, with his experience and advice, to preserve him from other rash steps.

Truth was, the old priest was just a little homesick, though in his imagination nostalgia grew to something far more portentous. Judea was a land of bitter memories. It was, nevertheless, the home of the Chosen People. It was a racking thought that he who had been their spiritual leader should waste his waning years eating the dreamy lotus in a land so paradisiacal that its very delights must be a temptation of Satan. There still were left good working years. It was not too late to serve his faith and his people and so save his soul.

There was, too, the yearning to see his family. He had always been afraid of his harridan daughter, but he was dotingly fond of his sweet little grandchildren, grown since he saw them from a long-shanked lass and a scampering lad to a lovely queen and the handsomest youth in Judea.

The Babylonian Jews made every effort to keep him among them. These efforts continued even after letters came from Herod, imploring Hyrcanus to return to share the royal authority with his grateful ward. They recalled to him how high he stood in their affection, that in Jerusalem his disfigurement would bar him from exercising his priestly office, and that kings ordinarily were not in the habit of repaying kindnesses, but rather preferred to ignore indebtedness incurred before their day of greatness.

Anticipating such objections, Herod sent other letters to Phraates, the Parthian ruler, requesting him to release Hyrcanus, and to Jewish leaders in Babylon, implying that to keep the old priest from his own home and family was a selfish attitude inconsistent with the piety they professed.

After these letters came a mission headed by Saramalla, bearing gifts and assurances of affection. The personal plea of the lovable Syrian, the mellow warmth of his invitation, proved irresistible. Hyrcanus burst asunder, as a slight thing, the ties that had bound him, as he had thought, irremovably to Babylon. Happy, amid the tears and prayers of his friends, he left for Judea.

Herod and his grandchildren received the venerable priest with every manifestation of joy; Alexandra, with a sullen greeting. But he did not mind his daughter's coldness. In her new womanly dignity Mariamne was sweet and affectionate, almost maternal in her solicitude for his comfort and health. Aristobulus canceled the years between them and was his comrade on excursions to places of historic and religious interest, absorbing keenly the scholarly lecture that accompanied each excursion.

Yet it was when with Herod that he felt happiest. At every feast Hyrcanus held the place of honor; at all sessions of the cabinet or council meetings he presided; his title was that of "Father." To all it was obvious that Herod was leaving nothing undone to honor this old Hasmonean and to convince him and everyone else of his gratitude and affection.

Partly, this was no pretense. Herod, before jealousy (or insanity) maddened him, was not a man lightly to forget favors. Nevertheless, as a son of the desert, he was an eminently shrewd, farseeing schemer. Were Hyrcanus to remain among the Parthians, he would be, as a living ex-high priest, preferable, perhaps, despite his incompetency, to such sycophantic creatures as Herod might see fit to install as high priests. On the other hand, Herod's demonstrations of friendship and honor which the priest accepted with simple joy were bound to make Hyrcanus unpopular with the anti-Herodian factions. Thus through his kindness the king was actually destroying him in the esteem of the old priestly clan.

Before many months passed, Herod disclosed his hand. With the train of Saramalla came a priest named Hananel. Commonly he was believed to be a Babylonian of no exalted family pretensions. Some thought he was originally an Egyptian. In any case he was not a descendant of Aaron, and therefore ineligible for the office of high priest.

Him, to the consternation of the Jews, Herod appointed.

In naming this obscure timeserver, Herod helped himself in several ways. First, there was no possibility that the new high priest could harmonize all discordant elements to renew the traditional duel between crown and temple, as were the case had he selected a more eligible candidate from one of the powerful Pharisaical families.

Besides, Hananel's appointment annulled simultaneously the requirements that the high priest be of the family of Aaron, that the office be of life tenure, and that it be hereditary.

In a word, the high priest was the king's good servant, and his alone.

It was a bold stroke, and a telling one. Actually there was nothing that the Jews could do but clamor. Except a son of the cowardly Antigonus II, no one had a really good claim to the office. Next to pleasing everybody, Herod reasoned, pleasing nobody was the most effective policy for avoiding factional dissensions.

While Herod served him with piety, to all appearances a devout Jew honoring his spiritual father, and the Pharisaical priests glowered impotently about their sacred duties, Hananel went calmly about his office.

There is a certain sang-froid about this unassuming rascal that is almost admirable. Truly he did himself well. That for two periods he served as high priest himself is historically certain. Less sure is the story that five of his sons became high priests and that the Caiaphas of the Crucifixion was his son-in-law. A still less creditable tradition identifies him with the high priest Annas of the Gospels, which, if true, would find him still in office almost seventy years after his investiture.

Tradition apart, there is no question but that outwardly he filled the office in a satisfactory manner and that, waiving legitimacy, he was no worse and certainly less harmful than many of his legitimate predecessors.

If the Pharisees squirmed at the sight of Hananel in his sacerdotal robes, their discomfort was trivial compared to the corroding anguish of Alexandra. It is difficult to conceive of a woman so utterly devoid of every feminine trait and maternal emotion as was the queen mother. She despised her father as a weakling. The amiable qualities that endeared him to others she sneered at as evidences of senility.

She regarded her children as pawns to be moved about or sacrificed in her game for dominance. Constantly she upbraided her son for the affection he showered upon Hyrcanus, for his friendliness toward Herod, for his lack of ambition and his failure to ally himself with the enemies of the king.

In the presence of Mariamne she assumed an attitude of hurt dignity. Meaningless incidents were magnified in an attempt to make the queen believe that Herod was deliberately dishonoring her mother. Suspicion, scandal, slander flowed in envenomed streams from her false lips. Most of all she goaded her daughter's soft spirit with the charge that she was too gullible. Herod had married her solely because of her family; he still loved Doris, and would make Doris' son, and not the child Mariamne was soon to bear, his heir.

The calumnies seemed to fall on unheeding ears. Mariamne was too much in love with Herod, too deeply devoted to the ideal of serving her race, to swallow such brazen lies.

Yet their repetition was disturbing. Merged with the recollection of flashes of Herod's old hardness (though never to her), with his frequent absences on the necessary details of the business of ruling, and with the royal actions that irritated her beloved people, they sank into the well of her unpleasant memories, later to be drawn up to poison her bliss.

To the queen mother, the appointment of Hananel was a cruel

blow. With any Pharisee she would gladly have connived. But
with an outsider, in no wise obligated to her and faithful to
Herod alone, this was impractical.

If only there were available some one of the true priestly class!

The ringing laughter of Aristobulus, awakened at some salty
jest of old Saramalla's, trickled into her chamber. In a flash
came the suggestion. Why not the high priest Aristobulus!

In that inkling was born a companion idea, characteristically
treacherous.

She bethought herself of Cleopatra. Through that queen's
influence she could win Antony's approval for her son's appointment to the most sacred office among the Chosen People.

There was a strange friendship between these women—the
fascinating siren of the Nile, ensnaring with her languorous
charms the men she could use, and the hard-grained Jewish
vixen, who destroyed with the less lovely expedient of plot and
calumny those who obstructed her greed. They had in common
an overweening selfishness and a fiery patriotism, an utter absence
of moral rectitude, and, in the hour of decision, a woeful lack
of physical courage.

In spite of their friendship each had stationed in the court of
the other, besides the recognized go-betweens, secret agents—
adepts in the arts of spying and blackmail. One of them, ostensibly a court musician, was speeded to Cleopatra bearing a burning indictment of Herod's ambitions and Mariamne's weakness.
Inevitably, Alexandra assured the Egyptian, Herod would clash
with her interests. Arabia, the rich valley of the Jordan, even
Syria, might come under his domination unless his schemes were
drastically impeded. In the past, the message continued, Egypt
had ruled this dominion; it was still Antony's to bestow on
Egypt's queen if he saw fit. But Herod was meanwhile building
himself up in Antony's esteem. The Roman must be brought to
realize Herod's designs. Of course, not too abruptly. Prevail
upon him, she urged, to order Herod to displace Hananel with
Aristobulus of the true priestly clan. Surely, she implied, Antony
could see no reason why Herod should not appoint the most
eligible candidate, even though it happened to be the king's
brother-in-law. If it were known that this was done at Antony's

own orders, no one could reasonably raise the charge of nepotism.

It was a subtle appeal that did not in the least deceive Cleopatra. However, she welcomed any opportunity to cramp the ambitions of the only man who had ever dared to snub her. She laid the situation before Antony, and demanded that he act.

To her chagrin, Antony was in one of his intractable moods.

He could see no reason why a head of a great empire should interfere in the internal affairs of a vassal state where the safety or welfare of the nation was not concerned. He was, moreover, in no mood to do anything that might embarrass his friend Herod.

As a matter of fact, Antony, except in his most debased moments, did have the redeeming trait of loyalty. His native shrewdness and greed, too, envisioned the gold flowing from the seemingly inexhaustible treasury of the Judean king. Why chance a diminution of that golden stream, just when his ambition and his extravagance needed so much money?

So Antony temporized; Cleopatra fumed with vexation; and Alexandra paced her chambers like a caged tigress. Spy after spy tremblingly returned with the same story of no success. Antony was stubborn and simply would do nothing.

Meanwhile—the realization was slow torture for Alexandra—organized opposition to Hananel was declining. The roar of resentment his appointment had aroused subsided to a sullen grumbling as the high priest, formally efficient, carried out his duties, replacing rebellious Pharisees with pliable Babylonians, Jews and turncoats anxious to curry favor.

It was the arrival of Dellius, Antony's contemptible panderer, that suggested a scheme, nasty even for Alexandra's vicious mind. To still his master's restless sensuality, this Roman made it his practice to travel periodically, as methodically as would a modern shoe buyer, to replenish Antony's harems with alluring young persons of both sexes. Cleopatra's jealousy and violent temper had more than once explosively terminated Antony's infatuation with young women. The immoral Egyptian, on the other hand—as did many of the depraved Roman matrons of the time (even the Roman state closed a knowing eye when the young Julius Caesar returned to Rome with a diplomatic triumph and the sobriquet, "Empress of Bithynia")—actually encouraged his intimacy with young men to preclude the chance of any feminine rival's challenging her supremacy.

Dellius, honored as Antony's representative, dined with the royal family. With appraising eye he measured the charms of the queen and her brother, regretting perhaps that such delightful morsels were not for his master's enjoyment. The crafty queen-mother recognized a kindred spirit. She spilled the wrathful tale of her failure into the agent's sympathetic ear, suggesting that Antony might become enamored of her children and then depose Herod if he dared oppose his advances. But how to arouse the Roman's lust. There was no way of bringing the pair to Antony.

The wily agent had an idea. On his arrival he had observed the Spartan swindler Eurycles, furtively slipping out of sight. They had been in shady deals together. The Greek, despite his utter moral worthlessness, was nevertheless a skilled artist. Let him paint the pictures of her children. For a consideration, Dellius would agree to bring them to Antony's attention together with his own enthusiastic commendation.

Without an instant's hesitation, Alexandra ferreted out the hiding sycophant. Under threats of disclosure—from Dellius she had obtained a summary of his more glaring misdeeds—she forced the Spartan to agree to paint the royal children.

It meant a tremendous moral debasement for all three. Herod himself, until late in his career, obeyed the injunction against the making of graven images. Yet three of the four remaining Hasmoneans, of royal and priestly blood, would proceed to violate a solemn law, punishment for which had traditionally been a shameful death.

Mariamne and Aristobulus grudgingly posed for the Spartan. Their scruples soon vanished when Alexandra assured them that their portraits were intended solely as a surprise gift for Antony which would raise Herod higher than ever in the Roman's favor. To keep the gift a real surprise they were made to swear to reveal what they were doing to no one, not even to the king. Since no Jew would ever see the pictures, nor know they had submitted to their being painted, no scandal would ensue, and their transgression would be venial and excusable.

Eurycles was really an artist, with the vicious knack of empha-

sizing the sensuous charm of his subjects. Before his disgrace, he
had painted many of the lascivious murals in the homes of
wealthy Romans.

In the portraits of his latest models he excelled himself. Even
Dellius, the cynic, discovered in them a voluptuous lure he had
never sensed in the actual presence of the persons painted. When
Dellius returned to Antony, his report contained but one topic,
the unbelievable beauty of Herod's wife and young brother-
in-law. Such pulchritude could have been derived not from men
but from gods. Better let the pictures speak for themselves. His
libidinous appetite provoked by the agent's panegyric, Antony
stared greedily at the miniatures. His desires were aflame, checked
nevertheless by the rein of his caution. The jealousy of Cleopatra,
the loss of Herod's friendship, and perhaps an almost forgotten
sense of shame precluded any designs he might entertain toward
Mariamne. But as for the equally desirable boy, neither Cleopatra
nor Herod should resent his patronage of him. At once he sent
Herod a letter, friendly in tone, reasonable in wording, requesting the king to send his brother-in-law "unless he thought it hard
upon him to do so."

The reception of the letter was a shocking blow to Herod. It
was the first definite evidence of plots within his own family,
engineered, he realized on rereading between the lines, by his
mother-in-law, but involving—he knew not to what degree—his
wife and her brother, for whom he had a genuine affection.

Alexandra he had never cared for, according her courtesy and
esteem solely as the mother of his wife. Consequently he was
quite indifferent concerning her attitude toward him and perhaps even relieved to discover evidence of her unfriendliness.
But the thought that perhaps those he trusted and loved were
plotting with her, against him, chilled the very depths of his
being.

In truth Herod was lonely for affection. When the love of his
subjects did not materialize, he immersed himself in the affections of those about him. Now stonily staring at the letter, every
equivocal syllable of which stabbed into his throbbing brain, he
faced the terror of losing the love of even these.

He was under no illusions as to Antony's purpose in inviting

Aristobulus. A less decent person might petulantly have sent the boy to his fate. Herod, in a diplomatic letter designed to avoid giving offence, explained that the presence of Aristobulus in Judea was imperative to the maintenance of peace. "If this boy," he wrote, "should only go out of the country, all would be in a state of uproar; because the Jews are in hopes of a change in the government, and to have another king over them."

Knowing only that her brother was in danger of being taken from her, though blissfully ignorant of the circumstances and cause of the summons, Mariamne hastened to Herod. With the shrewdness native to those essentially simple and wholesome, she urged that her brother be made high priest. Then it would be impossible ever to remove him from the country.

It is possible that Herod was more than a little suspicious that she could not have hit upon so apt a suggestion without coaching by her family, or indeed foreknowledge of Antony's request. The proposal was so practical, however, that he immediately acquiesced.

A council was hurriedly called together—the cabinet and family. He was aware, he informed them, that Alexandra had conspired with Cleopatra to dispossess him of his kingdom and eventually to hand it over to Aristobulus. He was shocked at such plotting because his own overthrow would drag down with him Alexandra's daughter and would besides plunge their country— through his efforts finally, after years of war and misery, restored to peace—back into new and more terrible wars. Though he was cognizant of her wickedness, he was determined, for the sake of her children, to overlook it.

More than that. It had been his constant purpose to have Aristobulus serve as high priest. Because of his extreme youth, that had been inexpedient. He had, on that account, brought in an obscure outsider, whom he could readily remove, rather than a native Jew, who, all might reasonably expect, would hold office for life. Even though Aristobulus was still only a lad of seventeen, the plot had hastened the king's purposes. Returning good for evil, he was prepared to proclaim that Aristobulus should immediately be invested with the high priesthood, to serve in such capacity for the rest of his days.

It was a clever statement designed to enhance the dignity and decency of Herod, and focus attention on the enormity of Alexandra's treachery.

Partly in excess of relief, more to gain time to regiment her scattered thoughts, the queen mother burst into tears. When she regained composure, she admitted with an air of penitent frankness that while she never had designs on Herod's crown, or threatened his safety, she was distressed at the apparent slighting of her son. Now that all her doubts were settled, she was ready to put herself and her interests in charge of her noble son-in-law, and to admit that in the warmth of her maternal solicitude she had acted imprudently.

The seemingly frank statements momentarily cleared the air. Yet neither Herod nor Alexandra deceived the other. The opening phase of a campaign was over. Each had suffered a reverse; each had won a minor victory. As they kissed the cup of friendship, each warily watched for traces of venom on its golden rim.

Informed that he was displaced, Hananel took the news in stride. Gradually he initiated the neophyte into the mysteries of his office, receding, as the youth avidly absorbed the functions of his new dignity, into a comfortable, well-paid life of ease.

The nation, as a whole, was delighted with the new appointment. Yet the element that had ranted against Hananel because he was ineligible now shrieked in pious horror because his life tenure in office was violated.

In the palace itself covert warfare had been covertly declared. Suspicion, fear, and hatred lurked in its marble recesses; violence crouched behind its velvet tapestries.

The opening campaign resulted in Alexandra's house arrest at the order of her son-in-law. True, there was no order openly issued to keep her within bounds. Yet, whenever she attempted to leave her quarters, spacious and luxurious, to be sure, Herod's Gallic guards formed an impenetrable wall. To every protest, written, since Herod sedulously kept away from her, she received the same answer. The king was solicitous for her health. Her nervous condition, the result of her injudicious correspondence with Cleopatra, he pointedly specified, demanded complete rest. He could not permit her to emerge into the heat of the day or the chill of the night. If she were to become ill, it might upset the queen, whom it was imperative at this time to protect from every distressing influence.

Baffled, Alexandra tried another approach. A mother's place, she insisted, was by the side of her daughter during the latter's trial. Her attempts to see or communicate with Mariamne met with little success. Usually she was informed that her daughter was resting; she was indisposed. Sometimes, more bluntly, the queen mother was told that her presence would disturb the queen. Every attempt to break the meshes that enwrapped her was futile. At every gateway was a guard of Herod's, incorruptible and immovable.

Had Herod immured her in the dungeons beneath the palace, the confinement would have been in many respects less galling and less humiliating. Being treated as a sick child who must seem to be pampered while she is at the same time restrained from doing her health harm was almost unbearable. On one pretext or another, she called in her trusted spies and confidants, and got rid of others whose faithfulness she distrusted. By thus playing at conspiracy, she derived some comfort. But it was at best cold comfort. Herod had managed to secure her where she could do a minimum of harm.

To keep Alexandra entirely from seeing her children would have been neither wise nor politic. Mariamne was very soon to give birth to a child. At the advice of the court physician, prompted needlessly by Herod, she rarely even asked to see her mother. On the infrequent occasions when Alexandra was permitted to enter her daughter's apartments, it was only for a short time, and always in the presence of others.

Apart from the more recent differences between Herod and Alexandra, this was an eminently sensible procedure. In the past, meetings between mother and daughter always culminated in the former's querulous insistence that the queen use her influence to further her family and her racial interests, accompanied by a denunciation of Herod himself, that left the ordinarily tractable young woman weak and depressed. It was easy then to prohibit interviews so dangerous to mother and unborn child.

It would have been a more difficult undertaking to keep

Aristobulus from seeing his mother. To have forbidden their meeting at all would have disclosed Herod's hand completely; to lay too many or too obvious obstacles in the way of their meeting would have been almost as revealing.

Herod made no attempt, therefore, to keep mother and son apart. Instead, seemingly solicitous and worried, he confided to Aristobulus that his mother was unwell, a victim to hallucinations, a prey to a persecution complex, and that it would be the part of discretion to humor her perhaps, but not to take seriously any complaints or accusations she might make.

The young high priest was in a turmoil of indecision and mixed loyalties. He idolized his sister; he admired and loved Herod; he was deeply grateful to his mother, now that he knew that she planned and was suffering for his advancement. Beyond these quite natural emotions, he considered the high priesthood not merely an honor, but rather a potentiality for leading his people back to ancient glory and piety. A boy despite the exalted dignity of his post, he saw himself another young Samuel. In his unformed mind was no thought of the inevitability of conflict between a young Jewish high priest and an Idumean king.

On him, as on a noble instrument, abused by a vicious performer, his mother played, and playing, marred the purity of tone and sweetness of soul. At first it was Alexandra who urged their meeting. Then, more and more frequently, he sought these conferences unsolicited, driven by a haunting fear she had implanted in his undiscriminating mind. And always thus ran the shuddering burden of his fear: "Herod made Hananel high priest. Herod then deposed Hananel and made you high priest. He can make and unmake high priests at will since he is in favor with Antony." In brighter key would resound dubiously at first, but strengthened by repetition, a new, more hopeful theme. "Still, if you yourself could meet Antony and impress him with your dignity, and honesty of purpose, and worth, the noble Roman would keep you in office and you would no longer need be concerned with the shifting favor of a subject king."

By persistent iteration of these ideas, Alexandra accomplished her purpose. Aristobulus still loved and admired Herod—this she could not undo. But he nevertheless entrusted his interests and his ambitions completely to his mother. He would be governed by her advice, and act according to her plans.

Before long they reached a decision. Alexandra would appeal to Cleopatra for help. So she wrote her Egyptian accomplice a long, detailed letter, dripping with venom toward her son-in-law, presenting in heart-rending terms her own misery and that of her children, and imploring that means for their rescue be effected.

Had she been able to smuggle the communication safely out of her apartments without Aristobulus' help, it is doubtful whether she would have thus disclosed her scheme to him. But her own servants and spies would have been searched. The person of the high priest on the other hand was sacrosanct. No guard of Herod would venture to lay an impious finger on him. With his mother's missive pressing against an uneasy heart, he hurried past the guards, thrust the letter hastily into the waiting grasp of a trusted spy, and fled to his own quarters, sick and trembling with alternate fits of hope and shame.

Alexandra may have visualized Cleopatra as an avenging siren, luring and goading her Antony to issue a peremptory summons to the presumptuous king to render an account of his misdeeds. If so, she was to be disappointed. Cleopatra really understood Antony, his swift reversals of mood, the intensity with which he clung to his loyalties, and above all the practical common sense with which he regarded his manifold yet insufficient sources of income. Much as she hated Herod, she knew that at present matters between the Judean king and his master were functioning for the latter too profitably to be interfered with.

She did, however, suggest a scheme whereby Alexandra and her son might escape, a scheme characteristically wily and macabre. Let it be reported that two maids of Alexandra's, residents of a coastal village, had died. Bierlike coffins containing the swathed forms of the high priest and his mother could easily, on the pretense that they were the bodies, be carried through the guards and brought eventually to the coast, where Cleopatra would have ready a ship for the final leg of their escape.

The plot appealed alike to the tortuous mind of Alexandra and to her dramatically inclined son. Spies and agents were contacted to act as mourners, as players, as bier bearers. The cast in the ghoulish farce was painstakingly rehearsed; every minute detail was perfected; every possibility of failure considered and provided against.

That is, all but the human element. A waiting-woman by the name of Aesop, bursting with the secret and anxious to regain the favor of a former lover whose ardor had grown cold, blurted out the plot to him. To the fickle lover, one Sabion, a scurvy rogue, the knowledge came at a desperately opportune moment. Herod had never ceased trying to track down all who had any part in his father's assassination. Recent disclosures pointed unmistakably, and probably rightly, in the direction of Sabion. Disclosure of the plot should convince Herod that his suspicions were baseless. Pausing only to swear to Aesop, already ruing her unbridled tongue, that he would never divulge their secret, he rushed to the king's presence and babbled the whole incredible tale.

The king listened without apparent emotion. Flinging a bag of gold at the informer, and stemming his torrential gratitude with the laconic reminder that his father's death was still a matter of investigation, he withdrew to his chambers.

As the full import of the information sank in, he could appreciate both its favorable and disagreeable aspects. Alexandra was foolishly playing into his hands. That was certain. It was Aristobulus who complicated the affair. Were he not involved, it would be simplicity itself to act as he pleased about Alexandra. Her grotesque act would surely proclaim her as a madwoman or a dangerous plotter who would acquiesce in the sacking of Judea by the scarlet woman of Egypt. Either judgment would suit Herod. It would simply resolve itself into catching Alexandra in the act of flight, making public the account of her plotting, and restraining her even more closely than hitherto.

But Aristobulus was almost equally involved. That made matters disagreeable. Were there more time, he might convince the youth of the absurdity and danger of the whole procedure. That time was lacking. He must let the plot proceed, and foil it while it was under way. As a preliminary countermeasure he redoubled the guards, placed cordons of watchers about the palace and city, and had every foot of the highway to the coast patrolled day and night.

Then came the eventful day. It was common knowledge about the palace that two maids, sisters from a seaside village, were dangerously ill. The clouded brow and dragging steps of Alexandra's Egyptian physician encouraged belief in the gravity of their condition.

About noon, a single dismal shriek, the traditional acknowledgment that death had struck, pierced the walls of Alexandra's quarters and wound its tenuous course along the palace corridors. Other voices wailed in response, for was it not the Law to "take up a wailing for us, that our eyes may run down with tears, and our eyelids gush out with water"? Disheveled figures, their outer garments rent in grief, began to emerge, in woeful quest of linen shrouds and of perfumes and odoriferous drugs for the embalming. Both girls had died, they told the guards. Meanwhile others, audible in grief, went their mournful way to procure minstrels, musicians, and professional mourners for the procession, and caterers to prepare the "bread of mourning and the cup of consolation" for the feast after the funeral.

Everyone despite his grief was in haste, for all preparations must be completed before nightfall. Such speed in disposing of the bodies, it might be remarked, would cause no suspicion. Bodies decomposed rapidly in the sultry heat of the Orient. Embalming was elementary among the Jews; the placing of the customary hundred weight of myrrh and lignaloes on the body, before it was wrapped in linen sheets, was only a brief deterrent to corruption.

That same night a funeral train wound its clamorous way through the western palace gate, past guards who stepped respectfully aside. At its head, the bearded masters of the funeral, with set somber faces; then half a dozen strutting pipers shrilling a wailing measure more discordant than funereal. Followed the biers, each borne high on the shoulders of ten doleful bearers. Then torch carriers whose sputtering brands made an uneasy play of light and shadow on the ghastly procession. Behind them came the minstrels and professional mourners, disheveled, dirty, tear-grimed with simulated grief, heaving in undulating cadence, like a stricken snake.

By a window, Herod smiled grimly at the swathed figures, the bandages suspiciously loose over the clothed figures, the napkins

fixed loosely on the face and head. The solemn masters, the gib-
bering bearers, the croaking mourners, every face in that false
throng impressed itself indelibly on the consciousness of the king.
Most were known agents of Alexandra. All were corrupt. With
them he would deal later.

He waited until the wailing died in the distant tortuous alleys.
A desert stallion, ready saddled, pawed impatiently at the gate.
Into the saddle he vaulted. With a band of Gallic and Idumean
guards he dashed through the courtyard, clattered through cobbled byways, later to join the direct route to the west.

The funeral trail gradually diminished its cacophony as it left
the capital behind. Alexandra had been able to ascertain (with
Herod's connivance) that there were three posts they must pass
before emerging into safety. The guards at the first two showed
a perfunctory respect for the grief of the mourners, but in no
way attempted to impede their passage.

At the third and final barrier something went wrong. The
wailing glissando of the players snapped at a harsh command;
violent arms jostled the panicky coffinbearers to the imminent
peril of their burdens. The biers were lowered with an uncere-
monious thump; the royal hand of Herod jerked away the napkins and pulled the ghastly figures to a pose of seated silliness.
A stentorian guffaw, echoed by the guards, sent a quite undeath-
like flush flowing along the bared faces of the duped victims.
Crimson shame suffused the face of the high priest. Alexandra's
was afire with defeat and hatred.

Beaten with spear shafts, the funeral cortège, its sorrow suddenly real and painful, scurried back to the capital. Under the
sardonic eye of Herod the erstwhile corpses clumsily unraveled
themselves from the enveloping shrouds. Stained with the dust
kicked up by the jubilant cavalcade, they halted until the boisterous mockery and the rumbling hoofbeats died away. Continuance
of their flight was not to be thought of. Herod must have taken
steps, they were certain, to prevent that. Together, in their
shame, they turned their steps toward Jerusalem. Thoughts, too
confused, too shameful, too violent for utterance raced through
their heated brains as they plodded into the dusty distance. Just
at daybreak they reached the city. The frowning western wall

casting its long, sad shadow, the castellated towers, bathed in honeyed amber, the pink distances of the vale of the Jordan, streaked with gold—all this prospect, prideful and heart-warming to the Jew, they did not note.

Grinning guards admitted them. They slunk into the queen mother's apartments, almost too stricken to be concerned with the consequences of their flight.

With the disgraced truants in his custody, Herod acted with exceptional forbearance. Violence on his part Cleopatra would have considered an affront to her. Mariamne, too, would have been hurt, especially had her brother felt the king's displeasure. In the eyes of the Jews, any attempt at conventional punishment would have served only to create two more martyrs, and thus intensify the ill will they bore the crown. Why, by force, hazard one's domestic bliss, and make one's enemies more relentless, he reasoned, when ridicule was a more effective, and, best of all, a single-edged weapon? While he saw to it that his creatures broadcast the story of the flight and recapture, in no wise softened in the retelling, throughout the land, he made no obvious attempt to punish either of the runaways.

Toward Alexandra his conduct seemed so natural, so generous, that it amazed his followers and his enemies alike and deceived everyone but the object of his attentions herself. He appeared most solicitous of her health. Night and day a stream of guards approached trembling maids—new servants, since the old trusted agents had unaccountably vanished—inquiring in mock concern about the results of her nocturnal misadventure.

Herod himself, almost too solicitous, frequently visited his mother-in-law, at every call reminding her in hurt tones that at her age her flight was physically most unfortunate. Moreover, he told the fuming woman, in a voice actually dripping with pained anxiety, the people were gossiping whether her mind were not affected, and if it would not be wise to restrain her son from her company and influence. And Alexandra knew that Herod was not lying; that her impetuous flight actually strengthened the King's hand.

Toward Aristobulus Herod pursued a quite different course. Bluffly waving aside the miserable boy's protestations of repentance, he assured him that his action was merely ill-advised, a mistake that any young man out of a disproportionate but quite understandable sense of loyalty might have committed.

As a result of the fiasco, the influence of Alexandra on her son greatly diminished; Herod's proportionally increased. It was, nevertheless, an expensive victory for the king. Alexandra's hatred he knew and could cope with; that Aristobulus might so soon prove dangerous he had not anticipated. His fixed policy was to have ready a counterstroke for every possible attack. The defection of Aristobulus, temporary and silly though it was, placed him among those whom Herod must make ready to dispose of should safety seem to demand it.

But for the present he could do nothing rash. Anything in the form of the open revenge he craved was too dangerous.

Hot summer merged into a scarcely cooler autumn. The rapturous Feast of the Tabernacles was nearing. Everywhere, happy throngs of celebrators combined the memory of the sojourn of the Israelites in the desert with gratitude for the bounties of field and orchard. Green booths made of interlaced branches sprang up as by magic; their jaunty occupants went about bearing green boughs. Everywhere was laughter and joy. As never before, hope and happiness welled in Jewish hearts. A usurper might be on the throne, but their own high priest was in the Temple. How admirably he conformed with the Messianic traditions! How completely he satisfied the omens and portents that fell from every lip and burst from each blissful heart!

In the palace of Herod, too, was an hour of joy. Mariamne had given birth to her first-born—a boy as both had wished—who was to bear the royal Maccabean name of Aristobulus.

The Day of Atonement dawned gloriously. Rejoicing crowds swarmed about the packed streets, their swaying green branches an ever-surging green sea. Herod, at a palace casement, happy as any peasant father, was awkwardly holding the infant in whom his hopes were centered. The baby's tiny hand closed faintly on a royal finger. Affection, simple and elemental, rushed into the father's heart. He beamed sympathetically on the clamorous green parade. Perhaps he could still make these people love him. Could they but appreciate his hope and his love for his child—

their king one day—there might be an end to sedition and conspiracy. An impulse—theatrical perhaps, but natural to the flushed monarch—impelled him to the balcony. He thrust the whimpering infant across the railing. In ringing tones he proclaimed, "Behold your king!"

Curious faces peered through the leafy screens. The moving sea halted; the jubilant chorus faded. A voice raised here and there caught the new fire. Another moment and Herod would have won.

Then something else happened. A spark animated the throng, darting through the packed crowd with the speed of lightning, touching the nerve spring of Herod himself in his vantage post above the streets. The cry, "The high priest! Our high priest!" sprang from lip to lip, from the remote fringes of the mass to the stony barrier of the palace, encompassing the king in a suffocating bank of sound.

His spirits sagged. Jealousy, fury, unreasoning rage blotted out the momentary flash of affection for his people. No such acclaim had ever greeted him. Forced smiles and sullen rebellion were his portion. Did then these Jews place greater faith in their high priest, whom he had made, than in their king? Were their hopes fixed on Aristobulus rather than on the son of Herod and Mariamne? Intensified cheers broke in upon his racking reverie. The procession of the high priest was nearing. Herod pushed the child into the arms of a waiting nurse. Half-unwilling, yet fascinated, he watched the approaching pageant.

It is not surprising that the Jews enthusiastically cheered their priest. The idea of a boy pope or boy archbishop is repugnant. A boy high priest somehow fires the imagination and stimulates the hopes of the most abject and downtrodden. The Messianic tradition seemed to imply a combination of majestic grace and youthful innocence; a generation later the magi would seek a "newborn king." Old Testament history, too, had established precedents for investing youth with majesty, and power, and piety; David, Samuel, Joseph, the youths in the fiery furnace—these and other names of youthful heroes were on every tongue, and, ringing above them all, the unfailing refrain, "Aristobulus!"

In appearance and decorum the high priest was in every way

worthy of the crowd's acclaim. Taller than most, with ebon locks framing an oval, olive face, and eyes burning with an inspired enthusiasm in his calling, tempered with an almost naive pride in his appearance, he was indeed a memorable figure.

His garments matched perfectly his proud, pontifical bearing. A violet sleeveless tunic, its skirt adorned with blue, scarlet, and purple pomegranates alternating with little bells was partly covered with the ephod, the bodice of fine twisted linen, which was in turn embroidered with threads of violet, purple, and scarlet, interwoven with gold. On the ephod was a breastplate, ornamented with twelve precious stones in four rows, each stone inscribed with the name of a tribe of Israel. Fixed to the ephod was also the mysterious urim and thummim (the doctrine and the truth), by means of which the high priest would contact the Deity. Shoulder straps fastened the bodice, front and back, each strap ornamented with an onyx bearing the names of six tribes. Completing the body costume was the cincture fastened above the waist, of the same precious fabric as the bodice. Crowning all was the high priest's miter, with the triple crown of gold, with the name of God that Moses wrote in sacred characters, and with the legend "Holy to the Lord."

The traditional splendor of his attire and the reverent fervor of the multitude bestirred in the young priest who knows what dreams of conquest and glory—emotions that the sensitive suspicions of Herod quickly divined. He tore himself away; almost he fled. In his innermost chamber, where the cheering reached him only as the faint eddies of a troubled dream, he formed his terrible resolve. Aristobulus was marked for death.

Once again it was Alexandra's intriguing that placed her son in jeopardy. Deliriously happy on hearing of her son's triumph, she ordered a day of celebration at Jericho in his honor—an occasion on which her house arrest would naturally be cancelled— and invited all the nobility from Herod down. It was a summons, however disagreeable in its possibilities, that the king could not afford to ignore. It might also present him with an opportunity to carry out a yet formless plot that was taking shape in the darker depths of his mind.

The party merrily rode or were borne down the weird landscape that tumbled from the chill heights of Jerusalem to the sultry gully of the Jordan. At a resting place Alexandra informed them that she had arranged a day of sports and games culminating in a grand dinner to be presided over by her son. From the defiant gleam that accompanied her pronouncement, Herod could infer that the celebration, particularly the banquet, was designed as a further step in the advancement of Aristobulus, at his expense and that of his child.

For the remainder of the journey he rode apart, communing deeply with himself. On that solitary, unhappy ride was born a plot, hideously simple and safe.

The games began in the cool of the early morning and continued into the stifling swelter of the forenoon. Impervious to the heat, the king cast aside his dignity and played, inducing the high priest also to be a participant. By degrees the sports grew more and more informal. Herod, we are told, played with Aristobulus in a "juvenile and ludicrous" manner. As the breathless heat grew more intense, the celebrators turned naturally to water sports. Hastily, garments were flung aside, and hot bodies dived into the fountains and fishponds in the palace gardens. Aristobulus, heated from play, burdened with the solitary dignity of the high priesthood, and yet a teen-age lad in his pleasures and tastes, looked longingly at the gleaming forms flashing through the cool waters. Herod, his sympathy seemingly aroused by the high priest's discomfort, urged him to shed his dignity and join the bathers. Aristobulus demurred faintly, then surrendered. In that heat, and looking into those sparkling pools, the boy in the high priest was dominant.

With a shout of defiance at his discarded dignity, he plunged into the pool, naturally oblivious of Herod's hardly perceptible signal to a little knot of bathers at the edge of the water. Long, long he swam about, as if eager to soak up all the limpid coolness before entering again the breathless heat that pressed upon Jericho.

The sun stumbled, a bloodshot toper, behind the stony hills of Judea. Shadows fell into the edges of the pool, and tarnished its brassy gleam. Gamesome swimmers like children desirous of making the most of the little time left them for play began to pull each other under. The sputtering victim would wreak his vengeance on another victim in turn.

Amidst the laughing shouts and the splashing, none of the bathers noted that Aristobulus had disappeared. Even the two Idumeans with whom he was last seen swimming seemed unconscious of his being no longer with them. Quite certainly, Herod in the shadowy gloom could not possibly have observed that the high priest did not return to the surface after his frolic with the Idumeans.

It was only when the king himself called a halt to the water sports that Aristobulus was missed. No one, least of all the king on the pool's purple rim, had seen him leave the waters. In the darkness he had perhaps slipped into the palace to adorn himself for the banquet.

His quarters were vainly searched. Soldiers, their torches leering evilly into the musky gloom, surrounded the pool. Prodding in the reedy depths, they found the limp body, shorn of all its priestly dignity, beautiful and boyish, with a look of startled puzzlement still staring from its sightless eyes.

The lovely halls, gallantly adorned for the awaited feast, became a house of mourning. Lamentation swelled through the softly lighted chambers; purple robes and gay gowns were rent in grief.

With immoderate rapidity the tragic news sped to Jerusalem. The rejoicing capital in an instant became a vast mausoleum, where fresh young hope lay entombed beyond possibility of resurrection. Because the reason for the tragedy was so obvious, grief was the less endurable. No one—friend or enemy—could doubt Herod's part. Without the need for proof, that was taken for granted. His enemies—and how their number multiplied!—called it sacrilegious murder; his friends, hard necessity.

Mariamne, when the hushed voices of her attendants whispered the news, stared stonily ahead. Even the slight burden of her baby, which an understanding nurse laid in her arms, could not start consoling tears.

But a sadness, a grief akin to terror, reigned in the apartments of Alexandra. Not for one moment would she admit the possibility of accident. She knew; the more terrible her abandonment because she knew. She could not go to the king and shriek "liar and murderer" as every nerve of her being impelled. She must conceal the splinter in her heart, and with its festering agony await her hour of revenge.

On the day of the funeral Herod was first among the mourners. With his own hands he placed the priceless incense within the tomb; near the still, shrouded figure he set the ornaments and implements the boy had cherished. Tears, in unrelenting stream, rolled down his haggard cheeks. His grief seemed very real.

No doubt it was. He regretted the murder for itself. He was not yet—in fact never became—inured to killing. He knew the grief this boy's death caused Mariamne, too ill with shock and sorrow to attend the funeral. Personally, he had loved this exuberant dreamy lad; and, personally, he was grief-stricken at his tragic, necessary end.

In her chamber, Alexandra, outwardly the most composed person at the funeral, wrote a long letter to Cleopatra.

CHAPTER XI

WAR OF WOMEN

WHEN HEROD DECIDED TO HAVE ARISTOBULUS
killed, he acted only after the most searching consideration of
the inevitable consequences. For this was not a crime of passion.
This was planned, deliberate murder. Domestic unrest must
certainly ensue. The Jews—somewhat illogically, it must be admitted—because of the violence inflicted on the candidate they
were grooming to destroy Herod, would be intensified, too, in
their hatred toward him. A united family, a loyal people, if they
were ever conceivable, were now not to be thought of. Herod
knew that ultimately Cleopatra, too, would nag Antony into
calling him to account for his action.

Nevertheless, while experiencing the keenest personal sorrow
at the death of the high priest, he consoled himself with the
conviction that there was no other way. In his eyes, the security
of his children justified both the crime and the risk.

Meanwhile Hananel, the imperturbable, resumed the high
priesthood, accepting with equanimity sullen reverence or sycophantic co-operation as he carried out the duties of his office.

A barren honor it had come to be! All hallowed dignity and
rhapsodic piety had fled. Only the circumambient ceremonial
trappings remained. Even these with their reputed miraculous
powers Herod kept in his own custody, to be let out on occasions
when the king thought expedient.

At length the Jews themselves had to concede that the office
was no longer either hereditary or of life tenure. They had

152

resented Hananel's irregular selection. But Aristobulus' equally irregular appointment while his predecessor was still alive they had welcomed and by their joyous acceptance had given Herod a useful precedent that he was subsequently to use with advantage.

As a matter of record, high priests henceforth would be picked usually from aristocratic families who supported the king, particularly from the house of Boethus, a Sadducean magnate, one of a number of that class who had begun to throw in their lot with the king.

Many had hoped that because of her brother's fate Mariamne might be used as a rallying point in a campaign against Herod. But no estrangement development. For one thing, her grief was softened by the birth of her second child, another handsome boy who was given the Hellenic name Alexander. The prosperity, the very safety of her children would depend on her husband's continuance in power.

So, even if she were disposed to believe that her brother was the victim of a coldly designed murder, her Hasmonean pride— her besetting sin—might, it has been suggested, cause her to condone the crime as a necessary, though deplorable, dynastic sacrifice, common in oriental courts, and not unknown in her own family history. But most probably because she was genuinely and wholly in love with her husband she was willing to accept in good faith, against evidence and general disbelief, not to say her own judgment, the version of accidental drowning.

Alexandra was a pitiful creature. Nowhere would she show her grief. Every tender, maternal instinct, every consideration of remorse, she choked at birth. She lived, and kept alive, only to await the outcome of the summons from Antony that she knew would come, must come.

As Herod considered the prospect, he, too, anxiously awaited the summons. He was certain that Alexandra had written to Cleopatra. An unhappy bungler was languishing in the palace dungeon for his failure to intercept her messenger.

A few years earlier the execution of the unlovable, rebellious Antigonus had aroused resentment even among the Romans, who had been his executioners. To kill a vassal king so dishonorably had been without precedent. How much more gravely would

Antony, egged on by his alluring, revengeful mate, regard the murder of a member of vassal royalty, and potential king, by a rival vassal.

For some months there was a premonitory calm as the Roman thunderhead withheld its bolt. Herod, husbanding his strength for the dreaded call, lived in semi-seclusion, avoided formal functions and public appearances, and delegated much of his authority. Yet in the increased alertness of royal agents, in the aggressiveness of the military patrols, a populace ready for revolution realized that the hidden hand was firmly at the helm. Most of the king's time was spent with the children and Mariamne, who found a new happiness in his tenderness. It was the last real happiness the ill-fated queen was destined to experience. Alexandra was meanwhile kept closely watched in her apartments. Hyrcanus, dazed and seemingly senile, wandered listlessly about the palace or paid periodic visits to the Temple, the only worshiper whose piety was visibly unaffected at the sight of Hananel in the robes of Aristobulus. Perhaps he never noticed the change!

At length the summons came. Dellius, vulture of ill omen, arrived, lacking his customary oily affability, with an order commanding Herod to appear for trial before Antony at Laodicea. The king had long anticipated his being called to account, had rehearsed every possible phase of the charge, and had perfected his defense. Accordingly, he was ready to start immediately, even though Antony's order necessitated a journey of over five hundred miles.

Practically no last-minute arrangements had to be made. The kingdom was so well organized and functioning so smoothly that even a lengthy absence in itself could not matter. Otherwise Herod could not possibly have justified the appointment of his uncle Joseph as procurator during the king's absence.

Joseph, at once brother of Herod's father Antipater and husband of the king's sister Salome, was spiritless, loyal, and stupid. That Costobar had made him a cuckold was a source of malicious pleasure to all the court, except the unwitting dupe himself, and, probably, the king and queen. In a less tightly knit political organism such an appointment, even for a short time, over a people as irreconcilable as the Jews might have had the gravest consequences. But for one reason, no one else would do: only Joseph was loyal to both Herod and Mariamne; only his unswerving fidelity to both could be counted on. Salome and Herod's mother, Cyprus, hated Mariamne. Alexandra detested Herod, and looked upon her daughter merely as a cat's-paw. Costobar's self-seeking was all too obvious. Saramalla was ill in Syria. Hyrcanus was in his dotage.

It was no common or easy responsibility that Herod thrust upon his deputy. The king realized he might never return. He knew that in the event of his death Mariamne would be torn asunder between the vindictiveness of his mother and sister and the calculating selfishness of her own mother. He feared, not unreasonably, that Antony, with lust already sharpened by the provocative miniature in his possession, might seize and ravish the last of the Maccabean queens.

Nor was there solace in the possibility that at his death Mariamne, supplanting Cleopatra as Antony's mate, might reign over a more extensive dominion than he could bestow upon her. Herod was always basically Arab, but with a strong infusion of Jew. The prosperity and reasonable growth, under Roman protection, of a strong Jewish-Arab state, one befitting the nobility and dignity of the children of Esau and Jacob, was the extent of his ambition. He was unwilling that more than this be attained at the cost of his wife's happiness. He could not visualize with complacency the spread of a Jewish-Arab commonwealth beyond its natural boundaries by any transitory honors or authority conferred upon his children at the whim of a fickle potentate.

After long, sleepless hours he had worked out the solution. As he left for the uncertain journey to Asia Minor, he delivered his final order to Joseph. If certain news of his death reached Jerusalem, the procurator was to kill Mariamne. Horrified, Joseph protested. In carefully prepared words, Herod explained. It would be an act of kindness to put her at rest, whom they both loved, rather than permit her to become the prize of unfeeling faction, or worse still another concubine for Antony, liable to Cleopatra's tigerish spite. Convinced, but still shocked, Joseph gave his word. He would kill Mariamne if Herod failed to return.

Outwardly calm, Herod bade Mariamne a tender farewell, and departed with a heavy heart.

The long, weary days on the road, with his uncertain fate at its terminus, gave Herod ample time for reflection. Fate, he felt, had not dealt kindly with him. His accession to the throne was not unlawful. By mismanagement, corruption, and violence the Hasmoneans had forfeited their right to rule, since under Roman dominion internal peace and efficiency were a requisite for holding power. That efficiency and peace he had brought the Jews. Roads were safe; life was secure; the name of Jew was honored. If people grumbled about high taxes, they forgot the safety and convenience the judicious expenditure of those taxes purchased, and that they had more than the means to pay. Every Jew would have to admit that not even in the days of Solomon was the kingdom so powerful, or life so safe and so easy. All this he himself was responsible for.

A glow of satisfaction lightened his brooding thoughts, but momentarily the clouds gathered again. Despite all he had done for his country, he had won only the hatred of the people he ruled. "Why?" he asked himself. Was it his defiance of the sanhedrin? In that he was fundamentally justified. The death of Antigonus II? The scoundrel deserved to die for bartering Jewish women for help from the Parthians. Even the Romans recognized, by the manner in which they executed him, the enormity of his crimes. For seizing the throne? By that very act he had ensured the perpetuation of the Maccabean dynasty through Mariamne's children. By the installation of Hananel as high priest? Who else was there that would not arouse factional strife? By the murder of Aristobulus? Necessary. Here his attempts at justification stopped before a blank wall over which he could not see, and beyond which he knew there lay but doubt and darkness.

For solace, he would linger longingly on the vision of the queen and the children. But invariably Salome with her sneering tongue, his carping mother, and Alexandra half-mad with spite would distort that picture and make it hateful. Then his terrible injunction to Joseph would return to him with almost the solace of a fearful last hope. Whatever else might happen, he had provided against Mariamne's unhappiness.

Herod was troubled and depressed as he reached Laodicea. But he showed no signs of his uncertainty. Wishing to impress Antony with his undivided loyalty to Rome and his complete willingness to submit to Antony's decision, he had left behind his Idumean retinue, who would fight to the death for him, and rode, a gallant, fearless chieftain, at the head of his Gallic guard, the gift, incidentally, of the man he was about to face.

Antony's manner of greeting did nothing to lessen Herod's concern. In place of the usual friendly, clamorous welcome, there was an embarrassed coldness. Obviously Cleopatra's nagging had put her lover in a frame of mind where Herod would have to satisfy a prejudiced, if unwilling, judge.

From Herod, the usual gift was not forthcoming. Not averse to bribery, when it furthered his interests, the king had that innate dignity which shrank from attempting to purchase his own life from a man whom he had reason to count on as a friend.

Antony, encountering neither the expected bribe to win his favor, nor yet a show of fear from a person who knew his death had been urged and perhaps promised, was at a loss. Ordering his attendants to leave, he faced the Jew. Herod was calm, dignified; Antony, trying vainly to whip up an indignation he was unable to feel.

There was in the appearance of the two every evidence that there stood rulers of men. Herod was dark, black-bearded in the Jewish fashion. A deceptive slimness, the result of a hard youth and abstinence from the sins of soft living, tended to emphasize an already tall figure. At first glance one was impressed by an appearance of unyielding dignity, of wiry strength, of hardness of character and emotion. Then in his eyes one caught a glint of something more. Desert pools, they seemed, under a starry desert sky, mysterious and fathomless, yet ready to reflect the glory of the heavens.

Antony's was a less regal, more brutally powerful figure. Cicero, it is true, described him as a butcher, or a pugilist. Though Cicero's choice of epithet was dictated by envy, it was an accurate description. Actually Antony tried to and did resemble the statues of Hercules, whom he claimed as his ancestor. He was ruddy, and bearded like his presumptive progenitor; his curly hair was tousled; his eyes were wild and impetuous. Taut muscles bulged on a massive frame; his entire appearance implied tremendous physical powers. As yet it was difficult to detect the incipient softness, the toll of drunkenness and lust, that would soon drain him dry of vigor and spirit. It was only when one observed his mouth, weak, and generous, and made for laughter, that one suspected the giant's softer side.

His torrents of accusations checkmated by the proud dignity of Herod, Antony felt his simulated indignation slipping away. Soon his accusations became questions, and in Herod's precise, unaffected answers—Antony little suspected how perfectly rehearsed those direct responses to the inevitable charges were— what was left of the Roman's anger disappeared. Face to face with the bold Judean, he experienced a comforting sense of camaraderie; the castigating voice of Cleopatra echoed but dimly in the depths of his subconscious mind. He was looking upon a friend whose gratitude and generosity never failed, who carried out a difficult assignment with skill and distinction. The reckless bearded Roman and the bearded suave Semite had too many interests in common, needed each other too much, for violence to disrupt their association. Two soldiers saw each other's problems, and brushing aside every unsoldierly consideration solved their problems as soldiers.

Antony announced his decision. Since he had confirmed Herod as king, it would be unbecoming to pry too minutely into his domestic affairs where the safety of Rome was not affected. To act otherwise would deprive Herod of his authority as king, and without that authority it would be impossible for him to act as Rome's agent and the symbol of Roman power and prestige.

With a simple word of gratitude, Herod received the decision. Timidly, almost, he signaled his attendants. They entered, staggering under a gift of gold whose munificence astounded even Antony, cloyed as was his sense of values by the extravagance of his consort.

Thereupon as old comrades they underwent the round of banqueting and roistering. Herod, sensing always Mariamne's sweet image, with restrained exuberance; Antony with unbridled license. Better than the feasts and the drinking bouts, and the dancers, Herod enjoyed sitting in judgment with his host. At heart the desert sheik weighing the differences of his tribesmen, he found the keenest delight in deciding the cases brought up before Antony. That Antony took time from his almost constant swilling to provide this kind of entertainment for his guest was an indication that his diplomatic acumen was still keenly alert.

The demands of the Parthian campaign cut short their pleasures. The army started to march—its pace determined by the comfort or the whims of Cleopatra, who was once more pregnant. Although Herod accompanied the army for a few days, he and the queen managed—to Antony's intense relief—not to see each other. Then with protestations of deathless loyalty and friendship they parted—Herod for Judea and Mariamne; Antony, for the perennial incertitude of a Parthian campaign, and the certainty of a barrage of recriminations and demands from Cleopatra.

Herod had reasoned rightly that Judea would remain calm during his absence. He had not, however, foreseen the ceaseless bickering and wrangling his departure would occasion. Salome was the prime offender. Though she was married to her uncle Joseph for some years and had borne him children, her ambition and envy saw in his easy-going disposition and lack of jealousy only a despicable weakness; his cooling, middle-aged ardor the sex-ridden princess considered a waning virility and rapid descent to a premature senility. She hated her sister-in-law, and Mariamne's mother, who—it must be granted—never tired of flinging in the face of the desert shrew her lack of royal blood. She was jealous even of her brother. A kinder fate, she felt, might have designated her husband as Antipater's successor, rather than the reckless upstart Herod.

With Joseph she could do nothing. He was too completely committed to a contented indolence in his own station, to an undisturbed loyalty to the king. Her paramour Costobar, however, possessed possibilities. He was ambitious, keen, ruthless. Could she weaken, or, better, destroy, her huband and Mariamne during Herod's absence, the king would fall an easier prey to later plots.

Cyprus, more unyielding, more fiery proud as the years passed, likewise hated the young queen who had entwined herself about Herod's heart to the exclusion of his mother and her family.

Alexandra, breaking from confinement when no one had the

hardihood to restrain her, added to the general ferment. Constant ill-will, bickering, recrimination drove Mariamne to the point of nervous exhaustion, where only the unfailing sympathy of Joseph afforded her a moiety of comfort.

All hating one another, these women nevertheless made common cause in their onslaught against the queen. Just as Herod cast off Doris when she stood in the way of his advancement, so they assured her, was he prepared also to abandon Mariamne. He was interested in her only as a breeder of royal offspring to strengthen his hold on the throne. Tales of reputed intimacies with Cleopatra in Egypt were resurrected, the story of his idolatrous sacrifice at Rome, his implanting of Hananel, the murder of her brother.

Desperately the queen tried to ward off the many shafted barbs until loyal, dull-witted Joseph could stand her anguish no longer. In one breath he blurted out the terrible promise Herod had forced upon him. Panic-stricken at his unintended disclosure, he feverishly argued that such an order demonstrated the quintessence of love. To destroy a dear one to save her from pain and shame proved Herod's supreme affection for his wife. He talked on and on. The words rolled in stumbling cadence from his quaking tongue. A stunned group heard, but understood nothing beyond his first impetuous disclosure. A horrid joy fixed itself in the bosoms of the elder women. Mariamne's heart became as lead.

From that moment the need of probing attacks was gone. Knowledge of Herod's order gave Mariamne's enemies new assurance, certain power. Their suspicions, their judgment, had been vindicated. Herod, they insisted, even in his death, would remove any possible barrier to his family's supremacy by ordering the murder of his logical successor. Mariamne would, in the natural order of events, rule Judea, at least during the minority of her first-born. She was, apart from her marriage to the Idumean, the legitimate Hasmonean queen. If she should choose to remarry, she could still bear children to Herod's successor. Should she remain a widow, she could rule happily a score of years, and live thereafter a contented, honored queen mother. This the supreme vindictiveness of her husband would not countenance. Therefore, he had ordered her butchered by the very person who pretended to cherish and defend her.

Poor, hapless Joseph wandered about the palace, cast off by Mariamne, laughed at by his own blood.

Meanwhile a rumor spread with incredible rapidity through the city. A caravan leaving Laodicea during the uncertainty of the outcome of the conference brought the report that Herod had been tortured and executed by Antony. Alexandra, frantic for revenge on Herod's kin, leaped at the rumor. She stirred up Joseph to aid her. Together they implored Mariamne to flee the capital and seek safety with a Roman legion outside the walls. In Alexandra's crawling mind a plan took shape. Antony would soon see Mariamne, and fascinated by her beauty would declare her regent. How she would take advantage of the queen's regency, Alexandra also had determined.

The city was in an uproar. Riots broke out in the country districts as well, harshly and instantly put down by the Herodian authorities. The turmoil was sullenly subsiding as letters arrived giving the lie to the rumors. Shortly after—the king had accompanied Antony only a short distance on his march against the Parthians—Herod himself returned.

It was now the turn of Salome, abetted by her mother. Catching the king's ear first they, as if reluctantly, told him their terrible secret. Joseph had abused his trust by repeated intimacies with the queen. Naturally they were unwilling to disclose their family shame, but the evidences of guilt were so overwhelming and the lusts of the guilty pair so revolting that their love for the king would not let them remain silent. Even Herod would have to grant that Mariamne's attempt to escape from the city, with the connivance of Joseph and Alexandra—an escape foiled only by the fortuitous return of her husband—was indisputable evidence of her guilt. That Mariamne had steadfastly refused to flee from the court they naturally did not tell him.

Imperiously Herod checked their charges. He was not prepared to condemn his queen until he himself would secure evidence of her treason. In his speech there was that quality of icy anger that discouraged further words. They had not told him the choicest bit of all—Joseph's disclosure. But that could wait. With timid words of affection and sympathy they stole away, gloating.

Chastened by his dangerous interview with Antony, exhausted with the breakneck haste of his return to Jerusalem, filled with overflowing love for his queen, who too had narrowly avoided death, Herod was in no mood to accept without question the charges of those who hated his wife. Still he could but be affected. He decided on a policy of watchful waiting. The first reunion with his lovely queen stemmed the carefully phrased questions he was prepared to ask. She was noble, young, beautiful. How could she possibly have sinned with Joseph—agreeable and likeable, to be sure, but dullish, garrulous, unromantic, and hen-pecked. It just did not ring true. His doubts were washed away.

Still there was a coldness, a restraint, almost a revulsion in her embrace. Hers was not the attitude of a true, loving wife greeting a husband who was returning to her from a mission so perilous that it offered less than an even chance of escape from death. Once more Herod tingled with jealousy. Once more he was prepared to hurl his inquisitorial charges.

The queen's icy charm, the aura of regal chastity that seemed to emanate from her lovely being again checked him. Still his cankering doubt was unendurable; her coldness, unaccountable. Quietly, without blame or rancor, he told her of Salome's vicious accusations.

For one brief moment Mariamne was shocked into silence. Tears welled into her eyes and with tears returned her voice, faltering and hesitant, as if uncertain as to what defense she could make against such horrid calumny. Confidence, born of innocence, restored her courage. With a convincing eloquence she denied the accusations. She took the most sacred oath that she was in every way guiltless.

Her defense completed, she turned to the attack. One by one, she enumerated the petty persecutions, the slanders, the mental torture, the nervous sniping to which she had been subjected.

Herod heard what he wished to hear. Every doubt vanished. A great love and pity filled his being for this exquisite harassed creature.

With protestations of his own love and faith, he halted the

flow of his wife's words. He again embraced her. This time there was no reluctance in surrender. Unbidden, the old familiar terms of endearment came to his lips, the sweet, homely metaphors of his courtship days in the Samarian hills. In silent bliss, too complete for expression, she accepted each loving word, every endearing epithet.

Yet her utter silence disturbed Herod. For an instant there returned a chilling shadow of vanished doubts. Why did she not respond to his loving words? A moment of troubled silence, and he again told her how great was his love, how unbearable his anxiety, when away from her side. Still the queen did not answer. She rested softly in his arms, returning his caresses, in wordless bliss. Echoes of forgotten fears dinned ever more persistently in his ears. Mentally, he squirmed. Her voicelessness was unbearable. Gruffly, almost, he demanded that she tell him that her love was as complete and single as was his own. With condescending patience, as to a sickly child, she put off saying the words he felt he must hear. When his persistence at length struck a very faint spark of resentment, she, more playful than petulant, said "Yet was not that command thou gavest, that if any harm came to thee from Antony, I, who had been no occasion of it, should perish with thee, a sign of thy love for me?"

Her words hit Herod as with a physical impact. He recoiled, flinging his queen from him. His eyes blazed insanely. Unwittingly, his hand groped for the dagger by his side. A hand raised threateningly, then fell limp, the jeweled steel dropping soundlessly on the thick carpet. Madness seemed to possess him; horribly he glared at Mariamne, shrieking his accusations. Now, he yelled, he knew she was guilty. Only if they had been intimate would Joseph have dared to disclose his dangerous secret, to kill any lingering affection she might otherwise have entertained for her husband. In unflinching pride, Mariamne listened to the reckless charges. When his madness tapered into an exhausted silence, without a word or a backward glance, she disdainfully passed from the royal presence.

Poor Joseph! The man who never hated anyone and wanted all men to be his friends was hustled off to execution, unattended by a single friend, regretted and pitied by no one.

While Salome and Cyprus basked anew in royal favor, Herod

ordered Alexandra to be closely confined in her palace quarters.

Openly Herod and Mariamne lived as hitherto. Formally they were reconciled. Actually there was a barrier between them that not even time could remove.

II

Meanwhile, at Antioch, Cleopatra was about to experience her hour of greatest triumph. Antony, abandoning the Parthian campaign because it meant separation from the Egyptian queen, had consented finally to formalize their long union by marriage.

It would be the Roman's third marital venture. Waving aside the law requiring that ten months elapse before the remarriage of a widow, he had wedded his first wife, the wealthy Fulvia, while she was pregnant of her first husband. Fulvia was a jealous shrew; Antony, a confirmed libertine, already seriously enmeshed with Cleopatra. Showing her first consideration for her husband's peace of mind, Fulvia died in childbirth while the bereft widower, hardly waiting the completion of the obsequies, flitted off to Cleopatra to embark on a course of extralegal paternity. To cement their reconciliation, Octavius yanked him back—to Octavia, beautiful and innocent as a doll and with as little fire. Desperately this lady tried to hold her wayward mate, even to the extent of foregoing the delicacies of the Roman festal halls in favor of a rigorous diet. For three years she managed to grasp the checkrein, presenting him with a daughter, and arousing hopes that his reformation was permanent. Vainly! He persuaded a kindred spirit to make an attempt on Octavia's virtue. When the outraged wife informed her husband, he simply sneered at her for her "Roman arrogance." In a moment of unbearable ennui, he slipped the leash and headed straight for the fleshpots of Egypt.

Divorcing Octavia, he lived openly with Cleopatra, acknowledged the paternity of their own children, and assumed the guardianship of Caesarion (Cleopatra's child by Julius Caesar). But he always balked at the final step—actual, legal marriage. "I cannot trust my whole life to a single woman. Hercules, my forbear, like me, left his blood in many places in order to found new dynasties."

Marriage aside, the degree to which Cleopatra was able to

enslave her paramour is almost incredible. At the Alexandrian games she made him act as "gymnasiarch," a functionary combining the duties of master of ceremonies with those of official "bouncer." On trips to court or to the market place she rode high in her chair while Antony trotted alongside, grinning among her eunuchs. He posed with her for paintings: he as Osiris and Dionysus, she as Isis and Selene. In public he called her his queen, his mistress. Her insolence grew apace with his abasement. Her bodyguard were Romans, with her name, in place of the Republican insignia, engraved on their shields. Disregarding Antony's embarrassment, she vowed she would dispense justice on the Capitol until such time as her Caesarion was old enough to assume his rightful place as ruler of Rome.

Still, up to now, Antony had always balked at actual marriage. Cleopatra, too, had hesitated to ally her fortunes irremediably with the Roman adventurer. But matters had reached a state where she must recognize the necessity of such a step. She was no longer a young girl. A ripe thirty-three, with all her beauty intact, mellowed and softened in fact by every physical precaution and beautifying device, she had nevertheless, in her growing children, arguments that predicated the need of a regular family life. Caesarion was in his teens; Antony's twins were emerging into childhood; within a half-year there would be another.

She demanded that Antony marry her. He demurred. He was still stubborn when she pointed out the obvious benefits of their marriage. Antony's rupture with Octavius was final; civil war inevitable. In the ensuing conflict, Antony's cause would be hopeless without Egyptian grain, Egyptian wealth, Egyptian ships —which meant in a word, Cleopatra's grain, Cleopatra's gold, Cleopatra's navy, since without Egypt as a center any assault on Rome would be foredoomed to disaster. Failing to move him with even such convincing arguments, she retired to her apartments and turned a deaf ear to his every plea to be permitted to see her.

Such treatment was bound to be effective. From a promiscuous lecher, Antony developed with the years into a connoisseur in lust. The synthetic passion of the dancing chits, the warmed-over glow of neurotic matrons now left him unsatisfied. Only Cleopatra with her controlled emotions that would complement every mood and desire of her exacting lover could satisfy his passion. Not to be deprived of Cleopatra, the exasperated satyr was ready to make any concession, even to marrying her.

The wedding was proclaimed throughout the East, for a date sufficiently remote to permit the most elaborate preparations, yet not so distant that the approaching maternity of the bride be too obvious. Nobles and commoners, even slaves, anticipated the event with a spirit of unmixed jubilation. That the marriage of a queen to a man with whom she had lived for some years, and to whom she had borne children, was in any way unusual never seemed to occur to the indulgent Orientals. To them it meant merely an occasion for festivity, which they were determined fully to relish. If a stray moralist chose to be cynical, he, for his safety's sake, was careful to keep his opinion to himself and to render the expected lip service to the ceremony.

The wedding day dawned in glittering Eastern glory. After guests had been assigned the choicer places, the parade ground was thrown open to the milling citizens, that they too might see and enjoy. On high golden thrones sat Cleopatra, adorned as Isis in a simple robe of chaste silver and pearls and beside her Antony in a royal purple cloak as Roman Imperator. Henceforth, a herald announced, Cleopatra must be addressed only as the "New Isis." Thereupon the marriage ceremony ensued, with its ironic prayer that the virgin would become fruitful and the new husband remain true.

The parents safely wedded, the twins entered the scene and were led to silver thrones only slightly lower than those of their parents. (Caesarion, it should be noted, was judiciously kept away: his father was not the groom; his destiny not Oriental, but Roman.)

First, six-year-old Alexander acknowledged the plaudits of the crowd. On his head he wore a high stiff tiara from the back of which flowed a white cloth which covered the neck. A pale amber-sleeved tunic of finest wool, over which was worn a flowing cloak of karakul fleece, thrown over one shoulder and hanging in graceful folds at the back, loose fitting trousers, and soft crimson sandals completed his dress. The occasion of the Median costume became apparent when it was announced that a marriage between the young prince and the infant daughter of the

King of the Medes had been arranged. At which news, the mob, at once clamorous and sentimental, shouted itself hoarse.

Then the other twin, Ptolemy, was presented as the crowd exploded into renewed salvos of approval. This child, as yet untrammeled with connubial expectations, was dressed in the garb of the Macedonian kings, with the traditional boots and mantle, topped with the cap encircled with a diadem—vesture familiar to all, from the representations of Alexander the Great, and a subtle reminder that he and his mother had their power grafted in the great Macedonian.

Wedding gifts were distributed to the children: Armenia, Media, and Parthia (as yet unconquered) to Alexander; to Ptolemy, Phoenicia, Syria, and Cilicia.

Unlimited food, wine, and entertainment for every one was proclaimed, and the crowd broke loose to a season of revelry and riot.

In the quiet of the nuptial chamber, the bride-mother asked for her wedding gift. Astounded, the groom heard her demand the possessions of Lysanias, Malchus, and Herod.

Cleopatra's desire for these three kingdoms is understandable. From the break-up of the world of Alexander, the great rivals Egypt and Syria regarded the very lands she now wanted as *terra irredenta,* the perennial cause for battle, and the constant battleground. The glory of her native Egypt must not be shorn of territory her people traditionally considered Egyptian. Besides, the rulers of these kingdoms were, all of them, her enemies. With one word, Antony could satisfy her country's ambitions and bestow on her peace of mind. What more fitting wedding gift than this!

Yet Antony could not grant her everything she wanted. This she knew, and that if she made her demands exorbitant he would grant her part.

Lysanias, king of Chalcis, at the foot of Lebanon, presented no problem. He was defiant, remiss in paying taxes, and questionable in loyalty. (It was pretty well established that he had aided the Parthians.)

His immediate execution was ordered and speedily carried out, and Chalcis was Cleopatra's.

It was not so easy for her completely to have her way with

Malchus, King of Nabatea, and Herod. The Arab king ruled over the territory east of the Jordan—today a wilderness, then teeming with grain and sheep, but more important still as the sole source of bitumen, a mineral pitch that in the hot valleys oozed from the fissures in the rocks. This product was useful as fuel and invaluable as an embalming agent. Unbaked brick covered with a plaster of bitumen made almost indestructible building material. Until Malchus organized the bitumen industry (amassing a tremendous fortune in the process) it had not been a profitable product. Without his directing genius it would probably again become unprofitable.

There was, therefore, no advantage in seizing the lands of this king. Not that Antony was not sorely tempted. The canny Arab had none of the openhandedness of Herod. Money from him— plenty of it—eventually always went to Antony, but only after bickering and squabbling, most distasteful to the Roman. Cleopatra must grant that to depose or destroy Malchus were merely to impair the source of greatly needed revenue.

Grant this she did. But she would remit no jot of her enmity toward Herod, whom she hated with a particular hatred. Unseating or killing him in view of his tremendous contributions to Antony was, of course, not to be thought of. But she would hem him in, contract his territories, make his life unbearable. Antony willing or no, this she would do.

On the whole, Antony's wedding gift gave her little reason to complain. He ceded her, in addition to Chalcis, the peninsula of Sinai, part of Arabia Petra, the coast of Palestine except Sidon and Tyre, Cyprus, an estate in Crete, the Cilician tin mines on the slope of Taurus as far as the cedar forests, and Lebanon.

Supplementing the original gift, at her insistent plea, he added the valley of the Jordan, including the city of Jericho.

The request for Jericho was a masterstroke of vindictiveness. Only there, and in its environs, grew the almost fabulously valuable balsam groves. Today, the world has only a vague knowledge of the nature of the balsam of biblical days. According to Arab tradition, the Queen of Sheba presented Solomon with a root, which, planted in the lavish soil by the Jordan, became the parent of the groves. It has been described as a tree or shrub resembling henna, with many leaves inclining to white, and resembling rue in scent. Its wood and berries were intensely aromatic—the oil derived from the berries almost unimaginably so. Used in the rarest medicines and perfumes, it was considered so valuable and curious as to be exhibited on at least two occasions before the citizens of Rome.

The confiscation of his groves would hurt Herod; the loss of the territory about the Jordan still more. To the end of his life he would seek in the tropical luxury and indolence of Jericho surcease from political and family worries. In the hot, lazy valley, the bitter heights of Jerusalem and the fretting turbulence of Jewish factions seemed remote indeed.

The loss of income he might have suffered; the deprivation of his favorite refuge would cut him deeply.

Cleopatra's malevolence did not stop at this. With Antony still enveloped in the waning glow of their belated honeymoon, she persuaded him to make Herod responsible for the collection of tribute from Malchus. She was well aware of Malchus' avarice and Herod's pride. She would hurt them in their most sensitive parts. If she could not destroy these wily foes, she would at least, by stirring up enmity between them, make it unlikely that they would ever combine forces against her.

Unconscious of Antony's decisions, Herod had been making some progress toward a genuine reconciliation with Mariamne. They really loved each other; they were sensible of the need of avoiding a clash between their widely divergent backgrounds and personalities for their own sake and their children's.

When the news of Jericho reached him, he seemed to go quite mad. Spitting threats at Cleopatra, at Alexandra for keeping alive the Egyptian's hatred, even at Mariamne, for being the innocent pawn in this unhappy wrangling, he shut himself in his chamber, shouting curses to the unheeding walls.

When a calm hour returned, he analyzed his position. Clearly, so long as Cleopatra lived, his fortunes rested on a shaky foundation. Were she done away with, his throne would be firm, his mother-in-law's plotting futile, his friendship with Antony secure, even a lasting reconciliation with Mariamne possible.

CHAPTER XII

AN EMPIRE LOST

THE HONEYMOON FESTIVITIES CAME OFFICI-
ally to an end with the resumption of Antony's campaign against
the Parthians. That Cleopatra should insist on remaining by his
side at least as far as the banks of the Euphrates should cause no
surprise. To do her justice, she was from her early girlhood as
much at ease in a rough military camp as in the perfumed barges
and silken courts in which she is customarily pictured. In some
respects she was a better soldier than Antony. She had a persistence, an eye on the main chance, that her volatile husband
lacked.

Like every Roman, except apparently Antony himself, she
appreciated how much depended on the success of this campaign.
Sixteen years before, Crassus had embarked on his ill-starred
expedition. Since that setback to Roman arms the Parthians
were riding high, toppling Roman fortresses, overrunning Rome's
allies. Antony just could not desist from making one supreme
effort to re-establish the prestige of the Republic before the fires
of rebellion scorched all Asia. Yet so obsessed was he with the
lure of the Egyptian that his preparations for this all-important
project were hasty, his plans shallow, his one wish to finish the
unsavory task and fly back to his wife.

History records that Antony fared more safely, but hardly more
gloriously, than his predecessor. A rear contingent of ten thousand men, left to guard the battering rams, was annihilated. The
main army, some three hundred miles within Parthia, had,

thereupon, hastily to retreat, suffering many casualties and recovering neither the prisoners nor the standards (their avowed objective) abandoned by Crassus. Fleeing at length across the Araxes into friendly Armenia, the harried legionaries kissed the earth in a frenzy of relief.

Heedless of the disgrace of the double defeat, unmindful of the fact that this disaster must inevitably alienate his lukewarm adherents, visualizing only the alluring form of Cleopatra, Antony goaded his weary soldiers from their comfortable winter quarters, across the howling passes, through the blasting cold of the snow-buried gullies, squandering thousands of loyal lives that had survived the horrors of the Parthian plains, for the sole reason that he might join her sooner.

When she bade her husband farewell, Cleopatra must have sensed some premonition of what fate held in store for him. With the most intense fervor she had pleaded with him to accomplish his mission in a manner befitting a Roman conqueror. Here, she assured him, was an unsurpassable opportunity of being not merely the leader of a dwindling faction but the idol of all Romans everywhere. Soothe the deep sting of Crassus' defeat with a glorious victory, and Octavius' supporters would melt away.

Still, she must have felt, too, that the sex-sodden general could no longer be inspired with the motive of glory. Had her condition been otherwise than it was she would have inevitably accompanied him. But to cross the rugged Armenian mountains and to attempt to live on the breathless plains of Medea would have been folly. Moreover, she wished her child to be born at Alexandria, the coming capital—unless her schemes went awry—of her world.

Returning, she rested at Apamia and Damascus before passing on to Jerusalem.

Here Herod, undoubtedly informed of her intended visit, entertained her in regal manner at the palace of the Maccabees (his own palace was not yet built), while Mariamne, the flawless hostess, seconded every effort of her husband's to persuade his venomous guest that he was a loyal, devoted vassal.

Secretly, however, Herod seriously considered having this most

vicious of enemies killed. The prescribed banquets and ceremonies over, Cleopatra dropped her friendly mask and peremptorily ordered him to accompany her to Jericho, where the
Nabatean monarch had also been summoned to await her arrival.

Nowhere in the world is there a more appropriate setting for
violence than on the twenty-three sweltering miles of road that
plunge from Jerusalem down to Jericho. Starting at the capital,
twenty-three hundred feet above sea level, the road twists its
agonized way through an arid wilderness of bare mountainside,
either bleak and volcanic or strewn with blinding masses of
jumbled limestone slabs; numberless caves, immemorially the
refuge of robbers, honeycomb the distorted hills. One solitary
khan with its rock cisterns—the inn of the parable of the Good
Samaritan—expresses all that is human; everywhere else, the landscape, weird, almost satanic in its implied threat, hastens the
unhappy traveler on his precipitous journey to the tropical valley
of the Jordan, thirteen hundred feet below the level of the sea.

Almost anywhere along this tortuous descent the queen might
have been done away with, the murder attributed to robbers, and
Herod's worst enemy—Antony's, too, for that matter—removed.

Unwilling to seize the entire initiative himself, Herod submitted his plan to his council. To a man they were horror-
stricken. Granted, they protested, that Antony would eventually
benefit by her murder, his impetuosity was such that none of
them, nor Herod, would be alive to share his appreciation. His
revenge would doubtless be immediate and complete. In ordering the queen's assassination, Herod would as surely be signing
his own and their death warrants.

Reluctantly, since he could never again hope for so certain
an opportunity, Herod conceded the reasonableness of their
protests.

A brilliant cavalcade starting by dark to encompass the journey
before the murderous heat of midday struck, wormed its way
along the serpentine twists, or involuntarily held its breath lest
the thundering hoofs loose an avalanche down its lowering cliffs.

Herod rode by the queen's litter in sullen silence. From time to
time a quizzical glance from half-parted lids would penetrate the
king's moody spirit. Whenever a wishful glance swept the lime-

stone caverns, a humorless smile formed on her painted lips. They found it difficult not to understand each other.

At Jericho the castle shunned by Herod since Aristobulus' tragic death was placed at Cleopatra's disposal. Several days elapsed, the queen leisurely recovering from her exhausting trip from Jerusalem, the vassal kings according to their several natures openly stewing or inwardly seething at her studied malevolence.

In her own good time, she ordered their attendance. A keen business woman, carrying on transactions with business men obligated to do her bidding, she wasted no time on preliminary bargaining. Imperiously she made her demands known. With her vast interests, she could devote but little of her time to local sources of income. Since this income was derived from enter-prises of a peculiarly specialized nature, she had no one on her personal staff to conduct them on a paying basis. Malchus might, therefore, continue to operate the bitumen industry; Herod, the cultivation of the balsam groves. In return each was to pay her annually two hundred talents—approximately two hundred and forty thousand dollars. In addition, Herod was held accountable for Malchus' payment as well as for his own.

Malchus, only momentarily abashed by the enormity of the demands, erupted in a frenzy of oriental clamor that ran the emotional gamut from sobs to rebellion. Tears drained past the huge hooked nose and soaked into the agitated black beard; malicious sparkles shot from jetty eyes; talon-like hands clawed at his rending robe; in a fit of despair the squat, swarthy figure groveled at the feet of the disgusted queen.

A tradesman and a miser at heart, he was hurt to the bottom of his acquisitive soul. The thought of the money he must pay was bad enough. But the impersonal manner of it all! Had he only been permitted to do a bit of haggling! This was outright robbery! Worse! Even a robber was amenable to a bargain, as the unscrupulous Arab well knew from his own manifold busi-ness ventures.

Herod, on the contrary, accepted the judgment in disdainful silence. With a glance of loathing, he grasped the still voluble Arab by the shoulder, forced him to make a dutiful obeisance to the queen, and, bowing, left the royal presence.

Later that day a messenger prostrated himself before Cleopatra. Entertainment had been prepared by Herod for the gracious consort of his patron Antony. Would she honor her Jewish hosts by condescending to grace their festivities before she resumed her tiresome journey to Egypt?

The Egyptian would and did. Perhaps the contrast between the sniveling, penny-pinching Arab and the stalwart, proud Jew poked fires slumbering since their first meeting six years before. Or perhaps she had the pernicious design of entrapping Herod as she had enamored every other male when it served her purpose. Whatever her reason, she proposed adultery, and, her offer declined, repeated her efforts with little attempt at secrecy.

It must be remembered that Cleopatra's strength rested largely in her ability to captivate men of power; that her wealth and position were safe only while there were strong men to protect them. Whether she actually considered Herod as a potential successor to her uncertain Antony or whether she planned to bring about Herod's destruction at her husband's hands is debatable. The other explanation, the desire merely to satisfy animal lust, belongs in the realms of the romancers. Her passions, though deep and strong, were always subservient to her interests. Not for the sake of transitory lewdness would she gamble with her career.

Herod, never a lustful man, was immune to her wiles. Courteously, but inflexibly, he checkmated every overture. The baffled Egyptian, twice thwarted by the handsome Jew, offered herself to Costobar. Failing to ensnare the king, she might ruin him by alleging an attack on her virtue (sic) by his kinsman. Costobar —his long irregular attachment to Salome legalized after the execution of Joseph—shrugged away the opportunity. The sword of Herod, and Salome's tongue, were too immediate, too deadly.

In a pique, Cleopatra left for Egypt. Herod courteously presented her with a parting gift—slips of balsam and a gardener who knew how to transplant and care for them in Egypt. (A generation later, it was to the balsam grove at Heliopolis with their Jewish caretakers that the Holy Family is said to have fled to escape the rage of this same Herod.)

At Jerusalem, Mariamne gave birth to her fourth child and

first daughter. Herod, meanwhile, accompanied Cleopatra as far as the border city of Pelusium, and then left her with every manifestation of loyalty.

After Herod's return to Jerusalem, the royal pair tried honestly to reassemble the battered fragments of their former bliss. The innate domesticity of the king recoiled at the exposure of Cleopatra's raw immorality; Mariamne, her eyes opened by the Egyptian's utter viciousness, found new virtues in a husband loyal enough to repel, and courageous enough to fight her blandishments. For the more than two years that elapsed between Cleopatra's visit to Judea, and Actium, Herod played honestly the part of a devoted husband; Mariamne, that of a dutiful wife. She became once more a mother. Her fifth and last child, an ingratiating little girl, the image of her mother, helped banish some of the memories of a distressful past.

Much of this interval Herod spent on the kind of work that was to become increasingly his particular field. He was unconcerned at the very deliberate progress on his own palace. Rather he threw himself into a task that besides taxing all his architectural and constructional ingenuity removed him from the pent-up hostility of Jerusalem to the clean, bracing air of the wilderness.

Years before, Jonathan the Maccabee had envisioned Masada as an impregnable fortress and sure refuge in any danger. Though its defenses were not yet completed, it served, even in its unfinished state, as a safe retreat for Herod's family when driven from Jerusalem by Antigonus II and his Parthian allies.

It was a fortress fashioned by nature itself. At the southwestern shore of the Dead Sea is a flat-topped mountain, higher than the nearby hills. Two paths, one from the lake, the other from the inland slope, struggle up its summit. The former, known as the "Serpent's Path," was almost impassable. The narrowest of slippery ledges, with yawning chasms on both sides, had to be traversed. Unscalable walls of vertical rock barred the direct approach so that some four miles of cruelly treacherous terrain must be crossed before the top could be attained. A steep but direct path led straight to the top from the western or inland side of the hill, a path completely blocked by a tower, built in earlier days, and strengthened by Herod to the point of impenetrability.

The top of the hill was peculiarly no rocky waste, but a verdant, level disk, about a mile in diameter. So fertile was its soil that a garrison could laugh at threats of starvation by planting its own food. The air was dry and invigorating with such unusual preservative qualities that a century later, when the Romans seized Masada in the final stroke that marked the end of the Great Rebellion, they found supplies left by Herod still fresh and wholesome. The entire summit was encircled by a wall of white stone eighteen feet high and twelve wide. At strategic intervals rose thirty-eight massive towers seventy-five feet high. Barracks and houses were built abutting this wall, leaving the greater part of the fertile plain for cultivation and grazing. Great cisterns were dug, assuring an unfailing supply of pure, cool water. From the center of the mountaintop rose Herod's palace, magnificently furnished and equipped with luxurious baths. Servants' quarters and other buildings were connected to the palace by a series of cloisters, each sustained by great marble pillars. On its completion, the fortress could accommodate ten thousand men and vast stores of provisions.

The tremendous labor of planning and directing entailed in building Masada was really relaxation for Herod. With a challenging task to stimulate his talents, and a happy home in which to rest, the echoes of a seditious Jerusalem hardly penetrated his consciousness. But, Masada barely finished, he was ordered to Ephesus, where Antony was calling the roster of his allies and vassals for the final duel with Octavius.

II

It was obvious to all that even the Roman Empire was not extensive enough to sustain two leaders with such diverse and limitless ambitions as Antony and Octavius. Clearly the time had come when one man must rule Rome if Rome was indeed to survive. And it was the choice of ruler that occupied the minds and schemes of men.

A long series of civil wars had killed almost every civic virtue except that of loyalty to Rome itself. Every ruler or attempted ruler had drawn to himself those who planned personally to profit by his victory, while their true loyalty was always essentially to the state, never to the leader alone.

In the camp of Antony were those who had no other choice, so hateful were they to Octavius that Antony's overthrow would spell their doom as well. Others were in a sense loyal to Antony and would incur considerable risk in his behalf, but still withheld their entire allegiance subject to their approval of his activities. Still others, like the intriguer Dellius, were ready to change sides at the remotest hint of disaster to their patron.

A very similar condition existed also in the army of Octavius.

In general, most open-minded Romans preferred Antony to Octavius. And understandably so. In every virtue but caution Antony was his rival's superior; in the degradation of their moral qualities there was little choice except that Octavius' was the meaner. Yet Antony had one terrible handicap, Cleopatra.

Summoned to Ephesus, along with Antony's other allies, Herod found himself left cooling his heels (at Cleopatra's express command) outside the city, and therefore unable to join in the violent dissension on the status of the queen that was occupying Antony's staff. Her opponents—numerous and outspoken—protested their entire loyalty to Antony. They would follow him as a Roman general in a civil war to establish his right to rule. But their first loyalty was to Rome. With Antony the husband of an Egyptian queen, furthering the prospects of her children, they would be fighting for a foreign dynasty against their own country, not as factionists but as traitors. Some few openly advocated her death; most insisted on her dismissal. A deputation arrived from Italy, intending to assure Antony that the road to Rome would be open the moment he put away his mate. Cleopatra had them ejected before they could reach Antony. Still, so strong and numerous were her enemies that Antony was reluctantly prevailed upon to order her back to Egypt. Whereupon she played her trump card. Antony's chief-of-staff, Canidius, listening quietly until the clamor of her opponents had abated, remarked dryly that since her gold and her supplies were maintaining and feeding Antony's army, who could reasonably object to her remaining with that army? The decree of expulsion was withdrawn. Against the better judgment of most of Antony's generals she was permitted to stay.

The deputation returned to Italy, sullenly resigned to the acceptance of Octavius. Deserters (Dellius among the first) flocked to his standard, all with information about Antony's forces. One in particular had come upon the information that Antony had left his will in care of the Vestal Virgins. Risking public horror at the sacrilege, Octavius strode into the sacred precincts and forcibly removed the document. Public reading of this before the senate stemmed public resentment that might otherwise have reached dangerous heights.

It was this will that quite destroyed Antony's chance of popular support in Italy, since it branded him as a traitor to Rome. The fatal script asserted that Caesarion was the true son and heir to the fortune and position of Julius Caesar, since Octavius was merely his foster son. It went on to bestow great legacies to the children of Antony and Cleopatra, and decreed that in the event of his death he should be buried at Alexandria—a certain indication to Romans that Antony was striving to supplant the Eternal City with the Egyptian port as capital city of the world.

With Roman popular opinion turned against him, dissension grew and disunion increased at Ephesus. Sickened by the endless bickering, Antony turned his back on the camp. In the words of Plutarch, "The whole tribe of players and musicians were ordered to repair to Samos; and while almost the whole world was venting its anguish in groans and tears, that island alone was piping and dancing." From Samos, Antony took his court to Athens, where entertainment was enjoyed of an even more vicious nature. Eventually, at the insistent pleas of those most loyal to him, Antony returned to Ephesus. To even his staunchest adherents it was clear that their hero was disintegrating rapidly and that they were fighting in a lost cause.

Herod, languishing on the outskirts of Ephesus, was sick with anxiety. Every effort to join his forces with those of Antony was blocked, personal permission to consult with his patron frustrated. He knew the orders came from Cleopatra, but there was nothing he could do to circumvent her designs.

Like a thunderbolt came the order, under the signature of

Antony, that Herod and his troops were not to participate in the coming battle. Malchus, taking advantage of the general turmoil, refused to pay tribute, and was raising the standard of rebellion among his own Arabs as well as attracting to his cause desert tribes whose allegiance normally was doubtful. In accordance with his agreement with Cleopatra, Herod was commanded forthwith to chastise the obstinate Arab.

The orders carried the accents of doom. Herod knew he was superior to Antony's other generals in loyalty and ability; he felt certain that as Antony's camp-mate he could check the withering influence of Cleopatra. Instead he was assigned the inglorious chore of bill collector to settle her bad debts. With world supremacy for his patron, and his own assured safety the issue, he must be wasting his powers in a squabble with an unscrupulous huckster.

Antony's mental corruption seems also to have begun to affect his paramour. Else there is no explanation of the insane errand on which she dispatched Herod. Were the all-important battle with Octavius not imminent, were the advice and military personnel of Herod not so urgent, her action might have been interpreted as a characteristic act of understandable spite. Under normal conditions a petty war between her vassals might eventually have been advantageous to her. Whoever won, she could seize the other's domain and in time reap the full benefit of his peculiar source of income. Even the victor would have wasted his own strength in winning her victory and have rendered himself the easier to absorb whenever she willed it.

Strangely, with her world poised on the outcome of a single battle, she could not see that this was no time to dissipate Antony's resources in a wrangle for petty revenge, and that in sending away Herod she was tremendously sapping Antony's chances in the struggle that was vital to her as well.

Dejected and furiously angry, Herod speedily moved his army into enemy territory. The ensuing campaign merits study as a military project, manifesting the influence of a skilful, inspiring commander over troops that exhibited the characteristic combination of invincibility and panic, of spirit and lethargy that marked Jewish armies throughout the Old Testament era.

The first onset at Diospolis in Arabia was a clear-cut Jewish

victory over an unready foe disorganized by the unsuspected
proximity of their opponents. A greatly reinforced Arab army
gathered at Cana in Coele-Syria. Apprised of the enemy's
strength, Herod, in accordance with established military procedure, gave orders to fortify his camp strongly and to await the
proper time for battle.

Having tasted easy victory, the Jews protested. They had
already beaten the Arabs once, could easily beat them again.
Away with this excessive caution, so untypical of their king, so
slighting of their prowess.

Herod had the gift, bestowed only upon the greatest of conquerors, of knowing when to lay aside the textbooks on strategy.
Intuitively, he felt that his men at the moment were irresistible;
that should the moment pass, they would again become dis-
gruntled, uncertain mortals. He addressed the turbulent warriors. He admired their zeal; he praised their spirit; he himself
would lead them in the attack they were so anxious to begin.

A cheering wave, the king at the crest, broke upon the Arabs.
Filled with consternation the Arabs fled, striking hardly a blow in
retaliation. In jubilant pursuit the Jews, too, broke ranks, to
hunt down a panic-crazed enemy and loot his camps. At sun-
down they returned, weary with killing, laden with plunder, to
fling themselves into a camp that needed no guards, no sentries,
since there was left apparently no enemy.

Drunk with jubilation, Herod for once underestimated the
astounding vindictiveness of Cleopatra. Not content with detach-
ing Herod's forces from Antony's host, she sent another army
under her favorite general Athenio to observe the conduct of the
war of the vassal kings, and, if expedient, to interfere in a manner beneficial to her. This army had difficulty in locating Herod's
rapidly shifting troops and arrived just in time to see the rout
of Malchus, or, as Josephus naively puts it, "Athenio very wist-
fully looked on."

That night Athenio's Egyptians, rank upon rank, poured into
the unsuspecting Herodian camp. Shocked out of dreams of pillage and glory by so sudden an assault, the Jews ran, a disorganized mob. Bands of nomad Arabs, hitherto inactive, related
racially but owing no allegiance to Malchus' tribesmen, joined in

the pursuit. Such Jewish units as tried to reform and fight they lured into terrain where their horses were a hindrance, and cut down. Retrieving what he could from the disaster, Herod recalled the remnants of his army into previously prepared mountain strongholds. For some months he could engage only in guerrilla tactics, harassing the enemy and attempting to raise the lagging spirits of his men by skilfully executed forays from his inaccessible retreats.

Earthquakes occur periodically in Palestine, but that of 31 B.C. was of unprecedented violence. Towns in a moment were tumbled into heaps of rubble; unnumbered cattle were killed; thirty thousand human lives were crushed out; starvation stalked the land. While Herod's troops were unharmed by the earthquake, the panic that swept the country infected the despondent Jewish soldiery. They deserted in large numbers, literally cutting their way through the saner elements that tried to restrain them, only to fall on the waiting swords of Arab patrols.

Partly to gain time in order to investigate whether the reports that his country was completely destroyed by the earthquake were really true, Herod sent ambassadors to Malchus to discuss terms of peace. The Arabs, emboldened by the exaggerated accounts to believe that Herod's army, too, had been in large measure effaced by the earthquake, killed the ambassadors.

This was a fatal blunder. The massacre of ambassadors, who in the eyes of the Jews held a rank analogous to that of angels, or messengers of God, filled them with a desperate fury. Since peace was impossible, they were determined to die dragging as many as possible of their enemy into the grave with them.

Herod, ever sensitive to mass emotion, saw his opportunity in the changed attitude of his men. Desperation, he knew, was unorganized and defensive, productive of last-ditch, costly resistance, but rarely of victory. He would take this desperation and transform it into a victorious, avenging rage.

First he called upon his commanders, praised their spirit, and intimated that the hour of victory was not far off. Something of his elation was communicated to these officers as they summoned their troops to listen to the words of their king.

From the opening syllables, an army listened enraptured to the ringing tones unfolding a speech that was a masterpiece of inspirational oratory. It began with the frank admission of their altered fortunes, which had lowered their spirits. It went on to point out that the war was necessary and just. The Arabs, on the other hand, were prompted by wickedness, and envy, and "ignorance of God," and the basest ingratitude, since it was Herod's plea with Antony that had saved them from utter absorption by Cleopatra. The depravity of the enemy, "who think gain to be the best of things, let it be by any means whatsoever, and injustice to be no harm, if they may but get money by it," was demonstrated by their slaying of the ambassadors. Men so base cannot possibly prosper, Herod's speech assured them. The enemy might be more numerous, but "with whom is what is righteous, with them is God himself, and where God is, there are both multitude and courage." But even aside from the righteousness of their cause and the assurance that God was on their side, the Jews from a military standpoint had no reason to be downcast, he assured them. They had decisively won the first battle and completely routed a foe that did not dare stand up to them, in the second. The treachery of Athenio and the earthquake, it is true, temporarily exalted the chances of the enemy. But why fear a foe whom they could always beat in fair battle? The only real advantage the Arabs could have would be the assurance that the Jews were too despondent to fight. If this, however, were only a false hope, it would be a serious handicap to the Jews' opponents. The fact that those in camp had escaped the ravages of the earthquake was in itself assurance of God's continued favor. "Consider that you have God at all times for your protector; and prosecute these men with a just bravery—who in point of friendship are unjust; in their battles, perfidious; towards ambassadors, impious; and always inferior to you in valor."

It was a masterly oration, designed to raise drooping hopes and inspire lagging spirits. Incidentally, it demonstrated a seemingly sincere trust in God and a conviction that the Almighty will not abandon a just cause, nor permit to continue to prosper those who violate his commandments. To what extent Herod's words were honest is a matter of opinion. Certainly, his speech rings true. Nowhere else in the Old Testament era did king or prophet inspire the Israelites with nobler sentiments more eloquently expressed.

The Jews, lifted from the depths of dejection to the pinnacle of elation, wanted to attack at once. Only with difficulty were they restrained. The king determined that they must recognize this as the decisive battle in a holy war. Before all the army, he solemnly offered sacrifice, made a prayer of submission to the will of God, and pleaded for his help.

Thereupon, Herod recrossed the Jordan and stormed a strongly-held fortress to make impossible any attacks from the rear, and also to give vent to the explosive spirits of his men. Spies, dispersed among the Arabs, spread astounding tales of the might of the Jewish army; prisoners were permitted to escape, after being allowed to see the strongest aspects of Herod's preparations.

These tactics were successful. The Arabs, despite their boastful attitude, had little stomach for battle and declined to be drawn in any great numbers from their strongholds. In every skirmish and lesser engagement the Jews won so effortlessly that the Arabian morale dropped lower and lower. Eventually, Herod maneuvered the Arabs into a position where they had to accept battle.

It was a brilliant victory for the outnumbered Jews. Five thousand Arabs lay dead on the field of battle, other thousands were trampled to death or cut down in their wild efforts to escape. During the battle, Herod's spies polluted the wells in the enclosure which the Arabs looked upon as an impregnable refuge. Consequently, those who reached this camp found themselves in a position hardly less enviable than that of their slaughtered fellows. Messengers of peace went to see Herod, but were refused admittance. After five agonizing days, four thousand blinded, black-tongued tribesmen surrendered. The remainder, making one despairing effort to break through to safety and water, were so weakened that they were no match for the exultant Jews. Seven thousand more, including Malchus, were put to the sword; the abject survivors willingly accepted Herod's rule.

The whole campaign was convincing proof that Herod possessed the qualities of warrior and commander in every kind of military or emotional contingency. He moved his men secretly and rapidly; he kept open his lines of supply; he adapted his strategy to the circumstances; he prepared for possible disaster, and translated despair into victory. More specifically, in the first battle he directed well-trained troops in formal conflict and won. Disregarding military tradition, he utilized the élan of an inspired army in an original manner to win the second glorious victory. His army shattered by treachery, he gathered and organized the remnants of his forces and waged brilliant guerrilla warfare. Assailed by a further unpredictable calamity in the form of an earthquake, by sublime oratory and at least apparent piety and confidence in God he lifted the spirits of his men from acceptance of inevitable doom to assurance of triumph.

It would appear that Herod had won for himself another kingdom. How valuable or lasting an acquisition had been determined far from Palestine. Actium had been fought, and—true to Herod's fears—lost by Antony.

With incredible stupidity he had let Cleopatra persuade him to risk all on the issue of a single sea-battle. With five hundred craft—three hundred of them Egyptian—he left the Pireus. Octavius' fleet at the same time sailed from Tarentium and Brundisium. The two navies sighted each other off the Greek coast, but neither was quite ready for battle. At Actium in Epirus, Antony moored the best of his ships and beached the others, destined even before the battle to be burned. Octavius, meanwhile, anchored his fleet on the northern side of the same gulf, opposite his enemy's ships. Gradually, and without molesting each other, land forces assembled—one hundred thousand infantry and twelve thousand cavalry for Antony, eighty thousand infantry and twelve thousand cavalry for Octavius. Across the narrow gulf the hosts faced each other, inactive, while the fleets groomed for battle.

Eventually Cleopatra reduced her fleet to sixty superb fighting ships. Supplemented by the Roman vessels, this fleet was numerically inferior to Octavius', but it was faster, and more powerful.

On the day of battle, as if by prearranged signal the fleets maneuvered for position. By smarter handling, Antony's ships darted into perfect battle array, while the enemy squadrons seemed ragged, almost disorganized by contrast. Lining the shore, an unbroken arc of burnished armor, the two armies watched their navy mates, Antony's men begrudgingly elated that the sea-battle they had so violently opposed seemed to augur well, the troops of Octavius fearful that the loathed Egyptian might yet be crowned in Rome.

In an instant an incredulous gasp broke from every intent observer. Actuated by a sudden flux of panic, Cleopatra issued an insane order to her fleet. Almost instantly, so efficiently had her men been drilled, all sixty ships hoisted sail and streamed through the sparring lines of Antony out to sea and over the horizon. By her action, Antony almost certainly lost the battle of Actium, but by no means the campaign. He might have gone ashore and staked his fortunes on a land-battle, with at least an equal chance of success.

Instead, blinded to everything but the flight of his queen, he transferred to a small swift galley, and with never a glance at his ships, valiantly trying to close the gap made by the desertion of their allies, he streaked in pursuit of his fleeing consort. The Egyptian fleet could not long keep ahead of the speeding ship. Cleopatra stopped her galley, named ironically the *Antonia,* and Antony came aboard. There were no words that could be spoken. For three days he hunched abjectly at the prow, face buried in hands, oblivious of weather or hunger, the image of despair. Until they rounded the Peloponnesus and reached Taenarum, Cleopatra kept prudently out of sight.

Their waiting heralds bore them the bitter news. The abandoned fleet had fought bravely for four hours before the bruised, unmanageable hulks surrendered. On land, the Antonian army, dismayed by the twin buffets of Antony's flight and Canidius' subsequent desertion, also made its submission.

For a time Antony tried to escape from himself in Cleopatra's company. Attempting to return to Libya, he found that province hostile, since his troops there had revolted. In utter despondency he sent Cleopatra to Egypt and withdrew to the desert accompanied by Lucilius (the attempted savior of Brutus). The dry, clean heat of the wilderness seemed only to stimulate his craving for Cleopatra. He rejoined her to spend a dismal winter at Alexandria.

Octavius meanwhile, smugly consolidating his conquest in the East, was stung by the outbreak of mutiny in Italy into the realization that his troubles were not over.

Herod, with his new-won kingdom, was pondering what his next step should be.

Unlike Pinarius Scarpus, the powerful governor of Libya, and Canidius, and a host of lesser chiefs, he did not at once make his obeisance to the conqueror. Instead he sent messengers to Antony with expressions of sympathy and offers of aid. Tangibly, he proposed that the defeated leader consider Jerusalem and the other Judean citadels as places of refuge in case Egypt failed him. All this, however, was conditional on Antony's doing away with Cleopatra. Herod's decision, while a tribute to his loyalty, was not as quixotic as it has sometimes been represented. Opposition to the otherwise popular Antony was based chiefly on his espousal of Cleopatra and the fear that Rome might eventually become an Egyptian puppet state. On the other hand, Octavius was supported chiefly because he stood for a truly Roman supremacy. The mutiny in Italy during the winter following his triumph at Actium showed that there was violent opposition even where he was presumably strongest. The East, which never took him to heart, would flash into rebellion under an Antony unhampered by his hateful mate. Should this rebellion have its inception and its headquarters in Judea, it would, if successful, tremendously exalt the dignity and power of the Judean state and the Herodian dynasty.

Herod's pleas were vain. Antony was too thoroughly steeped in his infatuation to react against it. Having done all that honor demanded, certain that to continue in his support of Antony would be suicidal, Herod realized that there was only one course: to attempt to make his peace with Octavius.

CHAPTER XIII

A KINGDOM WON
—A QUEEN LOST

IN JERUSALEM IT WAS TAKEN FOR GRANTED that Antony's collapse would tumble his satellites into the dust with him. Herod's enemies, emboldened by confidence in his imminent ruin, began to emerge from hiding. Active opposition, open expressions of enmity were, naturally, not in evidence. Why risk lives to attempt what Antony would be certain to accomplish! But a sense of gloating satisfaction, of jubilant anticipation could be sensed where there had been a rabbit-like timidity, a cowering acquiescence to the commands of one whom they hated and feared.

The king's friends seemed as fully convinced of their patron's downfall as were his enemies. Less and less they appeared in public, as if anxious to do nothing to aggravate public disfavor.

As for Herod himself, he was nearer to the cracking point than anyone suspected. He was—by all impartial standards—a good king. He had brought his subjects territory and prosperity; he had maintained their freedom of worship and assured them immunity from aggression. Yet in return he could find only suspicion and wrangling in his own family, unyielding hatred from his people, and now the threat of destruction at the hands of Rome, which he had ably and conscientiously served.

In justice, Herod might be said to have had two, and only two, objectives: a happy family life and a prosperous, peaceful kingdom. Every act of his had these as their ultimate goals. Every act, moreover, if we except the murder of Aristobulus and the tentative instructions to kill Mariamne—both induced under

187

stress of abnormal emotions deliberately aroused by agents hostile
to Herod—seemed normal and justifiable. And precisely because
his normal, justifiable objectives never were attained, he clutched
at any desperate means of accomplishing his ambitions.

How frenzied the cataclysm in Herod's mind, how he pondered
and raged, and pondered again, is not recorded. It is obvious,
however, that he ever after carried an insane taint, which from
time to time burst all reasonable bounds and turned an able,
constructive, visionary monarch into a fretful, fuming tyrant.

Mariamne, wise in her knowledge that her husband wanted to
work out his problems alone, unobtrusively hovered by, occasionally calming his turbulence with loving word or glance, but
generally leaving him the uneasy solitude she knew he wished.

Not so with Hyrcanus. Senile in his sympathy, he pushed his
way past the protesting guards into the royal presence. He caught
Herod at a most unhappy moment, just when the weight of
destiny pressed inexorably on his bowed shoulders. Unconscious
of the tortured features, the darting danger of the eyes, he began
haltingly to mutter his solicitude.

It was more than the haggard king could stand. "Out, old
fool!" he spat at the dumbfounded patriarch. Puzzled, Hyrcanus
stood stock still for a moment, then like a blind man began to
grope for the door. With gruff kindness, the guards hustled him
from the chamber as tears coursed down the seamed cheeks.

Herod, by nature kind and generous to the old man, almost
instantly regretted his brusqueness. But why didn't the old idiot
keep way! He wanted not sympathy or advice but only the
uninterrupted opportunity of thinking out his problem. Later—
very soon—he must recall the old priest and make amends!

Of a sudden, a suspicion slipped into his cogitations. Perhaps
—it seemed absurd on the face of it—yet it was not impossible
that a final, feeble wave of ambition was breaking over the last
of the male Maccabeans. If anything happened to him, Hyrcanus,
not the king's children, might inherit the throne. Racked between affection and doubt, Herod momentarily lost sight of his
major perplexity and began to brood on this new fear.

A discreet tap at the door cut short his speculation. Impatiently, he bade the applicant enter. The sight of the intruder

did nothing to raise his spirits. It was Dositheus, a hanger-on at the court, temporarily in the good graces of Alexandra but a subject of suspicion to Herod. His brother had been executed for treason; other relatives had perished in the heckling of Antony at Tyre; his surviving family were in no sense remarkable for their loyalty.

"A letter has been committed to me. My loyalty to you, Sire, would not permit my participation in any action that might run counter to your royal interests. I humbly ask your consent to deliver this letter if it is your pleasure that I do so."

The rascal spoke with an air of smug humility that did not deceive Herod. Snatching the letter, he read avidly with darkening brow. He rerolled the missive, carefully restored the seal, and thrust it at the groveling messenger.

"You may deliver this to its destination. Then wait for an answer, which you will bring to us before anyone else has an opportunity of reading it. At present you have given us no reason for increasing our suspicions of your conduct. You may retire."

The letter was Hyrcanus' final bungling step to doom. At Alexandra's insistence—at first, he refused—he let himself be persuaded to write to an Arab chieftain, Malchus, appealing for the latter's protection in the almost certain event of Herod's execution. Unfortunately the letter contained statements, inspired by Alexandra's virulent hatred, picturing Herod as a murderous monster.

At the king's command, Dositheus was accorded every facility for reaching his destination speedily. Malchus—not to be confused with his namesake, the late Nabatean king—received the messenger with characteristic desert hospitality. Quickly the answer was on its way. He would be honored to offer refuge to the noble Jews and to as many as chose to accompany them. More than that, he would gladly furnish them with an escort at the border, to prevent interference with their flight.

Holding this answer in hands cold with rage, Herod summoned Hyrcanus. Recalling his brutal reception at their former meeting, and convinced that the king called him to express his repentance, the priest immediately assured Herod that he harbored no resentment, and that his esteem and affection for the husband of his beloved grandchild could not be marred by any transient ill-humor on the part of a man depressed by affairs of state.

Herod stopped his well-intentioned protestations.

"Is this your letter?"

Hyrcanus stared at the damning document. Perhaps he had half-forgotten that he wrote it. His memory was failing; all his life he had made it a practice to dismiss unpleasant facts from his mind, and to assume them as having never taken place.

But even before he could formulate an excuse, Herod continued, "Here, too, is Malchus' reply. Your own answer will be made to the sanhedrin within an hour."

The council was hastily summoned. Their servility glazed with an unctuous dignity, they heard the king's charges and with one voice concurred with his demand for immediate execution. That same afternoon Hyrcanus meekly bowed his neck to the headman's ax.

In the grim interval before it fell, there may have flashed before his fevered eyes an exciting panorama covering the events of eight hectic decades: his unhappy childhood, three uncertain months on the throne which he gladly relinquished to his brother Aristobulus II, his partial restoration to office by Pompey, his exaltation to the high priesthood, his betrayal and mutilation by his nephew Antigonus II and the Parthians, the blissful interlude at Babylon, his entrapment in the fatal eddy of homesickness that whirled him into a vortex of greed and hatred. Quiet and security—all that he ever wanted—were scarce to be found in all that giddy panorama. He would have to wait for that; he would have to wait.

The flashing ax snapped his revery.

The execution of Hyrcanus was not the act of a reasonable man. No good could possibly come of it. Negatively, Hyrcanus was almost eighty-two, certainly too old himself to rule, surely too much attached to his great-grandchildren to consent to serve in their place. Such an act of insane fury, too, put Herod's friends on the defensive and convinced his enemies of his utter ruthlessness. Worst of all, it placed a bloody barrier between himself and Mariamne.

All her slumbering doubts and suspicions flared into a startled conviction: the invasion of the sanhedrin, the massacre in Jerusalem, Antigonus II's ignoble death, Aristobulus—the lost hope of Israel—and now poor, harmless, lovable Hyrcanus. The king must be a demon intent on exterminating every possible rival in whose veins flowed royal Jewish blood! He had not even hesitated—under the pretext of excessive love—to order her own execution! What assurance had she that her children might not be the next victims of their unnatural father!

Horror flowed over her like a tide. She would never again in fact be the king's wife. Between them would exist an unending enmity, open or covert, as her children's interests dictated.

When the red fit of fury dimmed from his mind, Herod was crushed by what he had done. In Mariamne's eyes, in her bearing, he could read the loathing she felt for him. Nor was there time to try once more to ameliorate this deepest of all differences. Octavius, after suppressing the outbreak in Italy, was resting at Rhodes preparatory to re-establishing order in the East.

Herod must see him now rather than await the otherwise inevitable summons from the Roman.

But first he must set his kingdom in order. His surviving brother, Pheroras, he named regent, with orders to attempt to seize the crown for himself and hold it in trust for Herod's children in the event that the meeting at Rhodes terminated fatally. His own mother, and Salome, together with his children, were sent to Masada—a far-sighted decision that ensured their safety from an enraged Jewry if he should lose his life. Mariamne and Alexandra, who had nothing to fear from the Jews, were placed in the luxurious fortress Alexandrium under charge of the treasurer, Joseph, and Herod's trusted camp-mate Sohemus of Ituria, who was further directed to kill the women if the news from Rhodes were bad—Alexandra, to prevent her from once more intriguing for the crown, and Mariamne to spare her from the revenge or lust of Octavius.

Aware of Pheroras' limitations, he reorganized the sanhedrin with temporarily, at least, greatly increased powers, and in a manner more befitting its traditional dignity. All his creatures, whose subservience had made the council merely a royal tool, he discharged with generous gifts and annuities, bestowed, however, in a manner that left them no doubt as to the king's opinion of their venality.

To be president and organizer of the new sanhedrin he selected the famous Hillel (70 B.C.–A.D. 5), descended on his mother's side from David, whose consistent preaching and practice of the doctrine of gentleness, of love of humanity, of confidence in God amidst misfortune, has left an imperishable imprint on Jewish thought and action. It was, no doubt, as a Babylonian and a courageous lover of peace that Herod chose him. Yet their willingness to serve is evidence that all pious Jews were not united against Herod, and that some, including the more perfect, were convinced that their faith and their race could prosper by co-operating with one commonly execrated as a foreign slave and upstart.

As vice-president, he selected the beloved Essene, Manahem.

Hillel rapidly reorganized the sanhedrin, exacting of its members acquiescence to his basic principle, "What is unpleasant to thee, do not unto others; this is the entire Law; all the rest is but commentary upon it."

The country, superficially at least well governed and peaceful, and the worst exigencies provided against, Herod started for Rhodes.

Octavius, the factional leader, is usually overlooked in a consideration of Caesar Augustus, first and greatest of Roman emperors, a resplendent monarch who established the Augustan age, graced by literary luminaries like Virgil, Horace, Livy, Seneca, and Pliny the Elder: an age when universal peace, the Pax Romana, spread sheltering wings across the known world; where paved roads ran smoothly from Italy and Germany and viaducts and bridges criss-crossed France and the Iberian peninsula; where stout walls held at bay the savage Celt in his misty hills; where the thirsty traveler slaked his thirst at Roman wells in Saharan oases and safely went his desert way under the protection of the imperial aegis; when, in a word, Rome was the noblest, most powerful, most luxurious municipality ever envisioned by man. Such truly was the land and time of Caesar Augustus, who, retaining the wasted shell of republic, propped it up with beams of empire; who dismissed a servile, senile senate, and replaced it with the rule of the strong man, maintained by the swords of the Roman legion.

But it was Octavius the factionist, whose evolution into the august Caesar was still in its embryonic stage, before whom Herod had to plead.

Frankly, there was little of the superman either in the appearance or in the reputation of the person who held his temporary court at Rhodes. Octavius was unimposing, short, almost dumpy in appearance. His features were regular, might even have been handsome had they not been marred by a sallow complexion, pimply skin, and decayed teeth. A chronic sufferer from colds in the head, he was cursed by a running nose and fits of sneezing. In person he was not clean; in fact, he had an almost feline dislike of bathing in any form.

Nor was there a compensating magnificence in his attire, which was shoddy, poorly fitting. Before his marriage, his mother and sister had made his clothes. Now, henpecked by his malicious mate Livia, he exercised household authority only to the extent that she begrudgingly plied her needle, and perhaps obtained her revenge in the secret amusement which his ill-clad appearance invariably occasioned.

He was absolutely without personal magnetism; he had only a modicum of generalship; he had the unhappy faculty of making most men immediately dislike him. If Herod is excoriated for the execution of Hyrcanus, let it be remembered that Octavius consented to the murder of his preceptor and friend Cicero, whom he called "father" with what seemed honest affection. Because of the number of brutal killings instigated by him, he earned the nickname "Executioner." Roman parents feared and detested him for his habit of snatching very young girls indiscriminately of patrician or plebeian origin, to sate his lust.

In one sense, even his reaching the pinnacle of power, whence no venturesome hand seemed anxious to pluck him down, might be attributed to the fact that he was the only really important surviving factionist. Since the almost forgotten Gallic invasion, Rome, while secure from foreign aggression, had had her coasts assailed, her countryside denuded, and her citizens butchered, in one Roman invasion after another. For some sixty years, begin-

ning with the class warfare between Marius and Sulla, Roman
blood had been wasted by other Romans. Pompey ruled his
brief moment and was slain in the sanguinary war with Julius
Caesar. Julius himself died with the daggers of Brutus and
Cassius in his heart. By suicide, this bloody pair cheated Octavius
and Antony of their revenge. Even vast Rome was too confined
for the limitless greed of these factionists until Antony foolishly
flung aside his chance for victory at Actium.

Now only Octavius survived; there was no rival worthy his
mettle in sight; and the Roman people, sick of six decades of
killing one another, were determined to prevent further rivalry,
even if the alternative meant complete submission to Octavius.

On the credit side of Octavius' ledger, it should be noted that
with all his many deficiencies he was an able statesman, with the
faculty of discovering client rulers and other subordinates who
would, for a price, be loyal to him, and with the knack of im-
parting to them the assurance that their efforts would be supported and their accomplishments appreciated. (Four of these
rulers might, in passing, be mentioned: Herod, Amyntas of
Galatea, Archelaus of Cappadocia, and Polemo of Pontus, all of
whom, except Amyntas, who died young, had long and prosperous reigns.) Moreover, the later Octavius—the Caesar Augustus—
was, if we credit Suetonius, abiding in his friendships and never
unreasonable or ungrateful to those who tried to serve him.

On his way, Herod rehearsed not only his manner of approach
but every word, every syllable, every inflection of the plea he
would make before Octavius. Abject submission, he knew, would
be unavailing. Rome had no place for failures or cowards. Bribes
and gifts, too, would be useless. These the hardheaded Roman
would consider an attempt to purchase power that would be mis-
used, or reparation for power that had been abused. Only in the
manly, direct approach, supported by pithy words—Octavius was
notably impatient with flowery address—was there any hope.

Herod's ship sailed into the harbor of Rhodes, moored a discreet distance but not too timorously afar from the Roman
galleys, and the king slipped ashore to learn his fate.

With little formality he was ushered into the presence of
Octavius, whose sniffling and sneezing happily abated in the
balmy, island sunshine. Before a word was spoken the king

removed his diadem, a felicitous gesture of acknowledgment that, while both Antony and Octavius had granted him the right to wear it, Antony's defeat now rendered that decree invalid. The implication was not lost on the statesmanlike Roman. He nodded permission for the king to speak.

Herod's speech was candor itself. He freely admitted himself a partisan and friend of Antony's. True, he had not been at Actium, but that was only because Antony had ordered him to fight the Arabs instead. He, moreover, did what he could to help his patron by sending him gold and grain, and he would gladly, out of friendship and gratitude, have done much more. "For (the account is Josephus') if a man own himself to be another's friend, and know him to be a benefactor, he is obliged to hazard everything, to use every faculty of his soul, every member of his body, and all the wealth he hath, for him; in which I confess I have been too deficient. However, I am conscious to myself that so far I have done right, that I have not deserted him upon his defeat at Actium, nor upon the evident change of his fortune transferred my hopes from him to another; but have preserved myself, not as a valuable fellow-soldier, yet certainly as a faithful counselor to Antony when I demonstrated to him that the only way he had to save himself, and not to lose all his authority, was to slay Cleopatra, for when she was once dead there would be room for him to retain his authority; and rather to bring thee to make composition with him, than to continue at enmity any longer.

"He, however, would not attend to my advice, but preferred his own rash resolutions, which have happened unprofitably for him, but profitably for thee. Now, therefore, in case thou determinest about me, and my alacrity in serving Antony, according to thy anger at him, I own there is no room for me to deny what I have done, nor will I be ashamed to own, and that publicly too, that I had a great kindness for him. But if thou wilt put him out of thy case, and only examine how I behave myself to my benefactors in general, and what a sort of friend I am, thou wilt find by experience that I shall do and be the same to thyself. For it is but changing the names; and the firmness of friendship that I shall bear to thee will not be disapproved by thee."

Octavius' response was immediate and sensible. He was fast

learning to think in terms of benefit to empire instead of personal
revenge. He would need men, loyal, courageous, and able, like
Herod. With his own hands he replaced the diadem on Herod's
head. His words were gracious and reassuring: "Thou shalt not
only be in safety, but shalt be a king: and that more firmly than
thou wert before. For thou art worthy to reign over a great many
subjects by reason of the sincerity of thy friendship. And do thou
endeavor to be equally constant in thy friendship to me, upon my
good success, which is what I depend upon from the generosity
of thy disposition. However, Antony hath done well in preferring
Cleopatra to thee, for by this means we have gained thee by her
madness. And thus thou hast begun to be my friend before I
began to be thine. On which account Quintus Didius hath
written to me that thou sendest him assistance against the
gladiators."

(Hordes of brutal gladiators bound for the celebration of
Antony's anticipated triumph at Actium had been held in check
by the Legate of Syria, aided by Herod's forces. It might be added
that Herod's purpose was to keep the gladiators out of Judea,
rather than to help Octavius.)

"I do therefore assure thee that I will confirm the kingdom to
thee by a decree. I shall also endeavor to do thee some further
kindnesses hereafter, that thou mayest find no loss in the want of
Antony."

The "further kindnesses" were not long in coming. All of
Palestine that Cleopatra had ruled plus Samaria, and the coastal
area except Ascalon, were added to Herod's kingdom. Doubtless
he took the greatest personal satisfaction in the restoration of the
balsam groves and in the acquisition of the four hundred Galatians who had been the Egyptian queen's body guard.

Octavius' protestations of friendship were unquestionably sincere. Thereafter only Agrippa and Maecenas were closer to the
emperor than the erstwhile Antonian partisan.

Shrewdly, Herod lost no time in justifying Octavius' good
opinion. He presented him with eight hundred talents; he gave
him a body guard of one hundred and fifty magnificently accoutered troops; he outfitted a Roman army, ignorant of the

desert terrain it had to traverse, with stores of water and wine without which it would have perished.

So, by the time Herod was ready to return to Judea, he was firmly established in the good opinion of his new patron.

For the first time in Herod's life, his personal safety, his throne, and the succession of his children were really secure. With a solid, dependable patron in place of Antony of the exacting demands and volatile moods intensified by Cleopatra's hatred, he felt he could now devote all his energy to attaining happiness for himself and peaceful prosperity for his people. Elated beyond expression, he rode through Jerusalem at the head of his cavalcade.

It was no jubilant capital that greeted its returning hero. The streets were strangely bare. What stray citizens were not indoors followed the procession with covert glares and muted imprecations.

But Herod did not seem to be disturbed. He could still rule a surly kingdom well, and drink his fill of happiness in a loving family and court.

As he ascended the snowy, marble steps that led from the north of the Temple to his palace, he found a little familiar group awaiting him. Pheroras was there, obviously relieved now that he could retransmit the onerous duties of regency; Salome, with a triumphant grin; Cyprus toothlessly cackling her joy; Costobar smiling without warmth; his older boys hopping with excitement; Joseph, his face a mask that betrayed nothing; Sohemus, trying to seem happy, but strangely ill at ease; Alexandra, in the background, glowering.

These Herod took in at a glance, their varying emotions imprinted on his retentive mind for subsequent analysis and interpretation. But he brushed past them to throw his arms about Mariamne.

She responded to his embrace with stiffened body and averted face. Her reaction was worse than a blow. The blissful future he had constructed during the seemingly endless journey home toppled into dusty shards of persistent doubts and vain hopes.

Yet he gave no indication of his cruel disappointment. Briefly
he expressed his joy at his restoration to his family and friends,
thanked them for their loyalty and efficiency during his absence,
and promised to render a complete account of his experiences at
a state dinner that same evening.

The banquet, elaborate as only the East can provide, passed
perfunctorily. It was, after all, but the prelude to Herod's all-
important report.

Leaning on his couch, eyes fixed on a goblet his hand was
slowly turning, he began to speak. It was as he had promised, an
official account of the results of the meeting with Octavius. More
immediately, it was a direct plea to Mariamne. With the warmth
of the born orator he reviewed the unhappy episodes of the past;
he touched with loving pity on the fate of the boy high priest;
he spoke with convincing regret on the necessity of removing
Hyrcanus. But all that was in the dismal, uncertain past. His
restless hand put down the goblet; his face turned toward his
wife. As he visualized a future filled with achievement and
joy, his voice caught a brighter, more ardent quality. With
Caesar's friendship his own efforts, loyally seconded by his family
and friends, were certain to bring prosperity to his country and
tranquility and happiness to himself.

A murmur of approval ran about the table. He touched
Mariamne on the sleeve. She drew away, imperceptibly to all
but him, and whispered some commonplace to her mother. Both
smiled. Almost gruffly, Herod strode from the banquet hall.

That Mariamne thrust aside a real opportunity for lasting
reconciliation is unquestionable. Had she for one instant forgotten her Hasmonean pride, had she determined to put the past
out of her judgment and evaluate her husband on his present and
future conduct, Herod's fits of madness might never again have
been stimulated; by a reasonable and glorious reign he might
have had the opportunity of atoning for the past and making
them both happy.

But pride was her besetting sin; compromise and forgiveness
were the virtues farthest from her make-up. That her husband
loved her deeply and idolized her children she must have felt;
that the terrible trials he had undergone and that the various

facets of his affection might express themselves in startling and inexplicable ways she would not concede.

Herod passed from the banquet hall to the portico overlooking Jerusalem. Black and brooding, with sickly pinpoints of light shuddering in the choking darkness, it lay below him like a sullen sea, restless and threatening beneath its murky surface. Dirty gray hanks of cloud brushed aside a protesting sliver of moon; dull, disturbing echoes from the lower depths made an uneasy diapason for discordant shrieks of unseen night birds. A chill, not altogether that of the piercing night air, made him shiver. Slowly, quietly he made his way to the royal quarters.

Mariamne was waiting for him in tearless fury. A torrent of invective gushed from her lips. She called him "murderer," "unnatural brute," "monster." Dazed by her violence, he did not know what to do. Humbly he begged her forgiveness for the past, abjectly promised to do her will—anything, to regain her love.

Still Mariamne was hardened in her pride. Stubbornly she rejected every overture, spurned every attempt at reconciliation.

At times, Herod's humility gave way to a desperate suspicion. She could not so despise him unless she had given her affection to another. Yet he quietly accepted every slight and rudeness in the hope that her attitude might change, her love reawaken.

Thus miserably almost a year passed before the climax came. Passing through the royal chamber in the still heat of the Judean siesta, Mariamne in the semidarkness brushed by the recumbent form of the king. In an uncontrollable burst of affection, he grasped her arm and attempted to pull her to his side. Startled by the unexpected presence, she struck wildly at the face of the king. He released her, dazed and hurt.

The enervating heat, the nervous shock wrenched open the floodgates of her vituperation. Every harbored grievance engulfed the shocked ears of the king; the murder of her kinsman, the mocking politeness and open scorn she suffered from his family, her regret that Octavius had not killed him, and, in a final reckless burst, her admission that she knew of Sohemus' orders to kill her. Almost sputtering with hatred, she rushed from the room into the blinding, stifling sunlight of the courtyard.

A fit akin to madness seized Herod. He sobbed in his fury, tore his robe into rags, staggered about the palace, almost naked, mumbling incoherent threats.

With the return to partial sanity he reached a terrible conclusion. Even though similar suspicions on a previous occasion had not been justified, this time he was certain of Mariamne's infidelity. Sohemus was a handsome soldier who had befouled his queen and made a cuckold of the king who trusted him.

Of one fact, he would make certain. Neither Sohemus nor the queen's attendants who must have known of her sin would live to gossip or gloat over his dishonor. Speedily he summoned his council. Sentence of death was passed, not only on Sohemus but on every servant who was in any way attached to the queen's person. The dungeon gates clanged on the unfortunate group. At the king's pleasure, they would be executed.

The case of Sohemus is a peculiar one. For many years he had been Herod's trusted guardian and companion in battle. Veteran of a score of campaigns, in his conduct he had been so conspicuous for fidelity that to him Herod entrusted the secret orders to kill Mariamne if he did not return. Despite his real attachment to Herod there was still in Sohemus a streak of the wily desert Semite. Petulant over her separation from her children, and aware of the trust her husband reposed in him, Mariamne with quiet persistence and studied innocence began to question what were the king's orders, in case his errand culminated disastrously. At first, loyal to his pledge of secrecy, Sohemus pleaded ignorance, or gave evasive answers. Then gradually it entered his not over-subtle mind that the friendship of the queen might be his salvation if the king was executed. Accordingly he whispered the tale of his horrible commission.

As a reward, Mariamne, shortly after Herod's return, requested for him a position in the king's cabinet as merited by loyalty and solicitude. Under other circumstances Herod might have declined to find a place for the mediocre mind of Sohemus in a council marked for brilliance. But it was the only favor Mariamne asked, the sole indication that she was willing to use her position as wife to influence a husband desperately hungry for her love. Herod happily granted her request—a fatal gift for

Sohemus when Herod recalled the circumstances of its bestowal.

Now Mariamne was provided with a new staff of attendants, every one a spy of Herod's. Afire with blinding headaches he avoided the queen, trying to find relief so that he might calmly consider the situation and find some satisfactory solution.

His wish for solitude was not respected. Constantly Salome was by his side, goading him with the charge that Mariamne was an adulteress, a traitress, who never loved him and used him only to sire a Hasmonean line of rulers. When, in fury, he ejected his sister, his mother would take her place, recalling old scandals and lies, wrung from the queen's former attendants frantically striving to purchase their lives.

So all day long the king's ears were assailed; all through the endless, sleepless night his brain was pricked with wavering accusations and imaginings that always at length focused on one object, the unfaithfulness of the queen.

Salome was too crafty to rely on the permanence of the king's anger and Mariamne's stubborn pride. The royal pair had been estranged and reconciled before. If another reconciliation were to take place, there would be little possibility of again sowing discord between them. Therefore she determined to take steps finally to destroy Mariamne.

Her plan was viciously clever. The king's cupbearer, carefully coached by her, went in to Herod. Rapidly and uneasily he told his tale.

"The queen, sire, has been most generous to your slave. She has also ordered me to offer you a love potion prepared by the queen's eunuch. Since I did not know how it might affect Your Highness, I humbly ask your permission before presenting this beverage to you."

Trembling, he backed away, as insane rage gripped Herod.

"Send the queen's eunuch to me at once."

The poor wretch, the one servant still faithful to her, pleaded complete ignorance. He was immediately put to the torture, but in all his agony there was nothing damaging to Mariamne that he could disclose except what Herod already knew, that the queen's hatred resulted from something that Sohemus had disclosed to her.

Herod burst into a tantrum of fury. Sohemus, he shrieked, would not have sold his loyalty and decency unless at the price of Mariamne's virtue.

Led blinking from the dungeon, Sohemus and the queen's attendants were executed.

That same day, Mariamne was formally brought to trial for adultery, treason, and attempted regicide. But not before the sanhedrin. Under Hillel this council had developed into a sane, reasonable body that would refuse to consider silly charges like those of Herod.

Instead, he established a jury of his own followers.

The trial began, a disquieting spectacle of a manly, loving king flinging the vilest accusations against a beautiful and virtuous queen, before a jury uneasy, unqualified, and subservient.

The king's charge was incoherent: a conglomeration of love potions, servants under torture, familiar malice, and unrestrained spite. Never did he seem so weak, so foolish, so pitiful as when he gasped the formless charges; never did Mariamne appear more queenly, more proud, more innocent than as she listened with eyes unafraid to the incomprehensible lies from the man who loved her so terribly.

Commanded to bring in a conviction, the jury declared her guilty, and passed the sentence of death to be carried out at a time designated by the king.

Sobered by the verdict, Herod shrank from naming the date for execution. Instead, on the private advice of the jury, he determined to place her for the time being in a fortress, in not too restraining confinement.

With an affectionate message, Mariamne might still have won a reconciliation with her husband, moodily hoping for just such a word. But the spies surrounding her could bring him only the unvarying report. She was unrepentant, irreconcilable; she was not afraid of death; she spurned the little amenities with which he strove to make her confinement more bearable, and on every opportunity expressed her loathing for the king.

The continual imprisonment of the queen began to have a disturbing influence on the people. In every part of the kingdom they were rallying about her. As yet there was no open rebellion,

but rather a sullen resentment that momentarily might explode
into action. Obviously only their reconciliation or her death
could restore normal conditions.

Salome and her friends were determined on death. Ceaselessly
they tortured him with fresh evidence of her recalcitrant spirit,
of her obdurate hatred, of the threat to public peace if she lived
and the danger of forfeiting Caesar Augustus' good opinion if
she provoked a rebellion.

At length, weary and sick, he named the day for her execution.

Almost joyfully, Mariamne heard the order; proudly she
walked before the people to hear her sentence and be slain.

There are few scenes in history more nauseating than Alexandra's reaction to her daughter's doom. As Mariamne, quietly
resigned, softer and sweeter at the hour of death, with all the
turmoil and tragedy of life irrevocably behind her, was preparing
herself for the executioner's stroke, her mother sprang out from
the weeping crowd. Hysterically she upbraided the queen for
her insolence and ingratitude to the king who was their common
benefactor and the father of their nation. Yanking her hair and
ripping her garments, she called upon the spectators to bear
witness to the nature of her daughter and the patience and justice of Herod, who, against his generous nature and warm affection, was forced to execute this vile adulteress for her evil deeds.

Mariamne turned her back on her mother. With a pitiable
little gesture she signalled to the bewildered executioner. The
headsman's ax fell mechanically, with the furious old beldame
still ranting at the crowd that all but trampled one another in
their effort to thrust the loathsome scene from their eyes and ears.

(Soon, perhaps out of shame for the despicable role played
by the only surviving Hasmonean, an account of Mariamne's
death, a rather clever dovetailing of a story from the Book of
Maccabees and the familiar account of the preservation of Alexander the Great's body in honey at Alexandria, was circulated,
that has persisted in Jewish tradition to this day. According to
this legend, instead of Mariamne's mounting the scaffold, she
eluded her guards and fled to the roof of the palace. From this
vantage point she addressed the packed crowd below, asserting
that she was the last of the Maccabees, who unfortunately was

linked to an Idumean upstart and slave. When about to be apprehended, she flung herself to the pavement. Herod, thereupon, had the shattered body preserved in honey and kept constantly in his own chamber.)

Herod, in his palace, was presented the report that his justice had been carried out. It might as well have been handed to a dead man. For two days he sat, insensible to everything. Salome and his mother wisely kept away; Alexandra was roughly thrust aside when she attempted to see him.

On the third day, the full horror of what he had done swept over the king. Screams of "Mariamne! Mariamne!" shrilled through the palace halls. Guards stared ahead, uncertain as to how to act with this madman. Spies pressed their uneasy bodies into the folds of the arras, hoping, unseen, to escape the fury that their actions had helped bring about.

Unquestionably, Herod was for a time insane. He sent for Mariamne's attendants, to request her presence; he implored his children to persuade their mother to come to him; he sent gifts to her prison, and hourly inquired for her health.

Every attempt was made to bring the king out of his mad mood. Feasts were proclaimed and assemblies called. But the sight of Herod at banquet, carrying on a conversation with the queen's vacant couch by his side, or ordering a messenger to ascertain her opinion before committing himself on a problem, only aggravated the concern of his friends and increased popular clamor.

Coincidentally, a pestilence—a perennial event in the slums of Jerusalem—spread into sections of the kingdom generally immune. In this the people generally, as well as the king, saw the avenging hand of God.

Herod fled to the wastes, ostensibly to hunt.

But he killed nothing. Wild beasts, slinking away, heard an even wilder voice shout "Mariamne" to the unheeding desert; barren cliffs recoiled with the familiar wail; cold stars blinked sightlessly at the strange figure that clawed and clutched at the resistless sands.

His attendants found him violently ill, blinded with an incessant pain at the back of his head. They carried him to Samaria, hoping that the friendly atmosphere might effect a cure.

Since medicines and diets proved unavailing, his doctors prescribed that he eat and do as he pleased.

Their prescription was not unsuccessful. His physical strength returned; his mind relapsed only occasionally. But in his soul there was always the searing image of Mariamne, the soft bride of Samaria, the joyful mother of his brood, the proud queen by his side, the victim that his suspicion had sacrificed, the restless, ever-present ghost that he never could expel.

CHAPTER XIV

BREAD AND CIRCUSES

DURING THE FIVE-YEAR PERIOD (29–24 B.C.) following the death of Mariamne, Herod, King of the Jews, gradually evolved into the Herod, friend of Rome and tyrannical foe of every national aspiration, who is depicted in Scripture. Where there had been irregularly recurring periods of madness, he would henceforth never be far from the border of insanity; with increasing regularity he would hurl himself over that border; and longer and more violent would be his tenancy in that deplorable state.

As he lay slowly recovering at Samaria, he fought with all the vigor and determination of a monstrously strong spirit to throw off the harrowing memory of his failure as a husband. But the recollection of Mariamne was too deeply ingrained. His despairing efforts to forget her only made her image the more vivid and lasting.

His remorse made him bitter. Originally endowed with a disposition generous by nature, and a purpose bent on making his subjects happy, he became hard and cruel. Because in him there was no room for peace and happiness, he would compel those responsible for and contributory to his anguish to share that suffering.

He would hate and persecute his enemies and false friends. But he would never deviate from his policy of being a ruler of whom Rome might be proud, and of bestowing upon his complaisant subjects a tenure of peace and prosperity.

He established the premise that he must consider himself no longer as a Jewish king, but as a Roman administrator; Judea, not as a national state, but as a Roman province.

From this principle he never deviated. Never once, however violent his fits of insanity, however ruthless his actions towards individuals, was his value as a Roman ally called into question, excepting on the solitary occasion when Caesar himself was deluded.

While these determinations were slowly and laboriously taking form in the weakened body and harassed mind of the king, Alexandra made her last, desperate bid for power. If she could gain possession of two fortresses, one commanding the capital itself, the other the Temple, she could reasonably expect to control Jerusalem and defy Herod.

Her plot had the one advantage of simplicity.

From the Temple fortress she could prevent the offering of sacrifice, a catastrophe the Jews would want to avoid at all costs. Pledging allegiance to her would be a small price, indeed, to pay for the privilege of continuing the ancient sacrifice.

Then with the fortress of Jerusalem itself in her possession, Herod would hesitate to risk his newly and hardly acquired favor with Augustus by confessing the necessity of laying siege to his own capital city.

The entire scheme reeked with blackmail. A saner, more decent reasoning process would have demonstrated that its only chance for success lay in the possibility of her conniving with creatures as debased as herself.

She summoned the commanders of the forts and presented her project with a degree of guile and arrogance undiminished by her fall from power. If Herod died, she reasoned, or went completely insane—neither contingency improbable—it would be well to hold these fortresses in trust for Herod's children, rather than to let some usurper seize them.

Or if Herod should recover, he would necessarily have to come to terms with her, and thus again assure the permanency of Hasmonean rule through her regency until Mariamne's children were of age.

Her arguments might have been effective but for two things:

all of the commanders were loyal to Herod and they despised Alexandra.

Stilling her suspicions with encouraging but essentially non-committal responses, they immediately sent an account of their interview to Herod. He uttered the brief command "Kill her," and Alexandra perished on the scaffold. Her last thought as she scanned the few faintly interested spectators must have been the tragic realization that her death hardly stirred a ripple on the surface of Jewish national emotion.

Her life had been one tireless, ineffective struggle to rule. She had seen her husband slain, her brother-in-law ignominiously executed. In her intrigue with Cleopatra she would willingly have bartered the virtue of her son and the chastity of her daughter; as a result of her plotting she had caused the murder of her handsome, gifted son and the execution of her aged father; her unbridled ambition had not stopped at reviling her innocent daughter on the scaffold with the vilest accusations.

She was a fanatical nationalist. Like her grandmother, the other Alexandra, she sought to establish a matriarchal dynasty. But she was essentially amoral, a hateful, meddling mischief-maker whose death—too long deferred—caused no regret but only a shameful realization of the depths of degradation to which the last descendant of a noble line had plunged herself.

Her execution was a sort of tonic for Herod. Still wan and miserable, but with renewed ambition, he returned to Jerusalem.

His first official act was characteristic of the new despotic Herod. The sniveling sycophants who had condemned Mariamne to death were summarily killed; they were reminders of a past that Herod was still trying to erase from his memory.

As always it was the bickerings and recriminations in his own household that gave him no peace nor rest. Salome, an amorous grandmother, had grown tired of Costobar and was having an affair with a certain suave Hellene named Alexas. Had Costobar, with his predecessor Joseph's fate in mind, been more tactful, he would quietly have divorced his waspish mate, and buried himself quietly somewhere in Idumea.

But he was a kind of Near-Eastern Pooh-Bah, conceited and snobbish, with the fatal facility of airing an assumed superiority before his wife's family. Never would he let them forget that whereas Herod's ancestors were mere Idumean chieftains, he was a lineal descendant of the priests of the Koze (an idol of the Idumeans before turning to Judaism), which made him a sort of minor deity. To be inferior in rank to Herod and to live under the shrewish domination of Herod's sister was galling to his pride, and he missed no opportunity of showing his chagrin.

Some years before, as governor of Idumea, he had almost blundered into disaster. To him the imposition of Jewish rule and manners on Idumeans, whose culture he held to be more ancient, was unbearable, almost as repugnant, in fact, as that he, an Idumean of the highest nobility, should take orders from a compatriot of lesser rank, who had abandoned the land of his forbears for Judea. Like Alexandra, he intrigued with Cleopatra, in the expectation that if Antony gave her Idumea he would be appointed its ruler. Yet while he carried on this intrigue, his mercenary spirit in his own land was shameless. No graft was too petty, no extortion too exorbitant for his grasping fingers.

But, as history shows, Antony did not give Cleopatra Idumea. Costobar's plotting was uncovered, and only Salome's plea saved him from the block.

Now his charms had waned; the star of Alexas was in the ascendancy. Reversing the Jewish law which permitted only the husband to divorce his wife, Salome sent Costobar a bill of divorcement, at which action Costobar took no pains to hide his relief.

Herod, informed of this affair by his spies, whose number and efficiency had tremendously increased since his return to the capital, was not displeased at his sister's action. Costobar he had never considered attractive or likable. He had found him valuable only in performing his less pleasant errands. There were others, not allied by past association, to whom he would prefer to entrust these duties in the future.

It was then no surprise when Salome came to him. Half-apologetically she admitted that her divorce was counter to Jewish law. But how could she continue to live with a criminal who was plotting the king's death? Unimpressed by her demure demeanor, Herod insisted on details. The details were vague; she had been unable to discover particulars, but she knew Costobar's friends Lysimachus, Antipater, and Dosithius were implicated.

Herod was familiar with the hatred and the spitefulness of his sister. There was to be a meeting of his council, he told her. Later, if she were able to produce more detailed information, he would investigate.

She grasped his shoulder as he turned away. Admittedly she could give only scanty details of this conspiracy. But she knew intimately of another crime, which would convince the king of the type of man she was accusing.

The story went back twelve years to the capture of Jerusalem. Costobar, assigned the unpleasant task of apprehending refugees, had, in general, carried out his bloody commission most thoroughly. He had, however, she informed Herod, let escape two important refugees, the Bene-Baba, or sons of Baba, members of an influential collateral branch of the Hasmoneans. More than that, he had secreted them from the searching revenge of Herod, who was particularly anxious to do away with these potential leaders of a popular uprising. When rumors of Costobar's lack of trust then reached the king's ears, the Idumean vehemently asserted his innocence, and the king's subsequent efforts to find the refugees were unavailing.

This story of deception and guile Costobar had confided to her. And she, unwilling to send her husband to certain death, had kept it from her brother's knowledge until this new threat to the king's life compelled her to speak.

The reason for Costobar's strange clemency is not hard to divine. His mind was always subtle; his ways always devious. Should there ever be a successful revolt, he would be specially marked for revenge unless Jews of unimpeachable integrity and great influence came to his aid. Besides, should Herod die, naturally or otherwise, the taint of the gentile in his offspring might be less desirable to the Jews than the unmixed Hasmonean blood of the Bene-Baba. So by saving and harboring the sons of Baba, he felt both his position and his life were safe, even though Herod fell.

But in amorous boasting he lost his subtlety.

Now with his associates he was thrown into prison under sentence of death. A military guard proceeded to their hide-out and hauled the bewildered Bene-Baba from their refuge. To make certain they would not again escape, Herod personally witnessed their execution.

Their death cast a pall upon the Jewish people. The victims were unambitious, unworldly; daily, except on the feast of the Great Atonement, they prayed for those whom they might unwittingly have offended. They represented the noble, unpolitical type of Jew. Their destruction brought with crushing conviction the realization that there was on the throne a new, pitiless Herod, from whom the common people could expect at best only an unquiet peace and measured competence.

With Costobar and Alexandra disposed of, and the sons of Baba dead, the last personal links with a Jewish past were broken and Herod felt free to establish a new Judean order, culturally Hellenic and politically Roman.

He began by renovating his palace in Jerusalem, to change or destroy every familiar memorial of its past.

The palace, originally built by Simon and enlarged by his son John Hyrcanus, even in that day (139 B.C.) excited the indignant envy of the ambassador of Antiochus at its display of gold and silver and its general sumptuousness. Under Herod's guiding genius, it became almost unbelievably ornate. Situated high above the city, amid extensive gardens and pleasure walks, its general form was that of two spacious marble wings built about an enormous central hall capable of holding one hundred dining divans for state banquets. Since the Jews contributed little to architecture, its construction was basically Greek, the furnishings being luxuriously oriental.

Josephus freely admits that his vocabulary is inadequate to do justice to the beauty and spaciousness of the almost endless succession of rooms. Everywhere were the richest furniture and choicest ornaments; even common utensils and vessels were silver or gold. The ceilings were high and exquisitely embellished; the floors were mosaics of rare stones cunningly patterned. In each room attention was focused on some one article or ornament of striking artistic merit, so that mere lavishness never intruded upon art. Rooms unexpectedly opened into porticos or walks in the form of open courts sustained by pillars of multicolored Italian marble. Lest the eye be surfeited with man-made art, there were groves of flowering shrubs and shade trees whence the songs of birds trilled above the ceaseless ripple of bronze fountains.

Mariamne's quarters were transformed into a cloistered harem, with as yet no occupant except flabby, bored eunuchs. Scores of servants, all skilled in the art of providing luxurious comfort, hovered about, chief among them a barber, whose principal function it was to blacken the beard and hair of Herod, in which the king took an almost feminine pride and whose incipient grayness filled him with alarm. Soothsayers and fortune tellers were there, testifying to the un-Hebraic atmosphere of the palace, rubbing elbows with spies, informers, and diplomats. Everywhere were stolid guards—incorruptible Germans, Thracians and Galatians.

Enclosing the palace grounds was a wall thirty-five feet high, with towers at strategic points, to assure safety and privacy.

Meanwhile Herod reorganized the army into an entirely mercenary unit. Special groups were formed of Celts, Thracians, Greeks, and Germans, as well as mixed groups of various nationalities. Palestinian Jews were strictly barred, but Babylonian and other Jews, though sneered at as "proselytes of the king's table," found it profitable to enlist.

All Palestine was organized for defense or offense as a Roman outpost. A ring of fortifications, accessible to one another and to central base fortresses, was constructed about the borders of the country, chief among them Jericho, at Antipatris on the plain of Sharon, at Cypros, Phasaelis north of Jerusalem, and Herodium in the mountains adjacent to Arabia.

To pacify the border country constantly raided by Arabs and other Semitic irreconcilables, Herod devised a system of settlement not greatly unlike that practiced in the early days of our own West. Military colonies—settlers aided by the government and protected by troops—were sent into fertile regions along the borders. As they established their homes and attracted other settlers, they soon became too strong and the region too civilized to encourage raiders, who were driven further into the wilderness. By this system, Herod gradually disposed of excess population in the crowded centers, opened new sources of profit and taxation, and rendered a large army unnecessary.

Officially he no longer called himself "King of the Jews" but "Friend of the Emperor" and "Friend of the Romans." His subordinates were known by the Hellenistic court titles of "kinsmen," "comrades," and "friends."

Of his older counselors, only his Rothschild, the banker Saramalla, retained his post. The rest were supplanted by Greeks like Nicolaus of Damascus, Herod's official historian, whose one hundred and forty-four books (now lost) are the basis of Josephus' account of Herod. Other figures of rising importance were Nicolaus' brother Ptolemy, Herod's adviser and administrator, the Greek Andromachus and the Roman Gemellus, tutors of Mariamne's sons, and the Greek rhetorician Ireneus.

The sanhedrin—no doubt to the relief of its members—was restricted to jurisdiction in religious matters. Its former judicial and political functions were allocated to a newly-formed private council, the "synedrion," composed exclusively of Hellenes and Hellenistic Jews.

Greek became the official language of the court; on coinage, legends in Hebrew were replaced by Greek.

For some ten years Herod was to consume his energy and to try to banish his unhappiness with building. In this policy he was also carrying out the wishes of the emperor and his adviser Agrippa. All over the Empire lesser kings were competing with one another in building streets, canals, harbors, aqueducts, temples, arenas, and theaters. But none of them could even remotely rival the achievements of Herod. Born architect and expansionist to begin with, by lack of domestic happiness and by remorse for Mariamne he was driven on unremittingly in his design to Romanize and denationalize Judea. This design grew into a cultural intoxication for what was pagan and Roman, in which was effaced his former interest in Jewish nationalism and monotheism. The thought of a personal, just Yahweh was repugnant; he became horrified at the idea that a Redeemer might topple over his Roman structure.

After the completion of his palace, Herod began work on a gymnastic amphitheater beyond the walls of Jerusalem and a theater almost in the shadow of the Temple. Public buildings of this type marked Roman progress everywhere, but their erection horrified the Jews.

Yet in his building of the gymnasium, at least, they could hardly accuse Herod of establishing a precedent. Under their own high priest Jason the less devout Jewish youths took passionately to athletics, "liking the glory of the Grecians best of all." The high priest Menelaus even sent a Jewish team to compete at Tyre, where athletic games were being held in honor of the god Baal, known by his newer title Hercules. For some years priests and people visited the gymnasium daily, while sacrifice at the Temple was neglected. But all this was part of a shameful past that sincere Jews did not want to recall.

As the amphitheater rapidly took shape, a sense of foreboding grew. This building without the walls was but the first step. What act of desecration would the tyrant think of next?

Tales were whispered to shuddering listeners of the cruel pastimes they would be expected to witness: of the bone-crushing naked wrestlers, the Herculean boxers wielding their lethal cestus-covered fists, the shrieking slaves and criminals consigned to the maws of savage beasts, the deadly duels between gladiators, the whole brutalizing display. Rabbis, sullenly wagging their heads, recalled how the Jews had been punished in the past when Jason and his successors "built a place of exercises at Jerusalem according to the customs of the heathen."

Could they restrain the Jews from committing the sin of their forbears? Would their young men be satisfied with the shrill voice of the silver Temple trumpets when they could listen to the sweetest of Greek singers at the amphitheater? Would the blood of sacrificial offerings rilling down the runnels to the Brook Kedron thrill them like the spilling of gladiatoral gore?

In 25 B.C. Herod announced the establishment of the Actian games, a quinquennial athletic and musical celebration in honor of Augustus. Jews and gentiles were invited to compete for prizes—not merely the traditional Olympic laurel wreath, but gold, and jewels, and money, to procure the finest talent in the world. Soon Greek and other non-Jewish athletes and musicians flocked to Jerusalem, swaggering about the streets, disdainfully jostling in their path Jewish residents, who generally were only too anxious to draw away from their polluting touch.

Naturally the natives decried the outrageous paganism of the games and the undisguised sensualism of the candidates. Yet they were in a dilemma. If they participated they lowered themselves to the level of non-Jews in contests essentially abhorrent to their ideals. Still there was a growing feeling that the strength, and skill, and courage of Jewish manhood were being challenged. Not to take up that challenge would be counted an admission of racial inferiority. Tales of their ineptitude and pusillanimity would be carried to every corner of the Empire. Jews scattered throughout the Roman Empire would be shamed, because the Jew in the homeland was unwilling or afraid to compete with the gentile.

The more sober, particularly the older Jews, remained at home where possible, willing to leave the streets to the strutting invaders until the games were over.

The more hot-blooded of the younger Jews were, however, incapable of practicing such self-restraint. Brawls became frequent; clashes were daily broken up by Herod's troops, who invariably ruled the Jews the aggressors.

A party of Jews decided to enter a Jewish team, of course without the sanction of their elders.

Unfortunately they were feebly equipped for the heroic task they assigned themselves. Jews made splendid soldiers and courageous patriots. Fighting for their country or even for gain they understood. But the idea of incurring physical risk in personal contact purely for sport's sake seemed foolish. The body, as the habitat of the soul, should not be endangered or pampered without reason. Games, traveling for pleasure, vacations, pastimes common in pagan countries, were unthought of in Judea, since there was in them neither national nor personal profit.

As was inevitable, the Jewish contestants made a sorry showing. Wrestling according to established rules, fighting with the hands, the complicated tests of skill and endurance were quite unfamiliar to them. Their opponents, to the huge delight of the gentile spectators, made their Jewish rivals seem ridiculous and disposed of them at will. Similarly, having had no occasion or opportunity to drive chariots drawn by two, three, or four pairs of horses, Jewish charioteers were humiliatingly inadequate.

The games were a triumph for the invaders, without a single victory to mitigate the Jewish rout.

In the musical festival as well, the Jews made a miserable showing. The strange, oriental intervals of the Davidical psalms grated on the exquisite ears of the judges. It was the godless lyrics of Pindar, and Sappho, and Anacreon that won the prizes.

In the ignominious defeat of the Jew, Herod recognized a further argument for supplanting a decadent, nationalistic culture with a vigorous one rooted in Rome. While the Jew hated games, he was consoled by the thought that they would occur only at five year intervals, and that the younger Jews were not likely to frequent the gymnasium, where their lack of practice would make them appear ridiculous. The theater, now completed, was a more serious threat. Its proximity to the Temple was an affront to the true worship; its frequent performances presented a constant threat to morals.

This theater was a splendid edifice of conventional design. The stage, or proscenium, consisted of two parts: an upper, from which the actors declaimed, and a lower for the traditional chorus. From the lower stage, a passage led into the pit, which, however, was unoccupied, on the theory that an empty pit improved acoustic properties by permitting the voice of the actor to carry to the farthest recesses of the building. On each side of the upper stage were painted houses depicting the main streets of Jerusalem. The background, while unchanged for an entire play, varied—it might be a market place, a rocky coast, a cave, a harbor with ships—according to the setting of the drama.

Tiers of boxes, one above the other, capable of seating some ten thousand, ranged in a semicircle about the stage. Outside the theater itself were colonnades or porticoes to shelter the patrons if it rained into the unroofed interior.

The Jews were reasonable in holding theater a threat to their faith and morals. The comedies were coarsely, designedly obscene. The tragedies, while literary masterworks of the greatest dramatists of the ancient world, were in a sense more pernicious. The gods of the drama were revengeful, mean, cruel without reason; Yahweh was just, merciful, and infinitely logical. In the Greek tragedies, the characters were helpless puppets, whose destiny was ordained by an unreasoning fate; the Jew himself determined his destiny by the judgment of his intellect and the choice of his free will.

No Jew, then, could attend the theater without hearing heresy and condoning blasphemy.

More objectionable still were the decorations of the theater—lavish gold and silver ornaments paid out of Jewish taxes, the numberless inscriptions in praise of Augustus, and, most of all, the trophies—full suits of armor—clearly a violation of the commandment against graven images.

Despite the protestations of the priests and godly citizens, the Jews stormed into the theater, howling with glee at the comedies, thrilled by the tragedies, or, when no play was being performed, just lazily sitting and gossiping in the warm sunshine, or strolling through the shadowy colonnades.

Some, whose consciences were not quite inert, excused their presence since Nicolaus had written a play, *The Chaste Susanna,* which glorified their religious history. But this was merely a sop to the scrupulous. The theme almost invariably was a convincing presentation of pagan fatalism, which excited the emotions, stampeded faith, and benumbed reason, until prayer and sacrifice in the Temple, since they merely quieted the soul and renewed the spirit, were quite neglected.

It was the trophies, however, to which decent Jews most violently objected, a fact that Herod was not long in learning from his spies. Perhaps his first reaction was that a little bloodletting might cool the ardor of the remonstrators. But while violence might discourage the clamor, it might also frighten people from the theater. As he viewed the throngs that packed every performance, and considered the popular neglect that was infesting the Temple with spiritual dry rot, he thought of another way. He invited the chief rabbis, representatives of the sanhedrin and other outspoken opponents of the theater, to the palace.

With gracious candor he explained his position. As Roman administrator he was expected to encourage Roman culture in all forms, including the drama. Therefore the building of the theater. He took pains to make it clear, however, that it was Rome's policy not to interfere with state religions in her provinces. Consequently he intended to have performed only what was recognized as great drama, excepting *The Chaste Susanna,* which he offered not as a play of real artistic merit, but because the Jews liked it and perhaps as the first of a school of national drama which might in time challenge the best of the Greek.

What then was their complaint?

Preappointed leaders stated the insurmountable objection: the theater contained idols and violated the Law of God. Emboldened by a mutter of approval, they continued. The idols were a clear violation of Rome's policy of friendship toward all religions, which Herod himself had cited. In erecting a public building adorned with graven images and idols, the king was not acting in good faith with Rome; and, should Augustus be informed of the fact, he would be displeased with his Judean administrator.

(It might be noted that in their arguments the Jewish leaders used a form of blackmail not dissimilar to that when Pilate was threatened, "If thou release this man, thou art no friend of Caesar.")

Herod sat for a space, apparently absorbed in doubt. An excited buzz of whispered comments, exultant and rancorous, circled about the chamber. Guards nervously clenched their swords as the clamor increased, and the king still slouched moodily on his throne.

Eventually he rose. He appeared to capitulate to their demands. Would the committee accompany him to the theater, where, in their presence, he promised to correct any violation of the Jewish law?

It seemed an unexpectedly easy victory. Borne in the king's own litters, they proceeded in festive mood to the theater.

Hitherto probably not one of the Jews present had known the building other than by hearsay; most had passed it only when necessary and then with averted eyes.

Moving from the dim, cool corridors to the amphitheater, golden in the sunlight, with the walls of their own Temple hard and cold beyond the proscenium, they were momentarily hushed by the beauty about them. Even to their jaundiced glances this pagan temple of a sinful art was astonishingly more impressive than the chosen domicile of the One God.

Suddenly, an excited finger pointed at the painted decorations. But, Herod objected, if they would come closer, they could see that the pictures were flat and therefore not graven images.

Momentarily the clamor subsided. As eyes became accustomed to the sunny glare, figures seemed to emerge from shadowy niches. With one voice, a roar of malignant triumph broke forth. "The trophies. They surely are graven images. Destroy the abominations."

The king spoke briefly to his guards. Robust arms lifted the suits of armor from their pedestals, and stood them in a glittering row before the angry Jews. One by one cloaks, then helmets, metal shirts, and greaves were removed, leaving wooden pegs, knobs, billets, and poles. These were the "Idols" the Jews had objected to!

Any trace of anger on Herod's part would have reinvigorated the spirit of the Jews. But rather in his face could be read a quiet satisfaction, like that of a rabbi who had finally convinced an unusually obtuse class. Urbanity itself, he invited his company back to the palace to partake of refreshments and continue the discussion. The Jews looked foolishly at one another. A priest declined, on the pretext that there was but little time to prepare for the evening services. With doubtful, backward glances they shuffled out of the theater and silently went their respective ways.

Herod remained in the theater for a considerable time, personally supervising the reassembling of the trophies. On the short ride to the palace, those of his guards nearest him were alarmed to hear the king who so seldom smiled unmistakably chuckling.

But thinking Jews, in particular those present at the theater, could see nothing humorous about their discomfiture. When the initial feeling of chagrin wore off, they angrily realized just how completely the king had made fools of them.

As the story of their mishap was bandied about the alleys and

arcades of Jerusalem, they were, it is true, unmercifully derided.
They had lost caste, and Herod became something of a popular
hero.

For the mob loves a winner and has no sympathy to waste on
a loser, particularly if his hurt is chiefly in his pride.

Herod's clash with the pietist leaders was more than it appeared
on the surface—a skirmish in which the dignity of the assailants
was the only casualty. The Jews had made the issue—Herod's
violation of the Jewish law and his deviation from Roman policy;
they had chosen the battlefield—the theater that they insisted
offered indisputable evidence of his transgressions.

By a trick, he had routed them. Theirs was no honorable
retreat in the face of overwhelming odds. With everything as
they wanted it, they had made themselves ridiculous and had
forever forfeited the respect of their coreligionists.

As a matter of fact, there was, during the two remaining
decades of Herod's life, no protest of similar magnitude. Occasional outbreaks under spontaneous leadership would ensue, but
none that was recognized as the protesting voice of a united
Judea.

A plot against Herod's life, incidentally the last on record,
was indeed the immediate aftermath of the theater episode.
Precipitate and bizarre, with only the desperate courage of the
conspirators auguring success, it was nevertheless indicative of
the extremities to which Jewish nationalists would go to remove
Herod. Ten men of no social or political importance, one of
them blind, bound themselves by the "cherem," the great ban,
to remove this scoffer at their faith by the certain sacrifice of
their own lives. Encouraged by the blind man, who knowing he
could not actually participate in the attack yet insisted on incurring their risks, they hit upon the plan of waylaying the king as
he passed along the corridor to the royal box, of hacking their
way through the guards necessarily spread thin in the restricted
passage, and of then stabbing him before they themselves were
cut down.

The plot almost succeeded. Herod was about to enter the
theater when an informer, breathless and wild-eyed, threw himself in front of the guards and gasped out the essentials of the

conspiracy. After placing a cordon about the theater, the king returned to the palace, where the wretch disclosed the names and descriptions of the plotters.

Trapped in the theater, in fact indifferent to their fate now that their plans had miscarried, they were one by one dragged before the king. On the person of each was his dagger. None, the blind man least of all, offered an excuse. Proudly, each insisted that he had sworn to do a pious action, not for personal gain, or private revenge, but to remove one who was a stench in the nostrils of the Jewish nation. Under torture they bore the same steadfast resolution. All went to their deaths gladly as martyrs to a holy cause.

The death of the conspirators had its bloody sequel. The informer, skulking to his hide-out with the price of betrayal close to his heart, was recognized by an excited mob. They trampled his gold into the offal in the gutters. Then they pulled him to pieces, casting his limbs and torso to the half-savage curs that served as Jerusalem's scavengers. A tumultuous parade led by a hairy giant bearing a stave surmounted by the traitor's head wound yelling and cursing through the mazes of the capital's slums.

Under other circumstances Herod might willingly have written off the murder of his informer. But he was thoroughly angry, not so much at the plot against himself, as with the attitude of the Jews in showing their rage because the plot had failed. His spies and informers had wisely refrained from being participants in the mob that lynched their fellow. However, hanging on the outskirts of the rabble, they had recognized several women hurrying to the scene of violence.

These were tortured until they disclosed the names of the ringleaders. Not only were the actual perpetrators put to death after horrible torments, but with them their entire families were wiped out.

Herod's pitiless cruelty in dealing with the plot against himself and the killing of his creatures had the effect of discouraging any further act of open hostility against his administration. But there drove into the land another danger, which he could not destroy with terror. Constant drought, following an almost complete absence of winter rains, stunted the crops. Insufficient diet produced debility that made the undernourished easy prey to the pestilence that rode on the heels of famine. Stores of grain in the capital and other centers were freely distributed and all too soon consumed. Herod tried to purchase food from adjacent parts of Asia, but there, too, starvation prevailed. Disease had meanwhile so weakened and decimated the farmers that fields ready for a new sowing were untended, and vineyards untrimmed.

Hellenes were certain that the capricious Fates had turned their backs on the king; Jews could interpret the disaster only as a manifestation of the displeasure of an offended God.

But Herod believed in no fates and had lost what faith he had had in Yahweh. He had instead complete confidence in himself.

Sicily and Egypt were the major granaries of the Roman world. From his agents Herod learned that there was an abundant harvest in the latter country. But Petronius, Roman prefect in Egypt, was no philanthropist. His purpose, like that of most Roman governors, was to amass a fortune speedily and retire. He would permit exportation of grain to Palestine but only on condition of immediate payment.

At once Herod melted his gold and silver. Saramalla, through his international connections, found buyers willing to purchase the royal jewels at bargain rates, for cash, and abundant money was quickly raised for huge shipments of grain and massive bales of wool to provide food and covering for the victims of the plague shivering with fever.

In the distribution of these necessities, Herod again demonstrated that he could govern with prudence and skill. What grain and wool remained after the needs of his own people had been satisfied he sent to those in distress beyond the borders. With his surplus cash he hired fifty thousand laborers, most of them regenerated Jews, some from other lands, to plant for a generous harvest.

This disaster cost Herod most of his wealth, but the manner in which he handled the emergency won him the admiration of Augustus. Within a year the emperor would have further proof of the many-sided genius of the man whose fate had hung in the balance at Rhodes.

In 24 B.C. the emperor ordered Aelius Gallus, procurator of Egypt, to pacify the Arabian nomads in order to secure a short and safe route between Egypt and Arabia Felix. Gallus, a conceited, unimaginative swashbuckler, appointed as his chief of staff Syllaeus, brother and vizier of Obodas, king of the Nabateans, whose country the Romans aimed to overrun and subjugate.

For eighteen months the Arab flitted about the desert, leading the weary heavily-armed Romans in pursuit of chimerical armies that never could be brought to bay. Only seven Romans were lost in battle. But thousands perished in heat and thirst as wells were unaccountably dry or polluted. Other thousands succumbed to typhus and cholera as supply trains with food and drugs, their guides vanishing in the night, circled aimlessly in the illimitable waste of blinding sand and black basalt. Supporting fleets were dashed to fragments on shoals and rocks where Arab charts indicated safe harborage.

Still the duped Roman pushed his despondent troops in endless chase of a foe never seen and always reported just over the horizon. Daily heat, thirst, and disease took their toll. In Rome there were grim mutterings of "Crassus" and a "lost legion."

Herod was not ignorant of the difficulties in which the Romans found themselves. At the outset of the campaign he could have provided Augustus with abundant evidence of the duplicity of Syllaeus and the unfitness of Gallus.

Instead he waited until the Roman's plight seemed hopeless. Then he dispatched five hundred picked, desert-trained horsemen to their aid. Within ten days the haggard remains of Gallus' army staggered into Alexandria, a shocking contrast with the trim, lean warriors who led them to safety.

Augustus was unstinting in his praise of Herod. Public proclamations of his appreciation and gratitude were posted in Judea and throughout the Near East. The king of the Jews was appointed perpetual consultant on the Empire's Eastern affairs. As an additional reward, the district of Trachonitis, east of the Sea of Gennesaret, was added to Herod's kingdom.

It might have appeared a gift of dubious value. The region was wildly mountainous with deep, fertile valleys; the inhabitants fierce robbers from the earliest times.

To Herod it was a challenge to show Augustus he could succeed where the Romans had failed. He sent three thousand troops skilled in guerrilla warfare to the district. For a season savage warfare raged in the gloomy gorges and on the bare hill-sides. Gradually the ardor of the robbers cooled as they lost their bravest chieftains, and they sullenly withdrew further into the wilderness.

Thereupon Herod induced Zamaris, a Babylonian Jew with political ambitions, to settle in the valleys with a hundred families constantly protected by five hundred scouts. Soon the colonists were turning the soil in valleys unbelievably fertile. After the first harvest, hastily erected barns were filled to bursting. Herod, by his organizing genius, had transformed a robber-infested wilderness into a prosperous granary.

For three years he had been feverishly busy. The intricacies of internal reformation, the establishment of military posts, the superhuman fight against famine and pestilence, the erection of the theater and gymnasium, the restoration of his finances, the campaign in Trachonitis, the conspiracy against his life and the contention with the Jewish leaders, and most of all the ever-present ghost of Mariamne had exacted strength that he could no longer afford to spend. The old madness, kept at a distance by his intense occupation with affairs of state, crept on him again. He hated Jerusalem, hated even the glorious buildings with which he had adorned it. The palace, especially the empty harem, drove him to a brooding despair.

His doctors recommended a change of scene. With curtains drawn to shut out the sight of the detested city and muffle the strident shouts of hawkers and the sonorous intonations of priests, he was carried from Jerusalem to Samaria.

There in place and people he found the way to quick recovery. The verdant landscape, the soft, caressing air, the ferial quality of life generally—poverty without penury, faith without fanaticism, robust humor masking unfailing kindness—made him feel that this land, not his flinty, spiteful Jerusalem, should be his home.

Mindful of Roman policy which frowned on disturbing innovations, he looked into history to justify the re-establishment of a Samaritan state.

What he found was encouraging. Samaria, so unexciting and ambitionless, had had its own stirring moments in history.

During the administration of Nehemiah in Jerusalem, Manasseh, son of the high priest Joiada, married the daughter of the Samaritan Sanballat, acting as Persian governor under Darius. Refusing to put away his foreign wife, he fled with her to his father-in-law. In Samaria, the Persians granted him permission to build a temple. With Manasseh as high priest the services and sacrifices of Jerusalem were duplicated in the Samaritan temple of Gerezim.

To a casual observer there was not the slightest difference in their services. Both Jew and Samaritan observed the same Law and used the same ritual. Even the worshippers seemed the same. In both cases, the Jews at Jerusalem and the Jewish refugees at Samaria far outnumbered the odds and ends of foreign peoples placed there by the Assyrians when the ten tribes were driven into captivity.

During the time of Alexander the Great, the Samaritans fell upon evil days. Incurring his displeasure, their leaders and many of the people were exiled and replaced by Macedonians. Later John Hyrcanus threw out the Macedonians and tried to enslave the remnants of Samaritans who fled to Shechem, at the foot of Gerezim. In the city itself the Jews did a thorough job of devastation; buildings were destroyed and the Temple leveled.

Since then only a heap of rubble on a flat hilltop some two miles in circumference, overlooking a fruitful plain, marked the site of Jerusalem's former rival.

History, therefore, warranted the rebuilding, perhaps not of a capital, but at least of a city that might serve as a secondary seat of government. The traces of past magnificence and the superb location were a temptation again to test his talents as a builder.

Herod could hardly have selected a more suitable location for his new city. From the hilltop the view was breathtaking. To the north the wide, fertile plain of Esdralon stretched to the distant, snow-topped barrier of Mount Tabor; in the west, the blue Mediterranean glistened through a cleft in the cedar-crowned hills; pleasant, rolling country climbed to the hills in the south and plunged into the tropical valley of the Jordan.

Planning the city was for Herod a labor of love for people who loved him. Even as the ruins were carried away, it began to take shape.

Strong walls and towers surrounded the hilltop, by nature steep and hardly accessible. In the center of the city was a sacred square containing a temple dedicated to Caesar Augustus. Next planned were a palace and gymnasium rivaling those of the capital. A water supply from never-failing fountains was established, and cool, comfortable houses were erected. Three terraces encompassed the hillside, each adorned around the entire circuit with rows of pillars to serve as a promenade for its inhabitants.

Settlers, poor Jews tired of the thankless task of harrowing their stony patches, and gentiles, fascinated by the magic city rising from the ruins, flocked to Samaria. To them, after first bestowing the choicest plots of land upon his beloved Samaritans, Herod assigned generous grants about the base of the hill.

The city was formally rededicated with the new name Sebaste (formed from the Greek for Augustus), a delicate tribute to the emperor and a name preferred by Jewish immigrants to the hateful "Samaria."

On his return to Jerusalem, some of his old madness began to reappear in the form of constant uneasiness, nocturnal roaming about the palace, and sudden tantrums of temper. His advisers took counsel together and urged him to marry. At fifty, they argued, many years of rule would normally remain to him. It was unfitting that a king should be without a queen; a harem, without occupants. Slanderers were whispering that as a result of his illness he was impotent. Even the Romans thought his celibate existence unnatural.

As if in answer to their plea, Herod fell in love. Most gracious of the young women of Jerusalem was another Mariamne, daughter of a certain priest Simon, himself the son of an Alexandrian Jew Boethus.

It is true that the name Boethus was anathema to the Jews, for the rapacity of the family was notorious. The Talmud explains their brief stay in power by the judgment, "The fear of the Lord prolongeth days, but the years of the wicked shall be shortened." Elsewhere in Jewish literature occurs the curse, "Woe to the Boethusim: woe to their spears!"

But this greed for power, the unscrupulousness that marks the dealings of the family, were in no way characteristic of the daughter. She was admittedly the prettiest girl in the capital. Her reddish hair, her pert, childlike face and slight figure in every way contrasted with the dark, majestic beauty of her predecessor. In spirit she was animated, sweet, easily moved to laughter or tears; in short, a variable, pliant mate eminently conformable to the shifting moods of the king.

It has been hinted that Herod on first seeing her was so obsessed with her beauty that he intended to seize her and thrust her into his harem. If this were so, it could not have taken him long to appreciate the advantages of a formal betrothal.

She was a Jewess, yet not allied to the hostile Jews of Judea. Marriage with her would therefore favorably impress those Jews not irretrievably hostile to him. Besides, she would not in any sense constitute a dynastic problem. Not by the remotest connection a Hasmonean, nor allied in any way with those who wished him ill, she or her family could be no serious source of danger or intrigue. It would be unlikely, too, that she, with her sanguine, volatile disposition, could irk his own quarrelsome family. There was no reason, then, why she should not share his throne.

Accordingly Jesus, son of Phabet and Hananel's successor, quietly stepped down from the high-priesthood; Simon was invested with the sacerdotal robes, and Herod, his graying hair and beard carefully darkened, took the blooming Mariamne to wife.

CHAPTER **XV**

"HEROD'S TEMPLE"

HEROD'S NOT INCONSIDERABLE STATURE IN THE
world of Augustus rested in large measure on his fame as a
builder. No other subject king nor even Caesar himself could
approach the extent and splendor of his constructions, or emulate
the genius that characterized every engineering and agricultural
project. Not only his own land profited by his talent, but remoter regions, Syria, Rhodes, and Greece. Irrigation by ingenious systems of canals transformed desert wastes into blooming
orchards and seas of heavy-headed grain; where peasant carts
had sunk hub-deep in mire or sand, paved roads resounded with
the dull thunder of traffic; robbers became only an unpleasant
memory as wilderness posts, stocked with food and water and
manned by wary-eyed guardians, made safe and easy the avenues
of commerce.

It was in the building and beautifying of cities, however, that
Herod was pre-eminent, even in an age of peace, when every
subject ruler deemed himself a builder.

To originality of architecture, it is true, Herod made no great
contribution. The Jew, and even more so his Idumean step-
brother, was traditionally no builder of large cities. Bucolic and
nomadic by nature, he chose a transitory tent or cave amidst his
flocks as his natural dwelling place. When circumstances forced
him through many generations to adapt himself to city life, he
was content to accept the local architecture as he found it. Under
Hellenic influences he found Egyptian, Babylonian, Canaanite
and Greek architecture more convenient, and so—particularly if

228

he were wealthy—he adopted that. But only in the Temple—to build which, incidentally, he had to call on non-Jewish aid—was there anything resembling Jewish architecture.

But Herod was gifted with artistic taste and a sense of fitness. Substantially his buildings were Greek, with Egyptian and Phoenician touches that added warmth and color to the cool purity of the Hellenic models and resulted in a form of architecture that for lack of a better term has been designated Herodian.

In Sparta and Athens, at Rhodes, on the coast of Palestine in the Phoenician cities of Ascalon, Tyre, and Sidon, in Syria at Damascus and particularly Antioch, he spent his genius with a lavish hand. Throughout Rome his name became a byword for progressive construction, for development of natural resources, for building of roads, aqueducts, and canals.

A word might be said also of the rapidity with which his many projects took form. In our own day we marvel at the speed with which manufacturing plants, camps, or housing facilities to meet a sudden emergency are erected. But in these there is too often a note of impermanency, a hint that with the passing of the emergency these structures, too, will pass. Herod, however rapidly his cities sprang up, always built, as he hoped, for posterity. Imperishable stone was his medium, possible expansion was provided for, nothing was skimped or cheapened, everything he undertook had the spontaneity of a dream and the indestructibility of a legend. Craftsmen by the thousands, skilled and well paid, moved from project to project; laborers by the tens of thousands—so generous were their wages—were willing draftees from the local populace.

Almost unique among his building ventures because of the difficulty and daring involved in its construction was the great port of Caesarea.

On the Palestinian coast, midway between Joppa on the south and Dora on the north, was a teetering stone blockhouse known as Strato's Tower, giving its name to a drab fishing village at the base of a cove roughly the size of the Pireus at Athens. There, Herod decided to construct a great, safe Judean harbor.

Such a harbor was of prime necessity. The Jews were depend-

ent for the disposition of their expanding produce and manufactured goods on slow and expensive land routes, for there was
on the entire coast not one satisfactory harbor. Joppa, the biggest
port, was shelterless. Ships anchored off shore. Loading and
unloading was done by scows, endangered by the prevailing south
and west winds and by capricious gales that roared suddenly from
the mountains.

The transformation of Strato's Tower to Caesarea began with
the construction of a massive rounded mole. A breakwater of
immense blocks of stone was built to a width of two hundred
feet, reaching out from the shore to a depth of twenty fathoms.
Adjoining this breakwater and protected by it, a stone wharf
one hundred feet wide was erected, and stone warehouses were
built thereon. The entire wharf was further protected by a high
wall superimposed on the breakwater which besides repelling
the breakers served also, on its broad summit, as a pleasant
marine promenade. Towers elegant and sturdy arose at intervals
along this wall; one of them was named by Herod, a master in
the art of dedication, after Augustus' stepson Drusus, who died
in Germany. Only at the north was there an entrance to the
breakwater, since, to quote Josephus, "The north wind there
was the most gentle of all winds." At the mouth of the breakwater were sturdy bulwarks; on the west, a round tower and, on
the east, two huge square rocks joined together. Tower and
rocks were surmounted by three gigantic colossi, possibly in
imitation of that at Rhodes. Within the harbor two anchorages
were provided, one for vessels of deep draught, the other, near
shore, for smaller vessels.

After the harbor was completed, the workers' quarters and
fishing shacks were razed, and a city began to emerge from the
flinty shore. In harmony with the harbor, it, too, was semicircular
in design, centering about a spacious forum at the waterfront—
a symbolic touch—for Caesarea was to be essentially a city of the
sea. From the forum, streets radiated like the spokes of a half-
wheel, climbing the gentle slopes to the distant walls and passing
through stout gates to the country beyond. Parallel avenues
intersected the radiating streets with artistic irregularity, while
subways for emergency use ran from all important centers to the
waterfront.

In planning his city, Herod consulted Vitruvius, who under the patronage of Agrippa had renovated Rome with happy results. All buildings were constructed of white stone, of a height and design approved by a permanent planning council, so that nothing might mar the symmetry of the whole.

South of the city, where the sea made a pretty little indentation, Herod erected an amphitheater on a natural slope, with the Mediterranean, blue and sparkling, as a back drop. In the temple were two colossi: one representing Augustus, the other Rome. The synagogue, impressive in its simple dignity, was located within the city itself, aloof from the pagan atmosphere of temple and playground.

During the erection of Caesarea (its completion would take twelve years) and other projects, Herod outdid himself in his attempts to win the affection of the Jewish people, and simultaneously vitiated his efforts at appeasement by acts of senseless violence.

As the behavior patterns became more distinct and widely separated, it grew increasingly clear that the king was a victim of a split personality. The splendid architect, the scrupulous custodian of the fortunes of his people, rendering Caesar his tithe and enriching his own country, suddenly and frequently is transformed into the hysterical tyrant; the one hand forces beneficences on his subjects, then the other strikes them down if they seemed unwilling to accept his gifts.

In his benevolent phase, he went about the country speaking softly, listening humbly to the complaints of his people. They charged him with breaking the Law of Moses by erecting temples to false gods. Patiently, he explained that these were the customary acts of a Roman official and that actually—since no intelligent Roman paid more than lip service to the state gods—these temples were monuments and public buildings rather than places of worship. He reminded them, too, that none of these temples was erected in Judea proper, but in foreign lands, to increase Jewish prestige, or in dominions added to Judea by the Romans.

Others accused him of imposing exorbitant taxes on the Jews, and of squandering Jewish money in order to establish his own position and strengthen Rome.

This charge, too, he could turn aside. It was true, he admitted,

that taxes were enormously increased and rigidly collected. But
they were actually moderate income taxes. If the Jews paid more,
their earnings were also immeasurably greater than before his
reign. None of his subjects could deny that in spite of heavy
taxation life was easier and that unattainable luxuries of the
Hasmonean times had become the necessities of the Herodian.

That Herod could expend such tremendous amounts on his
multiple projects without impoverishing his people is no mystery.
His annual personal income was between two and three million
dollars. This was derived in part from private sources. The
copper mines in Cyprus, leased from Augustus, under the man-
agement of his engineers, became extremely lucrative. The income from the balsam groves at Jericho—now his personal property—can be surmised when it is recalled that Herod as their
manager had found them profitable even after paying Cleopatra
almost a quarter of a million annually for their use. He bought
parcels of land of little apparent value and made them the
centers of new cities, thereafter selling or leasing them at a staggering profit. Estates of wealthy Jews condemned for sedition
became his, by law. He was, in brief, financier, banker, pro-
prietor, and shareholder in the most diverse undertakings, all of
which under his skilled direction added to his wealth.

Supplementing his vast private income were abundant public
funds derived in large measure from taxes for the sources of
which he had been primarily responsible.

By encouraging, and sometimes enforcing, the colonization of
reclaimed or newly acquired lands, he removed the poor and
underprivileged from slums and sterile farms and offered them
opportunities to prosper in agriculture or industry, and incidentally, by taxes they now could pay, to contribute to the
national income. Moreover, since the robbers had been eliminated, and the country was at peace, there no longer was need
for a large army. Military expenditures were thus reduced and
men otherwise destined for the army, to be supported by taxation,
instead themselves became taxpayers. And all the never-ending
building projects and the irrigation of deserts and draining of
swamps put Jews to work and took back part of their wages as
taxes.

Still, anxious to conciliate the protesting Jews, he remitted one-third of their taxes. Then further, to placate those who discredited his beautifying cities beyond the borders, he offered to beautify Jerusalem as a preliminary step to his as yet undisclosed plan of rebuilding the Temple.

It was a formidable undertaking that little short of razing and complete rebuilding could accomplish satisfactorily. Jerusalem was some three hundred acres in area with a normal population of perhaps two hundred thousand. It was unquestionably a dirty, ugly, overcrowded city. There were, of course, attractive, even sumptuous buildings, like the Temple, the wealthier of the five hundred synagogues, Herod's palace and theater, the Roman official quarters, and the homes of the Herodian Jews. Some of these were sequestered in pleasant grounds, behind grim walls. But the greater part of the city consisted of filthy slums, rabbit warrens of congested, miserable humanity. The color and gaiety of flower gardens were lacking, for the Jew detested the smell of manure; stoves to banish the chill of the icy nights were prohibited, for the sensitive Jewish nostril was allergic also to the odor of smoke; carriages and litters (except the king's and those of his court) were banned, and indeed could hardly have prodded their way through the narrow arcades that served as thoroughfares. Alleys twisted, climbed, and tunneled to such a degree that the stories of the mile-long Damascene "Street Called Straight" and the undeviating avenues of the new Herodian cities were completely discredited by natives of the capital, as gentile grandiloquence. Since life in the dismal, fetid tenements was almost unlivable, the Jew of Jerusalem spent his scanty spare time either on the roof top or on the street. There he was elbowed, jostled, and often robbed by a reeking gang of street vendors, who ordinarily pressed upon the gullible pilgrim trade such souvenirs as shoddy coats of many colors, clay models of the Temple that crumbled at a touch, cheap jewelry, and odorous sheepskin sandals. Through the ear-splitting cries of this gentry sounded the thin wail of the fortune teller, openly practicing her forbidden art, secretly peddling to ever present informers sorry bits of information blabbed by superstitious patrons.

Such was at normal times the Jerusalem Herod wanted to renovate. Wealth and power, regal and sacerdotal, lived within its self-created pale, apart from the contaminating touch and blasting breath of the masses, who, infested with filth, disease, and vice, squirmed, and cheated, and fought in their human ant hills.

At the season of the great festivals, the crowding and din must have been almost staggering. There were in the Roman Empire probably seven or eight million Jews—approximately one-twelfth of the population. Rome, Alexandria, Sparta, in fact every commercial center old or new had its Jewish quarters and its synagogues which contributed to the support of the Temple. Every Jew dreamed—and the prosperity of the non-Judean Jews frequently enabled these to fulfill their dreams—of spending the feast days in the Holy City. As a result there were as many as three million Jews, native and foreign, in Jerusalem for the Passover, with a consequent confusion, and crowding, and squalor that must have racked the systematic soul of Herod.

Yet he was forced to content himself with paving a few of the streets and beautifying public buildings, measures which in no way endeared him to the starving, squabbling proletariat.

Failing to conciliate the Jews by gifts and soft speeches, he became more embittered. Obviously, he could not win the affection of a race who regarded righteousness above achievement or glory. It galled him to realize that he, whose temples, statues and trophies moved the non-Jewish world to grateful amazement, could win from his own people not one solitary testimonial of appreciation or gratitude.

The old madness returned in the form of aggravated suspicion concerning Jewish loyalty and of ruthless extermination of every suspect. His spies were everywhere—in the mansions of the wealthy, in the hovels of the destitute. The tanner exchanging a meaningless pleasantry with the coppersmith in the next arcade was spirited away that night; the rabbi, expounding a complex text to a curious questioner, never returned from an errand of mercy. The king distrusted even his spies. A well-founded tradition pictures him in disguise, haunting dens of thieves, prowling about reeking slums to single out some miserable outcast whose thoughtless words could be twisted into treason.

Not content with ferreting out real and fancied traitors, he issued the astounding order that the entire adult population must make under oath a profession of fealty to him.

No Jew could in conscience consent to such a violation of the Mosaic Law. Certain of the scholarly group among the Pharisees, led by Hillel and Shammai, openly defied the order, whereupon Herod, politic even in his madness, blandly exempted them, as he expressed it, since he felt assured of their loyalty. Similarly, out of gratitude to the Essenes, he excused this sect, whose religious precepts forbade their taking oaths. But hundreds of Jews of unquestioned integrity died as martyrs. Other thousands, weaker in principle, shamefully mumbled the hateful pledge, groaning at the tyranny of a ruler who demanded not only the subservience of their physical beings but even the abasement of their immortal souls.

Despite his obsession, the other Herod, the architect and promoter, continued his projects. The sharp ring of the mason's hammer and the thud of the road builder's pile became the nation's theme song. Antioch was modernized with two and a half miles of streets paved with marble; a chamber of commerce was instituted; and a drowsy, decadent town sprang into a thriving business center. At a place ten miles south of Jerusalem where he had repulsed Antigonus he erected a palace-fortress named Herodium in honor of his victory.

Near ancient Jericho he constructed a Romanized town, with a winter palace, amphitheater and hippodrome. This proved to be one of his most profitable ventures. Vast crowds of Jews on their pilgrimage to Jerusalem traveled from Perea down the valley of the Jordan to Jericho, before the final stage up to the capital. Others from Galilee and beyond used the same route, lest their pilgrimage be vitiated by the touch of the soil of hated Samaria. Accommodations in old Jericho had been almost as unsatisfactory as those in the Holy City itself. The comforts and diversions of the new city, however, were such as to beguile the lukewarm pilgrim into delaying to the last moment the consummation of his pious journey, and to tempt even his more fervent brother to turn his back with almost unseemly haste on the

gleaming walls of the Temple that he might have a longer time
to luxuriate in the languorous warmth of the pleasure gardens of
the valley before resuming his weary way homeward.

While Herod as empire builder was enriching Judea and
beautifying other parts of the Empire, and, as half-crazed despot,
was alienating or eliminating the decently disposed elements in
his own country, a political situation developed, typically oriental
in its complexity, fraught with unsought danger for the king,
which, nevertheless, eventually redounded to his credit. A certain
Iturean prince and high priest, the tetrarch Zenodorus, who
ruled the valley of Chalcis, and Heliopolis in the shadow of the
Lebanon and adjacent country beyond the Jordan, set himself
up as chief of the robbers inhabiting the remoter districts of
Trachonitis across the Jordan from Galilee. The country was too
barren to sustain life, so the inhabitants preyed upon the Damascene caravans, profiting to such extent under the leadership of
Zenodorus that Varro, the Roman governor in Syria, wrote to
Augustus for instructions. He was ordered to destroy the bandits
and turn over their country to Herod. Varro's onslaught met
with little success. The robbers, living in caves hardly perceptible
because of their narrow, hidden entrances, but wide inside, well
provided with water and food, and approached only by twisting,
readily defended paths, repelled the attacking Romans with ease.

But when Herod took over his new dominion, he made short
work of the rebels. Guided by traitors, he surprised one encampment after another, wiped out those he trapped, and dispersed
the rest. Zenodorus, brazen and sly as well as ruthless, had the
temerity to go to Rome and accuse Herod of a technical violation
of the Pax Romana, since the king had seized the country about
Gadara, which Zenodorus, when still in power, had leased to the
Arabs. Laughed at in Rome, he returned to the East, nursing his
hatred. Agrippa meanwhile, on a tour of the Empire east of
Greece which had just been assigned him, met Herod and spent
the winter with him at Mytilene.

A delegation of Gadarenes sought audience with the imperial
representative. In Rome, Agrippa was noted for his sternness.
But here in the balmy Eastern winter, mellowed by the companionship of the Judean king with whom he was to be con-

stantly on terms of warmest friendship, he listened patiently to the charges of the protestants. In substance, these were a repetition of Zenodorus' allegation that Herod had seized lands which had actually been leased to them.

Agrippa did nothing, but his mildness encouraged the Arabs to violence. Under Zenodorus' leadership, they rebelled, destroyed some of Herod's outposts, and besieged the Judean troops in their camps.

Like Agrippa, Herod practiced restraint. He knew how proud Augustus was of his Pax Romana, and no subordinate was willing to interrupt Caesar's reign with civil war.

In 21 B.C. Augustus himself made a tour of the East. In Syria, where Herod had gone to greet him, a large delegation of Gadarenes demanded a hearing. Deceived by the mild bearing of Agrippa on the former occasion, they clamorously insisted that Herod had robbed them of their possessions, violated their temples and forced them to rebel. Therefore, the emperor must instantly repudiate Herod and restore to them their self-rule.

Without waiting to hear Herod's ready defense, Augustus turned his back on the rebels, and with every evidence of affection grasped the hand of Herod and confirmed him in his authority.

The Gadarenes were stunned. Nothing short of cruel death for rebellion could be their lot. During the night they committed mass suicide, some slashing their throats, others jumping from walls or cliffs, or drowning themselves. To make Herod's triumph complete, by a "happy incident" as Josephus calls it "Zenodorus' belly burst and a great quantity of blood issued from him in his sickness and he departed this life."

Herod was further honored by being named one of the procurators of Syria, and his friendship with Augustus and Agrippa seemed to be cemented in lasting form.

In gratitude, Herod erected a white marble temple near Panium in Trachonitis. The site was the place where the source of the Jordan oozed out of thick reeds. Here there had been a cave and a grotto (long neglected) to the god Pan. After Herod's time, the Temple became the center of Caesarea Philippi, renowned in New Testament chronicles.

II

Since Herod is known to have married ten times, it has been customary to depict him as a sort of oriental Bluebeard, whose wives cowered in their quarters haunted by terror, never certain when the ax would fall as their royal husband's vagrant glances found pleasure in their successors. There is, however, little authority for drawing any very definite conclusions concerning the king's amatory affairs. Certainly, it is unsafe to assume—the ten wives notwithstanding—that the lechery characteristic of the rest of his family was also an attribute of his.

Of only one fact can we be assured. He loved his first Mariamne, and in all probability no other, with all the depth of which his intense nature was capable.

Whether passion, caprice, convenience, propriety, or loneliness for Mariamne induced his other hymeneal ventures we do not know, and all authorities are puzzlingly reticent. The order of his later marriages, whether he maintained his wives singly or as concubines in a harem, what their fate was—all these are unanswerable questions.

His first marriage with Doris, sometime before 49 B.C. is, of course, recorded. That he put her away before marrying Mariamne I, and, to his misfortune, recalled her and their miserable son Antipater is also certain.

His married life with Mariamne I, beginning at the siege of Jerusalem in 37 B.C. and ending with her execution in 29 B.C., is fully described by Josephus. It is known that she bore him five children: Alexander and Aristobulus, who studied in Rome, later to return to meet violent deaths at the hands of their crazed father; a younger brother who had the good fortune to die in Rome; and two daughters, Salampsio, who later married her stepbrother Phasael, the son of one of her father's subsequent wives, and Cyprus, who seemingly died young.

Mariamne II was probably Herod's third wife and the only woman after the death of the first Mariamne in whom (apart from his extraconnubial flare for his daughter-in-law Glaphyra) he showed a lover's interest. By Mariamne II he had one son, Herod Philip, whose infatuation for his wife (and niece) Herodias led to the murder of John the Baptist.

Following his third marriage, the order of his wives is confused. It is known that at some time he married two of his nieces, his sister Salome's children by her first husband, Herod's uncle Joseph. This typically oriental example of close inbreeding was probably engineered by Salome, for there is no evidence that Herod himself was inclined to the incestuous practices common among Eastern despots. Perhaps she reasoned that children of purely Herodian stock might efface the memory of the half-Jewish boys in Rome. However, there is no record of children by his nieces. It is not unlikely that Herod consented to a purely formal union merely to placate his hounding sister.

Malthace, a Samaritan woman, became the mother of Archelaus, Herod's successor as king of Judea, who incurred the displeasure of the Romans during the disturbances in 4 B.C., was deposed, and died in exile. She bore him also a second son, the noisome Herod Antipas, referred to by Christ as "that fox," who stole Herodias from Herod Philip.

Another wife, Cleopatra of Jerusalem, whose beauty and gentleness are traditional, was the mother of Philip, who, as tetrarch of Iturea and Trachonitis, married the infamous Salome (Herodias' daughter), and finding the lustful lady too erotic for his tastes divorced her and spent his days among the Arabs he loved, dispensing judgment tempered with mercy from his divan of justice.

Other wives there were, too. Pallas, whose granddaughter became the wife of Herod Agrippa, who for the persecution of Peter and assumption of the Deity was summarily punished (Acts 12:23); Phaedra, mother of a certain Roxane; and Elpis, whose sole claim to posterity is that she brought into the world yet another, and seemingly less vicious Salome.

If, however, little is known of Herod's later marital adventures, this much is certain, that, excepting Mariamne I's unfortunate sons and Cleopatra's son Philip, he fathered a sorry brood, prone to violence, treachery, and incest, and petering out within four generations in the unsavory person of Berenice, married three times before twenty (her second husband, her uncle), then living twenty-five years in incest with her brother Herod Agrippa the Younger, and finally the mistress of the emperor Titus, who

despite the lady's forty-five years was so infatuated with her
beauty that his advisers only with the utmost difficulty dissuaded
him from making her empress of Rome.

Yet, after all, the names of Herod's wives and the sins of his
children shed only an uncertain light on the domestic life of the
king.

III

It was actually an edict in the winter of 20 B.C., ordering all
habitual thieves into exile, that led to the rebuilding of the
Temple. Herod's order was unquestionably well-intentioned and
reasonable. The loneliest lanes were safe to travelers; the hilly
border country, once honey-combed with lairs of robbers, supported prosperous, law-abiding colonists. Only in the centers
where non-Palestinian Jews congregated—in Jericho, and most
of all in Jerusalem—was thievery rampant. Rich Jews from
abroad, with their well-stacked gold bags, were easy prey for the
wily Jewish thief. Since other deterrent measures had failed,
Herod reasoned that, if the thieves were not in Judea, they could
not fleece the visitors in the Holy Land.

The publication of the edict brought a flood of spies and informers hurrying to Herod with tales of popular resentment.
Unwilling to credit them, Herod sought information first-hand,
a harrowing experience that convinced him that the passions of
the people were, indeed, at white heat.

Puzzled by the reaction of the Jews, Herod called upon the
chief rabbis for an explanation.

It was quickly forthcoming. A Jewish thief in Judea, they
claimed, could be punished and redeemed. But to send him out
of the country placed his faith in jeopardy. Herod listened in
perplexed silence, as the rabbis continued. The people, they
asserted, saw in the king's order yet further evidence that he was
determined to uproot the Jewish faith. Else why did he persecute pious Jews who refused to take the oath of fealty, and send
wicked Jews beyond the borders where there was no possibility of
their eventual redemption?

Herod must have felt the insincerity of the charges. He knew that the Jews themselves showed no charity or forgiveness toward the thieves, but only contempt, and obviously cared little whether or not they were redeemed.

Nevertheless, the edict was recalled. Thieves merrily continued their thievery, heedless alike of the wails of the despoiled outlander, and the disapproving sniff of his pious compatriot.

When Herod withdrew from a stand he felt was practical and reasonable, it was usually out of deference to popular feeling. Sane or mad, he wanted always to be appreciated by his people. Contributing, no doubt, to his periods of madness was the conviction that do what he might, punish or inveigle, he never could win and hold the love of his nation, any more than he could count on the affection of his family. Prosperity and conditional security he had given his people; yet they hated him. True, he had won popularity with the Romans, but at the price of a corresponding loss of esteem by the nation he ruled.

Yet he never quite gave up the hope of winning popular acclaim. Back in his mind was the quenchless yearning for the miracle that would burst the dam of Jewish distrust and overflow the hearts of his people with love for their ruler.

A project, dormant for some years, began to stir. He would rebuild the Temple, rendering the structure grander in style than any edifice he had erected for Rome, more beautiful in artistry and color than even Solomon's Temple. "Herod's Temple" would show him in his true relationship to his nation and would still forever the insistent voices that whispered "tyrant" and "pagan."

It was an undertaking that called for extreme caution. Every stone was hallowed, the shape and position of every tile steeped in tradition. Moreover, a third Temple was unthinkable. Had not the prophet Haggai quoted the Lord, "Great shall be the glory of this last house more than the first!" and "The desired of all nations shall come, and I will fill this house with glory"?

Despite the initial difficulties, and quite apart from the scarcely creditable theory that the plan to rebuild the Temple was a token of his repentance for an evil life and the desire to placate the God of the Jews, Herod could hardly have conceived of a sounder project from both a personal and a national viewpoint.

It is clear, of course, that he hungered for popularity with the Jews. True, there were crazed by-products of this craving, in his bursts of harshness, his suspicion, his senseless attempts to compel affection. But these were manifestations of a mind not wholly sane. In that healthy area of his brain that regulated his affairs with Rome grew the conviction that a magnificent Temple was not only desirable but essential. Roman cities, whether in Italy or abroad, were judged in large measure by the grandeur of the temple, dedicated to the local deities. Judea had its sumptuous buildings—mostly Herodian. But the Temple in the capital city, the one temple in which the entire nation and the millions of Jews throughout the empire paid homage to their one God, was a relatively shabby, run-down structure. It is reasonable then to maintain that Herod, for the sake of his Roman reputation, even apart from the hope of ingratiating himself with the Jews, must have felt the necessity of undertaking the erection of a temple that would glorify his reign and—perhaps the greater incentive—make his people proud of him.

Herod went to work warily. He first called together the leaders of every Jewish school of thought and political creed, and in a conciliatory address outlined his plan and the reasons thereof.

He began by recalling the many improvements which had actually benefited the people more than they glorified him. He boasted a little that "with God's assistance, I have advanced the nation of the Jews to a degree of happiness which they never had before." This new work which he had in mind, unlike his other undertakings, which had merely strengthened their security and prestige, would be a "work of the greatest piety and excellence that can possibly be undertaken." The dimensions of the present Temple had been, as the listeners knew, restricted by a Persian satrap; consequently it lacked the height of Solomon's Temple by some ninety feet. In the troubled days preceding his reign, there had never been the opportunity of reconstructing a temple comparable with the first Temple. Now, however, he told them, there is peace, and prosperity, and amity with the Romans. Consequently his sense of duty commanded him to restore its ancient glory and thereby make a "thankful return after the most pious manner to God for what blessings I have received from him by giving me this kingdom, and that, by rendering this Temple as complete as I am able."

Herod's tongue had lost none of its cunning; his tones retained their old ring of sincerity.

His hearers were frankly hostile to the entire project. Yet they could offer only one objection—the fear that he would raze the second Temple, which had been promised such glories.

Herod readily reassured them that such was not his intention. He solemnly promised not for one moment to interfere with the daily sacrifice nor in any way to incommode regular or casual worshippers.

It is easy to appreciate Jewish veneration of tradition. There was a continuity from the time when David chose the threshing floor of Ornan the Jebusite on Mount Moriah for the site of his first center of worship. The two subsequent Temples had been expansions of this original altar. King Solomon found it far too small, so he built a wall and filled the space between with earth to establish a site large enough for the House of the Temple, the Holy Place, and the Holy of Holies. This temple stood for four hundred and sixteen years (1004–588 B.C.) when it was looted and burned by the Babylonians.

After the return from the Second Captivity the altar of holocausts was erected in 536 B.C. and the rebuilding of the temple began. Delayed by Samaritan interference it was restarted in 520 B.C. and completed in 515 B.C. The second temple never could recall the awe and impressiveness of Solomon's. It somehow gave always the impression of being a makeshift, a temporary structure that suggested but could not reproduce the sublimity of the first —in part because it was larger in extent and barer in adornment, and lacked the height and nobility of its prototype. Then too, the Ark of the Covenant was missing, and the tabernacle, sealed by Jeremiah in some forgotten cave on Mount Nebo.

It had, however, to sustain the pious Jew, what the other finer Temple lacked—the prophet's ringing assurance that it would entertain the Messiah.

Many of Herod's guests were schooled in temple lore; most, if not all, were proudly patriotic. Under the onslaught of his promises to restore their Temple's ancient glory, their objections began to ebb. The insistent thought recurred—for the reception of their Savior a less shabby Temple would certainly be appropriate.

The Jews consulted among themselves, and instead of rejecting the entire plan as was their original intention they inquired as to how Herod could re-erect the Temple without interference with worship or ceremonial defilement.

Herod had anticipated this question. A thousand priests, he explained, could be trained as masons and carpenters, so that no unconsecrated person would tear down or alter any part of the holy edifice. Ten thousand lay workers would be on hand to do the grosser tasks where possible defilement was not an issue. He planned, moreover, to renovate the Temple bit by bit, so that at no time would there be any indication of rebuilding but rather a gradual emergence into a glorious house of worship that would surpass that of Solomon.

While a few of the Jews caught Herod's fire, the majority begrudgingly acquiesced simply because they could find no valid reason to continue their objections.

Sacerdotal craftsmen were taught their trades, and work began. At first there seemed to be a fair degree of enthusiasm. Within eighteen months the Holy Place and the Holy of Holies were rebuilt. Indeed, the rapid progress was a matter of pride to the Jewish workmen, who established the tradition that while the Holy of Holies was being rebuilt, rain or storm came only during the night, to demonstrate the Almighty's pleasure in his new Temple. Growing dissension and Herod's progressive madness, however, caused the ardor of the workers to lag.

Eight years were to pass before the completion of the outer section; Herod himself was destined never to see the fulfillment of his most daring dream. Scripture tells us that Christ's words were punctuated by the clang of the mason's hammer. Between the Crucifixion and the formal dedication thirty-four more years were to elapse; then, eight sad years and the Romans left not a stone upon a stone.

In arranging for the reconstruction of the Temple, Herod sought the aid of the best available Roman and Jewish architectural talent. The plans called for a temple proper area of six hundred feet square, plus a Court of Gentiles, making the entire dimensions one thousand by fifteen hundred feet. The entire area was laid out in terraces at varying levels, crowned by the Temple itself, as if on top of a hill, visible from every part of the city, and from a great distance. No Jew in Jerusalem could escape its imminence; the approaching visitor would first see it almost as though it were suspended in air; the departing guest could see and feel its power long after the rest of the city had faded from view. So, symbolically—in fact, in an almost literal sense— its gleaming white marble and resplendent gold proclaimed near and far the might and glory of Yahweh.

The outermost court, the Court of the Gentiles, paved with variegated tiles, encircled the other courts and buildings, and was separated from them by a high wall, inscribed with signs in Latin and Greek forbidding gentiles under pain of death to venture farther. It was this colorful, noisy court that was usually thronged with sightseers. Here, too, were sly sellers of sacrificial doves for the poorer pilgrims, and desks at which crafty money changers enriched themselves by exchanging temple currency for Greek, Roman or other foreign coins. Around the Court of Gentiles ran wide porticoes with two rows of marble pillars forty feet high and lofty ceilings of cunningly carved cedar. At the corners of the galleries were chambers for the temple guards.

Gates, each inlaid with precious stones, led the pilgrim once he had satisfied the searching eyes of the guards into a large inner court, the people's court, befittingly a little quieter and more ornate than the outer court. Three sides of this inner court were surrounded by buildings sixty feet wide, for various uses, includ- ing the housing of the sanhedrin. These buildings were sepa- rated by nine gates in the shape of towers. The entrance of each gateway was divided by a large bar into two bays each fifteen feet wide and thirty feet high, covered with wooden leaves plated with silver and gold. On a lower terrace in the center was a royal basilica.

Opening from the people's court were four massive donatory gates of which the one on the eastern side, the "Beautiful Gate" of the Acts (so heavy that it required twenty men to move it) was the gift of a certain Alexandrian Jew, Nicanor, who to perpetuate his name had the most clever craftsmen in the Empire construct a door seventy-five feet high and sixty feet wide of Corinthian brass embellished with scrolled plates of gold and silver emblems.

One of these gates led fifteen steps down into the somewhat constricted Court of the Women, which was the nearest a Jewish woman might approach to the Holy of Holies. Men were not excluded from this court; in fact, they could cross it on their way to the Court of Men (court of Israel). However, the benches at its western and southern ends were reserved exclusively for women. Near these benches were thirteen poor boxes, each super- scribed with its purpose, e.g., oil, wood, vestments. (It was here that Christ observed the widow's mite and the rich man's dona- tion.) At the corners were rooms fifty-five feet square. In one, lepers were declared clean or unclean; in others priests sorted wool; and here oil and other temple requisites were stored, and the necessary cooking and washing was done by pious women who also lodged in these rooms.

The three other gates from the people's court opened on the Court of Men, on a naturally higher level. This court surrounded the Court of Levites on three sides. On the north and south it was fifty-five feet wide—on the east, only eighteen. A gallery fifteen feet wide, supported by marble columns, ran about it and afforded shelter from rain.

A low wall which barred entrance without blocking vision sepa- rated the Court of Men from the Court of Levites, five steps up; this contained the great three-tiered, unhewn altar of holocausts, some fifteen feet high, and fifty feet wide at its base. Conveniently near the altar stood the huge laver for sacrificial cleansing. Nearby were four rows of rings imbedded in the ground to hold the beasts awaiting sacrifice. Also at hand were eight marble tables for cutting and washing the flesh of the slain beasts, and a little beyond were eight pillars with hooks where the victims were flayed. From the court arose a lofty porch, surmounted with pillars almost the height of the Temple itself, each encircled with vines of gleaming gold, containing huge bunches of solid gold grapes.

The House of the Temple stood on the highest ground. It was

constructed of matched blocks of flawless, snowy marble gilded
with heavy gold plates within and without. Larger in dimension
than Zorubabel's Temple, it crowned a magnificent porch rising
to a height of one hundred and fifty feet with a similar width,
and a depth of thirty feet. A doorway without leaves, mysterious
in its simplicity, led into a vestibule flanked by two square pillars
each formed of six-foot cubes of stone. On these pillars rested a
sort of triumphal arch covered by a golden vine with golden
grapes. Thence a door with leaves of carved wood, covered with
gold and silver foliage and draped with Babylonian dyed linen,
led into the holy place with its altar of incense, one perfect seven-
branched golden candlestick, and a table for shewbread. Beyond,
separated by two massive veils, was the Holy of Holies—empty.
Above soared the House of the Temple to an additional height
of over fifty feet.

At the sides were three-story towers, with small rooms for the
use of the priests. As hitherto, the high priest's robes were kept
in the custody of Herod, but a passage was constructed from the
tower of Antonia to the Temple, to facilitate their transfer.

As the work began to show progress, Herod and the Jews might
pardonably have taken pride in their new Temple. So well had
the priestly masons done their work that no seams were perceptible in the jointures of the great stones, and the general
impression was that of one tremendous block of marble. All were
delighted with the Temple's convenience and spaciousness, which
never violated tradition or distracted from piety.

Amid general rejoicing the people thanked God for the new
Temple, whose completed state they could now visualize. Also
they were mostly loud in their praises of the king whose work
this was.

In all humility Herod sacrificed three hundred oxen in thanksgiving. For a space, he felt he might still become a popular king,
his misdeeds and mistakes forgiven.

Perhaps he had reason to be optimistic. Trusted friend of
Rome, protector and benefactor of his own nation, he lacked only
domestic bliss to fill his cup of happiness.

CHAPTER XVI

MARIAMNE'S SONS

WHILE HEROD HAD MANY ADHERENTS WHOSE loyalty he repaid amply in kind, and doubtless even more implacable enemies whom he neither feared nor shunned, his affections moved in a far lesser orbit. He truly loved his first Mariamne, loved her even while he killed her, and loved her to distraction after her death. Besides Mariamne, he opened his heart only to her older sons, Alexander and Aristobulus.

In no way did their mother's disgraceful death diminish their father's affection for them. Rather, in his remorse, he showered upon them all the love and devotion which they had previously shared with their mother. Perhaps it was because he found in them so many reminders of Mariamne. They were, it is true, very much like the queen, handsome, spirited, vivacious, sympathetic, lovable, loyal. Only in a certain restlessness, in spells of moody dissatisfaction particularly perceptible in the younger son, did they recall their royal father.

With the abatement of the first wild eruption of grief and despair following Mariamne's execution, Herod sought and in a measure found solace in the companionship of his boys. Regularly he took them into the bleak sun-baked hills where sand-colored lizards scurried over the rocks and scarcely discernible vultures momentarily like floating spots of soot flecked the blazing bowl of sky, or to the shady aisles of the royal gardens at Jericho, where comforting heat enveloped them like a blanket. He picnicked with them on the pleasant slopes of Samaria and accompanied them on shopping expeditions through the fascinating bazaars of the larger towns. Together they observed the placid round of life in the gentle Essenian communities, and learned shepherd lore on the Judean pastures. In a word, he strove to bury his memories in their wonderment, and chatter, and delight. For seven years he spent in their company hours he could ill afford to spare, losing in their gay laughter the haunting specters of the past. Yet all the while the uneasy feeling kept assailing him that this could not last—that they were emerging from childhood and must be prepared for their careers.

More than usually harassed by this thought, he was returning from a romp with his boys in the hill country south of Jerusalem. Riding along the hard-packed road, with his sons on gaily cantering steeds by his side, he hardly heard their brisk chatter. Near the city walls he surrendered his mounts to waiting grooms. At the hour when the long shadows had already engulfed the dark heart of the city and only the temple lay cold and forbidding in the level light of waning day, he entered his litter. Coal-black Abyssinian giants gently placed the carriage of sandalwood upon their shoulders, adjusted the crimson canopy against the evening chill, and with practiced smoothness started for the palace, followed by a similar litter bearing the boys. Through a chink discreetly left in the velvet folds, the king could note the averted looks of fear and hatred as he passed, and the lightening of those same faces as they glimpsed the litter of the children.

He was not jealous. For the time being, the horrible memory of Mariamne's death had shunted away every suggestion of rage or violence against those he loved. Still it was obvious that the half-divulged emotions of the Jews revealed his sons as eventual claimants to the throne. It was high time, then, to decide upon their education.

The litter climbed the ramp to the gardens above the city. Before the palace with its colossal marble wings stretching ghostly arms into the twilight, the Abyssinians softly set down their royal burdens. Brushing aside servants who unobtrusively gathered to learn their master's commands, Herod bade the boys an affectionate good night. Almost abruptly, he strode through the great hall with its hundred dining couches, crossed chamber after chamber, and passed along corridors and colonnades of rare marbles. For a moment he lingered in the pleasure gardens, where fountains tinkled and little canals gurgled, and the mournful lay of nightingales drifted on the darkness.

Then he stepped into his own study. In the semigloom, softened by the light of a gold, boat-shaped lamp with perfumed oil, he pondered long and deep. All through the night he sat thus, and the false dawn had already flushed the palace towers with a promise of day before he reached the decision.

More than anything else in the world Herod would have wanted his boys constantly at his side. But his common sense overruled his emotions. He must consider their education.

Three choices presented themselves. He might have them taught at the court, elsewhere in Judea, or in Rome.

The first choice was naturally the most tempting. Yet he considered it the least desirable. Though distinguished scholars and artists abounded at his court, he well knew their fawning nature, their unwillingness to risk disfavor by imposing educational chores or insisting on discipline. He knew too their unquestioning acceptance of a philosophy of Hellenic materialism which would almost certainly make pagans of his sons. Too, he recognized the vicious tangle of intrigue that enmeshed everyone about him. Horrified he recalled the fate of Mariamne. He determined, at any rate, to keep his sons from the trap that had cost them their mother.

He considered, too, the possibility of their being taught elsewhere in their own land, but away from the blighting breath of the court. His own early tutors, the inoffensive Essenes, might serve, or perhaps learned and pious Jewish rabbis, too enrapt in their religion to be concerned about politics. Again he rejected this possibility. The Essenes were too gentle, too unworldly, properly to bring up young princes. In their disregard of things material, they might teach his boys a spirituality that would ill prepare them for a life in an emphatically unspiritual royal court.

Even more dangerous was the prospect of their tutelage under the rabbis. Would not then the Jews have the opportunity of cultivating them as a foil to their father? Would not the mass of the people, hating the alien Herod, plot to replace him with a king whose blood was Maccabean, who showed in appearance and temperament the lusty grace of their Hasmonean ancestry? For an instant the pallid face of the boy-priest seemed to swell out of the gloom of the king's study.

Herod shuddered and passed on to his final choice.

It would tear at his heartstrings, were the boys to leave him. Yet there was no other way. They must go to Rome.

Utterly exhausted, Herod threw himself on his couch and slept the day through.

Toward evening he called his secretaries, and long into the night letters were dictated, orders prepared, and all arrangements made for the departure of the princes.

It was Herod's intention to place his older sons and—in a spirit of fairness—their younger brother, who outwardly showed almost pure Herodian characteristics, and whom paradoxically Herod loved least, in the charge of his particular friend, Asinius Pollio, who had been consul when Herod came to Rome. (It was, incidentally, this scholar and philanthropist to whom Virgil dedicated his fourth eclogue, which treats of the coming of a redeemer born of a virgin, and celebrates a reign of righteousness and peace.)

In 22 B.C., seven years after their mother's death, the young princes arrived in Rome. Graciously, Augustus installed them in apartments in his own palace on the Palatine hill.

Perhaps they were at first a little homesick. Even the novelty and grandeur of life about them could not compensate for the lack of their father. The death of their youngest brother, whose constitution wilted in the miasma of the Pontine marshes, for a time depressed them deeply. But the kindness and tact of all about them rapidly restored their spirits. Never did they feel that they were entirely severed from their homeland. Voluminous letters and delightful presents came in endless stream from their father, who permitted neither the projected restoration of the temple nor other cares or worries to interfere with his constant interest in the welfare of his sons.

For six years—happy and exciting on the whole—they lived the lives of typical young Romans of the best society. With somewhat less than proper restraint, they committed the customary excesses of their class. More mature, and indeed less vicious, than Latins of their age, they were possibly less affected than their companions, and more readily avoided the worst results of their transgressions. Candid and openhearted, moreover, they exhibited none of the meanness and snobbery prevalent among Roman scions. They were, as a result, generally popular.

Both boys were quick to learn and anxious to acquire knowledge. They did much serious study—rhetoric, in which Alexander excelled; the science of geography as newly organized by Strabo; much natural history, for which their Palestinian wanderings had given them a practical basis; and, of course, Latin and Greek. Like most cultured Romans, they, no doubt, studied Cicero, but, surreptitiously, since his works were on the proscribed list.

They took the keenest pleasure, also, in the regular course of physical exercises prescribed for them on the Campus Martius, entirely heedless of the proximity to the playing field of the grim prison where their grandfather Aristobulus had been confined.

Of the two, Alexander was the brighter mentally, and physically the stronger. Particularly in the exercise of arms and in horsemanship—a Herodian heritage—he excelled his brother. Whereas Aristobulus was somewhat slow in speech, Alexander exhibited all the natural oratory and easy conversational gifts in which his father was so proficient.

Despite the superior talents of the older brother, there was a companionship and understanding between the boys, unmarred by any trace of envy or arrogance.

Thus with serious study and healthful exercise, interrupted by occasional periods of youthful dissipation, the princes reached the respective ages of eighteen and sixteen. Externally they were Roman rather than Jewish, almost pagan in the tolerant Latin manner, attached to their father for his generosity and his concern in their welfare, and retaining the memory of their mother with the exaggerated sentimentality characteristic of youth.

During his sons' sojourn at Rome, Herod had demonstrated a constant interest in their progress. Their frequent letters and the laudatory reports of their tutors were a joy to his fatherly pride and affection. He was not too deeply concerned even when his spies sent him accounts of their limited transgressions.

But he felt it was now time for their return. Affairs were prosperous and peaceful in Judea. The newly constructed sections of the Temple had been dedicated; all projects were functioning successfully. He had become almost inured even to the ceaseless bickering in his own court, and the unyielding, if impotent, opposition of a Jewish minority. He was sixty-three. His hair and beard were graying—a secret, he vainly thought, between himself and his court barber—and the lithe figure was developing an unmistakable paunch; the litter began gradually to replace the saddle. Worse, the dizzy spells, the irritable moods, the hours when a hardly restrainable savagery took possession of him became more frequent. There was, too, a dull little pain in the abdomen, not serious, certainly, but annoying in its persistence and failure to respond to treatment. It were time his sons would assume some of the responsibilities of rule. He had made that burden light for them. He was entitled to some recompense for his sacrifices.

He sailed for Rome, ostensibly to see his friend Augustus, actually to arrange for his sons' return to their native land. His respects paid to Augustus, he was escorted, a little fearfully, to his sons' apartments. Perhaps, he thought, they were like the young Roman nobles he had met, indolent, superficial, and vice-ridden.

Their reunion left him overjoyed. The young lads he had left six years before, at once thrilled and tearful, had developed into personable, affable young gentlemen, truly cultured, in appearance slenderly graceful, polished by contact with Roman ways without being tainted by Roman excesses. They, in turn, showed to their father an easy affection, unexaggerated and unrestrained.

Not since the first years of his marriage to their mother had Herod been so happy. He stayed the briefest possible period in Rome. He was anxious to show those cynical Jews how fine, how manly his sons were. So happy was he that it never occurred to him that the Jews might prefer to look upon them as Mariamne's sons.

Favoring winds sped their homeward journey. Before entering Jerusalem, Herod conducted his sons on a tour of the cities he had founded, the fortresses he had erected, the irrigation projects, and roads, and harbors he had established. Everywhere throngs, mostly impelled by natural curiosity, in part, however, by deeper motives, greeted the princes with clamorous acclaim, even when they saw, to the amazement of some, that Herod encouraged, rather than suspected, their enthusiasm.

More sensibly, Herod would have established his sons somewhere out of Jerusalem, gradually to absorb the business of rule. Away from the intrigue and hatred of the spy-ridden court they might gradually have become acclimated to the niceties of Judean procedure, so different from the majestic bluntness of the Augustan manner. Instead, he hurried them to Jerusalem. He was naturally anxious to discover whether the more intransigeant Jews of the capital were as ready to welcome his sons as the less sophisticated provincial Jews had been.

The king's fears were unfounded. Nowhere else had there been so general, so spontaneous a demonstration of enthusiasm. He declared a holiday, distributed presents, and released political prisoners.

But despite evidences of popular approval, it was not wise to bring the princes to the court. They were not ready for the change; their transplanting was too sudden, too violent. Their frankness, their naturalness were qualities that could be appreciated in the more temperate atmosphere of Rome; here, in the bickering court of Judea, where the plain word and simple act were of their very nature suspect, they were a source of danger. Circumspection, the quality the young men chiefly lacked, was a prime requisite where every innocent remark would be distorted and every innocuous action twisted to whatever end suited the plotting, royal entourage. Accustomed to vice that flourished unashamed and virtue that flaunted itself as brazenly, the princes refused to conform with the court standard that every activity, sinful or even virtuous, must be devious. From the rarer altitude of their Roman training, they began to show their disdain of their father's relatives. They criticized the circumscribed routine of the court, laughed at the battalions of spies almost tumbling over one another, and patronizingly chided their father for not clearing away the accumulation of familiar debris.

With surprising humility Herod listened to the complaints of

his sons. Calmly, he also turned aside the scorching tirade of
Salome and her warning that his sons—such, she reminded him,
was the current Jewish prophecy—would dispossess their father.
He declined to be disturbed. He loved and trusted his sons and
took too great a pride in their popularity and their charm to
visualize them as rivals.

Meanwhile the young men were restless and unhappy. They
tried to drive the enemies into the open. But the Herodians were
too subtle to fight back with the same weapons. Failing to arouse
open antagonism which they would know how to combat, the
boys turned on their father. They criticized his submission to
his relatives, his countenancing of spies. Bitterly they assailed
him when a trouble-maker called it to their attention that the
king's wife and female relatives were wearing jewels that once
belonged to their mother.

Over the complaints of his sons, and the clamor of his relatives,
Herod still retained his calm. His sons, he reasoned, were ill at
ease in the court, as was quite understandable with spirited young
men moved from the indulgent patrician life of Rome to the
heated atmosphere of the Jewish court. Yet here they must live;
to this kind of life they must adapt themselves. A stabilizing
influence must be applied and quickly.

Marriage for his sons seemed the proper solution. With family
concerns and interests beyond their personal problems, the
princes should soon adjust themselves to the unfamiliar routine
of court life.

To find a bride for the younger, more sensitive son was a relatively simple matter. Aristobulus had become a worshiper of
Salome's daughter, his cousin Berenice. He had braved even her
mother's acid tongue to be near her; he had guilelessly entrusted
amorous messages to her servants. That first these messages
passed the sneering scrutiny of Salome, then the more sympathetic inspection of his father, he happily did not know. For
Herod was not inclined to dismiss his son's love affair with the
mockery that his sister displayed. Where harmony in the family
was concerned, there was in Herod a mental blind spot. In spite
of his experiences, intermarriage was his cure-all for family
dissension.

He called Salome and Berenice (since the young lady had very much a will of her own) into conference, and proposed Aristobulus as husband for his niece. Having already calculated all its possibilities, Berenice expressed herself in favor, and Salome somewhat sardonically added her consent.

When Herod suggested (he was too wary to command) that Berenice had demonstrated a willingness to listen with favor to a proposal by Aristobulus, the young lover was delirious with joy. But his brother's failure to join enthusiastically in his happiness came near causing the first serious rift between them.

The wedding was celebrated not in the joyful Jewish manner in which Herod had married Mariamne, but with all the sumptuous trappings and pagan extravagance of an oriental festival. Yet above the magnificent turmoil and artificial jubilation, keen-eyed guests were not slow in appraising the group at the central dining couch—Herod, beaming with happiness; Aristobulus' dark face feverishly gay; Alexander, indifferently successful in masking his doubt; Berenice, pretty, self-possessed, calmly designing; and Salome's thin lips disguised in a fixed smile that momentarily threatened to twist into a sneer.

From the very first, the marriage was stormy. Berenice was a true daughter of Salome, deceitful, lustful, and charming. It was obvious that she intended only to master and humiliate her husband. If Aristobulus seemed inclined for a time to champ at the bit, the alliance of daughter and mother proved too much for him. Moods of dull resentment, from which he was lifted to slavish idolatry only on the rare occasions when Berenice chose to exercise her charm, drew him from his brother. Sometimes he contemplated suicide. Then Berenice, who had all her mother's power of alluring men, would suddenly excite him into a state of rapturous infatuation, only to cast him back into blacker despair.

Somehow between moments of bliss and long days of despondency, their marriage persisted. The Herodians were prolific breeders, and, in spite of the long periods when she ignored her husband's very existence, Berenice bore him four children, only one of whom, whose virtue may be assumed in charitable ignorance, led a normal, decent life. The eventual marital affairs of the other three were consistent with their maternal ancestry. A son, the Herod Agrippa of the Acts, married his cousin Cyprus, unhappily, it need hardly be stated; the daughter, the evil Herodias, first married her uncle, the gentle Herod Philip, and later another uncle, Herod Antipas, murderer of John the Baptist. Another son, Herod Pollio, after various indiscriminate connubial experiences, married his niece Berenice, the most depraved of all the Herodians.

Herod saw with concern that Aristobulus' marriage had not brought about family harmony. He recognized, also, that Alexander, deprived, perforce, of his brother's companionship, was developing a moodiness and irritability foreign to his nature. This, too, he thought, marriage might remedy. It is indicative of Herod's unquenchable faith in the happiness of marital life as a panacea for all mental turmoil that, despite the evidence of the misery domestic discord had brought to himself and those about him, he never lost confidence in its efficacy. He did not, however, attempt to foist upon Alexander a Herodian bride, since there was none eligible.

He bethought himself of Archelaus, by Augustus recently made king of Cappadocia. No ordinary, puppet knight, propped up by patronizing dictatorship, this Archelaus! On his mother's side he was descended from Darius, son of Hystaspes, of the royal Persian line. From his father, he inherited the purple blood of the Macedonian kings. One child had Archelaus, a daughter Glaphyra, renowned throughout the East for her beauty, her wit, and her intelligence. In her, Herod felt, Alexander would enjoy an antidote for the provincial pettiness and mean clannishness he found so irksome.

Herod betook himself with magnificent entourage to the Cappadocian court. Archelaus was a bluff, wholesome pagan, not readily impressed even by the magnificence of Rome. Away from his court, Herod, too, could be bluff and wholesome. They found each other kindred spirits. Quite candidly, Herod divulged the purpose of his visit. With equal candor, Archelaus expressed his personal consent.

But, he confessed, Glaphyra would have to be consulted. For Glaphyra was no veiled oriental beauty, eating sweets and putting

on fat in a harem under a eunuch's unwinking eye. Lacking a
son, her father had brought her up as a boy. She could hunt and
ride better than most men, and probably outcurse them all.
Popularly she was known as "clatter-mouth," at once the pride
and embarrassment of her subjects.

But there was no trace of indecorum in the young lady who
joined her father and Herod in council. Sweet and demure,
utterly feminine, with only a lurking twinkle to hint at a possible eruption, she listened to Herod's proposal, and with deceptive meekness placed herself at her father's disposal.

The vitality of the court, the lack of ostentation, the apparent
loyalty of retainers, and absence of spies affected Herod strangely.
Here he saw family affection, mutual trust, a joyous spirit of
service that he never experienced in his own court. He was filled
with self-pity. Perhaps in providing a mate for his son he was
cheating himself of a last chance of happiness. Taking advantage
of the informality of the court, he sent for Glaphyra and made
her a second proposal, of himself.

She was not altogether surprised by the offer. She had noted
in Herod the little kindnesses, the covert stares, the sudden flush
of pleasure more indicative of the lover than of the father-in-law.
But the wise young woman declined the proposal. She was too
inexperienced in court lore, she said, too ignorant of public life
to take her place as queen of a great kingdom. As his daughter-
in-law, she would learn gradually to fill her destined place.

Thus, she indicated her preference for Alexander, and at the
same time expressed her assumption that her husband-to-be
would eventually succeed Herod. Really, the canny princess had
come to the conclusion that it was better to be wife to the heir
apparent than one in a procession of wives of an aging king.

As she modestly turned to leave, something of the humor of
the situation took possession of her. She made the mistake of
laughing. It was a good-natured laugh with no trace of malice,
one such as customarily eased an awkward situation in Cappadocia. But in it Herod could detect only scorn. His pride
deeply hurt, he started for Judea to complete arrangements for
his son's wedding.

Salome's spies preceded him to Jerusalem, with the account of his rejection. Salome gloatingly met him with the news that he was reported to have made violent love to Glaphyra, and she not to have denied him the privilege of extramarital relations. Angrily, bidding her silence the rumors and under no circumstances to let them reach the ear of Alexander, he reported to his son the success of his mission.

The wedding was the most colorful event the East had experienced since Cleopatra greeted her Antony in the perfumed, silken-sailed love barge on the Cydnus. Rome, Greece, Syria, and Judea contributed their choicest fabrics, their costliest jewels, their most delicate viands. Supercilious Romans, pretentious Greeks, and artless Arabs, even the few Jews who found it profitable to risk ostracism by their presence, alike confessed themselves amazed at the gold strewn about so prodigally, the tables so laden with food as almost to bury their coverings, the delicate linen and begemmed dishes, the fountains running wine, the relays of dancers, of acrobats, of musicians.

Herod seemingly had reason to feel confident that the coming of Glaphyra might supply the leaven to aerate the morass of hate and suspicion into which the court had sunk. Certainly, during the nuptials, he experienced an atmosphere of general friendliness and joy that promised betterment. For all was cordial; enmities seemed to have lost themselves in the general spirit of hilarity. Even Salome was gracious, the more so since she appeared to have achieved a new conquest, the somewhat callow and boresome but immensely wealthy Syllaeus, vizier to the Nabatean king. Berenice, alone, prevented from attending by her advanced state of pregnancy, sulked in her apartments. But she was apparently not missed, not even by her huband, who spent most of the time pleasantly drunk.

Both sons now safely married, and one, at least, happily, Herod felt the need for a change. His pain had grown more aggressive, he tired more readily when not quickened by a task he enjoyed performing; his ears could no longer attune themselves to court discord; the laughing voice of Glaphyra, even Alexander's jovial presence, caused him acute embarrassment.

Hearing that Agrippa was about to undertake a tour of Asia, he intercepted him at Ionia and without much difficulty prevailed upon him to alter his itinerary to make an extended tour of Judea.

Once again Herod made the round of his achievements. With the delight of a child exhibiting his new toys, he took Agrippa to the cities he had built, especially Sebaste and Caesarea, to the massive fortifications Alexandrium, Herodium, and Hyrcania, along the hard-packed roads and never failing aqueducts, and to remote agricultural communities where once-barren hillsides bloomed and where deserts flowered. Banquets surpassing even the Lucullan delights of Rome, and entertainment, erotic and amusing by turn, prodded the jaded Roman appetite to laughter and admiration. If it had been Herod's primary purpose to escape the oppressive routine of palace life, he never missed an opportunity of impressing his guest with the skill and wealth and power of Rome's dependency under his direction. Though the rigorous Jewish minority, as always, abstained from taking part in any Herodian function, their absence could hardly have been noted, since the common people, everywhere, particularly the destitute multitudes living in the capital, eagerly took part in the revels, exhibiting to Agrippa every indication of a contented, loyal populace.

For his part, Agrippa was all graciousness and affability. He offered sacrifice at the Temple, provided sumptuous feasts for the already gorged mob, appeared everywhere with Herod, and always demonstrated his friendship with the Judean king.

Throughout the summer and fall he tarried in Judea, leaving reluctantly just in time to escape the winter sailing that he abhorred.

For Herod, the short winter sped by. Still a little giddy with the favor of Agrippa, he was left untouched by the mounting storm about him.

With spring stirring in his veins, he learned that Agrippa had embarked on a campaign beyond the Bosporus. Herod left hurriedly, hoping to overtake him at Lesbos. Head winds and choppy seas detained him many days at Chios, where he passed the time playing the munificent philanthropist to all who came to see him. Not content with individual beneficences, he left money to restore the municipal portico, destroyed in the Mithridatic war. After the storms abated, he left for Byzantium, only to learn that Agrippa had sailed through to the Black Sea. Sailing after with all speed, he caught up with him near Sinope, in Pontus.

Though Agrippa had been for six months incessantly in Herod's company only a short season before, he expressed the greatest delight, as did also his subordinates, at Herod's unexpected arrival. He appreciated the length and arduousness of the journey his friend had undertaken; he was grateful for the aid and supplies he was bringing. He was shrewd enough, too, to evaluate the order and stability of a kingdom that could function despite its king's absence.

Actually, Herod seems to have had an almost hypnotic effect on the otherwise not tractable Agrippa. The over-all conduct of the campaign and affairs governing the civilian population were entrusted largely to Herod. And, as in Judea, they were always together.

The campaign in Pontus—it could not have been a particularly difficult one—was soon over. Loath to lose the pleasant companionship of Herod so soon, Agrippa sent most of his fleet back and began an overland journey through Cappadocia and Syria.

For Herod it was a delightful tour. Where citizens needed money he supplied it; where buildings were in ruins he had them rebuilt on a more magnificent scale. Petitioners to Agrippa, wisely, and never vainly, sought Herod as their intercessor; communities that had reason to tremble at the wrath of their Roman master found in the Judean an intermediary to turn aside anger and win pardon.

At Lesbos, a delegation from the Jewish colony came to him with their grievances. Where elsewhere in the Roman Empire Jews were exempt from military service, here they were impressed. Moreover, lawsuits involving Jews were always tried on Jewish holidays when no Jew could appear in court, and the money set aside for use of the Temple was seized on various pretexts for the public treasury.

They found in Herod a sympathetic listener. He requested Agrippa to set a trial, and appointed his friend and biographer Nicolaus of Damascus to plead the Jewish cause.

This Nicolaus did so effectively, and before judges so obviously friendly to his clients, that the Greeks admitted all charges and offered only the excuse that it had seemed to them just that Jews voluntarily living among Greeks should live according to Greek law and should worship in the Greek religion.

Agrippa decided that, since the Jews had been so annoyingly persecuted, they might have whatever they wished as compensation, provided that their request did not conflict with Roman interests. Wisely they asked only for freedom of worship and exemption from military service.

That night they waited upon Herod to express their gratitude and esteem. "Protector of Jews" and "Guardian of the Temple" were among the laudatory titles with which they hailed their smiling patron. Aglow with happiness, Herod bade Agrippa farewell, took sail for Caesarea and hurried on to Jerusalem. Speedy as his trip had been, the story of his magnanimous conduct outraced him to the capital. Jubilant crowds, reeking, ragged, and colorful, spewed out of alleys and tumbled down from pestiferous tenements to greet and cheer their king. To the noisy mob that packed the assembly place he made his report on the state of the kingdom, pointing out how safety, justice, and prosperity flourished as never before. There was still he admitted, a little rankling rash on the body political, caused by taxes. This in part he would instantly alleviate by a remission of one-fourth their indebtedness; and he implied that further reductions would follow.

Still in an expansive mood he dismissed his guards and pushed his way alone through grinning throngs toward his palace. His thoughts on that hot, slow journey were happy thoughts. He was rebuilding his people their Temple; he brought them creature comforts they had never known; he made their nation the friend and favorite of all-powerful Rome. He was tired, and wanted to rejoin his sons. Perhaps he might even yield to them some of his authority. He was, after all, in his seventh decade, and he knew, in spite of the optimistic assurances of his doctors, that he was not well.

The crowds had thinned as he neared the palace; their voices had dwindled to hoarse echoes in the city below. He could hear the night wind brush through the olive branches, bending the scarlet cyclamen so that their blossoms shone a burnished orange in the moonlight; lance-like cedars seemed to prick the heavens awash with stars.

Noting with a half-shamed smile that the gray was beginning to show through the dyed black of his beard, he entered his palace.

It was a step out of hope and happiness into chaos. Spies stumbled over one another in their zeal to report the misdeeds of their suspects. From a chamber the strident voice of Salome rose above the laugh of Glaphyra. With a shock he realized that merriment had gone out of that laugh. It was a shrill, humorless complement to Salome's shrieking invective.

With the closing of the palace portal, he felt himself trapped in a net of intrigue and hatred. All the happy plans that had enlivened his stay abroad and made joyful his return home dropped from him with the travel-stained cloak he wearily surrendered to a servant.

He entered his study, bowed and bent, as under a physical load. All night long he listened to informers, and read reports, and tried to make sense of Salome's spite and Glaphyra's ridicule. A little before dawn, he called in his sons. Aristobulus was sullen and Alexander angry. When they left, some of the old madness returned. Panting, he hurled himself on the divan as dry, racking sobs convulsed his aging frame.

Normally, Herod had a remarkably orderly mind. Unless obsessed by jealous rage, or fits of madness, he could almost without effort group and classify and arrange the complexities and confusions inherent in the Herodian system which derived information from sources of their very nature venal and untrustworthy. From the welter of charges and countercharges he must attend to three matters involving Salome, his youngest and only surviving brother Pheroras, and Alexander and Aristobulus.

Salome's crime was that of making a fool of herself. She was in her fifties, and without regret had seen three husbands die. Nevertheless she was hungrily seeking a fourth, the while dallying with a variety of gallants, gifted rather with youth and physical appeal than with social position or wealth. Herod was relieved, then, when Sylleus, representing his master, Obodas, as the Nabatean king at Alexander's wedding, fell victim to her somewhat warmed-up pulchritude. Sylleus was safe and fat, a solid man, if rather bumptious. He should be able effectively to brake Salome's headlong carnality. Still they seemed genuinely in love.

Herod had entertained Agrippa, spent the winter between Jerusalem and Jericho, and sailed after his Roman friend, and all this while Sylleus had protracted his stay, to the increasing amusement of the court.

"The Nabateans are notoriously stingy," it was whispered. "Rather than incur the expense of making two trips, Sylleus, having attended the wedding, will remain to celebrate the feast of the first-born." A crude drawing depicting the love-making of an asp and a hippopotamus was passed from hand to hand. Cruelly it finally was left for Salome to see.

Salome's rage surpassed even her previous best efforts. Her cowering guest was literally scared into making a proposal. He thereupon started for home, a little dazed, and buried in gifts from his espoused.

But on the wearisome journey through the desert, the love-light began to glimmer. By the time the pink temples of Petra lay before him, it had quite gone out.

Retrospection threw him into a panic. He recalled Salome in her less amiable moods, her drooling sensuality, the history of her husbands. He trembled when he remembered that he had foolishly consented to become a Jew. If his countrymen found that out, they would stone him!

Emboldened by distance, he sent back a scornful and by no means secret repudiation of his engagement on the score that a) the lady had practiced deception; b) she was too old for him.

Glaphyra's interception of the message from Petra did not help soften the blow for Salome. Her "clatter mouth" was tireless in retelling the story; her laugh rasped the raw edge of Salome's hurt pride.

Beyond sending a courteously worded report of Sylleus' conduct to his king, there was nothing Herod would do to assuage Salome's feelings. He, too, was not sorry at her discomfiture. Though he did wish Glaphyra were a little more tactful!

However, he could not quite so lightly dismiss the case against his brother. Love had come late to Pheroras. An enthusiastic hunter, a tireless rider, a gambler, poet, and all-round favorite, he had never belonged to the court cabal; he admired without envying his royal brother and cordially detested his meddling sister and all her set. Until he was fifty, women had never attracted him. Then the belated onslaught of first love left him powerless and certainly senseless. A pretty former slave girl one-third his age, an actress, earning an honest penny between engagements by doubling as attendant at Alexander's wedding, caught his fancy. He lost interest in his companions and pastimes; he would win her, even at the price of marriage. It culminated in the bright little showgirl's being installed as Pheroras' wife.

Herod, on the point of sailing to join Agrippa, issued terse orders. Pheroras must divorce the actress. As compensation he would be married to Herod's own daughter Salampsio, a substitution made more alluring by a dowry of three hundred talents.

Never dreaming that his affable younger brother would even hesitate to accept so generous an arrangement, Herod left.

Pheroras indeed courted his niece dutifully, and more frigidly, no doubt, than she would have wished. But being not over-bright, she attributed his lack of warmth to avuncular restraint.

There was, however, no restraint in his efforts to rewin his lost actress-bride. In a short time, his ardor and persistence brushed aside every hesitancy on the part of the once-bitten damsel. He avoided Salampsio's angry tears and Salome's spite by fleeing to Galilee, where he remarried his lady.

Herod felt it would be impolitic again to annul his brother's marriage. He liked him and did not begrudge him happiness. Nor had he illusions about his own daughter. From Mariamne she had inherited a weak, full-blown version of her mother's beauty; in place of her parents' pride and strength of character she had only vanity, giddiness, and a tendency to whine constantly. A fortunate escape for Pheroras! he conceded.

Yet he must keep up a pretense of authority. Pheroras would be punished by banishment from court (which he detested and rarely attended).

As for his tearful, hurt child, her three hundred talents would attract suitors by the score. Too much so! The choice had better be left to him. He scanned the field rapidly and decided that Phasael, son of his oldest brother, the late Phasael the tetrarch, would be the winning candidate. Phasael was handsome, vain, and quite without a will of his own.

News of the betrothal was made public and Salampsio quickly dried her tears.

These matters involving Salome and Pheroras were after all family scandals that hardly touched Herod himself. What deeply upset him were the accusations against his sons, involving disrespect, complicity, and even treason. From Salome down to the most debased spy had come reports and complaints, massive in their accumulation even if not impressive in their content. The gist of the charges was that the sons were outspoken, that they mocked their father for dyeing his hair and beard; and that, with Glaphyra, they were attempting to turn Augustus against Herod.

Superficially there was some basis for the accusations. Filled with the fashionable cynicism of Rome, the princes lost no opportunity of belittling the ceremonious sham that functioned at Jerusalem. With perfect good humor they laughed at their father's attempts to disguise his age, just as Roman youths joked about their elders' similar efforts.

The charge involving Glaphyra also was even more farfetched, and simmered down to the fact that she could consistently outrail her husband's relatives.

Calmly, Herod heard all the evidence, weighed all the testimony, and reached a decision that was reasonable and sane. He was convinced that his sons were indiscreet, that they hated court life, and that they loved him. Enough the cosmopolite to understand that his sons' training had not prepared them to accept the patriarchal attitude toward age, but rather the air of breezy superiority prevalent at Rome, he could overlook their jesting about his appearance.

Something like a smile flashed across the gloom of his face as he reviewed the charges against Glaphyra, "That she mocked Salome and Berenice, and said they would be slaves when she became queen; that she boasted of her father's influence with Caesar; that she habitually insulted Berenice for carrying tales to Salome; and that she encouraged her husband and brother-in-law in their disregard of Jewish customs."

Herod was certain that his sons' worst fault was indiscretion, but that their love and loyalty to him was undiminished. He would have liked completely to ignore all charges. But this he could not afford to do. To repudiate the spy system would be to close to himself, and to himself only, the chief avenue of information. If merely in self-defense, he must keep his spies, to circumvent the spies of others.

He rewarded the informers for their vigilance, put off Salome with vague promises, and resolved to call his sons into conference as soon as possible, to impress upon them the urgency of discontinuing the battle against customs and practices as they inevitably must be.

It was Herod's misfortune that he must make this and every other important decision alone. His trusted counselors were gone. Saramalla had long since dozed out his life in a sunny Syrian village. The Essenes had been made so unwelcome by Salome that they no longer visited the palace. The more moderate Pharisees, who once maintained friendly relations in the hope of a solution favorable to their faith, were kept away by fear of their radical brethren. To lean on for council was only Nicolaus of Damascus, a materialist and an opportunist, and the horde of sycophantic court parasites, informers, and spies. Consequently every decision Herod had to make, every problem he must solve, left him a little more tired, more depressed.

An accusation came from a new and unexpected quarter. Egged on by his wife, who was getting bored with the bucolic monotony of Palestine, Pheroras was prevailed upon, unwilling and unhappy, to support Salome in the charge that his sons, abetted by Glaphyra's father, were plotting to poison the king and divide his power between them.

It was a nonsensical charge based on the flimsiest evidence. If his informers had hoped that their lies would result in insensate rage and revenge, they were disappointed. Herod was indignant only that the charges had been made.

Yet this charge had one fatal effect. It reawakened the king's suspicion that however innocent his sons were at present it was still possible that they might some time in the future be guilty.

To forestall this, he committed what was possibly the crowning blunder of his career: he recalled Doris' son, Antipater, to court.

CHAPTER XVII

RETURN OF THE FIRST BORN

FOR MANY YEARS, DORIS AND HEROD'S FIRST-
born, Antipater, had been living in rustic seclusion, generously
provided for by the king, under the stipulation that they in no
way presume on their relationship or indicate any hope of additional gain therefrom. They scrupulously kept the letter of their
agreement. All the same, they never for a moment were content
with their lot. Doris was proud and vengeful; her son she tutored
only in the injustice done them.

The years passed and she heard of Herod's prosperity and
power, while she and his son remained unnoticed in their gilded
prison. Because of Herod's liberality, they, too, could afford the
luxury of maintaining a spy or two at the palace. Consequently,
she was not unaware of the less pleasant incidents that occurred
in the court. Moreover she was obsessed with an inflexible hope,
nourished by envy and resentment. She felt certain that Herod
must eventually recall her, and lived in the bitter bliss her
dreams of revenge provoked. After each crisis she eagerly awaited
a summons to return. In her pride, she felt that Herod must turn
to her; she could not appreciate the possibility of his having
ceased to love her. Her hopes rose highest after Mariamne's
execution. But she angrily saw herself passed over in favor of
other wives or concubines. She was not too blind to know that
her beauty was slipping away and that physical allurement as an
agent to regain her husband's affections could no longer be
depended on.

She revised her schemes; Antipater would exact revenge for both of them.

For a time, as she heard of the popularity of Mariamne's sons, she was sick with disappointment. Then the tide began to turn. She gloated over the reports of friction between them and Salome; she felt an insane joy in Aristobulus' unhappy marriage and Glaphyra's gift for trouble-making. The time must come, she knew—since she had studied her husband from his early manhood—when in his mortification he would recall his oldest son.

She was almost calm when the summons did come. In a singularly matter-of-fact manner she bade Antipater farewell, with but two brief rules for conduct at the court: "Antagonize no one; and cultivate Salome." She felt no need to elaborate; she knew her son, too.

She was well aware that Herod had recalled Antipater, not out of affection, but out of vexation with his favorite sons and the wish to humiliate them. Antipater was likewise under no illusions. He knew, particularly since the invitation did not include his mother, that he was merely the rod to punish Herod's children, and that at the outset at least his father would esteem him merely as an instrument of correction.

Antipater was fitted, however, to play to perfection any part that might benefit him. Of all the Herodians he was the most despicable, a fact that he began to demonstrate from the day of his arrival. Servile, obsequious, hypocritical to the core, he was all filial devotion and grateful affection toward his father. To his half-brothers he was pleasant and conciliatory, never flaunting their relationship, so that they, too, were taken in. Openly he impressed the court as a sort of simple, agreeable country cousin, still lost in the wonder of unexpected transition; actually, all sense of decency had long since been buried in a sea of boundless opportunism. Perhaps the most fitting epithet is that expressed by a gentle Methodist missionary of a century back, who arrived at the shocking conclusion that "One would not be mistaken, if he called the life of Antipater a mystery of wickedness."

Only Salome saw through his disguise, and, disgusted with the inept whirligig of spite and discord that produced nothing, she welcomed an ally. They were often together. But beyond a

questioning wonder that Salome should exhibit a human trait,
this excited no special comment. It was after all natural for an
elderly aunt to help her nephew keep afloat in a social sea that
was somewhat beyond his depth.

But it was Antipater who soon played the leading role, though
seemingly an obscure one. Through insinuation and innuendo,
by cleverly timed half-truths and seemingly embarrassed silences,
he did more to poison his father's mind against his brothers than
Salome with all her vilification. In the midst of a paean on the
excellent qualities of the princes, he would let fall an invidious
hint on their apparently treasonable activities, not to harm them,
he took pains to impress Herod, but because he loved his father
so deeply he felt compelled to inform him of the strange conduct
of his sons. Others, he went on, might regard their activities as
treasonable. He himself knew, of course, that they were merely
the impetuous reactions of sons in whom the memory of their
mother's violent death still rankled. It was only that Herod might
forestall the effects of their resentment that he, against his will,
laid this information before his father.

At judiciously spaced intervals and in varied guises the process
was repeated, until by dint of repetition Herod was completely
won over. Antipater became his constant companion—his
acknowledged favorite; his other sons were snubbed or openly
rebuked.

In spite of his success in displacing his brothers in his father's
affection, Antipater seemed to everyone but Herod as merely a
bumpkin. His training had been so egocentric and his previous
opportunities for social life so narrowly limited that he was an
obtrusive misfit in the Hellenic elegance about him.

To begin with, there was nothing prepossessing about his
appearance. His considerable height was diminished by an awkward stoop; his sturdy limbs were marred by a crablike shuffle.
His features were regular, and might have been distinguished
were it not for a crooked smile and a disconcerting habit of casting his eyes everywhere except upon the person with whom he was
speaking. His voice had an unctuous quality; he flushed readily,
and perspired a good deal. The cultural life of the court was
scintillating rather than profound; still, it was so far beyond the
range of Antipater that he seemed and showed that he realized

he was relatively illiterate. His awkward Greek accent and his fluttering attempts at elegance would certainly have made him a laughing stock, had it been profitable to laugh.

Yet all had to concede he had been uncommonly lucky. Characteristics which would have aroused ridicule, or, at best, pity in Herod, were considered by the king as evidence of modesty and humility, virtues so conspicuously lacking in the rest of his family.

To everyone else, however, his lack of grace, his cringing hypocrisy, and his complete inferiority to his brothers were quite transparent.

Salome, the farseeing, knew it would be only a matter of time before the king, too, opened his eyes. Therefore, there was but one course of action open. She would remove her accomplice, before he was suspected, to a place where he could continue, though absent, to operate his evil designs.

She went to Herod, reminding him that he had given his other sons the advantages of a Roman training and the benefits of intercourse and friendship with the noblest Romans. But the son who obviously loved him best and with least cause, after vegetating for years in rural seclusion, was pushed, quite unready, into the refinements of a royal court. Though quite unhappy here, this son concealed his misery for fear of seeming unappreciative of his father.

Herod was hurt. He felt he had failed to do justice to this child of his first love. In catering to his own craving for affection, he had neglected to think of his son's happiness. But, he assured Salome, he would atone for his selfishness. Antipater would also go to Rome, and speedily.

That same day, Antipater was summonded to Herod's study. Prepared by Salome for the offer of a Roman sojourn, he managed, nevertheless, to affect a grateful surprise. Coyly he hesitated an appropriate time, since he disliked being separated from his father. Quite overcome by such filial devotion, Herod assured him that their mutual love would be best served, and their future relations most securely cemented, were Antipater to live, for a time, in Rome.

They embraced; Herod genuinely touched, Antipater's cheeks wet with ready tears.

It was Antipater who spoke first. Though he had never made

a request of his father, there was one favor he would ask as a
parting gift.

Expansively, Herod bade him ask—the favor was already
granted.

Haltingly, Antipater began. His father knew how dearly he
loved him. But a son's affections belong also to a mother, who
during their long exile had schooled him in the love of a father
he had never seen. Now this forsaken mother must live out her
years in bitterness, separated from those she would never cease to
love.

He paused, overcome by synthetic emotion, or perhaps because
he sensed that there was no need to continue.

The upshot was, as the ancient chronicler quaintly puts it, that
Antipater managed to "bring his mother back into Mariamne's
bed."

Fortunately—or possibly Salome had realized the opportune
moment for her proposal—Agrippa, returning to Italy from his
Asiatic tour, was still within reaching distance. With Antipater
alone—the other sons very definitely shunted into inferior positions—Herod hastened after and overtook him. The blunt Roman
must have been startled at sight of the king's uncouth charge.
Nevertheless he received him cordially, and bearing Herod's gifts
and expressions of esteem for Caesar continued his journey with
his unexpected companion.

On the leisurely sail Antipater learned much of Roman life
and manners that later served him in good stead. Agrippa was
practical and candid. He offered his pupil an unvarnished version of what to expect at the capital and instructions as to how
he should best conduct himself. The lesson was not lost. Antipater was receptive; he had a retentive memory and an adaptive
faculty.

Strangely, the poor relation whom the provincial sophisticates
snickered at in Jerusalem almost immediately cut a wide swath
in the more glittering society of the Imperial City. His allowance
was truly princely. Whatever doors could be turned with a
golden key opened wide at his touch. Through other more dis-
criminatory portals he passed with letters from Agrippa or Herod.
Wealth and influence, and something besides, a naïveté, a seem-

ing country wholesomeness, made his presence a welcome one among the jaded Roman aristocrats. Society found him refreshing, the more so because he never seemed aware of his powers to charm. Only simulated dignity that more nearly resembled cocksureness marred the perfection of his impression. True, the more vigorous Roman element with whom his younger half-brothers had consorted snubbed him as a rustic and sneered at his air of self-importance. But Antipater wrote off this society as little loss. His slickness was gaining him access into more influential circles. Before long, he ingratiated himself even into the company of the familiars of the empress Livia.

The transformation of the Judean yokel into the social lion of Augustan Rome was truly remarkable. At ease alike in the gambling rooms and brothels with reckless young Romans, or in the halls of elegant dilettantes, where, to be sure, he maintained an appreciative silence, he enjoyed best the hectic, venomous coterie that attended on the empress. Here he could observe and enjoy, a participant in none of the never-ending cabals and plots, yet a friend and confidant of every plotter. Here he was in his element, noting and studying the hateful arts of deception and treachery as practiced by masters.

Only one little worry still assailed him. He did not underestimate the charm of his brothers. With reason, he feared that during his absence they might regain the good will of their father.

Naturally cunning, he studied well the refinements of double-dealing in the most perfidious court circle in the world. The possibilities of remote plotting, of contaminating a father's mind and stunting paternal love from a distance appealed to his devious brain.

From Rome to Jerusalem flowed a constant stream of messages and letters, so affectionate in tone that Herod had always before him the picture of a loving, devoted son. Buried in each communication was also the smouldering spark of doubt, the insidious hint, the veiled suggestion, which implicated his brothers and kept alive the king's distrust. Little by little, hints gave way to open charges of attempted poisoning, of threatened rebellion, yet all worded with such seeming concern for his father's safety and with such regret and sorrow at his brothers' perfidy that

Herod never for a moment suspected the trickery that motivated the charges.

Antipater was too shrewd to trust to the chance efficacy of his letters alone. Salome was sent a duplicate of every letter he wrote to the king, and knew therefore how most tellingly with manufactured evidence of her own to give substance to every hint or charge of treachery brought by Antipater.

For two years Herod lived in mental and emotional agony. The son of his first love, long neglected, almost forgotten, through letters, warm and convincing in expressions of loyalty and tenderness, and insistent, if sometimes vague in detail, on the treachery of the princes, was presenting constant evidence of filial love that the king knew he hardly deserved. On the other hand, Mariamne's boys, on whom he had lavished almost excessive affection, were plotting his death and coveting his throne. He wanted with all his soul to discredit the evidence. But to him, it was too patent. Every accusation was corroborated by Salome; hints dropped in Rome were affirmed by testimony from his sister in Jerusalem.

Ordinarily acute where threats to his safety were concerned, Herod could be singularly blind to treachery on the part of his own family. That there might be an obvious nexus between Antipater and Salome never occurred to him.

The princes, meanwhile, did nothing to allay their father's suspicion. When he praised the zeal and accomplishments of their absent brother, he was met with prideful insolence. A hint at the charges hanging over them resulted in a chilling silence, more hurtful to the king's ardent spirit than physical violence.

At length Herod resolved to act. But with the memory of Mariamne's trial ever haunting him, he was determined that this trial must be scrupulously judicial. Not again would he venture to be plaintiff and judge. Augustus, himself, in a fair trial, would pass judgment.

Hastening toward Rome in 12 B.C., Herod met Augustus at Aquileia. The Judean presented a sorry spectacle. Harried in mind, weary and heartsick, he poured out his soul to the Roman. Sobbing, he implored a trial for Mariamne's sons on the charges of treason.

Caesar was shocked at the change in his friend. With comforting words he assured him that justice would be done, and ordered the princes to Rome.

Three weeks later the trial opened in the presence of some twenty of Caesar's trusted advisers.

It is quite likely that, moved by the anguish of his old friend, he was in no mood to be lenient with the princes. The appearance of the defendants, however, made him less certain of their guilt. Sullen they seemed, and defiant, yet giving the impression that they were hurt, rather than guilty. With a not unkindly gesture, Caesar bade them follow their father and himself into the council chamber. For a space, father and sons alike were made acquainted with those whom they had never met. But, for the most part, they were among friends: military comrades of Herod's; fellow students and roisterers of his sons during their Roman sojourn.

Thereupon Caesar, as presiding judge, in a manner calculated to ease the nervous excitement of Herod as well as the stunned resentment of his sons, explained the case, asked his advisers to be humane in their monitions, and promised that he would prefer, if possible, to reconcile rather than to punish.

After which he called upon the father to prefer his charges.

Herod, in the frenzied interval between meeting Augustus and the trial, had prepared his case with all the skill of a practiced pleader, augmented with the vindictiveness of a benefactor whose kindness has been repaid only with disdain and treachery. He began calmly enough, by asserting that it was from Caesar himself that he had been granted the authority to name his own successor. As a result of his exercising that indisputable right, the defendants became so embittered that they plotted to kill him and seize for themselves, by violence, that kingdom which he held in trust for Rome. To prove that his sons' resentment was unreasonable, he elaborated on his kindness to them, recalling how he had given them everything they could desire—preferment over his other children, a Roman education, marriage into the best families. Only after their conduct became intolerable had he recalled his first-born, so long slighted by his father, yet so loyal and grateful for that father's belated atonement.

The speaker became less coherent as he contrasted Antipater with his other sons. It was evident that despite his disappointment and resentment he still deeply loved the sons whose lives might well be the payment exacted for their father's denunciation.

More and more he realized the impact of his action. How, after all, was this trial different from Mariamne's? Caesar's lips might pronounce the sentence, yet it was Herod who was actually sentencing his sons to death just as he had killed their mother. His voice lost its fine resonance. The peroration, which he had planned as a resounding indictment, was spoken so low that only with difficulty could Caesar and those nearest him follow. Weakly, he faltered a moment. Then, with a visible effort to regain his self-control, he brought his charge to an end with the statement that even though his was the power of life and death, he preferred to delegate that power to the discretion of Caesar. Instead of acting in a manner natural to an abused father and outraged monarch, so great was his love for his sinning sons that he would debase himself to their level, before their common judge.

For a moment he stood, almost dazed, staring at Caesar with unseeing eyes. With quiet sympathy, the emperor led him to his divan, into which he sank, a dead weight, as though completely exhausted.

A pitiful murmur swept through the chamber, combined of embarrassment and furtive tears.

But it was the princes who were most affected. They stared at the unkingly figure slouched in the divan, arms limp, eyes glassy, the beard ordinarily sleek, and black and prideful, now crushed, scraggly, gray, and streaked against his chest, his mouthy breathing rasping through the room.

They were decent, loving men—if proud—and true sons of Herod and Mariamne. Mostly, they were affected by their father's collapse. Refute him, they could. But that would make him appear weak and gullible before Caesar. Yet if they said nothing in their defense, would not that be looked upon as confession of their guilt? For a moment they whispered unhappily with each other, then burst into tears.

But they were mistaken in assuming that their failure to

defend themselves was construed as an admission of crime.

Understandingly, Caesar and the other observers read in their distress, not the speechlessness of the criminal, who with every avenue of escape blocked sinks into defiant silence, but rather the stunning shock of hideous, untrue accusations against innocent young men. A wave of sympathy engulfed the judgment chamber, stirring at length even the almost inert form of Herod. Raising himself on his elbows, he faced his sons. His lips moved, but no words followed. It was his eyes, suddenly alive, that flashed their message to his sons, appealing to them to repudiate his accusations. He was once again the tender father praying that his suspicions be proven false.

Aristobulus, red-eyed and shaken with sobs, could only with difficulty regain some measure of self-control. It was Alexander, whose natural gift of oratory had been developed in the Roman schools, that spoke for both. Though his low, vibrant voice was readily heard by everyone, he seemed to be speaking to his father alone—an intimate utterance intended for no alien ear.

Simply and gratefully he expressed his appreciation that the trial was held before Caesar, itself an indication that their father wished them no harm. The thought of continuing to live under their father's suspicion was nevertheless so unbearable that they would prefer to be slain in their innocence. The accusation, to them, was inexplicable. Merely because their father was alive and enjoying his substance, it surely did not follow that his own sons would want to do away with him. The crimes they were accused of, their father must realize on reflection, were in no way characteristic of them. When, for instance, had there ever been any real reason to believe they were skilled in preparing poisons? Plotting with others? Were they not always condemned for being too straightforward in their criticism and their enmities? As for corrupting servants! Was it not well known that their tastes were simple, and their servants few and devoted to Herod, excepting perhaps those dubious characters who were recommended by Salome and whom they themselves distrusted?

Admittedly, distrust, and slander, and calumny are present in all courts. But a sane, just ruler like their father would want to listen to all sides, the accuser and the accused, before passing judgment. This, no doubt, is the reason why their kind father requested this trial before Caesar, in order that, having presented the charges against them, they might be given the opportunity, before the highest authority in the world, to clear their names and be reunited with their father. Granted, they had talked too freely, but never against Herod; only against talebearers, detractors, and those who would make their father appear ridiculous. True, they were faithful to their mother's memory. Yet they had never denounced the manner of her death; that would have been an aspersion upon the father they revered. They would reserve the right to defend their mother's good name from vilification, as they had done in the past, and as they would likewise do for their father, were it ever his misfortune to meet with reverses.

Alexander slightly raised his voice and turned to Caesar. How, he continued, could they consistently be accused of plotting to kill their father to win the throne which, by their very violence, they would forever lose what chance they might otherwise have of inheriting? Parricide is so detestable a crime that Caesar would certainly not reward the murderers by bestowing a crown and kingdom upon them.

Once more he turned to his father, a tremor in his tones.

If Herod was now convinced of their innocence, they would plead with him to expunge the accusations from the record. If he was, notwithstanding, still suspicious of their guilt, they would then ask Caesar to pronounce the sentence of death upon them, as they would not want to live.

It was a convincing refutation, all sincerity and candor. More than that, the situation touched the heartstrings of the listeners, most of them friends of the disputants. Some wept openly. All hoped fervently that the distressing scene they had witnessed would result in the reconciliation of father and sons. Herod was most affected. Tears streamed down his cheeks. He rose from his divan. Apparently he was about to throw himself at his sons' feet in a tumult of repentance.

This Caesar could not allow. It would be unseemly for a king to grovel before his subjects. With restraining arm he warded Herod back to his divan and ordered all to their places.

It was clear, he pronounced, that the sons were innocent of the charges brought against them by their father. Still, they were not entirely blameless. Careless in their pride, they had made no effort to avoid indiscretions, or to refute the accusations against them, which were making their father so miserable. In the future, they must avoid every occasion of suspicion, and by their dutiful attitude convince their father of their esteem and gratitude. Herod, on the other hand, should ignore anonymous or unfounded accusations against his sons, and discuss frankly with them whatever actions on their part might appear to him questionable.

Smilingly, he embraced father and sons. A jubilant company sallied from the council chamber, Herod and his sons, arms entwined, the last to leave. At the door they came face to face with Antipater, breathless and snuffling with pretended joy.

It had been his intention to be on hand at a time when his father, despondent at the proven duplicity of his sons, might be most susceptible to a show of affection. Even though matters had taken a turn he had not anticipated, he could readily adapt himself to the altered circumstances. If there was no occasion for showing sympathy, he could just as effectively share his father's joy, and, even, with a little luck, merit credit for having made it possible.

A flash of annoyance passed over the face of Herod; Alexander and Aristobulus shot black looks at their hypocritical brother; Caesar's glance was compounded of amusement and disgust.

Antipater was nowise upset by his dubious reception. He knelt before his father in filial affection; he embraced his unresponsive brothers. Neither annoyance nor dislike could stem the slithering cascade of words. He was so happy, he averred, that he had played a not unimportant role in bringing about this lasting reconciliation between his beloved father and his dear brothers. Had he himself not reported the calumnies that were on everyone's lips in Rome, his father would have heard them eventually from less trustworthy sources. By his forthright action he had brought matters to a head. The charges, as he knew they would be, were proved false, and due to this thoughtfulness his father and his brothers were again united. He pleaded with Herod in the future to disregard similar charges, which were certain to be made, even though to all others they might sound convincing. He admonished the princes to abandon their ambitions, natural though they might be, and to leave their future condition to the generosity of their common father.

Cunningly, he reopened the old, seemingly-healed wounds, refanned the noxious fumes of suspicion in hearts that had so newly been soothed with the balm of reconciliation.

That evening, Herod was again received by Caesar. The conversation was of Judea and its future. Herod's complete control was reaffirmed. The country was his to dispose of to one son or to distribute among several. The emperor, however, negatived Herod's proposal that the matter of future authority be settled immediately. He realized that Herod was physically and emotionally tired. It would be more satisfactory, he insisted, if Herod made his decision in his own country before his own people.

In departing, Herod left his gift—three hundred talents for the emperor's treasury. Augustus, in turn, bestowed upon Herod half the copper mines in Cyprus and made him director of the remaining half.

Caesar was most cordial in bidding Herod farewell. Never had he been so considerate, so understanding. Yet, though Herod did not suspect it, and even Caesar himself was not fully aware of the fact, the Judean had effectively removed himself from the ranks of energetic, reliable Roman vassals. The man Augustus could and did feel sympathy for a deluded father, and affection for a distressed friend. Imperial Caesar, however, could but realize that a subject ruler was a dupe of plotters, and evidently slipping into his dotage. Never again would Caesar have unquestioning faith in the judgment of Herod, or unmixed confidence in his skill and vigor.

But of this Herod was happily unaware as he sailed homeward. In his company was also Antipater. Wisely that individual had surmised that the proximity of Caesar was not conducive to his safety. Besides, he felt the time was nearing when Herod would make a choice among his sons and it was not his policy to delegate his interests to chance or to the agency of others. He knew, too, that Herod could not ask Caesar again to sit in judgment on his sons. The next time Herod himself would be judge, and Antipater was determined that his presence should speed that day.

On their way homeward, they tarried for a time at Sebaste with Alexander's father-in-law, bluff, old King Archelaus of Cappadocia. Several weeks passed and Herod seemed in no hurry to return home. The genial welcome of his host, the clean, informal court atmosphere, the prevailing comfort and gaiety gave him the first respite from excitement and intrigue that he had experienced in years. He became again the considerate father Mariamne's children had known, the unruffled commander his troops revered.

As for Alexander and Aristobulus, they were learning to know their father. Wholesome, natural affection was blotting out the last sordid traces of incertitude and distrust.

Antipater, only, found their sojourn trying. He knew that Archelaus disliked him, or, even worse, despised him, referring to him before everyone except his father as "Herod's oaf" and "the Judean booby." Cordial to all others, the Cappadocian king treated him with a cold formality that barely missed being insulting.

Vainly, he implored Herod to hasten home. The Judean king was enjoying himself too much. Nor, as he was somewhat mystified to discover, was he much concerned with what Antipater wished or did.

Not until news arrived about a revolt in the remote district about Trachon was Antipater able to persuade his father, over the protests of his host, to return to Jerusalem.

As a matter of fact, the disturbance was an unimportant uprising, easily put down by the local military commanders. Antipater had, however, magnified its potentialities and emphasized what might be Caesar's reaction to rebellion in Judean territory, to the point where Herod consented, regretfully, to return to Jerusalem.

As they gradually approached the city, Herod lost his gaiety and became listless; the younger sons became irritable, as though the capital were flinging afar its toxic aura and tainting all normal, healthful emotions.

But Antipater was rapidly regaining his complacency. By the time they entered the palace only he seemed pleased to return.

Herod and his other sons were spiritless and dejected. A king
and his princes were coming home, but rather, they conveyed the
impression of recaptured prisoners, returned to confinement from
which further escape was impossible.

It took Herod a week of intensive work to reassemble the
scattered reins of government during which he tried, honestly,
to bar himself to spies and informers. Of course, Salome in her
sisterly visit did not fail to exaggerate the apparent lack of interest in Judean affairs demonstrated by the princes at Sebaste, and
their evident reluctance to return to the kingdom which their
father had, at least at times, intended them to govern. As a
corollary, she felt bound to remind Herod that it was Antipater
who, among the amusements and distractions at the Cappadocian
court, constantly bore in mind his father's interests in Judea.
Perhaps, she reminded Herod, he had noticed how assiduously
Antipater had thrown himself into his work since his return, and
how reluctant his brothers were to take up again the duties of
their station.

His sister's innuendoes were on his mind as he prepared his
speech.

It was meant to be a most important address: a report on the
present state of the kingdom, comments on his recent meeting
with Caesar, and, above all, provisions for the government of his
country after his death.

Particular pains were taken, too, that the setting be appropriate and impressive. To lend the occasion a quasi-religious
significance, a high platform was erected within the Temple, in
the Court of Strangers, where Jews might hear the proceedings
from the women's court or the court of Israel, while gentiles
could attend in the Court of Strangers, without their presence giving offense to Jews. The platform of cedar and sandalwood was
covered with a velvet canopy of Tyrian purple, embellished with
the golden grape motif characteristic of the Temple. Roman
emblems were conspicuously missing. Obviously Herod intended
to speak as King of the Jews, on topics that concerned Jews.

Hours before the time for the address, the place of assembly
was densely packed. Close about the throne chair were the Sadducean elite, comprising the high-priestly clan, and the chief

merchants of the kingdom. Nearby, and apparently on the best of terms with them, were the Herodians (gentiles and half-Jews mostly), besides Greeks and Romans attached to the court and hangers-on from a dozen African and Asiatic kingdoms. The chief Pharisees also were present—in fact thrust themselves into places where they could be readily seen and observed. In exhibiting their utter disapproval of the proceedings, they would at the same time maintain their positions as leaders of the opposition. Seemingly miscast in the glitter and commotion, a placid delegation of Essenes, Herod's guests from Engaddi, occupied places of honor before the platform.

Every foot of space not reserved for guests or arrogated by sneering Pharisees was packed with perspiring, squabbling Jews and gentiles in their respective sectors, pushing, catcalling, showering one another with coarse witticisms or abuse. Reverence appropriate to the place and dignified attention that the significance of the assembly should warrant were absent. There was rather the atmosphere of a street fair and the boisterous vulgarity of a holiday night in the slums.

A turbulent yell, an explosion of pent-up excitement more than an expression of loyalty, rolled through the holy place as the king in regal garb, followed by his sons, passed along an alley framed by the impassive faces and burnished shields of the Gallic Guards and ascended the platform. A hush, part interest and part concern, fell upon the massed courts. Wealthy Sadducee, conniving Hellene, ambitious Pharisee, or miserable commoner knew alike that what Herod had to say would seriously affect their positions, perhaps their existence.

The speech was neither impressive nor effective. With only a passing reference to the present, unprecedented prosperity of the kingdom, Herod passed on to what purported to be an account of his recent meeting with Caesar. How cordial their relations were, how personally friendly, how Caesar put unquestioning faith in all Herod's actions and would unswervingly sanction all his decisions—such was the tenor of his comments. It was a most expansive account of a love feast, and Herod enjoyed the telling. But the listeners it informed only that Caesar and Herod were the best of friends, which they had already taken for granted.

During the long narrative of his Roman adventure (which omitted the really important items of his accusation of his sons, and Caesar's judgment) the crowd became restless. They instantly recoiled to attention, however, when he introduced the topic of the royal succession.

A clear, reasonable exposition of future policy might have saved the day. Instead, attempting to be witty, Herod became merely facetious; striving to be detailed, he was merely garrulous. His sons, he announced, would be his successors. Antipater, as first-born, who had moreover unfailingly shown ability and affection, would rule first; and after him, Alexander and Aristobulus—in whose favor the king, incidentally, pronounced no encomiums, such as had attended the mention of Antipater. There was no further elucidation of this decree.

The listeners were perplexed. Did Herod intend that Antipater would rule for life, and that, in the event of the latter's death, Alexander and his brother should inherit the throne rather than Antipater's children? Or was Antipater to be supreme ruler and his brothers petty kings under him? Or were they to rule in turn? Or did Herod, abstruse when he meant to be subtle, have still another plan in mind?

Pausing to let the import of his decision sink in, the king continued in a vein of ill-timed humor. He had, he assured his subjects, no intention of resigning his crown. Was he not at an age when men know best how to rule? Besides, his health was excellent and he intended to live for a long, long time. From past experience he knew not only how to govern a kingdom, but, his sons could rest assured, how also to control a family. One promise only would he make, that those, and only those, who demonstrated their loyalty to him would be guaranteed happiness. He closed on a solemn, almost ominous note, "I pray to God to preserve what I have determined."

With a smile for Antipater, and a knowing leer for his other sons, he descended from the platform, and, almost jauntily, moved along the avenue of guards to his litter beyond the Temple.

In his wake followed Antipater, a smile of triumph on his full lips; then his brothers, shamefaced and dejected.

No one, except Antipater and the Pharisees, felt elated over the speech. Obviously Herod was growing old mentally. Even a glib flow of words could not disguise the paucity and confusion of ideas. The one decision he made betrayed the indecision that possessed him. It was recalled that he was sixty-four, and that during his life he had experienced violence and treachery that would long since have beclouded the reason of a less able man.

The crowd was slow to disband, as is the way with crowds disappointed in their purpose of assembly. Slowly, as if unwillingly, individuals and small groups began to detach themselves from the purposeless mass. Then, suddenly, with all the impetuous violence of a mountain squall, black clouds rushed together and broke. A chill, drenching rain streamed upon the unsheltered mob. In an instant, bedraggled, morose bands lunged to the tenements or palaces of Jerusalem.

Only the limp purple trappings of the platform with the golden grapes hanging at crazy angles were reminders that a king had spoken to his people.

CHAPTER XVIII

PLOTS AND CONFESSIONS

HEROD'S ATTEMPT TO RESTORE HARMONY IN his family by allotting all three sons a share in governing his kingdom after his death proved a signal failure. Alexander and Aristobulus felt that they, the legitimate Judean line, had been slighted. Their father's slurring remarks and patronizing attitude galled their pride. They were hurt also at the realization that Herod, by recognizing Antipater as coregent with them, placed Doris on a level with their royal mother.

Antipater, while concealing his chagrin, was disappointed in not having completely ousted his brothers in his father's design.

No one could suspect from his conduct, however, that he was anything but delighted by Herod's decision. He openly lauded his wisdom, and, on being apprised that his brothers seemed not to share his complacency, expressed himself as shocked at their ingratitude.

Once again Mariamne's sons had not learned the lesson of repression. They openly showed their bitterness. The injury done them they discussed with whoever would manifest a willingness to listen. In Herod's court all would and did listen, and what was heard invariably found its way, not unembellished, to the king's ear. Most unwisely they even forwent their animosity long enough to express their views to Antipater, who, with guileful sympathy, drew from them the full story of their resentment.

Naturally, he too went to Herod, grieved, as he expressed it, by his brothers' duplicity, yet bound in gratitude to reveal to his father their hatred and their plotting.

He was disappointed at Herod's reaction. He had undoubtedly expected indignation, searing anger, and violent revenge. But Herod seemed hardly to hear. At the conclusion of the unsavory narrative, his eyes closed, his head drooped, he seemed in a coma.

Alarmed, Antipater called the royal physician. While he willed the king's death, he appreciated the implications, were he alone to be present at his demise.

Once again the physician prescribed his unvarying remedy. Withdrawal from court life and new, fresh interests alone could assuage the fever and ease the tension under which Herod existed.

This time Herod was disposed to accept his advice. He was spiritless, tired to death. Undoubtedly he was feeling his age. His pain left him little respite during his waking hours; his drug-induced slumbers were haunted by the victims he had sent to their doom.

Herod would immediately have thrown himself into new building ventures. His physician, however, demurred. Something not so strenuous, something novel, would more quickly restore the king's strength and enable him, so much more effectively, later to undertake architectural projects, were he so disposed.

In matters not pertaining to the court, Herod could be reasoned with. At the suggestion of Nicolaus, he undertook the reorganization of Olympic games.

These contests had fallen upon evil days. Never quite abandoned, they had been performed in a sort of uninspired rote. But all their glory and glamour had departed. Financially a failure, they depended for mere existence on the grudging generosity of donors, gambling by doubtful means, to attain a degree of notoriety.

In the year 10 B.C., the third year of the one hundred and ninety-second Olympiad, Herod called together the managers of the Olympic games. He expressed his willingness to finance the competitions, to provide the arena, and to guarantee their perpetuation at five-year intervals. Unhesitatingly the managers elected him perpetual manager and surrendered full direction into the munificent hands of the king.

Gleefully, as a child with a new toy, Herod issued his orders. The games were to take place at Caesarea and the participants would perform naked in the traditional Greek manner. In addition, for the first time in the history of the games, prizes would be awarded also to those finishing second or third in the races.

After a remarkably short time, the arena was made ready and invitations issued to athletes and artists everywhere in the empire.

On the opening day, Herod led the procession of officials and participants into the arena. He wore a flowing purple robe and a diadem studded with jewels. His face bore a smile; his manner was gay.

He might well have been pleased. His initiative and generosity were lauded throughout the Roman world. Even Livia, Caesar's odious wife, sent donations of furniture from Rome.

The games were outstandingly successful. Greece and Rhodes sent their athletes as a patriotic duty. Leaving nothing to chance, however, Herod had engaged the ablest gladiators and professional athletes from Rome.

True, the more squeamish Jews were uneasy at the unwonted exhibition of nudity; and the actors and mimics—their first appearance before Jewish spectators on Jewish soil—were more celebrated for the smartness than for the decency of their performances. Perhaps even the amateur athletes found some of Herod's Olympic innovations a little disquieting. Among the Greeks, only in boxing contests, with the iron gauntlet, the cestus, was blood likely to be spilt. Herod, however, arranged for life or death struggles between gladiators and with wild beasts.

But these were minor discords, hardly heard amid the general paean of praise.

If the games and contests were hectic by day, Herod made sure that the nights would be doubly delirious. Buildings were brightly lighted; vessels in the harbor had their rigging and masts strung with colored lamps; booths and arcades were gay and noisy; food was abundant and free, while fountains literally ran wine.

When the games had ended, the participants and spectators left, delighted for the most part, and sated. To some extent, the games restored Herod's waning reputation.

When Herod had guaranteed to pay all expenses, no one had anticipated from a minor king such astounding prodigality, surpassing, in quality at least, anything that Rome or Alexandria could effect.

Herod smilingly accepted the acclaim and proceeded to reimburse himself by levying an assessment on the grumbling but still profited tradesmen and innkeepers of Caesarea.

Instead of exhausting him, the conduct of the Olympic games seemed rather to whet Herod's appetite for further activity. He had thoroughly enjoyed himself. The boisterous pagan atmosphere, the excitement of the games, the gladiatorial contests, the concerts and entertainments, the beauty and the noise were memories too delightful to be spoiled by the thought of returning to court. He threw himself into another building spree (incidentally his last)—memorials largely to his family and benefactors.

In the Capharsaban plain he diverted the course of a river to form a loop about a promising building whereupon he built a city in a fertile depression. Trees were left standing in such profusion that a traveler approaching over the enclosing rim could hardly see the buildings through the foliage.

Perhaps in this city, significantly named Antipatris in memory of his father, he expressed an unconscious revulsion against the Jews, whose cities were usually bare in appearance, and who hid their trees in interior gardens.

On a height above Jericho, overlooking that city and the jungle of the Jordan valley, he built a charming cluster of villas and rest resorts, named "Cyprus" after his mother.

A number of memorials were established to honor his brother Phasael. In several places monuments were erected extolling the latter's heroism and his sacrifice; the massive tower of Phasael was raised to dominate Jericho; in the fertile country north of that city a fortress town, also named Phasael, was established as defense and refuge against possible trans-Jordanian marauders.

There was something symbolic in the character of these projects that expressed the softer side of the vexed monarch. The fruitful wisdom and benevolence of his father, the tenderness of his mother, the sturdy bravery of his brother were all suitably expressed, not in forbidding obelisk or frigid mausoleum, but more fittingly through the warmth of living wood and populated stone.

Nor were his old friends at Rhodes forgotten. The Temple of Apollo, partly in ruins and unrepaired because of lack of funds, was restored, and a silver talent was contributed for the upkeep of the Rhodesian fleet.

Seeking also to honor Augustus, Herod constructed a Nicopolis —a shrine of victory—at Actium, scene of the decisive triumph over Antony.

The foregoing might be designated labors of love and policy. These completed, and Herod still seeking excuses not to return to Jerusalem, he looked about for something further to occupy his time.

It was brought to his attention that the main street of the great trading center, Antioch, was in poor condition. Herod personally supervised its repaving and furthermore built arcades along both sides to make trading more comfortable.

All these expensive projects constituted a serious drain on the royal treasury. Further taxes, while not unreasonable in the light of the increase in income many of his projects occasioned, would cause dissatisfaction among a nation which willingly paid only its tithe to the Temple. This dissatisfaction, in his uncertain standing with Rome, Herod could not afford to arouse. He therefore returned of necessity to Jerusalem, where he had reason to believe gold was available.

In the process of rebuilding the Temple he had steeped himself in Jewish history and tradition. It was generally accredited among learned Jews that David's sepulcher, which also contained the tomb of Solomon, was actually a storehouse of treasure. A persistent rumor had it that, during the reign of John Hyrcanus, that king helped himself to three thousand talents of silver therefrom, but left far more untouched.

To tap these resources, belonging to the nation, and justifiably available for national use, seemed to Herod a reasonable procedure. Neither superstitious nor particularly impressed with reverence for the resting place of the poet-king, he had no qualms about undertaking what would have meant to most Jews the violation of a shrine. Still, it was politic to keep his purpose a secret.

Not without agitation, Herod with Nicolaus, his new adviser Ptolemy, and a few trusted guards opened the sepulcher. Hastily and fearfully, awed in the presence of dusty death, they looked about the close chamber. Of actual gold or silver there was none, though there was some evidence that the tomb had been previously rifled. Golden furniture and antique jewelry were scattered about in abundance, however. Refraining from prying into the actual tombs, they hurriedly snatched the jewels, dragged what furniture was portable to a waiting wagon, and sped back to the palace.

When day broke Herod was a little ashamed of his apprehensiveness. The massive tombs of David and Solomon were sealed, untampered with for centuries. Was it not likely that if precious objects, and probably money originally, were so profuse in the sepulcher, the actual tombs, far too roomy for their occupants, would contain what was priceless?

That night, accompanied only by two Gallic guards, he returned to the sepulcher.

What actually happened is a matter of doubt. According to a prevalent tale, quoted by Josephus, flames darted from the violated tombs, annihilating the guards and terrorizing Herod. But Herod's official biographer and companion on his first venture into the sepulcher, Nicolaus of Damascus, does not mention the king's desecration of the tomb. He does admit, nevertheless, that Herod erected a propitiatory monument at the entrance to the sepulcher.

In any event, the objects filched from the sepulcher were insufficient to defray the cost of Herod's building ventures. Of necessity, he had to remain in Jerusalem to start the machinery for raising new revenue in as quiet and painless a manner as possible.

Unfortunately, this required his residence at the palace. There nothing had changed unless for the worse. In brief, the procedure was substantially as before—Alexander and Aristobulus moody and angry, Salome and Glaphyra snapping at each other, Antipater accusing his brothers before Herod while he appeared at the same time to apologize for their misconduct.

By this time the squabbling and plotting had attained an intensity that was almost comic in its pettiness and nastiness.

Salome's daughter hated and spied upon her husband Aristobulus, carrying to her mother choice morsels of scandal that Salome munched and gobbled with feverish relish before regurgitating them for the king's scrutiny. They were in truth juicy gobbets. The princes often discussed their mother lovingly, the while they hated their father.—Once they attained power, Herod's sons by his other wives would be appointed country school teachers.—Herod's wives and the women of the court who flaunted Mariamne's clothes and jewels would be made to wear sackcloth and be thrown into sunless dungeons.

But another affliction bore down upon him from a new quarter.

It may be recalled that on a previous occasion Herod, with his unshaken faith in the efficacy of inbreeding as a means of fortifying family loyalty, had arranged a marriage between Pheroras and his daughter Salampsio, and that Pheroras, who possessed the lone redeeming quality of stubborn affection for his commoner actress-wife, had jilted the royal damsel, whose distress was soothed by her subsequent betrothal to her cousin, Phasael's son who bore his name.

With the passage of time another effort was made to induce him to put away his wife and marry Cyprus, Mariamne's daughter. Worked upon by Herod and Ptolemy, Pheroras at length gave in. Bidding his wife and baby son a tearful farewell, he agreed to marry Cyprus after thirty days.

But the interval was too short for him to forget his wife or to find a counter attraction in the vapid prettiness of his niece. He defiantly left the court and rejoined his wife and son.

Herod naturally was angry. Even more was he offended by what he considered his brother's ingratitude. He made no secret of his sentiments. Heedless words of excoriation were picked up, and repeated. Pheroras' former associates turned against him. He became an outcast, despised for his courage and laughed at for his constancy.

Had Pheroras been disposed to accept his disgrace quietly, and gone off with his wife and child where his disfavor would have been forgotten, much misery would have been forestalled. This, despite the pleading of his wife, he would not do. Stupid as he was, intrigue ran in his veins. He secretly visited Alexander, confiding to him, on the authority of Salome, that Herod was infatuated with Glaphyra.

His purpose should have been obvious to any one less gullible than Alexander. What he intended was that the prince in his rage would slay the king outright, or else proceed to make use of the more customary oriental method of poison. He had failed, however, to reckon with Alexander's open nature. The prince would exact full justice, but he must first be assured of the guilt of the accused. With difficulty holding his fury in check, he strode into his father's chamber and taxed him with the charge.

Although Alexander was passionately devoted to his wife, his agitation was understandable. It was true that Herod and Glaphyra were fond of each other. The king found her gay, basically common-sense chatter restful, even while he suspected her husband of plotting his death. But it was equally true that, since his first impetuous proposal at the court of her father, his attitude combined the tenderness of a father with the spirit of banter of an older brother quite untinctured by the desire of the lover.

Momentarily Herod was stunned by the monstrous falseness of the accusation. Recovering his composure, he summoned Pheroras and Salome. Not a word had he for his son. Instead he turned on his cowering brother. In a blasting indictment beginning "Thou vilest of men!" he correctly exposed Pheroras' design, accused him of plotting to excite Alexander into committing the murder Pheroras himself had not the courage to commit, and attributed his own escape only to the innate goodness and moderation of his son.

Pheroras, his plot so clearly exposed, could only stammer that it was Salome who had prompted his action.

Goaded by her brother's excuse, Salome leaped to her feet in almost demented rage, tearing at her hair, beating her breast, shrieking that her brother sought her downfall only because she loved Herod and was constantly on the alert to forestall the dangers that threatened him.

She gave a rather well simulated performance that not quite achieved its purpose. For once, however, she slightly overplayed her part. She, too, had not anticipated Alexander's reaction, and had not had time to devote the amount of study necessary to give the right histrionic emphasis to her role. For the first time, Herod really saw her for what she was, a vicious, oversexed trouble maker. Half-amused, he let the precious pair assail each other. Then, tired of the brawl, he dismissed them and turned to his son with a gesture of reconciliation.

Pheroras' standing in court was irreparably damaged. Salome, too, had lost face. Quickest to take advantage of this new state of affairs were Herod's wives and their partisans. Emboldened by Salome's disgrace, they snubbed her, sneered at her, and revived the old story of her repudiation by Sylleus. They went further, hinting that in her senile infatuation she was shamelessly communicating with her errant lover, and that it was she who was encouraging the unrest he was causing in Arabia, reports of which had just been made public.

It did seem as though Pheroras' malicious charge might result in a lasting reconciliation between Herod and the princes. The better element at court became emboldened; spies and informers drifted away or made themselves inconspicuous.

That this reconciliation did not come about was largely Alexander's fault. Had he striven to retain the confidence of his father with only a small part of the zeal his enemies demonstrated in arousing Herod's suspicions, Salome would in all likelihood have been exiled to some remote fortress, the schemes of Antipater been nullified, and the pain of the closing years of Herod's life made tolerable by the love and companionship of his sons.

But Alexander had too great a measure of his mother's pride. Like her, he resented being unnecessarily hurt; and, like her, he could not forgive injury until the culprit had been made to feel his guilt. To expect a sick, morbid old man, racked with uneasiness and starving for affection, to undergo a purgatory of expiation was just, perhaps, but hardly reasonable.

Failing to pierce the cold civility of Alexander, Herod turned to Antipater, who with the true opportunist's adaptability was at once properly humble and grateful.

It was not long before Antipater took the opportunity to plunge the king once again into a morass of doubt and suspicion.

Three young eunuchs, the king's cupbearer, steward, and valet, protégés of Alexander, by their ingratiating manners and skilled service had won the favor of Herod. Alarmed at the possibilities, Antipater, coming upon his father in one of his blacker moods, suggested that Alexander might have had a motive other than filial devotion in presenting his father with these clever slaves. Was it not possible that they were the creatures of Alexander placed by him in posts where constant close contact would make them ideal spies, or even agents to poison their master or to perpetrate whatever other act of treachery the princes had in mind?

Instantly the eunuchs were apprehended. Under torture they testified that the princes really hated their father; that they said he was sick and old, and unfit to govern the kingdom; that his silly attempts to simulate youth by dyeing his hair and beard made him a laughing stock; that so many in the kingdom favored the princes that they were about ready to depose their father.

Herod's rage was boundless. Excepting the archconspirator Antipater, he suspected everyone. Those about him, even his thitherto trusted spies and informers, he accused of seeking the opportunity of doing away with him. The rack was never idle; the ax-man's arm was weary. Those, on the other hand, who absented themselves from court were by that very fact condemned as fugitives from justice. Nor did they escape the king's vengeance. The assassin's dagger fell in the remotest corners of the kingdom.

A reign of terror raged, surpassing in fury anything the country had known.

In the palace, indescribable panic prevailed. In an agony of terror, servants informed on one another. The informer was in turn informed on, and likewise put to the torture to elicit further confessions. During his saner intervals, Herod would be filled with revulsion against the contradictions and absurdities the rack wrenched out of its gasping victims. Yet Antipater was always at hand to keep his sense of reasonableness from taking root.

Some of Herod's more courageous friends counseled moderation. That very act rendered them suspect. Two of his oldest associates, companions of the raid on David's sepulcher were exiled: Andromachus, because his son was a friend of Alexander's, and Gamellus, who had been a fellow student with the princes at Rome. That he did not kill them outright was due to a lingering caution that it would not be expedient to execute men so generally esteemed in Rome as well as in Judea.

With them out of the way, Antipater was able to give full vent to his sadistic instincts. He personally officiated at the torture of the better type of servants and attendants, hitherto considered above suspicion. That most of them died without disclosing evidence detrimental to the princes only increased his zeal and that of the king.

One servant did, indeed, under torture make admissions that seemed to Herod to justify the bloody process. He asserted that Alexander, knowing his father's pride in his figure and his skill in archery, purposely stooped when walking with the king so as not to overshadow him, and that he often intentionally missed the target to let Herod feel he was the better marksman. But this Alexander did, not out of kindness, but to make the king careless. Moreover, Aristobulus had made very definite plans to kill Herod from ambush and flee to Rome. The servant further testified that he had in his possession a letter from Alexander to his brother, protesting that Herod had bestowed upon Antipater a dominion with a revenue of two hundred talents a year.

These charges at least were something tangible. Alexander and Aristobulus were thrown into prison.

Still Herod, wishing to justify his actions and at the same time unwilling to believe the worst of his sons, was uncertain. It did seem unreasonable that they would plot to murder him and then flee to Rome. And unless there was proof of Alexander's ulterior motives, his stooping and poor shooting were the actions of a tactful, considerate son, rather than those of a conspirator.

He sought further evidence through further torture. Now, the friends of the princes were chiefly the victims. Most died in silence. One, however, in his agony, alleged that Alexander had written to Caesar asking to be invited to Rome that he might expose the details of a plot against the Empire between Herod and Mithridates, the Parthian king. Furthermore, a poison potion intended for the king, so insidious that it was infallible, had already been concocted at Ascalon.

Herod believed the charges and felt better justified. His agents sought high and low in the coastal city, but no poison was found.

Thereupon the princes, in their cells, made frantic at the slaughter of their friends, took steps to halt the butchery. Four letters were addressed to Herod by Alexander. In gist they contained a full confession that they had plotted against their father and that further torture could bring to light no more information than they were prepared to present. Pheroras was a ringleader in the conspiracy, abetted by Ptolemy and Sapinnius, supposedly the king's most faithful friends. Salome not only detested her brother, but in her unbounded sensuality had forced her way into Alexander's chamber and insisted on his sleeping with her.

The letter was an artless attempt to establish the absurdity of their father's suspicions. By exaggeration, by stating what was so palpably unbelievable, Alexander hoped to restore his father to his senses.

However, he failed to appreciate Herod's frame of mind. Between the agony of his illness and his bewilderment he was incapable of logical thinking. He knew that most men hated him and wished him dead; in his physician's increasing perturbation he could read his impending doom. During the night, hideous phantoms invaded his dreams, sons and enemies, gigantic in stature, bending over his inert body with dripping sword.

As a consequence, an overpowering resentment against those who might attempt to anticipate or hasten his natural departure stifled every humane impulse.

When Glaphyra learned that her husband's scheme had miscarried (she had opposed it as too chimerical), she decided to take matters into her own hands. Over the objections of her husband, who was unwilling to air his father's folly before a fellow monarch, she sent for Archelaus. Though reluctant to travel to Jerusalem, which he detested, and unwilling to fraternize with Herod's family, he would not ignore his daughter's plea.

He was shocked at Herod's condition. The light of madness flickered in the king's eyes; he was feverish, and irritable when he discussed his sons, and abject in his grief that his friends had turned against him.

Sorrowing for his stricken friend, Archelaus considered what

might be the best way of ameliorating the king's mental and
emotional condition, and thereby restoring harmony in his family.

To reason with him would be of no more avail than with a
suffering baby. Therefore he would try to shock him into reasonableness by intensifying the very processes that had brought
Herod to his deplorable state.

Affecting indignation at the perverseness of the princes, he
vowed he would dissolve his daughter's marriage and take her
back to Cappadocia. More than that, he would wish to be present
at his son-in-law's execution. The princes should be killed outright, without trial or testimony, as one would step on a scorpion.
They were obviously unnatural sons, who had never even as
children loved their father. Their immediate execution alone
could solve Herod's difficulties.

His vehemence first amazed, then outraged Herod. He found
himself defending his sons, refuting Archelaus' charges with a
return of his old polemic skill, seemingly convincing his stubborn
adversary of the innocence of his sons.

After a suitable time, Archelaus reluctantly, it appeared, admitted he had misjudged the princes and agreed with Herod
that they had been unjustly treated.

Yet he felt that Herod's suspicions must be given another
direction lest they revert to their recent objectives. He should
more wisely perhaps have selected Antipater as the victim. But
that individual had avoided him where possible, and on the few
occasions when compelled to be in his presence, had acted so
much the highborn oaf that Archelaus could not conceive of
Herod's ever being willing seriously to consider Antipater
dangerous.

Accordingly Pheroras was picked. He had come to Archelaus,
whining and imploring him to intercede with Herod, that he be
recalled to the court. He agreed, as the price of reconciliation
with his royal brother, to admit that he had been the chief conspirator. In the company of Archelaus, Pheroras confessed his
misdeeds to Herod, and threw himself upon his mercy. Herod,
too happy to harbor resentment, readily forgave him and restored
him to the court.

After an exchange of presents, he accompanied the Cappadocian to Antioch, where he was convinced of the advisability of going to Rome, to report to Caesar the happy solution of the problems concerning which he had ill-advisedly sent a detailed, if disjointed, account to his emperor.

Josephus is mute concerning the outcome of Herod's meeting with Caesar. It is likely that the Roman was more than a little tired of Herod's recurrent family squabbles and that as a result their old friendship was wearing rather thin. At any rate, Herod returned home in no very agreeable mood.

Nor was the news that greeted his arrival calculated to ease his petulance. The land of Trachonitis was aflame with revolt.

The history of the friction between Herod and Trachonitis was long and involved. Inhabiting a barren, rugged terrain, rutted with ravines and perforated with caves, stretching rather indefinitely east of the country beyond the Jordan from the oases of Damascus to the wastes of Arabia, the Trachonites had been from time immemorial nomadic marauders, preying on the caravan routes that rimmed their country. Some years previously, Caesar had deposed the ineffective Zenodorus as their ruler and had bestowed his dominion, a thankless gift, on the more energetic Herod in the hope that the latter might bring about order in a district whose subjugation would otherwise entail the expenditure of more Roman legionaries than the country was worth. Herod had done unexpectedly well in the almost incredibly difficult task of transforming migratory thieves into peaceful, or at any rate pacified, husbandmen. But not for long. The soil for lack of water bore too sparsely to sustain the lives of the fledgling farmers who were perforce driven to rebellion, which Herod's commanders had little difficulty in suppressing.

But this was only the beginning of Herod's problem. Some forty of the chief rebels fled into Arabia, where Sylleus, still smarting from his near-escape from marriage with Salome, gave them refuge and moreover a fortified base from which they raided caravans and settlements and surprised Syrian and Judean outposts.

Herod might have pursued the robbers into Arabia and destroyed their base. But that would have involved the invasion of a country, like his own under imperial rule, and would surely have compromised his now rather tenuous hold on Caesar's favor.

Instead he hit upon an expedient calculated to lure his enemies from the security of their foreign stronghold to seek retribution in territory where Herod's troops could destroy them. Aware that the Trachonites religiously observed blood feuds that demanded retaliation in kind for violence done their families, he ordered that the relatives of the forty be executed.

But what Herod had not known was that the forty had grown to almost a thousand, that in place of a piecemeal disposal of two-score desperate fanatics he had to deal with a thousand ably led, magnificently equipped desert warriors against whom his available forces were quite inadequate.

Still careful to do nothing that might distress Rome, Herod put his case before Saturninus, the Roman commander in Syria, pleading that first the robbers be delivered to him for judgment, and then that Sylleus be made to repay the sixty talents loaned to Sylleus' nominal superior, Obodas.

Sylleus lost no time in submitting his defense. He denied that he harbored robbers, and disclaimed responsibility for money loaned to Obodas.

Saturninus, a vacillating opportunist, decided in favor of Herod. The money was to be repaid within thirty days. And Herod and Sylleus would mutually return Arab and Judean natives to their own land. Since no means for enforcing the terms of the judgment were indicated in the decision, Sylleus was not yet ready to admit defeat. Ordering his subordinates to ignore the judgment, he sped to Rome to appeal to Caesar directly.

When the day of payment passed and Herod had neither the robbers nor the money, he appealed once more to Saturninus, who half-heartedly granted him an ambiguous warrant to enter Arabia and destroy the robbers, under the strict injunction that his actions might in no sense affect Arabian lives or property, or imperil Roman peace.

Herod tried earnestly to act within the limits of his authority. With an overwhelming, perfectly disciplined army he stormed the robbers' citadel, annihilated its defenders but scrupulously avoided harming any native. An Arabian hot-blood named

Naceb, however, took it upon himself to harass the withdrawing Herodians. In the ensuing skirmish some Jews and about twenty Arabs, including Naceb, lost their lives.

On his return to Judea, Herod submitted a complete report of his actions to the Roman commanders in the East, who granted that his conduct had been correct in every detail.

Sylleus, however, had the advantage of being at Rome, accessible to Caesar. As soon as messengers brought him news of the Arabian episode, he prepared his story. An adroit liar and talented actor, he had the further advantage of a receptive audience. Dressed in the disheveled mourning of the East, he set before Caesar a creditable but quite false account of Herod's activities. Twenty-five hundred of the leading Arabs had been slaughtered, he alleged—all Arabia was laid waste. Arab possessions were being systematically looted and taken to Jerusalem. That his countrymen were too greatly disorganized to offer effective resistance was due to the weakness of Obodas; were he himself there, he assured Caesar, his countrymen could have driven out the invader. But relying on Caesar's ban on warfare between subject states, he felt safe in journeying to Rome to acquaint the emperor with Herod's earlier, less serious infractions of peace.

It was a convincing performance, by which Caesar was completely taken in. Of those who attempted to defend Herod, he asked but one question to which he demanded a categorical answer: "Had Herod led an army into Arabia?"

The outcome was a sharp letter reprimanding Herod; the gist of it, that the Judean king's status had changed from that of Caesar's friend to that of Caesar's subject.

After the successful outcome of his interview with Caesar, Sylleus lost no time in apprising his Arabian followers of the result. Accordingly, the sixty talents were not repaid and the Trachonites abandoned the torpid pursuit of farming for the jollier pastime of Jew-baiting.

Meanwhile a new turn of events in Arabia further raised Sylleus' star. Obodas, long ailing and ever incompetent, at length died—some said his death was hastened by poison administered by one of Sylleus' followers. Aretas, formerly named Aeneas, of the party hostile to Sylleus, assumed the office of king. It seems likely that the new king took over the government, not out of personal ambition, but to restore order and to forestall seizure of the throne by Sylleus. But the latter with mingled gifts and protestations of horror convinced Caesar that the new ruler had been most remiss in respect for Rome by seizing power without Roman sanction. On account of Sylleus' second exhibition of histrionic skill, Aretas' ambassadors, bearing not only gifts but also evidence of Sylleus' complicity in the death of Obodas, were sent home without a hearing.

To Herod, Caesar's rebuke was a stunning blow. He was no longer Caesar's old, revered friend. In the terse, bitter terms of the denunciation he read his demotion to the level of the myriad knights and petty despots who owned their uneasy thrones at the sufferance and whim of a heartless, all-powerful overlord.

That Caesar's decree was irrevocable Herod would not admit. Imperial condemnation of a trusted companion on the unsupported word of a crafty intriguer was too unreasonable and too greatly perplexing to be permanent. Unquestionably, he concluded, his representatives in Rome had failed him; perhaps they too, like almost everyone else he had faith in, were plotting his downfall. He would send his ablest diplomat, Nicolaus of Damascus, to Rome, to intercede with Caesar.

Nicolaus was not only an able biographer but also a diplomat of the first order. Herod was impatient for him to start for Rome. But the ambassador refused to be hurried. A hasty, ill-prepared attempt to win back Caesar's favor would, he insisted, be futile. Caesar, as he grew older, was increasingly possessed with a passion for order. To present a convincing case for Herod, he must be able to demonstrate that his client's actions and affairs were in order; specifically, that Herod was blameless in the Arabian affair; that peace was re-established in Trachonitis; and that some final decision was reached in the king's domestic difficulties.

Gathering and organizing transcripts of Saturninus' permission to enter Arabia and of the numerous other documents that would vindicate Herod took time. Besides, the exchange of Trachonitian malcontents for hardy Idumean farmers and shepherds inured to livelihood in inhospitable lands would take time.

Almost a year elapsed before Nicolaus was ready to start—a

year during which Herod's physical malady grew almost unendurable. Yet bodily pain was the least of his suffering. Family disorders of unprecedented intensity distressed him more than disease. Madness brooded over him, darkening every hope and emotion, leaving unanswered only the question whether insanity or disease would first claim the royal victim for its own.

While Nicolaus was collecting the evidence that would exonerate Herod, the position of the princes grew steadily more dangerous.

It was, in part, their own fault. They must have realized that their father was a doomed madman, crazily craving for attention and affection, and, lacking that, likely to turn with unreasoning fury on those who withheld it. Yet they kept aloof from the general court life, living entirely with their own entourage, constituting a court within a court, and never disdaining to show their contempt for the rest.

About this time an international adventurer, the Spartan Eurycles, found his way to the Herodian court. Utterly unprincipled and invincibly charming, he wormed his way into Herod's good graces. Also apparently playing no favorites, he lived in Antipater's quarters, became intimate with Alexander, and even won over Glaphyra, ordinarily so levelheaded, with his tactful devotion. In a fit of confidence, Alexander unbosomed himself to the wily Greek, told how his father snubbed and persecuted him, in brief, the whole sorry story of his unhappy existence, and his yearning to fly somewhere where all his past life would be only an unpleasant memory.

Eurycles decided that friendship with so heedless a young man could be dangerous. To clear himself of any suspicion of sympathy for Alexander, he at once carried the report of the prince's indiscreetness to Antipater, embellished with the warning that his brother would kill him at the first opportunity. At bottom a coward, Antipater relayed the story to Herod, substituting the king's name for his own, as the primary object of Alexander's violence.

It was a tangible accusation by an apparently disinterested witness, and readily convinced Herod. He ordered a truly regal gift, an order for fifty talents, for Eurycles, who, pocketing the gift, lost no time in leaving the gilded dust of the palace behind him. His next stop was at Cappadocia, where his highly colored account of the important role he played in establishing amity between Herod and his sons resulted in an additional if less munificent gift from Archelaus. After these profitable infamies he sped happily to his native Sparta.

More than anything else, the realization that his sons projected flight was galling to Herod. In his bewildered emotions they were the prime objects at once of his love and of his resentment. Their escape would cheat him of an outlet for either affection or revenge, the passions that ranged most violently through his confused mind. He almost begged for information against his sons. He hired spies in droves; he himself listened at doors and curtains, hoping yet afraid to catch the unwary word that would further confirm his suspicions.

Evidence, though inconclusive, was not long in coming. During one of his peevish moods he discharged two of his ablest, most reliable guards, young giants named Jucundus and Tyrannus. Them Alexander, partly for their skill in hunting, more out of sympathy, added to his staff. Word of this action, carried to Herod, was evidence of conspiracy.

The guards were arrested, first half-starved, then racked in the presence of Herod and Antipater. In his agony, one claimed that Alexander had indeed tried to induce him to kill Herod while he was hunting, and to make it appear that the king in plunging from his horse had accidentally fallen upon his own spear.

The story was so palpably untrue that even in a half-rational moment Herod must become aware of its absurdity. His condition had long prevented his hunting on horseback. Moreover not on the hunt or elsewhere would discharged servants with reason to harbor a grudge be granted the opportunity to stage so elaborate a plot. Antipater, of course, saw how unconvincing the confession was. Assuming horror at their wickedness, he had the guards quickly executed before the king could regain his composure.

Still seeking evidence, especially that concerned with the anticipated flight of his sons, Herod was informed by a servant punished for dishonesty that his master, the commander of the all-important fortress Alexandrium, was plotting with the princes. The specific charges were that he had agreed to aid them with reserves of gold stored in the vaults of the fortress and to give them refuge within its walls should they break with their father.

Under torture, the soldier persistently denied complicity. A son, however, in an effort to ease his father's sufferings, admitted the truth of the charges. In substantiation, he presented a letter, presumably in Alexander's hand, though actually written by Diophantus, Antipater's pet forger (eventually executed for forgery), containing these damnatory words: "When we have finished by God's help all that we have proposed to do, we will come to you. But do your endeavors, as you have promised to receive us into your fortress."

Neglecting even to order the commander's execution—a detail attended to by Antipater—Herod ordered his litter to bear him immediately to Jericho, where his sons were sojourning.

All down that long precipitous road, harrowing phantoms stormed through his mind. Night fell, but Herod's thoughts were blacker than the night. Impatiently he rejected the suggestion that he rest at the half-way inn until morning. The torches of the guards caught answering glints from the stony immensities that loomed overhead, or sought vainly to search the abysmal deeps of the precipices that skirted their path. From the well-like depths a single star glittered in solitary splendor framed in an ebon casket of jutting cliffs. Again the entire heavens were a tide of glimmering gold, rolling off into infinity. Oblivious of the night, its grandeur and its danger, Herod lay motionless, a cruel smile on his pallid lips. Daylight was caressing the domes and flowing along the marble walls among the moist, sensual green of the groves like a river of warm silver as the train passed through the gates of the soft, sinful city.

Jericho was in every sense a Herodian city. Most of its inhabitants were his sycophants and henchmen, court favorites, petty officials, servants and tradesmen whose livelihood depended on royal patronage.

Hardly pausing to refresh himself, Herod ordered the mass arrest of all not known actively to be his followers. The same afternoon, those apprehended were publicly tortured. Naturally confessions were wrung from many of the miserable victims. An excitable mob, their blood-lust whetted by the spectacle, fell upon the accused with stones, killing some of the proscribed and an occasional torturer who too slowly evaded the rocky deluge. Such evidence of loyalty at first pleased Herod until, getting out of hand, leaders of the mob began to raise the cry, "Kill the princes. Stone to death the enemies of their father."

This Herod did not like. He was clearly not disposed to allow revenge to be so summarily snatched from himself. The guards made short work of the chief rioters, and the rest slunk away to less perilous pastimes.

That evening the princes were seized and ignominiously incarcerated in common dungeons with spies as prison-mates and all their words and actions reported.

Alexander bore his imprisonment with dulled resignation. But to Aristobulus, more high-strung than his brother, nerves rasped by unhappy married life, his lot was unendurable. In desperation he sent for Salome, at once his aunt and mother-in-law. Disregarding his sharp-eared fellow prisoners, he appealed to her for help since she too was in jeopardy. Herod knew of her indiscretions with Sylleus; he was certain, eventually, to be revenged on those who had been friendly with the chief cause of his fall from Roman favor.

Salome knew that the meeting and Aristobulus' conversation would be reported to Herod. She appreciated, too, the truth of her son-in-law's excitable utterances and her own peril. Accordingly, she boldly hurried to Herod, and concealing nothing, since he would soon hear the entire story from other sources, she attributed her action to her solicitude for her brother.

Aristobulus' action resulted only in stronger repressive measures. The brothers were separated and kept chained in their cells.

While such treatment eased Herod's craving for revenge, it did nothing in presenting new evidence of guilt.

With a silly slyness, born of madness, he thought to entrap them into a confession of guilt, or at least to involve them in contradictory stories. Their chains were loosed; the princes moved to comfortable quarters, and, still kept apart, were ordered to write full accounts of their recent relationship with their father.

The scheme failed. The statements of the princes were essentially identical, even to the sole incriminating admission that, while they loved their father, they were in danger at the court and wanted to escape.

That admission satisfied Herod as a token of more serious unconfessed guilt. The arrival of Archelaus' ambassador, the sage Melas, gave the king, as he thought, the opportunity to justify himself.

He sent for Alexander. Where had the princes intended to flee, he questioned. To Archelaus, answered Alexander, who promised to send him to Rome, if such action seemed reasonable. But, added the prince earnestly, he had no thought ever of harming his father as Herod might himself have discovered, had not Antipater killed the guards before they could be further questioned.

Rending his garment in the traditional manner, Herod pronounced Alexander's statement a full confession, and ordered him to accompany Melas and himself to Glaphyra.

Her life since Herod fell into disfavor with Caesar was quite as miserable as Alexander's. She was truly in love with her husband. The court scoffed at their affection and sneered at the domestication of the gay young beauty. But the strong sensitive prince and the lively, lovable princess, in their relationship with each other at least, led normal lives, cherishing each other and their children, and regretting only the fates that circumscribed their opportunity for a full measure of family bliss. She was really fond of Herod too, and willing to attribute to his mental and physical weakness, and to the intereference of others, his harshness to her husband.

But Herod was no longer capable of being moved either by filial affection or by the tears of the girl, with whom alone of all the court he could be his natural self.

For that was past. With only brief intervals of tortured sanity to intensify the agony of a tottering mind and a literally corrupting body, he could no longer be quieted or cajoled.

In cold fury he demanded of Glaphyra whether she was aware

of her husband's treachery. It was a question that could not be answered in a manner to help Alexander. She fell into spasms of hysterical weeping. The months of uncertainty, the momentary elation when she learned she was to see her husband, culminating in her realization of Herod's mad hatred, quite unnerved her. Choking with grief, she could make no articulate reply.

Impatiently he turned to his son. Did his wife know of his intended flight? The reply was indicative of the affection that linked the unfortunate lovers. "How is it possible that she, whom I love better than my soul, and by whom I have had children, should not know what I do!"

This loving answer only intensified Glaphyra's distress. With intense effort she composed herself to speak. While she knew of no wicked design on the part of her husband, she was ready to make any confession that would help him.

Over the protestations of Melas, Alexander was hustled back to prison, and the ambassador himself dismissed. A scribe was sent for. Long the three were closeted; Herod suggesting, and Glaphyra sobbingly elaborating, confessions that she hoped might save her husband, with the scribe meticulously taking down every fatal word that poured from her trembling lips.

The confession, futile from any sane viewpoint, satisfied Herod as incontrovertible evidence. An agent was sent to Archelaus with an informally worded version of his daughter's confession and of his own responsibility in his son-in-law's guilt.

Nicolaus was given a more legalistically worded account of the same episode with the strictest injunction to present the confession to Caesar, while Nicolaus' primary purpose, the vindication of Herod, was almost forgotten in the king's furious insistence that Caesar be informed of the depravity of the Herodian families.

CHAPTER XIX

TWO TRIALS

ON ARRIVING IN ROME, NICOLAUS WAS RE-
lieved to learn that his task of discomfiting Sylleus would prove
easier than he had feared. The Arab, cocksure because of his
easy triumph before Caesar, had become overbearingly domineer-
ing with his followers. Already his shoulders seemed to stoop
with the press of the royal mantle; his commonest words assumed
a pontifical resonance; his actions smacked of infallibility. In a
more regal figure such assumptions might be condoned. But no
garb or office could ever transform Sylleus into anything more
impressive than the caricature of a Levantine huckster. Naturally, he alienated even his few sincere supporters. Others, less
loyal, by agents of Aretas were bribed to desert him. The more
timorous sensed that his star was waning, and quit him before
they, too, would be blotted out in its eclipse.

Nicolaus surmised how matters stood and bided his time, re-
newing old friendships and gathering support for his king among
the nobility closest to Caesar.

At the opportune occasion he pleaded for an audience with
the emperor. That this was immediately granted was not necessarily an indication that Caesar's attitude toward Herod had
changed. Rather was it an act of courtesy to a man with an
empire-wide reputation as diplomat, scholar, and aesthete, typify-
ing the highest form of Hellenic culture, an excellence to which
the Romans, despite their addiction to learning and elegance,
were conscious they could never attain.

Caesar knew, of course, that more than courtesy prompted the

request for an audience. He ordered both Aretas' ambassador
and Sylleus to be present. After the customary exchange of
amenities—sincere in this instance—Nicolaus presented his plea.
Aware of Sylleus' loss of prestige, he devoted his arguments to
exposing the rascality of the Arab rather than the innocence of
Herod. Had he attempted the latter, he would, in effect, have
made Caesar a defendant. Instead, taking advantage of the growing Roman rancor toward Sylleus, he proceeded to demonstrate
by facts garnered by himself, and especially by letters and documents pilfered by the Arab's absconding partisans, that the pretender had caused Obodas and many of his followers to be killed;
that he had misappropriated state funds; that in addition to the
debauched life that made his name a byword in his own country
he had threatened the security of the empire's social order by
committing adultery with noble Roman ladies; and, finally, that
his account of Herod's misdeeds in Arabia was a framework of
slander and calumny.

Not until the reference to Herod did Caesar interrupt. Possibly he was a little conscience-stricken at his cavalier treatment
of his old friend and wished either to atone for or to justify it.
Was Sylleus' charge true, he questioned, that Herod had led an
army into Arabia, had slain over two thousand of the natives, and
looted and laid waste the land?

Here Nicolaus was on familiar ground. His rebuttal was a
masterful exposition of Herod's good faith; he exhibited the
affidavits and documents he had so punctiliously assembled in
Judea.

He read on, dispassionately and objectively. There was no
need for histrionics; the record was all too palpable evidence of
Sylleus' mounting guilt. An angry red began to suffuse Caesar's
countenance. He hated to be made a fool of, particularly by an
Arabian trickster. Interrupting Nicolaus, he turned angrily to
the cowering culprit and demanded to know how many Arabs
actually had been killed. Sylleus uttered a mumbling response
that his informants had misled him by exaggerating their number. In cold fury Caesar ordered him first to repay Herod the
money owed him; following the repayment he was to be executed.

Aretas' party thought this a favorable occasion to put forth the claims for their candidate. They were mistaken. Caesar had not forgotten Aretas' unwarranted assumption of power. Denying their claims, he hinted broadly that Herod should have Arabia added to his dominions as propitiation for his unmerited suffering.

This unexpected development placed Nicolaus in a quandary. Herod has placed upon him the strictest injunction to put before Caesar the record of the princes' misconduct and to plead for permission to try them on charges of treason, with death the verdict should they be found guilty. Yet he knew how sick was Caesar of Herod's family squabbles, and how speedily he might rescind his intention of extending Judean sovereignty to include Arabia. Aware of Herod's insensate lust for revenge, he appreciated also his king's spiritual affinity with the non-Hebraic Semites. Perhaps a fresh interest in Arabia might drive out of his mind the fever of distrust and fear that possessed him in Judea. Momentarily he played for time, with well-worded expressions of gratitude, grappling for the inspiration to solve his dilemma.

Two of Herod's most recent favorites, an unnamed Greek and the Roman Volumnius made his decision for him. Sensing an opportunity to convince Herod of their zeal, they pressed forward and laid before Caesar copies of the king's charges against his sons.

Caesar's face was expressionless as he read the by now familiar denunciations. With a glance of sympathetic understanding, he tried to allay the dejection that Nicolaus could not conceal. But nothing further was said concerning Herod's overlordship of Arabia.

After a round of banquets in which Caesar outdid himself in cordiality toward his Judean visitors, Nicolaus and his party embarked for Palestine. They carried no formal answer for Herod, since Caesar had indicated that he would deal with him directly by means of an imperial letter. They did bring back, however, more than an inkling of Caesar's attitude. Before they left, all Rome was laughing at the emperor's pun (more effective in its Greek form), "Safer Herod's sow than Herod's son."

When the letter did come, it bore no sign of Caesar's displeasure or waning confidence. Friendly, almost paternal in tone, it reminded Herod that, as a king in whom Rome had the deepest faith, he had the power of life and death over all his subjects including his sons. If these sons were guilty of attempted parricide, he was certainly justified, even duty-bound, to order their execution. If, on the other hand, their offense was only attempted flight, they should be censured and an effort made to remove permanently the causes of the misunderstanding that prompted their strange impulse. The trial, Caesar suggested, should take place at Beirut, in Syria, a Roman colony, where local prejudices would be unlikely to influence impartial judgment. The judges, moreover, should not be Herod's dependents but men of repute and probity, men like Archelaus and Saturninus, the Syrian procurator. The letter closed on the friendly note that Herod's happiness was very dear to Caesar, who hoped that a sane, impartial trial would be the final solution of Herod's difficulties.

One who retained even a semblance of common sense could have discerned Caesar's determination to act as peacemaker between father and sons. But Herod could no longer think rationally or act reasonably. Ordinary prudence would have prompted his awaiting the arrival of Nicolaus. Instead, even before his ambassador disembarked at Tyre, he precipitately rounded up a jury of about one hundred and fifty. Needless to say, Archelaus was not among them. Saturninus and his sons he had to invite. The rest were little-known courtiers completely dominated by him, too cowardly and unprincipled to wish to see justice done, anxious only to please their patron.

There were chambers in Beirut, including a Roman court of justice, where a trial of such importance might fittingly have taken place. But Herod with one of his queer, dark quirks chose an old and disused market hall, where once among other commodities slaves had been auctioned. Perhaps its high stained walls that melted into a discolored ceiling, its dimly-lighted proscenium, and its stone benches that crowded upon the platform in close tiers recalled to him the chamber where the sanhedrin convened to invoke Yahweh's thunder. Perhaps he saw in himself the reincarnation of some irate minor prophet hurling doom at those who polluted family purity.

The trial itself was a travesty. The defendants were not present. (They languished in a village prison near Sidon.) Neither were they defended by a representative.

Herod himself was the only witness against his sons. As he rose painfully from the judge's seat, the ravages of madness and disease were all too obvious. The once erect figure sagged; streaks of dirty gray marred the sleek, dyed blackness of hair and beard; the face was at once ashen and heated; his robe, ill-fitted and grimy; his whole appearance abject and pitiful. In the querulous, unregal figure that prostituted his own sense of justice in making his shameful demands, Saturninus and his sons saw only the demoralization of a noble and talented character. To the other jurors, however, it was merely a spectacle to incite humor that must for safety's sake be suppressed, and a forecast of waning power that they could make profitable use of.

For a space Herod stared at the jurors as if unconscious of his purpose. Then, with a visible effort, he gathered his thoughts. Once he had embarked on his tirade, an overwhelming torrent of hatred inundated every physical pain and every natural affection. His charge was one long philippic of vituperation. In a voice rasping with passion, and at times unintelligible in the vehemence of his oration, he scoffed at leniency, derided the presence of mitigating circumstances, and insisted on the death penalty. He read the confessions of his sons, lingering with perverse pleasure on their admission of attempted flight. When he reached the passage where he himself was reproached for his conduct, his voice, climbing to a hysterical shriek, sobbed out a repetition for a sentence of death.

Even in his mad rage there resided in Herod a legalistic substratum that impelled him to justify his demands. He read that passage in Caesar's letter which might seem to imply that it was, under certain circumstances, his duty to kill his sons. Above all, he quoted God's explicit injunction in the Old Law, "If a man have a stubborn and unruly son, who will not hear the commandments of father and mother, and being corrected, slighteth obedience, the people of the city shall stone him and he shall die."

Spent with emotion, his voice dropping to a tone of apparent composure, he recapitulated his evidence and demanded a verdict

of guilty of treason and attempted parricide, not only because
the laws of Caesar and God warranted this, but also as a deterrent to other vicious sons who might else be hardened in their
criminal course by the immunity of the royal princes.

His attempt at moderation exhausted him more than his
violence. He slumped into his seat of justice, head drooped, eyes
staring at the dank stone floor, fingers clawing at the arms of his
chair.

No order forthcoming from Herod, Saturninus took it upon
himself to call for a tabulation of votes. In virtue of his position,
he cast the first vote. The conduct of the princes was to some
extent reprehensible, he admitted. Yet he had sons of his own
and appreciated how horrible it would be to condemn one's
children to death. He, therefore, voted for moderation.

His three sons, his legates, voted as did their father.

Following the four votes against the imposition of the death
penalty, there was a pause. The Herodians expected the king to
nullify by word or gesture the impression created by the expression of official Roman opinion. But Herod still sat leadenly, the
perspiration beaded on his forehead and the writhing fingers the
only evidence of life. Clearly, he saw and heard nothing going on
about him. Yet it was obvious that in the trial of his sons he was
suffering the remorse of the damned.

It is conceivable that leaderless, and lacking encouragement
from Herod, the jurors might have followed the Roman example
and voted moderation. Once again, as at Rome, Volumnius, who
seems to have been the evil genius of Herod's later years, took it
upon himself to interpret the royal wish. Leniency, he harangued
in strident tones calculated to pierce the shell of Herod's stupor,
was unthinkable. A verdict of death was the only possible decision for crimes so unnatural. If a loving father and generous
king was willing to sacrifice his sons at the altar of the common
weal, would the jurors not also be traitorous if they attempted
to circumvent his express commands?

Recognizing in Volumnius the mouthpiece of Herod, and a
little fearful lest their hesitance be unfavorably interpreted, every
other juror, in almost indecent haste, urged the death sentence.

The sordid business finished, the jurors awaited a signal of dismissal from Herod. But the king was as before, his beard flattened against his chest, his fingers contorting perhaps more slowly, clearly oblivious of everything save his own agony.

One by one the jurors melted away. Saturninus issued an order, and a Roman guard bore the unresisting figure of the king to his quarters.

The next day, with strength seemingly restored, Herod, picking up his condemned sons in transit, moved on to Tyre, where Nicolaus had been instructed to await his coming.

On landing, Nicolaus was informed of the result of the trial. Oppressed with a sense of utter futility, he prepared for the royal interview. He had carried out his delicate mission with tact and skill. Yet at every turn he was defeated by Herod's precipitateness or by Herod's underlings. His inability to bring to Herod Caesar's gift of Arabia was due to the presumption of the royal henchmen. Caesar's well-intentioned letter, inspired, he felt certain, by the friendship the emperor bore him, was vitiated by Herod's heedless passion. There remained only the remote possibility that he might sway the king from carrying out the last, bloody stroke of his malevolence.

Yet Herod upon arriving greeted his ambassador with unfeigned friendliness. The king seemed calm, almost chastened, and quite rational. The meeting was long and, from Nicolaus' viewpoint, satisfactory. He advised leniency and forbearance. He reviewed the years of persecution and frustration to which the princes had been subjected. He recalled their affection for their father and their honest, if unguarded, criticism, and he painted a realistic picture of the effect their death would have upon their father. It was true, he granted, that they had been rash; and it would certainly be advisable to keep them under restraint for the time being. Nevertheless, clemency rather than severity was Herod's only profitable course. Only by the exercise of clemency could matters still be brought to a happy solution. Death, on the other hand, would preclude all possibility of reconciliation and result only in sorrow and self-recrimination. Forgiveness, moreover, was the counsel of Herod's friends at Rome, and most certainly the wish of Caesar.

It would appear that Nicolaus had caught Herod in one of his more reasonable intervals. The king was deeply touched by the words of his friend. He could not bring himself to see his sons; but he did issue orders to loose their chains and to treat them as royal hostages rather than as criminals.

Saddened, Herod and his entourage repaired to Caesarea.

This proved to be a tragic mistake. To the Syro-Roman colony at Beirut, to the cosmopolitan populace of Tyre, Herod's problems were topics of momentary interest but certainly of no political significance. On the other hand, Caesarea with its Herodian army and large Jewish population was seething in an undercurrent of fear. In this city Herod's spies were numerous and unhampered. No hint of dissatisfaction, no bit of bold talk but was carried back to Herod's attentive ears. His calm left him; distrust and suspicion once again possessed him. The princes were returned to prison; the royal gates were barred to Nicolaus.

But so powerful was Herod's control, so prevalent his informers, that there was little talk and no real danger of an uprising.

One old soldier, however, Tero by name, a trusted veteran of all Herod's campaigns, could not be constrained to remain silent. Friend to the king and to Alexander as well, and "being by nature both loquacious and unafraid," he excoriated the spies and informers, whose profession he insisted was to destroy the king's peace of mind; and he orated with deepest emotion and no little rude eloquence on the undeserved plight of the princes.

Everyone listened to him with approval, so well he expressed their feelings. Yet the townsfolk and soldiers were discreet. None dared openly to support him, with the result that the fuming informers could bring to Herod only an account of intangible unrest and one man's rashness.

A little drunk with his own mission, Tero, as a privileged veteran, demanded access to the king's person, that he might place directly before him the reaction of the army and people toward his treatment of the princes.

That a blunt-spoken, opinionated common soldier should so readily be granted an interview with an oriental despot is not so strange as it might appear. With his soldiers, Herod, like Napoleon, usually felt at ease. In the company of veteran comrades he exhibited a disarming graciousness that encouraged con-

fidence and candor. Their company also afforded him an escape
from the atmosphere of intrigue that permeated the court. In
his last years, indeed, it was only among his soldiers that he could
lay aside the worries and regrets that beset him.

Despite the reports he had heard of Tero's activities, Herod
greeted him warmly.

Tero plunged at once into his diatribe. The speech as Josephus
sets it down is no doubt too rhetorically perfect to be the authentic product of an unlettered warrior. Yet in all probability it
contains the gist of Tero's remonstrance.

"Whither is thy understanding gone and left thy soul empty?"
he asks the king. "Whither is that extraordinary sagacity of thine
gone, whereby thou hast performed so many and such glorious
deeds? Whence comes this solitude and desertion of thy friends
and relations?" Would he kill these sons and leave himself
"destitute in thine old age; but exposed to one son who hath ill
managed the hopes that thou hast given him?" The very silence
of the people proclaimed their horror. The army, men and officers, were sympathetic to the young men. How could the loyalty
of the troops be assured when their commander-in-chief acted
in a manner so hateful to their desires!

Up to this point Herod, not unused to the grumblings of his
soldiers, had listened with a sort of half-humorous tolerance,
hesitating to interrupt a speech in which the orator was so deadly
in earnest. But the instant the loyalty of the army was questioned, fury seized him. He sprang at the unresisting soldier's
throat, the while yelling for his guard. Tero was thrown into
prison, and along with him some dozen others whose names he
had let slip during his incautious address.

Shortly thereafter, Herod became more composed and repented
his hasty action, especially since disloyalty, if it did exist in the
army, would only be intensified by such summary treatment of
the most popular military personnel. The matter might have
been speedily settled with eventual good results, had not another
complication arisen.

The king's barber was one Trypho, a perfumed exquisite
whom Tero had made the particular butt of his contempt, elbow-
ing him into the mire, spitting upon his elegant garments, and

aping with ribald exaggeration his effeminate mannerisms. As
soon as Trypho heard of the arrests, he lost no time in informing
Herod that Tero had tried to bribe him to cut the king's throat
while trimming his beard and thereby to win a reward and
honors from Alexander.

Instantly Herod was again stirred to an insane rage. Orders
were issued to torture Tero, his son, and the miserable barber
who, too late, saw his calumny recoil upon himself. Tero's son
bore his own torment with the greatest fortitude. But the sight
of his father in terrible agony was more than the young man
could stand. He agreed to make a confession that would satisfy
Herod on condition that his father's sufferings be terminated.
Insanely anxious not to miss one particle of evidence against his
sons, Herod agreed.

The youth thereupon asserted that his father had planned to
kill Herod at the close of their interview, but had been prevented from carrying out his design by the king's grappling with
him and calling the guard. That his own life would be forfeited
his father knew, but he was willing to make the sacrifice to save
Alexander.

The story, of course, was a desperate lie.

But Herod was incapable of distinguishing truth from false-
hood. He saw only that his last prop, the loyalty of his old com-
rades-in-arms, had collapsed, that in their love of his sons they
were willing to betray him.

For the first time he became panic-stricken. Only his army
stood between him and the vengeance of the people. He must
purge the army of the old, once faithful elements—must kill his
sons without further delay. Then with a new army he could
enkindle a loyalty that would be devoted to himself alone.

He reassembled his personal jury (that of Beirut, excepting,
naturally, the four Roman officials). Three hundred of the foremost veteran officers, along with Tero, Tero's son, and the barber
were charged with treason. Their names were read—their presence at the trial was not deemed necessary—and collectively they
were found guilty.

The king's agents scoured the slums—the scum of the city,
beggars, known criminals, petty servants, and discharged soldiers

were ordered to hurry to the circus, provided with stones and shards.

A mass execution ensued, with three hundred of Herod's most faithful friends, along with one rascally barber, stoned by a howling, sadistic mob.

Alexander and Aristobulus were, meanwhile, spirited away to Sebaste and quietly strangled in the city where, thirty years before, Herod had married their mother. Their bodies were borne by night to the crypts of Alexandrium, where rested many of the noblest Hasmoneans.

News of the death of Herod's sons hung like a pall upon the entire Jewish people. National mourning was observed, the more sincere because it was covert. Although the princes were almost pure Hellenes in their attitude toward Hebrew faith and culture, they were still Mariamne's sons. With them alive, there remained the hope of a restored Hasmonean dynasty.

But the sorrow that drenched Judea in unfeigned tears was not only nationalistic in character; the victims, despite their lapse from the faith of their mother, intimately recalled Mariamne to the older generation and were symbols of pride and hope to the younger patriots.

Of the reaction of the Jews Herod was for the time being unaware. The tragic events at Alexandrium and Sebaste aggravated his illness; their recollection banned recuperative sleep. Without stopping at Jerusalem, he was carried to Jericho, where for hours on end he lay in baths of warm oil—a treatment prescribed by his latest physician for the alleviation of his agony.

When this treatment also proved ineffectual, he tried by intense activity to overcome his illness. He proceeded on to Trachonitis, a still lawless district, where robber bands harassed and often murdered pious Babylonian Jews who of necessity journeyed through that region on their way to observe the Passover in Jerusalem. A considerable body of troops had hitherto been unable to keep the robbers in check.

With a stroke of genius, reminiscent of his haler days, Herod hit upon the solution.

There was in the country about Babylon a sort of Jewish Robin Hood with a following of some five hundred desperate spirits

renowned for the uncanny accuracy with which they could shoot
arrows while riding on horses as brave and fearless as themselves.
The Romans tolerated the freebooters, who incidentally would
allow no violations of the law but their own. The poorer Jews,
of course, idolized their dashing compatriots. Only to the more
grasping Jews and Babylonians were they a vexation.

Herod entered into negotiations with their chief and offered
them tax-free land near the Old Testament site of Bashan in
return for which the outlaws were to patrol adjoining Trachonitis.

The offer was accepted—the Babylonian pickings had become
lean.

Within a remarkably short time the land was rid of robbers,
while other Jews, attracted by the offer of tax-free land, came in
great numbers. Eventually towns and gardens would flourish
where there had been only bandit-ridden barrens.

This was Herod's last constructive project. His activity left
him completely exhausted, his spirits sapped, and his will weakened. By now he knew his illness was incurable; he could not
conceal from himself the fact that he was, for lengthy periods,
insane.

The conduct of the kingdom he left largely in the hands of
Antipater, though not without misgivings. He was moved with
pity, almost maudlin at times, when he considered his fatherless
grandchildren, soon to lose also their grandfather. It was intolerable for him to contemplate that, unprotected after his death,
they would be in the power of Antipater, who would conceivably
regard them as rivals, the more so since they were certain to have
a popular following.

The children, Alexander's two sons and the three sons and
two daughters of Aristobulus, he kept by him constantly, tearfully exhibiting them to visitors with pitiful observations on
their unhappy lot.

Forgetting how little domestic ties had availed his own family,
he thought by judicious espousals of the children to safeguard
their future lives. Alexander's older son, who very much resembled Mariamne, was espoused to the daughter of Herod's
brother Pheroras, thus being placed under the aegis of Herod's
immediate family. The older son of Aristobulus was espoused

to Antipater's daughter, and one daughter of Aristobulus to Antipater's son, being thus doubly insured in safety. Herod Philip, Herod's own son by that other Mariamne, the high priest Simon's daughter, he espoused to Aristobulus' younger daughter.

Antipater was only mildly disturbed by Herod's provision for his grandchildren. He knew Herod would be long dead before the espousals could be consummated. Nevertheless, he detected some danger in the manner in which Herod kept alive popular sympathy for the children. He knew that, with his other rivals disposed of, Herod's ingrained distrust was bound to be directed almost exclusively at him. Still, though his father was rapidly deteriorating physically and mentally, this was no time to assert his complete independence. He thought the occasion opportune, however, to test his strength against the king's. Should he fail, he could graciously admit his error; if successful, he would certainly impress the Jews and discourage opposition.

In a letter interlarded with pious platitudes and professions of filial devotion, he tactfully questioned the wisdom of his father's wholesale espousals. He proposed that he himself, in place of his son, be espoused to Aristobulus' daughter. His son would instead be espoused to the daughter of Pheroras, a scheme whereby Alexander's older son, whom he deemed potentially the most serious threat to his safety, would be shut off from a profitable union with the House of Herod.

Momentarily angry, Herod read the impudent proposal. Nevertheless, from the hot springs beyond the Jordan, a weary acquiescence was sent to Jerusalem.

In the royal palace Antipater began actively to chart a sinuous course; its immediate objective, to hasten Herod's death; its ultimate goal, the throne of Judea.

CHAPTER XX

PENUMBRA

ALTHOUGH ANTIPATER WAS GREATLY ELATED by his unexpectedly easy victory over his father, he was shrewd enough not to overemphasize its significance. Doltish and unimaginative he doubtless was. Yet he had a saving sort of back-country cunning that usually checked any temptation to act impulsively. It was an uncomfortable thought that had Herod been well and present he would not have dared oppose him. Rather, he would have hypocritically applauded his father's concern for his grandchildren and looked about for some safer, less direct means of hamstringing their chances. As it was, he had merely won a minor success in what might well be only the first skirmish in a long war of attrition against rivals, who had on their side youth and charm, which he could match only with aging skill and shopworn tricks.

If Antipater faced his problem squarely, there was no gainsaying that Herod loved his grandchildren and clearly planned to provide for their future, if need be at the expense of Antipater. Moreover, the king's obvious intention of placing them beyond reach of Antipater could readily imply that in time he meant also to put them above him. It was clear at least that Herod did not entirely trust his son. In the past, whoever Herod had not trusted invariably came to a violent end.

Ambition, even personal safety, demanded that Herod die speedily. Cancer was definitely too slow. He toyed with the idea of something swift, and certain, like poison, administered by someone else who hated Herod. The idea intrigued him. The longer he entertained it, the more attractive it grew. An unpleasant smile overspread his cunning features. In imagination he had just returned from Herod's funeral—dignified, adequate obsequies, yet not so magnificent as to exaggerate the accomplishments of the deceased, or to overshadow the capabilities of his successor.

Now projecting himself beyond that sad ceremony, he saw himself enthroned in regal splendor, face to face with the problems of government. Before him were ranged the various factions and elements he must work with or against: Rome, the army, the court, the Jewish political parties, the common people.

Herod, he reflected, had remained in power by pitilessly suppressing the Pharisees, the one party which was in a sense religious and potentially dangerous, and by exterminating anyone at court—not excluding his own family—whose loyalty he saw fit to suspect. With the other powerful political party, the materialistic and cynical Sadducees, he had on the whole, in recent years at least, maintained friendly and mutually profitable relations, placing their representatives in the high priesthood, and dividing with them their income from the Temple charges and other monopolies. Toward Rome, Antipater ruefully recalled, Herod's policy was that of a vassal prince, so loyal and efficient that Caesar repaid him with his personal friendship. The army, of course, loved the king as their brave, trusted leader, who willingly shared their dangers and made the problems of the meanest soldier his own concern. Or such, at any rate, had been their relationship until the recent execution of their veteran officers. The masses, despite a multiplicity of taxes, were prosperous, thanks to Herod's encouragement of trade, farming, and building. Nor had he the possibility of nationalistic dissatisfaction to deal with.

This then, Antipater diagnosed, had been the policy that sustained Herod through thirty-five years of unchallenged rule. He had unceasingly persecuted the Pharisees, the one faction most prone to be troublesome; he had filled the court with those he considered his friends, and eliminated those he suspected. He had worked endlessly for friendship with Rome, won the esteem of his soldiers by courage and leadership, and kept national pride sluggish by filling the bellies of the masses.

This recipe for ruling a nation had been successful, Antipater admitted, in Herod's case. But he knew it would not work for him. Vain though he was, he never discouraged his informers from carrying to him even the most derogatory reports concerning himself. As a result he knew exactly what was thought of him. Naturally he was too conceited to agree. On the other hand, he was not so naive as to discount popular or official disparagement of himself and his ability. In the first place, he was actually handicapped by his experiences at Rome. There, those whose opinions really counted derided him as an upstart or reviled him for a country lout.

Caesar was always frigidly courteous; the mean little kindnesses Antipater received at the Roman court were for his father's sake, not his own.

Still, Rome held the policy of legitimacy in high regard; and he had the advantage of being Herod's son, co-regent and designated successor.

With the Sadducees he anticipated no difficulty. He would be quite content to continue Herod's profitable agreements with them.

The hostile attitude of the army was, however, a real problem. He knew he had no military ability to win their admiration; he realized how much the soldiers despised him for his part in the death of the princes. That the remaining older men in the army were still unappeased over Herod's brutal treatment of the veteran officers was at best uncertain solace, for the younger officers now in control hated Antipater as heartily as did the older personnel.

How to win the people was unquestionably his greatest difficulty. He reviewed the taxes they had to pay. For the government of Judea, taxes were exacted on land, cattle, fruit trees, and produce brought to market. Water, city maintenance, meat, salt, wood, and real-estate taxes were collected for Rome. A poll tax went to the personal support of the Judean king. A truly crushing burden, unless lightened by means of income devised by a ruler with a genius for organizing and developing national resources!

Such a talent Antipater had to admit he did not have. Nor, had he possessed it, would he have been willing to make use of it. A keen self-analyst—only with himself was he ever honest— he properly evaluated his constitutional indolence, his impatience with the manifold details of national economy, and his fixed conviction that the state was obligated to support its king in unbounded munificence without presuming to demand commensurate services on his part.

That left the Pharisees. On them he based his chief hope for a successful administration. Though quiescent for years under Herod's harshness, they had of late grown bolder, and once again set themselves forth as spokesmen for the people and guardians of the national weal.

It was not only their knowledge of Herod's incurable illness that encouraged them to emerge from hiding. A sort of conviction that the present era of universal peace was only the prelude to a milennium, when man would rise above the weakness and sin that kept him from perfection, pervaded the entire Roman Empire.

The world was tired. Universal peace was peace under duress. Augustus, with more power than any other man before his day, brooded over the untimely death of his prodigy-son, Marcellus, and bitterly pondered the shame his vicious wife and their more vicious daughter brought to his old age. Virtue died young, like his boy; sin only, and suffering, had strength to survive in a corrupt world. Yet a spirit of hopefulness, almost of yearning, was everywhere. Virgil, dead some dozen years, had sensed this in the eclogue wherein he foretells the birth of a miraculous child conceived by a virgin. The Persians, the Medes, the inhabitants of the great Chaldean plain looked for a sign of redemption in the stars.

In Judea the conviction that redemption was at hand was most intense. Instead of the vague stirrings that stimulated the pagan world, the hopes of the Jews were based on very specific prophecies. The time of waiting for the coming of the Redeemer had elapsed; the circumstances were right—the scepter had passed from Judah—and even the place of his birth was known, a strange setting for the advent of a king, the hillside slum of Bethlehem. All Judea was in a fever of excitement, hoping and expecting that the Savior would soon come to restore the scepter that had been snatched away by the impious hand of the doomed king.

Everywhere were evidences of this national unrest. Pseudomessiahs, dirty and defiant, sprang up in the desert regions. Thickheaded Galileans, obsessed with the messianic complex, howled rebellion from the green hillsides, until the Romans laid them low. Robbers infested the rocky barrens between Jerusalem and Jericho. As preparing the way for the Savior, they were abetted even by those they victimized.

Behind these disturbances were the Pharisees. They expounded and clarified the prophecies. Soon he would come, and, as everyone took for granted, uproot the Roman and restore the crown of Judah.

Antipater's only connection with Jewry was his marriage to a daughter of Antigonus, the last sorry king of the Hasmonean line. Thereby, his children at least were eligible according to Jewish standards. He was by no means convinced that the prophecies meant anything. The notion of a Messiah was, in his case, a matter of superstitious hope rather than rational belief.

Yet, Messiah or no Messiah, he could not afford to deny the possibility of his coming, nor to blind himself to the effect that this real or imaginary figure had on the emotions and actions of the country. He fully appreciated that the Pharisees, in the present state of the country, were too powerful to be disregarded. He determined to cultivate their friendship, and, that won, to worm himself into their confidence.

Ordinarily this would have been almost impossible. Where the Pharisees hated and feared Herod, they despised Antipater. But a situation had arisen which compelled them to let him in on their plans, even eventually to dictate their policies. The wife of Pheroras, Herod's only living brother, was a devout Jewish woman, completely dominated by the less scrupulous wing of the Pharisees. To hold her interest, they asserted that, according to one interpretation of the Scriptures, her children and their descendants would occupy the throne of Judea. Though childless for years, and past the normal age for childbearing, she swallowed the prediction without reservation. As a result, her frequent tentative pregnancies were a fixed occasion of merriment among her acquaintances.

But the lady herself was never discouraged or disillusioned. More and more completely she gave herself over to the hoaxsters. When a number of them were penalized for lack of respect to Herod and Rome, she paid their fine. Pleading the delicate state of her health, she gave up attendance at court functions and shared her time equally between the Pharisees and her family.

The former found in her enthusiasm an unfailing source of cash as well as a personality backed by whose prestige they could function more openly and safely. Some of her family were not so happy about her zeal. She considered her husband's daughters (fortunately, he had no son) by a previous marriage unsuitable associates for the royal presumptive. Accordingly, she ejected them from their luxurious quarters and reduced them to the level of bond servants.

Had Pheroras been a more assertive character, he would have put a stop to such inane fanaticism. But he was still so in love with his wife that he was willing to compromise for the sake of connubial peace at any cost. Besides this disinclination to resist, he was hemmed in by his wife's mother and aunt, both formidable dowagers who not only seconded every ambition and action of his wife but, to forestall any dormant inclination on his part to kick over the traces, attached themselves permanently to his household.

Antipater was not slow to take advantage of these circumstances: a rabid faction with reason to hate the king; a weak brother of the king, completely dominated by his wife and her family; and a deluded, desperate woman, willing to believe or risk anything to protect an almost miraculous child as yet not even conceived! And all these elements beset with the single idea of doing away with the king! Properly directed, Antipater opined, they could not only fulfil their primary purpose but, in the process, secure the throne for him as well.

He wrote to the wife of Pheroras, disclosing in terms obscure to the casual reader but unmistakable to her that he was fully aware of the plot against his father and that as the husband of a Hasmonean princess he, too, shared the national longing for the restoration of the rightful rulers. He was so sympathetic to her plans that he would share her confidence. As a token of his good faith, he would send his mother, Doris, to her court as a hostage.

Whether his offer would be considered legitimate or a form of blackmail and whether Doris would be looked upon as his spy or as a co-conspirator was immaterial to Antipater. He had at any rate succeeded in forcing the conspirators to put themselves in his power, which necessarily implied under his orders.

So Doris left her ailing, indifferent spouse and was enthusiastically welcomed by her new associates; and Pheroras' palace buzzed with the conspiracy.

Naturally the fullest secrecy had been planned. But it was inevitable that with four women, one at least of them fanatical, and all imperious, plus an indeterminate number of factionists, many of them heedless and boastful, it was impossible to keep their activities entirely under cover.

From her informers Salome received some inkling of what was going on. Her common sense told her the rest. Doris—Pheroras' family—the Pharisees—such diverse factors could possibly unite only in a common hatred of Herod.

Her anger—as she grew older her irascibility became almost boundless—got the better of her caution. She broke in on the conspirators and violently accused them of plotting to kill her brother. They laughed her to scorn and informed her that her quarrelsome person was not relished in so pious a household.

Salome could recognize a repulse but not defeat. She hastened to Jericho to Herod and repeated her charges. Sick and weary, he refused to believe her. He had listened to her denunciations so often, and always the outcome was anguish and remorse.

While the conspirators had pretended to ridicule Salome's accusations, she was so close to the truth in her rash denunciation that they were decidedly uneasy. Now that they reflected, their sudden intimacy was unquestionably suspicious.

They changed their tactics. Publicly they made it a point to bicker. On properly spaced occasions they engaged in violent quarrels in the course of which invectives, malicious, and true, were exchanged, to add verisimilitude to the fracas and at the same time to relieve their native spleen, kept under duress because of their unholy pact.

They continued to meet secretly. Various schemes for killing Herod were discussed. Except poison, every method was rejected as uncertain or as dangerous to the perpetrators.

Even the administration of poison was a matter of enormous difficulty. Despite popular misconception, poison was a cruder, less effective weapon than it is today. Synthetic poisons, similar to those originating in the chemist's laboratory, were rare; concoctions of poison from mineral and vegetable ingredients were unreliable and often difficult to disguise and administer. Moreover, so poison-conscious was Herod, so thoroughly were the crude materials and the manufacture of the venom controlled, that even to obtain a lethal dose in Judea was a precarious business. The first of the final steps, the actual procurement of the poison, was assigned to Antipater.

By now, Mariamne began to get wind of the plot. As daughter of the high priest she could not afford to let his Sadducean party be excluded from a share in the spoils should Herod come to grief. She, too, wedged her way into the conspiracy and added further to the confusion of interests.

Salome, rebuffed but undismayed, kept doggedly on the quest for evidence. Soon she gathered enough at least to embarrass the plotters. Herod had to listen when she presented proof of treasonable action by certain Pharisees—all of them of minor importance. In the dragnet was caught also the eunuch Bagoas, whose jubilant insistence that when Pheroras was regent (for his son, of course), he, too, would be able to marry and have children helped bring their misconduct to light.

They were speedily executed—without the trial that Salome anticipated would disclose the real extent of the conspiracy.

Still, enough was made manifest to compel Herod, quite unwillingly, to call his sister-in-law to task on the dual charges of having abused her stepdaughters and of endangering the affection between his brother and himself.

Herod's sentence was surprisingly mild. He commanded his brother to put his wife away—of further investigation or punishment, not a syllable.

It would appear that in the interval between the execution of his sons and the arrival of the magi in Jerusalem Herod was singularly considerate of his family. All the distrust and fury formerly characteristic of his domestic relationship seemed engulfed in the agony of his disease. Perhaps, in his sane hours, he was so horrified with remorse over his cruelty to those dear to him that he shrank from intensifying his bitterness by further bloodshed. However it was, all his ruthless vigor, his insatiate lust for revenge, appeared to have been sapped by his suffering, with the consequence of his easy judgment on his sister-in-law and his reluctance to seek more evidence of guilt.

To everyone's amazement, Pheroras, instead of welcoming the opportunity of getting rid of his wife and her villainous relatives, absolutely refused to divorce her. The common opinion, "The little man is taking advantage of Herod's kindness," was hardly just. Pheroras was both the weakest and the best of the Herodians. Physically slight, with no particular gifts or abilities, he had talents and virtues largely negative. Save one. He feared no one except his wife. And he loved her, even more than he was afraid of her.

He would deplore, he explained, the loss of his brother's friendship, "but he would rather choose to die than be deprived of a wife that was so dear to him," demonstrating through the words of Josephus that clichés are no modern discovery.

Herod was puzzled. He did not enforce his sentence. Instead he ordered Antipater and Doris to have nothing to do with Pheroras and his family. To make compliance with his wishes more easy, he bestowed priceless jewels upon Doris and gave a hundred talents to Antipater.

Their response to his generosity was compounded of just the right proportions of dignified submission and grateful devotion. The king was certain that by his generosity he had forestalled any possibility of their treason; inwardly they gloated at his gullibility. The secret meetings continued and the details of the plot were perfected.

As the full implications of his actions dawned upon Antipater, he became alarmed. Even though his father was sick and clearly incapable of sound judgment, the possibilities that the plot might be uncovered were too grave. There were too many conspirators to begin with, and too many others suspicious or actually aware of what was going on. Salome was neither ill nor deluded, and an unlucky chance might readily divulge the entire plot to her. Definitely, it was safer for him to be elsewhere, removed by distance from any possibility of suspicion, should his plans misfire.

He communicated with a friend at Rome. Soon an order came, seemingly sanctioned by Caesar, requiring Antipater to report at once to the Imperial City.

With lagging steps and eyes ready to burst with tears, he brought the order to Herod. He urged defiance of Caesar's will; it was inhuman to tear him from the side of his beloved father, ill and beset by plotters.

The act fooled Herod completely. He urged instant compliance with Caesar's wishes; he was gratified that the emperor had shown such an interest in his son. By degrees, and with seeming misgivings, Antipater let himself be persuaded of the wisdom of his father's advice. Out of the king's sight, he gaily made his preparations for the journey.

Along with him went a present for Caesar, and a copy of Herod's will wherein Antipater was nominated as heir presumptive and Herod Philip next in line of succession should anything happen to the first choice.

As the ship breasted the soft swells of the tepid Mediterranean, it bore a well-matched pair of scoundrels: Antipater, a pampered passenger sipping Syrian wine on the moon-washed deck—and below in the choking hold the doomed rogue Sylleus, who, having failed to carry out Caesar's command to repay Herod, had been trapped in a further attempt against the king's life and was being sent to Rome by Saturninus for judgment.

There is little evidence, however, that the fate of the other conspirator had a sobering influence upon Antipater, whose complacency increased as the Palestinian coasts were left farther and farther behind.

Antipater's flight turned out to be a prudent move. Rumors of plots and charges of conspiracy so flooded the court that Herod was forced to do something. Unable to discern clearly amid the labyrinthian tangle of accusations and denials, he felt that

Pheroras' wife was the focal point of the disturbance. He gave Pheroras one last chance to get rid of her, with the penalty of exile in Transjordania in the event that he refused.

Pheroras, wavering in most things, was adamant in his devotion to his wife. With a bitter pride not native to the hen-pecked husband he entered into exile, vowing never to return to Judea while Herod was alive.

That this vow was not taken merely in a moment of bravado was soon apparent. Taking a turn for the worse, and hoping to be reconciled with his one surviving brother, Herod in the friendliest terms invited him to return. But Pheroras nursed his resentment in the bleak uplands and rejected the invitation.

As Herod recovered, Pheroras, softened by years of easy living, became violently ill. Herod, overlooking his slight, hastened to his brother, greeted him with fraternal affection and put him in the care of the royal physicians. (It was, incidentally, due to this demonstration of brotherly love and forgiveness that Antipater at length, by devious and complex routes, met his doom.)

Pheroras partly recovered. But he was exhausted and spiritless. His wife, still obsessed with the vision of royal offspring, was becoming panicky. Her latest assumption of pregnancy had been as fantastic as the others. Pheroras was no believer in the Pharisaical prophecies; nor could he be persuaded that his wife was another Sara to give birth to a son in her old age. Besides he was too sick to be amorous.

In desperation she turned to an Egyptian attendant who was reputed to be familiar with all the magic of the Nile. A love potion, said to be unfailing in its results, was concocted and guttered down the invalid's protesting throat.

That night Pheroras toppled over and died, possibly of a cerebral hemorrhage.

The body was brought to Jerusalem. A sumptuous funeral train accompanied it to the royal sepulcher, with Herod, probably one of the few genuine mourners, overcome with honest grief for the last of his brothers.

Shortly thereafter ugly rumors began to percolate to the court —confused reports that Pheroras was poisoned by an Egyptian potion that had actually been intended for Herod.

These rumors took on the guise of creditability when two of Pheroras' devoted freedmen gave Herod a more detailed account of the administration of the draught and its apparent effect.

Herod was perplexed. He was aware that direct inquisition of the widow might precipitate disorders. Sick and bewildered, he was unwilling to risk a violent reaction.

Instead he sought to obtain information by torturing his brother's servants and slaves. Only confusion resulted until one maid in her agony moaned the hope that God would inflict Doris, who was the real cause of their suffering, with similar tortures.

Thereupon Herod intensified the tortures until, little by little, the sordid story was disclosed, not of any poisoning of Pheroras, but how Antipater had gleefully told of Herod's gifts, while plotting his death—how the women, to divert suspicion, pretended to hate one another—of Mariamne's contrivance with the Sadducees—the deadly hatred of Doris for her husband—how Pheroras' spouse and her family schemed with the Pharisees, while Antipater plotted with anybody who would be willing to kill his father, complained of his slowness in dying, and denounced his brutality to his soldiers and his cruelty to his children and friends —of his procuring a poison which Pheroras was to administer to his brother, the while hypocritically running away to remove himself from suspicion.

It was Salome's hour of triumph. Doris was stripped of her newly acquired jewels and ejected from the court; Mariamne was summarily divorced and her father replaced as high priest by Matthias; troops were dispatched to arrest Pheroras' widow.

But that lady was not unaware of the turn matters had taken. She fled to the roof top and, eluding the restraining arms of her pursuers, flung herself to the pavement below. Almost miraculously, she landed on her feet, stunned and shocked, but otherwise unhurt.

The king was strangely gentle with his sister-in-law. He spoke with loving remembrance of her husband—how dear he had been to them both; sadly he enlarged on the duplicity of his son and the grief his conspiracy had brought to everyone; he recalled the cruel delusion the Pharisees had practiced upon her.

It was probably the reminder of her barrenness rather than the kindness of the king that unloosed the torrent of words that disclosed the whole diabolical scheme.

An Egyptian doctor, she testified, brought the poison from Egypt at the orders of Antipater, who gave it to Pheroras. The latter, distressed at the thought of killing his brother, passed it on to her. Such, however, was his subsequent anger with Herod that he expressed his willingness to poison him whenever the occasion arose. He later repented after Herod had demonstrated his love while Pheroras was ill. Knowing he had not long to live and unwilling to face his Judge with a brother's assassination on his soul, he reviled Antipater for tricking him, and ordered his wife to burn the poison in his presence. This she did, reserving, unknown to her husband, enough to do away with herself should Herod later on charge her with her part in the plot.

Thereupon she produced the box containing the remainder of the poison.

Under torture the mother and the brother of the Egyptian doctor corroborated her evidence and identified the container.

At this pat instant, Bathyllus, forger, panderer, and trusted freedman, arrived from Rome. Seized and searched almost before he was aware of what was happening to him, he was found to have on his person another dose of poison addressed to Doris and Pheroras (news of whose death had not yet reached Antipater), to be used in case the first potion was ineffectual. He bore also a letter for Herod wherein Antipater accused Herod Philip and Archelaus, son of the Samaritan wife Malthace of plotting against their father, endeavoring to have the king removed by Caesar and—overlooking Antipater—to have themselves named co-regents. But, he piously continued, he would not have the princes severely punished, for they were young and impulsive and probably influenced by their mothers.

Another letter brazenly deplored how expensive was the process of attempting to press the case against Sylleus (executed some months previously)—how the costs already exceeded two hundred talents, but that he was certain his generous father would quickly reimburse him.

Herod wrote back immediately in most affectionate vein urging his son to hasten home, since he realized the fatal nature of his malady and desired to discuss the affairs of the kingdom with his successor.

The letter was entirely disarming in tone save for a vague hint that he was not quite satisfied with Doris' conduct.

Jubilantly, Antipater bade his Roman cronies a nightlong farewell and was deposited glum and boozy on the ship that would speed him to Palestine. The tangy air gradually cleared his mind. By nightfall he was in the highest spirits. Already he knew just what would be his first activities as king—whom he would remove, whom kill. By the time the vessel docked at Tarentum he had compiled a list of the proscribed, including all his co-conspirators except his mother.

Here he received his first shock. A letter from an agent at the court informed him of Pheroras' death—an event of which Herod's letter had made no mention.

Even before the ship made its second stop at Cilicia his enthusiasm for a speedy return began to wane as he deliberated on the possible ramifications of Pheroras' death and his mother's lapse from favor.

He called a conference of his followers. Some advised his tarrying at Cilicia pending more explicit information on affairs in Judea; others, more persuasive, convinced him that his presence at the court would soon set matters right, and that failure to obey what was probably Herod's dying request would almost certainly preclude him from the succession.

Though still apprehensive, he conceded the wisdom of this advice.

During the last stage of the voyage the ship ran into foul weather. Delayed by head winds and battered by roaring seas, she laboriously inched her way to the Palestinian coast. In this reversal of the elements, Antipater, always a prey to superstitious fears, could see only a warning, withheld by a malicious fate until too late to benefit him.

Seasick and despondent, an unkingly figure, he stumbled ashore at Caesarea.

It was not a sense of guilt alone that made him apprehensive. Everywhere he was met by studied neglect or glowering glances.

Nowhere could he see a trace of the subservience a prospective
ruler might expect. Those more effusive in bidding him farewell
on his departure for Rome were nowhere to be seen. As he
moved inland, the populace became more overtly hostile. Yells
of "murderer, hypocrite, parricide" were his unfailing greeting;
stones hurled with more enthusiasm than accuracy added a note
of physical danger.

Still he could not turn back. Like a fish in a weir he could
move only forward to the mouth of the trap where destruction
lurked.

If he had anticipated a warmer welcome from his partisans in
Jerusalem, he was once more disappointed. True, there was no
sign of open hostility. Ordinarily Jerusalem was one of the
noisiest places in the world. Buyers and sellers trying to out-
bawl one another, open-air schools with scholars screaming out
precepts at the shrill top of their voices, howling wedding processions and funeral trains vanguarded by shrilling flutes and
shrieking professional mourners, hammering coppersmiths, fishmongers, quarrelsome housewives, and bellowing peddlers merged
into the cacophony that was the characteristic song of the city.

Today it seemed almost deserted. The sun was hot and bright;
clouds of pigeons drifted overhead on their daily flight to the
moist reeds of the Jordan; the dome of the Temple as always
glittered blindingly above the too-white towers; dust ascended in
clouds of tangible thickness from without the walls.

Yet an air of death seemed to pervade all. Chance passers-by
huddled against the windowless backs of the houses, or furtively
slipped down some convenient alley to avoid even seeming to
witness the return of the royal son and heir.

It must be granted, however, that Antipater had prepared for
this final stage of return with dignity and a sort of desperate
courage. His guard was gorgeously accoutered; he himself was
robed in royal purple. Emerging from the deserted streets they
marched up the broad stone stairway, passed the carved rearing
lions, and paused at the closed bronze gate of the palace.

It swung open. The porters admitted him, but turned away
the guard.

Pale, under the purple, Antipater passed through entrance

halls sweet with the heavy scent of orange blossoms, through tapestried chambers silent save for the drowsy tinkling of little fountains, to the throne room.

That it had more the air of a judgment hall, with armed troops lining the walls, and unsmiling prosecutors and counselors grouped about the throne, was, for the moment, unnoted by Antipater. His eyes lit at once upon the stern, sorrowful face of his father, then flicked for an instant, apprehensively, upon his companion, the saturnine Varus, doomed one day to lose legions and life in the Teutoburger Wald.

Sweating with uncertainty and fear, he rushed up to embrace the king. Herod, with long unused strength, rose to his feet and thrust the hilt of his sword into the chest of his son so violently as to stagger him. Guards, none too gently, straightened him up and forced him to face his father.

Herod lost no time with preliminaries. In words of biting impact he charged him with murdering his brothers and plotting to kill him. The trial would take place the very next day. Meanwhile, he was granted a single day of freedom to see Doris, and his neglected wife. That day must suffice also for the preparation of his defense.

Antipater's trial, compared with previous trials Herod had ordered, was dignified and just. Witnesses were called; Salome jubilantly told her story; servants who had been tortured repeated their evidence. A letter, stolen from Doris, which Antipater had foolishly written to his mother during his period of indecision at Cilicia questioning whether it would not be wiser to throw himself on Caesar's mercy, since it was probable that his father was aware of his perfidy, was introduced.

Antipater realized how weak was his defense. He threw himself at his father's feet, sobbing for mercy.

Herod painfully pushed himself out of his seat, and leaning heavily on the shoulder of Varus began his charge. Never once did he look at the figure groveling below him. In broken tones that barely carried to the limits of the room he deplored the actions of his children, repeated all he had done for them despite which they continually plotted his downfall. He was above all hurt that Antipater had the presumption to try to hasten his

death, which in any event could not be far off, when he already
knew he was his heir, and actually almost his equal in power and
authority. He reminded the court how generously he had treated
this ungrateful son—fifty talents a year income and thirty talents
for his expenses in Rome.

The memory of his injustice toward his other sons and his
misguided munificence to the culprit was too much for the sad,
sick old man. Almost in a state of collapse he was helped back
into his seat.

But Antipater was fated not to benefit by his father's weakness.
Nicolaus at once resumed the case, recapitulated the testimony,
and link by link forged a chain of evidence from which he could
not squirm.

Nevertheless Antipater made a skilful attempt at defense,
almost purely a personal plea to the king. He reiterated his often-
proclaimed affection for his father, recalled how diligently he had
worked in the interests of the kingdom, and tried to establish the
folly of risking his life to acquire that which he already was
assured of. The evidence, he intimated, had been concocted
during his absence when he was unable to protect himself. Moreover, much of the most harmful testimony was procured under
torture when men would say whatever they thought might lessen
their agony. Somewhat illogically he offered to submit to torture
himself to test the truth of his assertions.

Herod, like many others—for Antipater had a crude eloquence
that could be effective—was moved to tears by his son's plea. It
was clear that he was on the point of weakening; that Antipater,
in spite of the evidence, might win the royal pardon.

Nicolaus would not let this perversion of justice take place.
Keeping to the personal note set by Antipater, he contrasted the
minor indiscretions for which his brothers had been executed
with the deliberate infamy of the defendant, who had the shame-
lessness further to try the mercy of the king whose love and
generosity he had so maliciously flaunted and whose death had
been his one design. Even a serpent, the counselor continued,
would not so treacherously turn on a benefactor. He demonstrated how Antipater had been the prime cause of his brothers'
deaths, which he intended, not for his father's safety, but for his

own advancement. This pretense of sorrow and love was designed merely to delude his father and to restore himself once again to a position from which he could harass the king anew.

He closed by reviewing the incontrovertible testimony that Antipater had plotted continuously and deliberately to bring about his father's death by poison, had in this procedure defiled the minds of his own mother, of Herod's brother and sister-in-law, of many others close to Herod or influential in preserving the peace of the kingdom, and then, having set in motion such tremendous forces of mischief, had cravenly fled to Rome. His final words, directed at Varus, were a plea to disregard Antipater's willingness to undergo torture—a false test by the defendant's own admission—but rather to destroy "this wild beast."

Antipater had expended his last strategem, used his final argument. In rebuttal he could only fall on his face and appeal to God by some sign to proclaim his innocence.

Varus coldly ordered that what was left of the potion be brought into court. A criminal, already condemned, drank it and died immediately.

There could be only one verdict, "Guilty of attempted regicide and parricide."

Brokenhearted, Herod ordered his son thrown into prison.

And in Chaldea magi were beginning to speculate on a strange, new star that was blazing low in the western sky.

CHAPTER XXI

WE HAVE SEEN HIS STAR

THE STORY OF THE NATIVITY MIGHT WELL BE
considered a pageant in two episodes. In the first we see a stony
Judean hillside, mellowed by moonlight, with flocks huddled in
the hollows and gaunt shepherds keeping their nightly watch
against marauders. The hushed heavens are aroused by the beating of innumerable wings. A celestial hymn settles like a sooth-
ing benediction upon the startled watchers. The angel's voice
directs them to the cave, where they worship the newborn king,
leave their humble presents, and go back to their flocks. It is all
very idyllic, and consoling, and simple.

The second episode is one of wealth and power and treachery
and murder; of a star and dreams; of the slaughter of children
and the flight of the King.

As Matthew tells it:

"Now when Jesus was born in Bethlehem of Judea, in the days
of King Herod, behold, there came magi from the East to Jerusalem, saying, 'Where is the newly born king of the Jews? For
we have seen his star in the East and have come to worship him.'
But when King Herod heard this, he was troubled, and so was
all Jerusalem with him. And gathering together all the chief
priests and scribes of the people, he inquired of them where the
Christ was to be born. And they said to him, 'In Bethlehem of
Judea; for thus it is written through the prophet, "And thou,
Bethlehem, of the land of Juda, art by no means least among the
princes of Juda; for from thee shall come forth a leader who shall
rule my people Israel."'

340

"Then Herod summoned the magi secretly, and carefully ascertained from them the time when the star had appeared to them. And sending them to Bethlehem, he said, 'Go and make careful inquiry concerning the child, and when you have found him, bring me word, that I too may go and worship him.'

"Now they, having heard the king, went their way. And behold, the star that they had seen in the East went before them, until it came and stood over the place where the child was. And when they saw the star they rejoiced exceedingly. And entering the house, they found the child with Mary his mother, and falling down they worshipped him. And opening their treasures they offered him gifts of gold, frankincense and myrrh. And being warned in a dream not to return to Herod, they went back to their own country by another way.

"But when they had departed, behold, an angel of the Lord appeared in a dream to Joseph, saying, 'Arise, and take the child and his mother, and flee into Egypt, and remain there until I tell thee. For Herod will seek the child to destroy him.' So he arose, and took the child and his mother by night, and withdrew into Egypt, and remained there until the death of Herod; that there might be fulfilled what was spoken by the Lord through the prophet, saying, 'Out of Egypt I called my son.'

"Then Herod, seeing that he had been tricked by the magi, was exceedingly angry; and he sent and slew all the boys in Bethlehem and all its neighborhood who were two years old or under, according to the time that he had carefully ascertained from the magi."

The story of the evangelist is a masterpiece of concise narration and flawless characterization. It does not, however, close the door on further conjecture and speculation. The magi, for instance, have variously been depicted as kings, as wise men from the East, as priests, as magicians. History tells us that the magi were the sacred caste of the Medes. After Cyrus had consolidated Media and Persia, they became more numerous and powerful, and provided the priesthood for the religious functions of Persia. They were not magicians, since their religious tenets frowned upon sorcery. Nor were they of royal blood, although they at one time revolted and placed one of their number on the throne, where he ruled as King Smerdis. He must have been highly unpopular. The people rebelled, killed him, and proclaimed a holiday of thanksgiving for being liberated from magi rule. For a time the magi fell upon evil days. Gradually they regained most of their influence and established their headquarters in the magi city of Pasargadae near Persopolis, until the courtesan Lais prevailed upon Alexander the Great to set fire to their city. Scattering them did them no harm. In the Parthian empire they, according to Strabo, constituted one of the two councils of the empire.

The ancient cult of the magi—always dignified and ethical in contrast with most pagan cults—was codified by Zoroaster during the reign of Darius Hystaspes, the fourth Persian king, him by whose permission the second Temple was built.

Zoroaster's early history is uncertain. There is some reason to believe that he was a Jew, perhaps a disciple of Daniel's. At any rate there is a rather close resemblance to the Jewish religion in Zoroaster's teaching. In fact the term "sun worshiper," commonly applied to the magi, is inaccurate. The sun, or its terrestial symbol, fire, was not physically worshiped; it was merely the visible sign of an invisible, omnipotent, eternal Presence. Without the sun there could be no life; therefore, only the sun could suitably typify God.

Apart from the almost divine honors paid to the sun or to its mundane counterpart, fire, which Zoroaster is said to have dropped from heaven upon the altar, there are the following similarities to Hebrew ritual and belief: The mode of sacrifice is almost the same; beasts were clean or unclean; orders of priests resembled the Jewish classes of high priest, priests and levites; the priesthood was supported by tithes; one God, Creator and Sustainer of all, was adored; the immortality of the soul, the resurrection of the dead, and an eternity of happiness or misery were taught.

The sacred book, the Zend-Avesta, or "Fire kindler," is in some measure similar to the Old Testament. It contains accounts of the Creation, of Abraham and Joseph, and psalms.

The magi believed, too, in a star the advent of which would

foretell the virgin birth of a king whose reign would usher in a golden age of peace and justice for all mankind.

The magi of the Gospel saw their star between one and two years before the birth of Christ. As astronomers and astrologers, they were familiar with the heavens and because of the Zoroastrian prophecies they were ready to attach direct significance to any new star or other unusual phenomenon in the sky. Three days each month, St. John Chrysostom states, generations of magi scanned the heavens for the star which would be in the "shape of a wondrous child with a kingly crown on his head." To the magi who adored the Christ Child it was given to experience the fulfilment of the ancient prophecies.

The presence of the star has been variously explained. Some have called it a comet; others, a "nova" or new star. Kepler discovered that the conjunction of Jupiter and Saturn, occurring normally once in eight hundred years, actually took place three times shortly before the birth of Christ. Other astronomers point out that there was a conjunction of Venus and Jupiter about 6 B.C.

None of these explanations could quite account for the zeal of the magi. As astronomers, they would not have been deceived into believing a comet or conjunction of planets to be the long-awaited star. Moreover, a star would not move more than one degree a day. Nor could it disappear and reappear as did the star of Bethlehem.

"A star shall rise out of Jacob and a scepter shall spring up from Israel" Balaam had prophesied, and this was the star, "his star," that they followed, a star that, according to tradition, was suspended near the earth, and moved directly ahead of them, instead of in the normal elliptical astral orbit.

Tradition names the magi Melchior, Casper, and Balthasar; a charming legend provides the additional information that they were respectively white, brown, and black, descendants of Noah's sons, Japhet, Sem, and Ham, thus signifying the universality of the new creed. The threefold gift also is sometimes offered as evidence that the magi were three in number.

As a matter of fact, one cannot be certain of their number. Inscriptions on tombs in the catacombs show sometimes two, again as many as eight. An oriental tradition asserts there were twelve to correspond with the number of the apostles.

However many there were, they with their guards and servants must have constituted a large, well-armed caravan. For a few men, the journey would have been too hazardous. Three or even twelve magi, traveling without a sumptuous caravan and many guards, would have been too insignificant to set tongues wagging in Jerusalem and quicken the respectful interest of Herod.

After they had seen the star, the magi must have spent feverish weeks in rereading and interpreting their sacred books, and in assembling the guards, and camels, and supplies necessary for a journey of indefinite length and duration.

Starting probably from Chaldea (it is sometimes said one of the magi, an Arabian, met them on the way), they crossed the unchartered sandy wastes west of their land, scrambled through rock-strewn dry river beds, or forded swollen freshets, and skirmished with the savage Kurds who ranged down from the mountains. Then, having crossed the desert, they descended to the lowlands of the Tigris. Hugging its reedy banks, they skirted wasted Babylon, paused briefly where Cyrus had won the battle that established their homeland, and were saddened as they passed the site of the catastrophic conflict in which Darius' empire was conquered by Alexander. Then they turned north, with the star, and crossed a plain, then blooming, now since the destruction of the irrigation canals arid and dead. At a place marked by the tumbled debris of Nineveh, they crossed the river on a bridge of boats and moved across the burning flats of Mesopotamia. Eventually, after stopping briefly at Aleppo or Palmyra, they left the desert at Damascus. Here they paused, while the star hung motionless overhead, to review the prophecies of the Hebrews, and to inquire at the synagogue what the Jews knew concerning the birth of a Savior. Refreshed and encouraged, they proceeded, the star ever before them, crossing the rugged depths of the Anti-Lebanon, and entered Judea from the north. They veered with the star to the east of the Sea of Galilee and kept to the great caravan route along the east bank of the Jordan until they crossed the river at the ford near Jericho.

There the star disappeared.

They must have stared with stunned amazement at the suddenly dark blot in the sky. Myriads of lesser lights still flickered, but to them, without their star, the heavens were a pool of unrelieved gloom. They had come over a thousand miles—had been weary months on the road—and here, in the very land where they expected to find their king, their hitherto faithful guide had deserted them.

Still, to return to their homes, disillusioned, was unthinkable. God could not so cheat them. In the synagogue at Damascus they had caught more intimately the spirit of the Messianic prophecies. Before them, up the twenty-five tortuous miles from Jericho, lay Jerusalem with its Temple and its high priest, where they were bound to learn the truth.

Without pausing to rest, they ordered their caravan up the flinty road. Furtive figures loomed momentarily in the roadside murk, appraised their strength, and slunk away. Little stones, dislodged by the feet of hidden observers, rustled down the steep slopes. The humid heat of the Jordan changed gradually to the biting chill of the uplands. The guards, anxious-eyed, tried vainly to pierce the impenetrable gloom, as they wrapped their inadequate cloaks more closely about them.

But the magi seemed unaware of discomfort or danger. They must hasten to Jerusalem to consult the high priest and inquire of Herod what they knew of their star and the new born king.

Early in the morning, when the level sun was just igniting the golden top of the Temple and rinsing its marble towers a dazzling white, they entered Jerusalem.

Their entrance caused a sensation. The long line of blooded camels, the regal bearing of the magi, the imperious aloofness of their attendants, and the air of opulence and power that clothed the entire caravan made even the bored inhabitants, accustomed to ostentatious display by visitors, gasp.

News of the splendid train and their strange mission was soon brought to Herod. For a brief spell, his pain had not been too unendurable. A new doctor had recommended the more remote curative springs beyond the Jordan, and the king was in the capital, arranging his affairs before testing the efficacy of hot sulfur baths on his agonized body.

Both hospitable and curious, he immediately granted the visitors the audience they requested. Without mincing words, they asked the momentous question, "Where is the newborn king of the Jews? We have seen his star in the East and have come to worship."

Had the magi been less impressive or the question more timidly worded, Herod might have had them tortured to discover the source of their information and the particulars of their journey and purpose. But in these dignified strangers he recognized his equals, who must be dealt with on a regal plane. He summoned all the high priests, past and present, and all the learned rabbis. Since the ruling Sadducees were not distinguished for scholarship or piety, he extended an invitation even to the hated Pharisees and diffident Essenes, who would more likely be steeped in scriptural lore.

Herod was too prudent to inquire whether the Messiah was already on earth or still expected; he merely asked what the Scriptures maintained was his birthplace. Privately, while the priests were preparing their answer, he questioned the magi concerning the precise time when they had seen the star. "Two years before our arrival in Jerusalem," was their answer.

The priests meanwhile had agreed that according to the fifth chapter of Micah he would be born in Bethlehem. "But thou Bethlehem Ephratah, though thou be little among the thousands of Judah, yet out of thee shall he come forth unto me, that is to be ruler in Israel, whose goings forth have been from old, from everlasting." Confirming this prophecy, there is in the Talmud an imaginary conversation between a Jew and an Arab in which again Bethlehem is designated as the Savior's birthplace. Moreover, from the prophecy of Daniel, the time of Redemption was at hand.

While deeply disturbed by the implications of the priestly exegesis, Herod was outwardly unaffected. Gracious and affable, he wished the magi success in their quest and invited them to return and inform him should they find the new king that he, too, might worship him.

The magi could not have been other than impressed by Herod's courtesy. But they tarried only so long as propriety demanded.

They were impatient to conclude the final stage of their pilgrimage.

The scant six miles to Bethlehem were soon traversed. Pausing to refresh their camels at a well outside the village—traditionally Mary's Well, the same well where Mary and Joseph had slaked their thirst during their night of vain search for lodging—they suddenly saw in the roiled waters the distorted image of their beloved star. Joyfully they followed it the last few hundred yards until it came to rest over an otherwise undistinguished hillside dwelling.

In their zeal, they clambered up the stony steps, past the first-story cave given over to the beasts, to the upper floor, where they found the holy family, and, like the shepherds more than a year previously, they adored their king.

Then they gave the gifts customarily tendered to royalty in the Orient: gold, the element symbolic of royalty; frankincense, the fragrant resin used only in divine worship; and myrrh, in which the bodies of kings reposed.

The magi were almost unimaginably happy. The camels were stabled in the local caravansary; lodgings were sought for their followers; they themselves intended to remain indefinitely with their king.

Sleep crept slowly into their overwrought minds. Recurrent happy dreams prevented sound slumber. Dawn was near when they listened to the warning voice that made rubble of their joyously fashioned dream castle. They must leave at once for their homeland as secretly as possible, without returning first to Jerusalem.

It is reasonable to assume that the magi must immediately have warned Mary and Joseph of the danger to the Holy Child. But the warning was not necessary. Joseph, too, had had his dream, in which he was told to take the child and his mother and flee to Egypt.

The dual flight was probably simultaneous.

The magi could have fled east to the Jordan, avoiding the main route from Jerusalem to Jericho. But this route for a large caravan would have been hazardous and impracticable, along little-used, almost impassible trails. More likely they hastened south through Beersheba, then eastward along the Moabite high road, beyond the Dead Sea, and then, in relative safety, homeward.

Not much is definitely known of the magi after their flight. It is said that they were subsequently baptized by the Apostle Thomas, and that their remains, discovered in Persia, were first brought to Constantinople by Saint Helena, then transferred to Milan in the fifth century, and deposited in Cologne, their present resting place, by the German Emperor Henry VI in 1163.

The same morning that the magi fled, Joseph discharged the little debts his family had incurred, and thanks to the gifts of the magi was well able to purchase a donkey, supplies and other necessities for a hurried flight to Egypt. Avoiding the highways, he took to the lonely trails between the dunes and the sea, and within about two weeks reached his destination.

Scripture tells us only of the beginning of the flight and of the return to Nazareth after the death of Herod. Tradition, however, and unauthenticated narratives have provided fascinating, if inconclusive, details of the journey and the stay in Egypt.

The apocryphal Arabic "Gospel of the Infancy" states that the holy family rested at Matareah in Egypt. "They came to that sycamore which is called Matareah, where the Lord Christ caused a spring to bubble forth, and here the Lady Mary washed His swaddling clothes. But from the perspiration of the Lord which she washed out, there came the balsam into that region."

Some of the early Fathers as well as the apocrypha mention Heliopolis, where "a tree called persides bent down to adore the Son of God and idols fell and were shattered" as had been foretold by Isaias. (The leaf, fruit, or bark of this tree was said to cure illness.)

In a garden at Matareah, some six miles from Cairo and near the site of ancient Heliopolis, there is still an ancient sycamore known as the "Virgin's Tree." Close by are two springs from which flow sweet water, although all other nearby springs are brackish.

More than persistent tradition substantiates that the Holy Family remained in this vicinity. It was here that the slips of balsam given by Herod to Cleopatra were planted and, under the care of Jewish gardeners, flourished even as they did in Jericho. Alexandria and other urban centers had large Jewish populations—in fact, of Egypt's eight million, a million were Jewish. But most of these were cosmopolitan Jews, sentimentally attached, no doubt, to the land of their origin but interested mainly in commerce and trade. It was among the simple, devout children of the soil that the Holy Family would prefer to sojourn.

Back in Jerusalem, Herod derived a grim satisfaction from the failure of the magi to return to the capital. He was not upset at the news of their flight. That they should slip away so secretly could be due only to their chagrin at having been deceived by the star. After their bold demands and outspoken confidence, he would hardly expect them to skulk back and admit that their thousand-mile, year-long expedition had been inspired by a cruel deception.

Later, however, he learned that the star had reappeared and that the magi had offered royal gifts to a child in Bethlehem. Bitterly he cursed his failure to send priests with the magi or at least to have them trailed by his informers. More of the no-longer-new story was ferreted out—of the vision and the adoration of the shepherds, of the prophecies of Simeon and of Anna. But which was the child? Who were the parents? Neither threats nor beguilements could make the loyal people of Bethlehem tell.

Thereupon Herod reacted in a manner characteristic of his last frenzied days. If the villagers would not reveal the identity of the child he sought, he could still remove that child and punish his obstinate subjects at the same time by ordering the indiscriminate slaughter of all male children under the age of two. Before the inhabitants of Bethlehem were aware of the king's intent, his troops were among them, slashing and stabbing the innocent victims.

In all, some twenty children were sacrificed to Herod's mad wrath. Macrobius informs us that among them was one of the king's own children, put out to wet-nurse with a woman of

Bethlehem. The Protoevangel of St. James adds that Zacharias, the father of John the Baptist, was also slain for refusing to disclose the hiding place of his son.

Because Josephus does not mention the massacre at Bethlehem, some have seen fit to throw doubt on the biblical narrative. Yet Matthew's short account, even better than Josephus' histories, pictures the characteristics of the dying tyrant, his restlessness, his rage, his guile, and his cruelty.

He gathered "together all the chief priests and scribes," a commentary on the subordinate position of the Jewish priesthood under Herod. He "summoned the magi secretly," an action in keeping with the policy of a ruler who listens to no counselor and transacts his affairs behind barred doors.

"When you have found him bring me word, that I, too, may go and worship him," has the same note of disarming sincerity that lured the wily Antipater to judgment only short months before.

When he saw he had been "tricked by the magi," he "was exceedingly angry; and he sent and slew all the boys in Bethlehem and all its neighborhood who were two years old or under." This is precisely the kind of action a king would commit who could brook no rival, who had not refrained from killing his own sons when he suspected them of ambition, and who believed that wholesale bloodletting was the specific for every royal evil.

Josephus was born forty years after the event and depended for his information in large measure on the works of the royal biographer Nicolaus. Perhaps he was quite unaware of the murder of a score of impoverished children in a wretched hamlet. Or, knowing of it, it is quite likely that in a history devoted to the important events of the king's reign he might purposely have omitted a discreditable minor crime which had seemingly no historical significance.

Yet it is precisely by this relatively lesser crime of a maddened, dying tyrant that the name Herod has been lifted from almost complete obscurity to an undying notoriety.

CHAPTER XXII

NIGHT FALLS

EVERYONE ABOUT THE COURT BUT HEROD HIM-
self knew that he would speedily die and that the prolongation
of his life would result only in the intensification of his suffering.
But the king clung to life tenaciously, almost hopefully. Now
that the rival king had been ostensibly done away with at Bethlehem, he was anxious to try the mineral baths at Callirrhoe, which
he was certain would alleviate his pain, if not entirely cure him.

Antipater was imprisoned in the palace at Jericho; Herod had
not wanted to order his immediate execution after his guilt was
established. He was determined to make a public spectacle of
his son's punishment, as a deterrent to other conspirators and a
warning that no one, not even those closest to the throne, might
with impunity raise a hand or harbor a menacing thought against
the sacrosanct presence. To make the execution the more impressive, he was awaiting Caesar's sanction, although he knew he was
well within his rights to proceed without Rome's approval. Pending the arrival of Caesar's decision, the king prepared to leave
Jerusalem for the hot springs.

His departure was again delayed. New evidence of the depth
of Antipater's depravity came to light.

Caesar's malicious daughter Julia had a maid named Acme, a
blackmailer and harlot, in every way an appropriate member of
her mistress's entourage. This unsavory damsel sent Herod a
letter she claimed to have found among Julia's papers purported
to have been written by Salome. The letter was a violent indictment of Herod, charging him with the grossest cruelty and

351

malfeasance, and imploring Julia to use her influence to have him removed. Ordinarily, Herod would have assumed that the charges were the authentic work of Salome and that his sister was actually plotting against him, possibly in the interests of her nephew Herod Antipas, with whom she had of late grown very friendly.

Fortunately for Salome, the blackmailer, unaware of Antipater's fallen fortunes, was foolish enough to write him a letter also—naturally it was intercepted—which was in effect a confession of their complicity. "As thou desirest," she wrote, "I have written a letter to thy father and have sent that letter and am persuaded that the king will not spare his sister when he reads it. Thou wilt do well to remember what thou has promised when all is accomplished."

Reading the letters together, the king was horrified. He realized how unquestioningly he would have condemned his sister had he seen only the forgery. He recalled how he had given credence to other letters, just as palpably spurious, on the testimony of which he had turned against Mariamne's sons. Faintness, a feeling of utter futility swept over him. He dictated a hasty report of the conspiracy to Caesar and again changed his will.

He named Antipas as his successor, possibly in atonement for what he would have done to him had he accepted as genuine the letter Salome was accused of writing. Just as illogically, he completely passed over Archelaus and Philip, because Antipater had written disparagingly of them. To Caesar he left a thousand talents and divided five hundred talents among his family and dependents. Salome was willed the treasures of the palace; and other loyal adherents were generously remembered with gifts of money and real estate.

Reports of the king's worsened condition leaked out to the people. Patriotic Jews sensed that now was the time to strike a blow for their freedom. With the king deathly sick, and seemingly senile, the Jewish nation must assert itself by undertaking a token rebellion that would serve as an admonition to Herod's successor that Jewish faith and Jewish culture could no longer be humiliated, and that even the king must realize that the laws of Moses and the reforms of Ezra take precedence over the might of Rome and the authority of royalty.

In Jerusalem, in the immediate precincts of the Temple, a plot got under way.

No action of Herod's had been quite as hateful to the Jews as his placing a great eagle of gold above the main gate of the Temple. It is not likely that in putting it there he intended anything beyond an expression of appreciation for Rome's sympathy and assistance. Certainly, he meant no slight to the religious convictions of his people. After giving unselfishly of his money and skill in rebuilding and beautifying the Temple, he would not likely be willing to vitiate all the favorable reaction of his nation by a single defiant gesture.

But the Jews were intolerant of any mistake of Herod's. They gave him no credit for the splendid edifice he was constructing for them, and cursed him for the one unfortunate error in judgment. The king, in turn, was too proud to conciliate his people, and too cautious to risk offending the Romans by having the eagle removed.

So it remained, to the Jews a hateful reminder that they could not even enter the Temple of the All High without first passing beneath the symbol of Roman overlordship! Worse still, it was a graven image and violated the direct mandate against the making of a replica of any living creature.

The Sadducees, who held all the Temple concessions and discovered in the despised image an incentive for pious or curious Jews to attend Temple services more frequently and naturally spend more money there, had understandingly not protested. Apart from the profits involved, they prided themselves upon their cosmopolitan culture and were accused, not unreasonably, of having Greek statues in their own homes. They then would be unlikely to see harm in a single, innocuous eagle over the portico, which was not really a cloistered section of the Temple.

Not so with the Pharisees and their followers. Two of them in particular, Matthias and Judas, came to the conclusion that the eagle must be destroyed. They were not young, fanatical zealots, but scholarly, gentle, pious Pharisees, respected for their learning and revered for the sanctity of their lives. Daily they taught near the Temple. Great numbers of listeners, especially of young men, were attracted by the clarity with which the law was expounded—and the simple eloquence which advocated fear of God and of no other.

To these Pharisees, Herod's condition was an opportunity they would not miss. Now while the foe was weak and mentally disorganized, they must strike a blow which, whatever the results to themselves, would ignite anew in their coreligionists the long dormant flame of love of God and Temple. They could not lead armies or organize revolution. But they could destroy the graven image and spare their beloved Temple at least that infamy.

They had no delusions of victory. They knew that nearly every successful revolution is prefaced by abortive rebellion, whose victims are the martyrs that inspire future heroes to conquer. To their fellow rebels they had nothing to offer but the certainty of death.

But, being Pharisees, they taught the certitude that the soul was immortal and the promise that those lost in the just cause would enjoy an eternity of happiness. With surprising ease, they found followers willing, even eager, to sacrifice themselves for the purity of their faith.

It might have been possible to destroy the eagle secretly, by night. But that would have been interpreted as an act of vandalism. The Pharisees proposed to act openly, defiantly, to proclaim to the nation the insignificance of human life when weighed with the Law of the Eternal.

In midmorning, when the Temple was crowded with worshipers and visitors, and the stalls of the Temple with merchants at their busiest and noisiest, the Pharisee band pressed through the throng that choked the gateway into the courtyard. Among them were grim youths, sturdy and purposeful, some armed with axes, others with loops of knotted rope about their shoulders. Immediately the Temple was in an uproar. Money-changers bawled their protests as the crowd upended their tables and sent heaps of Temple currency clinking erratically across the court; whirring doves and bleating lambs were liberated from their enclosures; a few futile protests from the Temple guard were ignored. Obviously well rehearsed, the more agile of the intruders clambered up the wall. Thence, ax in hand, they were let down on ropes, and with frantic vehemence hewed and chopped at the massive golden eagle until it dropped in glittering slivers and thumping chunks on the pavement below. Beggars and hangers-on, lunging and snarling as they dived for the precious fragments, attracted the attention of the king's guard.

Brutally they pushed asunder the tangled mass still scratching for some possibly undiscovered bit of gold, and by liberal use of the butts of their weapons smashed a way through the clamorous devotees and isolated the actual perpetrators.

These made no attempt to resist or flee. With the light of martyrdom already in their eyes, they were pushed through an ever-increasing and ever more excitable throng, past the palace gates and into the presence of Herod.

With complete candor, they admitted their action. How could they do other than obey the Law of God! To Herod's amazed comment that they, knowing they were soon to die, should still look so happy, they answered that it was because of the assurance of eternal happiness after death.

Herod knew that argument with men of such fixed ideas was a waste of time. He considered the prisoners crazy fanatics, but he did not minimize the possibly dangerous consequences of their rebellion. This could easily be the beginning of a revolution; and revolt in the land, however unsuccessful, was always the reason for the king's removal. Only by immediately discrediting the actions of the rebels and by intimidating witnesses and sympathizers could he kill the cancer of rebellion before its deadly roots could spread throughout the kingdom.

He happened to be in more than usual pain on the morning of the outbreak. But he made a tremendous effort to compose himself. He stood at a window of his palace. For a moment he stared with hatred at the tightly-packed mob, partly curious, mostly antagonistic and emboldened by the destruction of the eagle.

The agony in his throat convinced even Herod that this was destined to be his last public speech, and in a sense it was one of his most effective. Disparaging every motive of religion or patriotism, he denounced the action of the prisoners as senseless, sacrilegious violence within the sacred confines of the Temple. He demonstrated that in rebuilding the Temple he had shown himself a far more devout Jew than those whose assumed piety led them into instigating a riot on Temple grounds. He explained that the golden eagle was not, in the strict sense of the word, a graven image, but merely a courteous gesture to Rome, which had aided and encouraged the renovation of the Temple and which everywhere among the three million Jews outside Palestine guaranteed Jewish freedom of worship. Now these rabid young rebels and even more culpably their older leaders had risked the destruction of the Temple in Jerusalem, and the secure practice of the Jewish faith throughout the world, by insulting the pride of Rome.

He felt that he must, by the severest penalties on all those showing the lightest sympathy toward the evildoers, convince the Romans that he was aware of the heinousness of the offense.

Herod's words bore an unexpectedly ominous ring. By a single impulse the edges of the mob began to seek escape, and those jammed closer to the palace to put more space between themselves and Herod's threats. But vainly! The converging streets and alleys were blocked with squadrons of Jew-hating Galatians and Germans, fully armed and seemingly eager for the word that would send them hurling into the dense mass they enclosed.

Between the troops and Herod, the Jews knew they were trapped. Leaders attempted to allay the panic and met in hurried conference. Representatives pleaded with the king to limit his displeasure to those actually guilty, and to let his listeners, his loyal, well-disposed subjects, disperse to their homes. With seeming reluctance he agreed. Cowed, and the lesson of sacrifice and devotion at least temporarily lost on them, the mob scurried away.

The ringleaders of the forty prisoners—Judas, Matthias and those who wielded the axes—were condemned to be burnt to death; the others, beheaded.

This extraordinary demand on Herod's wasted system resulted in almost complete collapse. His condition—probably intestinal cancer with complications—was pitiful. The entire surface of his body itched; inwardly he seemed consumed by slow fires. As a result of an ulcerated grand alimentary canal, his breath was so offensive that attendants quickly succumbed to nausea. Worms seemed to be constantly generated in his corrupting body, and quickly as they were removed others would appear. Always hitherto abstemious, he became the victim of a ravenous appetite. The command "Food, food" was constantly on his fevered lips, yet his stomach revolted when he tried to eat. He could not walk; his legs were swollen as though with dropsy. In trying to breathe he choked and gasped; a torturing cough racked every agonized organ. Those about him, however much they disliked him, wished for him the mercy of an early death. But Herod himself endured the pain, always trusting in the miracle of a cure. He gave orders for his litter to take him to the curative springs in the wilderness beyond the Jordan.

The streets were ordered cleared of pedestrians; vehicles and beasts of burden were hustled into prearranged corrals; chariots raced up and down the narrow thoroughfares, trampling under anyone unfortunate enough to be unaware of the edict; soldiers lined the avenue to the gates and blocked off every intersecting lane and alley. To be seen on a roof-top—ordinarily threshing floor, guest chamber and sitting room for the denizens of Judea— meant death.

With all precautions against violence taken, Herod gave the order for departure. He could, of course, no longer ride, and lay almost supine in a litter as his bearers carefully picked their way along the cobbled streets to the city walls.

Herod was leaving his capital for the last time. It was possibly a premonition of this that made him lift himself painfully on one elbow and fix his tortured eyes on the gleaming walls slowly sinking into the dusk of early evening, for one backward glance at the city where he had met with so much unhappiness. Through silvery green groves of olive trees and down the steep slopes his litter passed with infinite precaution. At every groan of the recumbent figure a band of fear tightened about the hearts of the bearers. One stumbled. An alert guard leaped into his place, and, pausing only to steady the litter, cut down the unfortunate slave.

A night under the stars seemed only to aggravate Herod's

agony. The season was the lovely Judean spring. Fields and green patches among the rocks were aflame with the red blossom of the wild mustard; crimson poppies and scarlet anemones swayed to the moist breeze in gay clusters; oleanders and peach orchards shook their airy blossoms into the blue immensity of sky. But Herod saw none of this. He was in a panic of haste to get to the sulfur springs in which he had placed all his hopes for a cure.

The springs of Callirrhoe—today highly regarded by Arabs for curing rheumatism and arthritis—were said to have been discovered by a Negro slave of King Solomon. Situated in the hottest, dreariest part of Jordan, they have little, in appearance at least, to arouse a cheerful frame of mind in the patient.

The heat rose in almost solid banks as the litter wormed its tortuous way across the wastes through the black stone desert to the entrance of the springs. A sudden gash, like a knife-thrust in the earth, yawned in the seared surface of the desert, and the king was carried down a deep gorge. Outside was the white glare of the sun; here, an eerie light compounded of semigloom and the brooding rocks caked with rust and green from the mineral waters, dripping down the cavernous sides. After a cruel passage to the bottom of the rift, the king's party reached the ten sulfur springs, heaving in heavy, oily undulations like a witch's broth in basins crusted with poisonous green. Pathetic eagerness and desperate hope glittered in the king's eyes—otherwise he seemed almost dead. With the utmost care, he was stripped and slowly lowered into a spring. The instant the reeking waters touched his body, he gasped, writhed, then vomited and slipped into unconsciousness. His alarmed physicians pulled him from the spring, hastily bundled him in a robe, and hurried him out of the gorge. His features were ashen, his breath and pulse hardly perceptible. In desperation, they put him in a bath of warm oil. Momentarily he regained his senses, then moaned that he was blind, and fainted again. This really seemed to be the end. His attendants, pagans all, began to intone their various chants and wails for the dead.

The uproar revived him. But he had lost all hope of recovery.

He ordered a generous bonus for every soldier and servant in his suite, and munificent gifts for the officers and doctors.

A sort of sullen resignation took possession of him. He started back to Jericho, to prepare for death.

During his final weeks, his agony was aggravated by the realization that his death would be the signal for nation-wide jubilation among his subjects. He could do little to abate his sufferings, but he could at least make certain that the day of his death would be a day of general mourning. Still retaining a glimmering spark of his superb organizing skill, he commanded that lists of the chief men from every town and village be brought to him. On these lists, he checked the names of some three thousand noted for piety, or patriotism, or simply for lukewarm adherence to his policies. These men he ordered rounded up and confined in the rose quartz hippodrome at Jericho. This done, he called Salome and her husband, and issued his command to be carried out posthumously.

"I know well enough that the Jews will keep a festival upon my death. However, it is in my power to be mourned for on other accounts, and to have a splendid funeral if you will be but subservient to my commands. Do but you take care to send soldiers to encompass these men that are now in custody, and slay them immediately upon my death; and then all Judea, and every family of them will weep at it, whether they will or no."

In his last days, Herod clearly reverted to the pagan philosophy of his ancestors. He no longer thought of death as a transition into an eternal state of bliss or misery, but rather as a pageant: a season of national mourning with himself as the central figure. In accepting the inevitability of his fate, he also discarded what shreds of Jewish faith had not been lost in his long years of contention with the Jews. By design, influenced at least in part by madness, he chose to meet death, not as the patron of the Temple, but rather as an oriental despot.

There remained still the matter of Antipater's execution. Shortly after the king had completed arrangements for the slaughter at the hippodrome, his ambassadors arrived from Rome with the report that Acme had been executed and that Caesar had also confirmed the condemnation of Antipater. However, in keeping with his policy of non-interference in Herod's family affairs, he suggested that, as Herod willed, Antipater might be banished instead of executed. For a very brief time the king was cheered by this evidence of Caesar's faith in him.

But not for long. The gnawing hunger, the hopelessness and the agony possessed him completely. He decided to kill himself. Seeking the opportunity, he cursed the watchfulness of his attendants, who knew they would be held accountable for any lapse in vigilance. He asked for an apple and a knife with which to pare it.

Thinking himself unobserved, he raised the knife for a quick thrust into his heart. The action did not escape the keen vision of an attendant, a cousin named Achiabus, who grasped the king's arm and wrested the knife from his emaciated fingers.

The resultant shriek of baffled rage, the pleading cries of Achiabus, the yells of the other attendants made such an uproar that it reached even the ears of Antipater in his not over-luxurious cell in the servants' quarters of the palace.

He thought his father had died. Shouting with joy, he demanded that his guards release him, promising them the richest rewards when he became king.

The chief jailor was not fooled. He realized that his treatment of the prisoner had not been sympathetic and that he would not long survive Herod should Antipater be restored to power. He hurried to the sick chamber and with embellishments and exaggerations reported what Antipater had said and promised.

All the wretched king's fury, all his pain, were concentrated in one unearthly bellow that Antipater be immediately executed.

In the grim faces of the guards that strode into his cell, Antipater could read his doom. Sagging to his knees, whimpering in a corner, he submitted tamely, while calloused fingers gripped his throat and squeezed the breath out of his body.

The death of Antipater served as a sedative for his father. He gave orders that his son be buried without honors or ceremony at Hyrcanum. Then he made the final draft of his will.

This completed, he fell into a coma from which he never quite emerged. Every moment might be his last. Meanwhile a million Jews slept little, torn between a quite understandable wish for his death, and a harrowing fear of what would happen to the hostages.

Five days later he died, after having lived seventy troubled years, thirty-four of them as king of a nation that prospered under him and detested him.

According to the custom, the will was read as soon as the body was delivered to the embalmers.

Archelaus, son by his Samaritan wife Malthace, was willed the title of king of Judea, Idumea, and Samaria, with an annual income of six hundred talents. His full-brother Antipas was left the lesser prize of Galilee and Perea, and an income of two hundred talents; while the best of his children, Philip, son of the gentle Cleopatra of Jerusalem, had to be (and was) content with the hinterlands of Batanea, Gaulonitis, Trachonitis and Paneas, with an income of one hundred talents a year. Salome was remembered with choice bits of property as were his numerous other relatives. His parting gift to Caesar was two million drachmae in ready cash; Julia was bequeathed jewels and costly garments.

The captives in the hippodrome were released as soon as the terms of the will were made known. Salome could not afford to antagonize the new king by usurping his authority. Archelaus would not jeopardize his chances of confirmation by Rome through an act of senseless butchery that would have only the mad whim of a dead monarch to justify it. So Herod's death was doubly a cause for joy. The nation as a whole celebrated its release from tyranny and each smallest hamlet had its particular reason for rejoicing in the safe return of its noblest citizens.

Archelaus, as new regent, took charge of his father's obsequies. Obviously, he was going to make sure that they would in every way be in keeping with the dignity and renown of the departed. For over three weeks the long train moved mournfully from Jericho to the royal tomb at Herodium. First came the body so skilfully embalmed that the composed features, the dyed hair and beard seemed those of a man in his prime, rather than components of the rotted hulk of a disease-riddled septuagenarian.

It reposed on a bier of gold encrusted with every known variety of gem. Over the prone limbs was spread a purple robe edged with gold; the right hand was clenched about a golden scepter; a royal crown rested, at long last peacefully, on the dead king's head. Immediately about the bier were Herod's sons and his numerous less intimate relatives, clad in deepest mourning. Following them marched in somber step his probably sincerest mourners—his fanatically loyal body guard. Behind these were solidly ranked Germans and Galatians, other foreigners whom Herod could trust. The regular Herodian army—Jews and Greeks —in battle array and some five hundred servants carrying spices for the entombment and other requisites for the ceremony brought up the rear. At length the procession reached Herodium and the body was laid in the tomb.

What little real grief there was had been worn thin during the interminably dreary march from Jericho. The seven additional days of official mourning proclaimed by Archelaus were as a result slightly on the gay side, especially since, to court the favor of the Jews, he enlivened them with public banquets. The new ruler was evidently trying hard to make a good impression. Much as it went against the grain (both as Samaritan and as Arab he had reasons for disliking his subjects), he strove to establish, first, that in religion he was a conformist, and, secondly, that he intended to rule moderately and with the single purpose of serving his people. Poor Archelaus! No sooner had he been initiated into the distasteful rite of offering sacrifice in the Temple than a clamor assailed his ears: "Reduce taxes! Cancel duties on commodities! Liberate political prisoners!"

Outwardly gracious, he granted these demands.

Made bold by what seemed surrender, representatives of the people proclaimed a period of national mourning for those executed in the episode of the Temple eagle. Archelaus took no official cognizance of this proceeding. A demand, practically an ultimatum, followed, that Archelaus punish all who took part in the trial of the rebels and that the high priest be removed. Seething with rage, but still cautious, the king chose only to pretend to be unaware of the insubordination of the nation.

He had to abandon that pretense when rioters cast stones at

him and almost annihilated a cohort of troops sent to quiet them. Belatedly he called on the army to restore order. In the ensuing riots three thousand Jews—almost to a man the number he liberated at Jericho—were killed.

Almost furtively, he stole off for Rome to obtain Caesar's confirmation of his kingship.

Caesar's favor was no boon. Archelaus was lost even before he left to be invested. Herod's mantle was not so light as to rest easily on lesser shoulders. There would be further insurrections. Rome would intervene and crucify two thousand Jews at the gates of Jerusalem. At length, the longed-for exile in Gaul, enlivened by his half-brother Alexander's wife—the twice-widowed, but still vivacious Glaphyra, for whom he would put away his own sullen spouse—a place to end his days quietly in the unexciting atmosphere of the provinces while Roman overlords, among them a certain Pontius Pilate, would dwell in the palace of the Herods.

To evaluate justly a character so enigmatical as Herod's is no grateful task, particularly in view of the fact that most of our knowledge is derived from the single source, Josephus. This Jewish historian wrote some forty years after Herod's death, when grisly warfare had effaced nearly every vestige of his administrative talent and when the combination of Jewish stubbornness and Roman savagery had resulted in a diaspora and an enslavement where cultural appraisal of Herod's statesmanship and character were almost impossible.

Critics vary widely in their evaluation of Herod. Caesar Augustus maintained that he had "too great a soul for so small a dominion." Agrippa, one of the few men who could really call him friend, felt that Herod "deserved all the kingdom of Syria and that of Egypt also."

At the opposite pole there is the allegation that he "stole to the throne like a fox, ruled like a tiger, and died like a dog."

Modern commentators differ as widely. Mahaffy, probably impressed by Herod's Hellenism, calls him "the most fascinating of men." Renan glibly comments that he was a splendid Arab but the slave of conspirators in his harem. Contemporary Jewish

opinion is often less favorable. Jacob Minkin (himself scrupulously fair) quotes the opinion, "He hindered nothing, he effected
nothing, and when he died, he just passed into nothingness."

Herod's career must be viewed in the light of world conditions
of his day. Rome was the only ruler; all other sovereigns reigned
by suffrance. Moreover, Rome was concerned in the affairs of
subject nations only to the extent that they affected her welfare.
The "colonial theory" that colonies existed primarily for the
benefit of the mother country was no seventeenth-century innova-
tion. Rome practiced that theory in her relations with subject
nations.

Accordingly Herod, a king by the grace of Caesar, compelled to
administer his kingdom in a manner to benefit Rome, should
not be measured by the same yardstick as that applied to the
governmental stature of a Frederick or a Victoria.

Rome made two basic demands of her tributary kings—that
they rule their lands profitably (for Rome), and peacefully. If
the subject king could enrich himself as well; if he tyrannized
over his people short of goading them into rebellion; if he lived
a lustful, vicious personal life, Rome was not concerned. Prosperity and peace were all she demanded, and every ruler had to
effect these requisites or he ceased to rule.

It is in consideration of Herod's achievements above these
minima that the term "Great" can be applied or withheld. To
maintain that only rulers of powerful, free states can be called
"Great" is to confuse greatness with wealth, and extensiveness,
and overwhelming might.

Rather should the answer be found in the subject's accomplishments in the fields of administration, of war and national
defense, of statesmanship, and in his personal life and ethics.

As an administrator, Herod eminently deserves the name "The
Great." He built cities, roads and harbors; he founded colonies
and improved agriculture; he encouraged commerce and increased manufacture. In a word, he raised the Jewish standard
of living to a level it had never known, and in the process he
established the reputation of Jewish workmanship and Jewish
business practices in a pre-eminent position throughout the
empire.

As a soldier, he had in his preroyalty days shown military

talents of the highest quality. He was a first-rate strategist, an inspiring leader, a fearless soldier. Along Judea's borders were savage marauders, who might readily have required a lesser ruler to call in Roman help. But Herod raised the Jewish army to such a level of efficiency that trouble with his unpleasant neighbors was rare and never really serious. This army served also to discourage rebellious activities on the part of his own people.

In statesmanship, a peculiarly difficult field, since he, with no independent powers, was compelled to enter the lists with blunted weapons, Herod, by personal magnetism, by an instinct for statecraft, occasionally by guile, maintained his country in the topmost rank of Rome's favored subject states, so that the title "Rex et socius" conferred upon him by Caesar was fully merited.

It is when one considers Herod's emotional and ethical composition that the answer is less clear.

The matter of carnal appetites presents no difficulty. In an age when sensuality and lust were considered the royal prerogatives, he was amazingly abstemious. As host for distinguished guests he could take a gourmet's delight in a pie of flamingo tongues or a dish of braised cow's udders. But he was equally, probably better, satisfied squatting before a campfire sharing his soldiers' breakfast of goat's milk, meat, and cheese.

In drink—at a time when the most gracious of Roman poets almost deified wine—he was equally abstemious. The not wholly creditable tradition that he tried toward the end of his life to stupefy himself with drink when his agony became too cruel, even if true, would not allow us to discount his many years of marked sobriety.

He was not a lustful king, nor is it quite just to refer to his plurality of wives as a harem. Most of his marriages were arranged for policy or family interest, and only Mariamne ever truly aroused his ardor. It is significant that not even his most violent detractors thought of accusing him of abnormal sexual practices, although such practices were almost a corollary in other royal courts, not excluding the imperial court of Rome. Indeed, for his time, Herod was a remarkably temperate king.

In the more subtle nuances of deportment and character, however, there is less certainty. True, in Herod's early career there is little reason to suspect the later complications that make him such an elusive personality. At first, his seemed a straightforward, militant, generous, sometimes romantic spirit, lacking, perhaps, only a sense of humor. Then early in his married life appeared a taint, a sort of spreading blight, expressing itself in acts of such insensate brutality as only almost inhuman perversity or fits of madness could explain. There is little doubt that there was in him a streak of madness which was aggravated and intensified by his unhappy domestic and public life.

Herod was handicapped from the start. At least ostensibly an Arab and a foreigner, he ascended to the most provincial throne in the world. With the sincerity of his religious belief suspect, he presumed to rule over a people that was a religious entity rather than a nation. Religious Jews chafed under his authority and he responded by placing non-religious Jews in the high priesthood. Jewish nationalists tried to sabotage his activities and he replaced them with foreigners and Jewish Hellenists.

Had his domestic life been happier during his early manhood, his madness might have been diverted into less lethal channels. But Doris was an opportunist. Mariamne, the one true love of his life, was at heart a proud Hasmonean, who, despite the unquestioned affection she bore her husband, could not help subconsciously regarding him as an upstart who had usurped power from her kinsmen. She was, regretably, not always tactful enough to disguise her inbred resentment.

The decent members of Herod's family were generally well-meaning but impotent; the rest, who composed the more clever element, were as vile a lot as are pictured in historical annals.

The Arab, unlike other Orientals, could not acclimate himself to court cabals and family intrigue. He craved unquestioned loyalty, unshared affection. He demanded and offered hospitality and friendliness. His reaction to aggression was violent and immediate.

Herod was, ethnically, such an Arab. Even the faintest shadow of suspicion that his wife might have been unfaithful fomented the latent madness in him to acts of horrible rage; the rash deed perpetrated, almost bottomless remorse filled his soul and could be blasted away only by other bursts of fury. Thus violence begot violence; successive waves of ferocity and remorse almost submerged all that was good and generous in him, so that in his final days frenzy all but possessed him completely.

Unfortunately, his religion was such that it afforded him no lasting solace. He died a pagan, but this was after madness had conquered his reason. From his speeches, which certainly sound sincere, there is every evidence that he believed, and from his youth had believed, in a personal God. It is likely, too, that after his marriage with Mariamne he was willing to identify this God with the Yahweh of the Jews. It was in large measure out of respect to this God of the Jews that he rebuilt the Temple. Reverencing the dictates of this God, he insisted on the practice of the Jewish faith by his children, even to the extent that they were housed with other Jews during their studies in Rome.

But at every turn, those who pretended to venerate this God opposed him, hounded him; only the Sadducees, whose religion combined lip service with an obviously materialistic philosophy, were willing to get along with him.

Herod might have lived a happy, normal life had he had the services of a good priest, a good psychiatrist, and a good wife. Even lacking the others, a truly complacent, understanding wife might have sufficed. But, unfortunately, only Cleopatra of Jerusalem seemed to possess the needed qualities, and her marriage came only after madness had too commanding a lead.

Yet, with due admiration for his achievements and a sympathetic understanding of his weaknesses and his sins, it seems only just to add to the much maligned name of King Herod, the epithet "The Great."

List of Principal Characters

Agrippa—Adviser to Caesar Augustus; friend of Herod

Alexander—Oldest son of Herod and Mariamne I; executed by father

Alexander—Son of Aristobulus II; husband of Alexandra; defeated by Marc Antony

Alexandra—Daughter of Hyrcanus; mother of Mariamne; mother-in-law of Herod; married Alexander, son of Aristobulus II

Alexandra Salome—Wife first of Aristobulus I, then of his brother Alexander Jannaeus

Antigonus—Brother and victim of Aristobulus I

Antigonus II—Son of Aristobulus II; most cowardly of Hasmoneans

Antiochus—Syrian emperor; captured Jerusalem; looted Temple; persecuted Jews

Antipater—Father of Herod the Great; counselor of Alexandra Salome

Antipater—Vicious son of Herod and Doris; Herod's final victim

Archelaus—King of Cappadocia; father of Glaphyra

Archelaus—Son of Herod and Malthace; Herod's successor

Aristobulus—Brother of Mariamne I; High Priest; murdered by Herod

Aristobulus I—Debased son of John Hyrcanus

Aristobulus II—Brother and successor to Hyrcanus; poisoned by Pompey's agents

Bene-Baba—Sons of Baba; last survivors of collateral Hasmonean line; executed by Herod

Berenice—Daughter of Salome; married (unhappily) Aristobulus, son of Mariamne I

Berenice—Last and most depraved of Herod's descendants

Caesar Augustus—Emperor of Rome; first (as Octavius) an enemy, then a friend to Herod

Cassius—Ally of Antony; financially aided by Herod

Castobar—Wily Idumean sheik; Salome's second husband; later her victim

Cleopatra—Queen of Egypt; attempted seduction of Herod; later his bitter enemy

Cleopatra of Jerusalem—Wife of Herod and mother of Philip

Crassus—Successor of Gabinius; looted Temple

Cyprus—Mother of Herod the Great

Doris—First wife of Herod; later conspired to kill him

Eleazar—Brother of Judas Maccabeus; killed in battle

Esop—Maid who told lover of Alexandra's attempted flight

Eurycles—Miniature painter and rascal

368

Eurycles—Spartan adventurer; reported statements of Alexander to Antipater

Felix—Treacherous Roman; defeated by Phasael

Gabinius—Pompey's agent in Judea

Gemelus—Roman tutor of Mariamne I's sons; exiled by Herod

Hananel—Babylonian priest; High Priest before and after Aristobulus

Herod the Great

Herod Philip—Son of Mariamne II; married and divorced his niece Herodias

Hillel—Scholar; proponent of love of fellow man; head of Herod's sanhedrin

Hyrcanus—High priest and king; father-in-law and victim of Herod

Johanan—High Priest; grandson murdered in Temple

John Hyrcanus—Nephew of Judas Maccabeus; last good Jewish king

Jonathan—Brother of Judas Maccabeus, and High Priest

Joseph—Uncle, brother-in-law, and victim of Herod

Joseph—Brother of Herod; killed, and body dishonored by Antigonus II

Judah—Leader of Galilean rebels; killed by Herod

Judas Maccabeus—Patriot; "Hammer of God"

Judas—Executed for part in destroying Roman Eagle in Temple

Julia—Daughter of Augustus; exiled for evil life

Julius Caesar—Appointed Antipater (father of Herod) procurator of Judea

Lucillius—Marc Antony's companion in desert

Malchus—King of Petra; refused Herod refuge, then repented

Malchus—King of Nabatea; incurred enmity of Cleopatra; defeated by Herod

Malthace—Samaritan wife of Herod; mother of Archelaus and Herod Antipas

Manaham—Essene; tutor of Herod

Marc Antony—Murderer of Caesar; lover of Cleopatra; friend of Herod; enemy of Octavius

Mariamne I—Herod's second wife and great love; executed by him

Mariamne II—Herod's wife; daughter of High Priest Simon of Boëthian family

Mathathias—Founder of Hasmonean line; father of Judas Maccabeus

Mathathias—Title assumed as High Priest by Antigonus II

Matthias—Executed for destruction of Roman Eagle in Temple

Menelaus—High Priest; attempted theft of sacred vessels of Temple

Messala—Friend of Marc Antony and Herod

Mithridates—King of Pontus; ally of Julius Caesar

Nicarnor—Syrian general; inveterate enemy of Jews

Nicarnor—Alexandrian Jew; donor of the "Beautiful Gate" in the Temple

Nicolaus of Damascus—Herod's biographer; works now lost

Octavius—Later Caesar Augustus

Onias—Saintly Jew; killed by partisans of Hyrcanus for "neutral" prayer

Pacorus—Royal cup bearer and Parthian conspirator

Phaedra—Wife of Herod; mother of Roxana

Phasael—Brother of Herod; tricked by Parthians; committed suicide

Pheroras—Youngest brother of Herod; defied king by marrying actress

Philip—Son of Herod and Cleopatra of Jerusalem; best of Herodians

Philipsio—Married Alexandra, sister of Aristobulus II; killed by father who then married Alexandra

Pollio—Pharisee scholar; advocate of moderation in relations with Herod

Ptolemy—Son-in-law and murderer of Simon Maccabeus

Ptolemy—Financier and chief banker of Herod

Quintus Didius—Legate of Syria; aided by Herod in revolt of gladiators

Sabbion—Rogue who informed Herod of Alexandra's plan to escape

Salampsio—Herod's daughter; married step-brother Phasael

Salome—Vicious sister of Herod

Sameus—"Righteous" man, who warned Hyrcanus of danger from Herod

Sanballat—Samaritan enemy of Jews

Saturninus—Roman commander in Syria; attempted vainly to save Herod's sons

Shamnai—Pharisee; joined Hillel in refusing to take oath of loyalty to Herod

Simon—Traitor priest-captain of Temple

Simon—Father of Mariamne II; later High Priest

Sohemus—Trusted friend of Herod; later executed

Sylleus—Nabatean adventurer; later executed by Augustus

Tero—Outspoken old soldier who protested Herod's treatment of sons; executed

Tyranus—Guard of Herod; accused of treason

Tryphon—Syrian general; killed High Priest Jonathan

Varro—Governor of Syria; aided by Herod in overcoming robbers

Varus—Roman judge in trial of Antipater

Vitruvius—Renovator of Rome; consulted by Herod in building Caesarea

Volumnius—Roman opportunist; helped bring about conviction of Mariamne I's sons

THE HERODIAN FAMILY

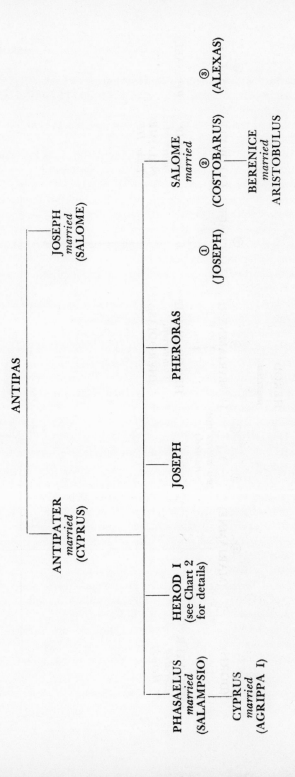

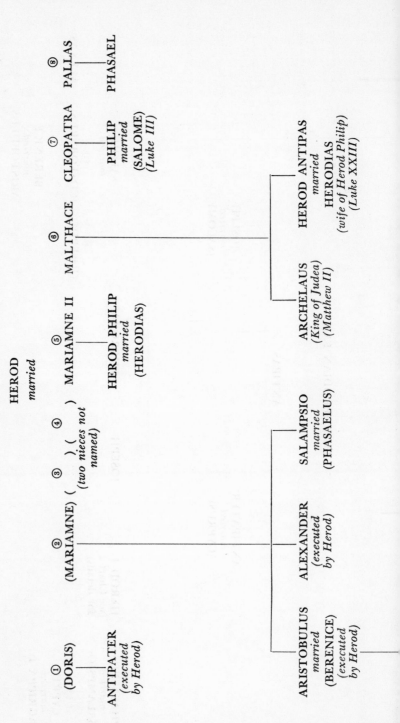

KING HEROD'S KNOWN FAMILY

HEROD
married

① (DORIS) ② (MARIAMNE) ③ ( ) ( ) ④ *(two nieces not named)* ⑤ MARIAMNE II ⑥ MALTHACE ⑦ CLEOPATRA ⑧ PALLAS

ANTIPATER
(executed by Herod)

HEROD PHILIP
married
(HERODIAS)

PHILIP
married
(SALOME)
(Luke III)

PHASAEL

ARISTOBULUS
married
(BERENICE)
(executed by Herod)

ALEXANDER
(executed by Herod)

SALAMPSIO
married
(PHASAELUS)

ARCHELAUS
(King of Judea)
(Matthew II)

HEROD ANTIPAS
married
HERODIAS
(wife of Herod Philip)
(Luke XXIII)

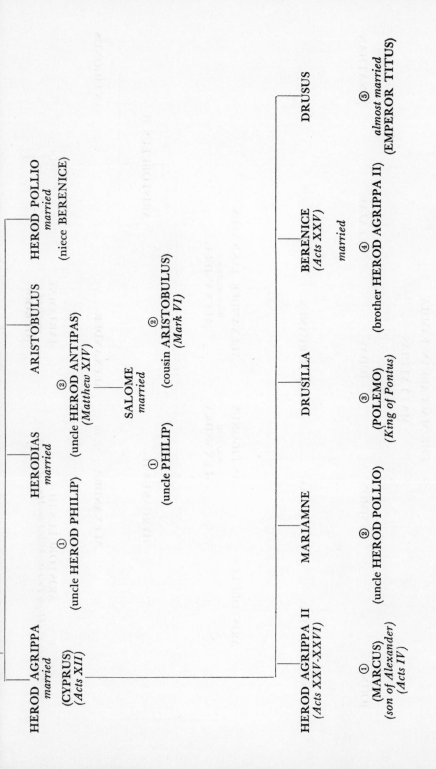

HEROD AGRIPPA
married
(CYPRUS
(*Acts XII*))

HERODIAS
married
① (uncle HEROD PHILIP)
② (uncle HEROD ANTIPAS)
(*Matthew XIV*)

ARISTOBULUS

HEROD POLLIO
married
(niece BERENICE)

SALOME
married
① (uncle PHILIP)
② (cousin ARISTOBULUS)
(*Mark VI*)

HEROD AGRIPPA II
(*Acts XXV-XXVI*)

① (MARCUS
(son of Alexander)
(*Acts IV*))

② (uncle HEROD POLLIO)

MARIAMNE

DRUSILLA

③ (POLEMO)
(King of Pontus)

BERENICE
(*Acts XXV*)

married

④ (brother HEROD AGRIPPA II)

DRUSUS

⑤ *almost married*
(EMPEROR TITUS)

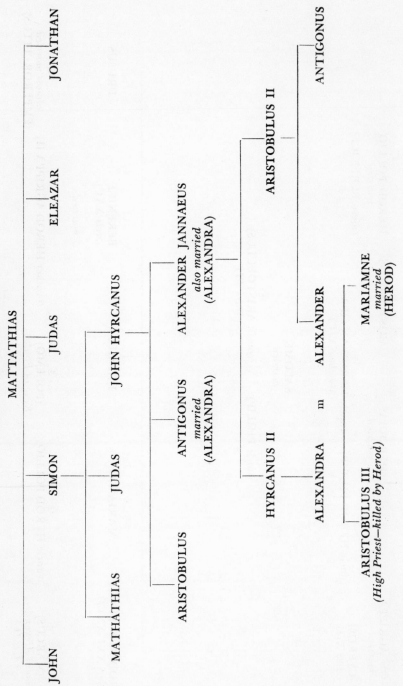

THE MACCABEAN FAMILY